PENGUIN BOOKS

THE INTERNATIONAL DIRECTORY
OF HAUNTED PLACES

Dennis William Hauck is an internationally recognized authority on paranormal phenomena and is a regular contributor to dozens of popular magazines and scholarly journals devoted to that subject. He is the author of several other books dealing with paranormal studies, including *Captain Quirk* (Pinnacle 1995), a biography of William Shatner detailing his UFO abduction experience after the end of the *Star Trek* series, and *Haunted Places: The National Directory* (Penguin 1996), a directory of over two thousand haunted locations and sacred sites in the United States. Hauck has also translated several old alchemy manuscripts and his most recent book is *The Emerald Tablet* (Penguin 1999), a look at an ancient alchemical document that presents a formula for experiencing the transpersonal consciousness that is part of many paranormal experiences.

Hauck is science consultant to the Mutual UFO Network, and an investigator for the American Society for Psychical Research, the International Ghost Hunters Society, the Borley Ghost Society, the American Ghost Society, and the Ghost Research Society. He is a professional member of the Association for Transpersonal Psychology, the Institute of Noetic Sciences, and the Center for Research in Science. He has served as a consultant and media contact for numerous motion pictures, including *Mysteries of the Gods* (Hemisphere Pictures 1976), *Close Encounters of the Third Kind* (Columbia Pictures 1977), and *The Haunting* (Dreamworks 1999). Currently, he is a consultant to several television production companies and has contributed to specials and documentaries on many different networks. Fluent in German with a reading knowledge of both Russian and Spanish, and with contacts with paranormal researchers in twenty countries, the author is uniquely qualified to produce this international directory of haunted places.

THE

INTERNATIONAL

DIRECTORY OF

HAUNTED PLACES

Ghostly Abodes, Sacred Sites,
and Other Supernatural Locations

DENNIS WILLIAM HAUCK

PENGUIN BOOKS

PENGUIN BOOKS
Published by the Penguin Group
Penguin Putnam Inc., 375 Hudson Street,
New York, New York 10014, U.S.A.
Penguin Books Ltd, 27 Wrights Lane,
London W8 5TZ, England
Penguin Books Australia Ltd, Ringwood,
Victoria, Australia
Penguin Books Canada Ltd, 10 Alcorn Avenue,
Toronto, Ontario, Canada M4V 3B2
Penguin Books (N.Z.) Ltd, 182–190 Wairau Road,
Auckland 10, New Zealand

Penguin Books Ltd, Registered Offices:
Harmondsworth, Middlesex, England

First published Penguin Books 2000

1 3 4 5 6 7 9 10 8 6 4 2

LIBRARY OF CONGRESS CATALOGING IN PUBLICATION DATA
Hauck, Dennis William,
The international directory of haunted places / Dennis William Hauck.
p. cm.
Includes bibliographical references and index.
ISBN 0 14 02.9635 2
1. Haunted places—Guidebooks I. Title.
BF1471.H38 2000
133.1'09—dc21   00–029341

Printed in the United States of America
Set in Janson
Designed by Victoria Hartman

CONTENTS

INTRODUCTION

Belief in ghosts or spirits is part of human culture, and the telling of ghost stories has been traced back to ancient times. Today, according to the George H. Gallup International Institute, more than half the world's population believes in ghosts and at least a third of that group have actually seen one. Whether we like it or not, ghosts and spirits are still part of modern civilization, and most of us believe there is a lot more going on in the universe than our practical scientists and social leaders would admit. This rejected part of human experience, which is another side of reality, will not go away simply by closing our eyes to it.

As we enter the new millennium, more and more people are opening their eyes to the Other Side. The number of paranormal experiences being reported has quadrupled in the last decade, and most organizations and researchers are swamped with new cases. Witnesses are much more willing to talk about such things, and they are actively looking for answers about what is really going on. The media and entertainment industries recognize this trend and have responded with an avalanche of articles and films on the subject. The surge of interest in the paranormal coupled with the growing emphasis on the global economy and emerging cultures makes this a truly planetary phenomenon. For the first time, local folklore is giving way to an international perspective that emphasizes the similarities and belief-altering components of these experiences. Though the cases presented in this book span many different cultures and religions, they are remarkably similar in their basic characteristics. Except for changes in location and language, they could easily be included among the two thousand true-life hauntings from the United States that I chronicled in *Haunted Places: the National Directory* (Penguin 1996).

For these reasons, I thought it time to focus on the best cases from throughout the whole world. For the purposes of this study, I have divided the world into three sections. The first is *Europe*, which includes Great Britain, Continental Europe, Scandinavià, Russia, the Mediterranean countries, and Africa. The second section is *The Americas*, which consist of North, South, and Central America, including the islands of the Caribbean and Atlantic. The third section covers *Asia*, including Eurasia, the Indian Ocean, Pacific Islands, and Australia. Each section is divided into individual countries, which are further divided into provinces or states listed in geographical order from east to west.

Every culture has developed its own terminology for dealing with paranormal manifestations. That culturally specific vocabulary is reviewed at the beginning of each section. The most general English term for a ghost is "apparition," which is an entity or spirit that has a recognizable human form. Apparitions are usually visible, though their presence can also be heard or perceived in some other way. Apparitions seem possessed of intelligence and can be quite purposeful in their activity. "Crisis apparitions" appear to warn people of impending disaster or the death of a loved one.

Many apparitions seem to have unfinished business of some kind. Often an apparition haunts a specific location because it is tied there by some emotional event, although such events need not be traumatic. Many apparitions appear because they loved a certain location, such as a librarian returning to a library or a gardener who refuses to leave a garden. And apparitions need not always be of dead people. Some cases on record seem to be caused by living persons projecting their likeness to another location and witnesses perceiving it as a ghost.

Many people are puzzled by the large number of headless ghosts or apparitions with missing limbs or just visible from the waist up. We must remember that some of these apparitions have been reappearing for centuries, and in that time many characteristics of their original environment have changed. The original elevation of ancient roads can rise as much as twenty feet due to grading and paving operations. Some landscapes have fallen considerably over the years due to erosion and the work of earth-moving equipment. Very few buildings have escaped remodeling and renovations over the years, and ghosts walking through a wall in modern times might just be walking through a passageway that existed many decades ago.

In some cases of headless ghosts, the person was actually beheaded or severely mutilated or the head buried away from the body for some reason. These ghosts purportedly roam through eternity looking for their lost heads. In actual fact, decapitating a living person seems to be one sure way of making a ghost. It is believed a severed human head might remain conscious for four or five seconds. They would certainly be the most terrifying few seconds of a person's life, charged with enough emotional energy to impregnate a castle wall or guillotine for centuries. As for other headless apparitions, perhaps it is best to reflect for a moment about exactly what it means to be "without a head." Such an archetypal image carries the idea that only the raw instinctual energy of the body is at work, while the higher part of a person, his or her intellect and spirit, has moved on.

✦   ✦   ✦

This book is intended for the mildly curious as well as the serious researcher, for seasoned tourists and armchair travelers alike. However, before actually visiting any of the sites listed here, please review the following words of caution:

✦ Always confirm and update directions locally. Every effort has been made to insure the accuracy of the information presented in this directory, however, the author assumes no responsibility for errors, misprints, or changes. Check business hours and locations of public places such as museums, libraries, and historical sites before visiting them.

✦ Some areas listed in this directory are in hazardous or isolated locations. Most desert locations should be avoided in the summer months. Some trails are intended for experienced hikers only. Deserted caves are full of hidden dangers. A few locations are in high crime areas. As a general rule, do not bother people unnecessarily and leave those alone who do not wish to be disturbed. Be careful and always check locally before visiting any of the sites.

✦ Respect local customs and beliefs. Never desecrate holy ground by taking unauthorized souvenirs or damaging property. Remember, a disrespectful attitude at a site sacred to anyone is an act of vandalism. At some of these locations, there are harsh penalties for frivolous behavior.

The *Haunted Places* series of books is an ongoing project, and the author would appreciate any correspondence, corrections, or comments. Please write to: Dennis William Hauck, P.O. Box 22201,

Sacramento, CA 95822-0201 USA. For information on current investigations and resources for experiencers, visit the author's Web site at www. hauntedplaces.com.

◆   ◆   ◆

Many individuals have contributed to this book. I especially wish to thank John Mason for his stunningly surreal photographs and stories about British locations. Sacred sites photographer Martin Gray has also provided some exceptionally beautiful pictures for which I am truly thankful. I am also indebted to Raymond Fenech for his research and photographs of Malta hauntings, and Jolling Luinberg for his research and photographs of ghosts in the Netherlands. I also owe my thanks to Lorraine Butler Glessner for sharing her experiences and photographs from Mexico, J.A. Hitchcock for her stories and photos from Okinawa, Deb Dupre for sharing her experience and photos from Salzburg Castle in Austria, and Judy Farncombe for sharing her psychic impressions and photos from Snowshill Manor in Gloucestershire. Pamela Heath supplied some splendid photographs from her trips to England and Italy.

I also want to thank Andrew Bennett for his material on the Chingle Hall haunting in Lancashire; Martin Lightburn for material from his *Gazetter of British Ghosts;* David Haslan for his information on the ghosts of Nottinghamshire; Dale Jarvis for information on the ghosts of Newfoundland, Canada; Lynne James for the material from the Cornish Connections; and Charles Ambridge for sharing his experiences in his haunted home, Treasure Holt in Essex. Donald Macer-Wright also shared his experiences at Littledean Hall in Gloucestershire and investigator Randolph Liebeck provided his reports and photos of the site.

The same heartfelt thanks goes to my Canadian colleagues, researcher and author W. Ritchie Benedict for sharing his files about Canadian ghosts and author John Robert Columbo for his insightful criticisms and sharing his carefully researched material on Canadian hauntings. I also want to thank my Toronto collaborators, Matthew Didier of TorontoGhosts.org and Patrick Cross of the Sci-Fi band.

A special thanks goes to author Tony Walker of White Rabbit Press for letting me use material from his *Ghostly Guide to Britain and Ireland* and to author Tom Slemen for his material on the ghosts of Liverpool and Merseyside. Alan Cleaver graciously shared his research on Berkshire hauntings, I am indebted to Paul Lee and John Fraser of the Ghost Club and Vincent O'Neil of the Borley Ghost Society as well as Jacqueline Taylor for her information on the ghosts of Yorkshire, England.

I would also like to thank Liz Vincent for her investigations and photos of places in Picton, Australia, Scott Pearson for his photo of the hotel ghost from Gawler, Australia, and Jack Sim for his material from the Brisbane Ghost Tours. Thanks too to Jesse Glass for his material from Japan.

I also wish to acknowledge the invaluable assistance of Bruce Schaffenberger for researching and photographing some of the European and North American entries included here. My colleague Richard Foster also provided considerable material.

Many organizations assisted in assembling material for this book. They include the Borley Ghost Society (629 E. 625 S #33, Ogden, UT 84404), the Ghost Research Society (P.O. Box 205, Oak Lawn, IL 60454), the Ghost Club (c/o Peter Underwood, Savage Club, 1 Whitehall Place, London, SW1A 2HD, Great Britain), the International Ghost Hunters Society (IGHS, Crooked River Ranch, OR 97760), the International Society for Paranormal Research (ISPR, 4712 Admiralty Way #541, Marina del Ray, CA 90292), the Australian Ghost Hunters Society (AGHS, P.O. Box 49, Seddon West, Victoria, 3011 Australia), and the Paranormal Society of the North Atlantic (PSNA, 11 Howley Ave. Ext., St. John's, Newfoundland, A1C 2T3 Canada).

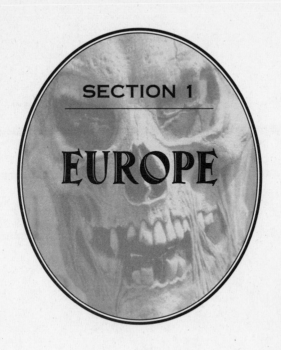

SECTION 1

EUROPE

The cases presented in this section include not only Great Britain, Ireland, and Continental Europe, but also Scandinavia, Russia, the Mediterranean countries, and Africa. This region is considered the birthplace of Western civilization and is also the most haunted area on the planet. Written descriptions of spirits go back over five thousand years in ancient Sumeria and Egypt, and the belief in the eternal soul probably goes back to prehistoric times. "Khu" is the earliest hieroglyphic word for ghost; according to the ancient Egyptian tradition, the khu left the body at death and then haunted the deceased person's family. The khu also had the ability to possess a person or animal and disrupt a person's health and mind, just as is the case with modern spirits. In modern Egypt, Ethiopia, and the Sudan, most people believe that an entire race of white-faced spiritual beings called "zars" parallels the activities of the human race and occasionally interacts with us.

Despite the ancient roots of the belief in spirits, no nation has had more experience with ghostly phenomena than England, and the English treat their ghosts with more respect than any other people. Virtually every city in England has its own poltergeist club or spiritualist society, and it is from England that most of our terms for ghostly

activity have originated. "Specter" is the general British term for an apparition, although among ghosthunters, it carries the connotation of a spirit with an evil or vengeful purpose. Our word "bogey" or "bogeyman" is derived from the north English word "boggart," which is a kind of shape-shifting creature that crawls into your bed to frighten you. Often black and hairy, they hide under the bed or in closets until it gets dark. In Lancashire, farmers hang horseshoes on their doors to keep boggarts away.

"Revenants" are ghosts of time, recognizable apparitions that return from the dead after long periods. Revenants always wear clothes dated to the period in which they lived, though it may take centuries before they decide to show up. They also follow certain color codes. "White Ladies" are the truest revenants, in the sense that they are connected to a specific house or location through some historical tie-in. "Brown Ladies" are tied to the earth and also have strong historical ties to a location. More often than not, they are looking for justice or seeking some other kind of recognition. "Blue Ladies" tend to be beneficent and tranquil presences, while the "Green Ladies" are the best spirits of all, full of nurturing energy and healing power. The rare "Pink Ladies" or "Red Ladies" are associated with acts of bloody violence. But be most careful around "Gray Ladies." They are a type of vengeful revenant that can stir up some real trouble and are most often found in British castles and old manor houses. Gray Ladies are usually noblewomen who died long ago in some kind of horrible accident, traumatic incident, or violent crime.

A "wraith" is the apparition of a person who just died or is on the verge of dying. Wraiths always carry the exact likeness of their human counterparts and most often appear to family members. Seeing the wraith of yourself means you are about to die. It is the same idea as the "co-walker," an apparition that is identical to a specific living person and first shows itself shortly before that person's death or at his or her funeral. "Spunkies" are the ghosts of unbaptized children. They wander the countryside searching for someone to give them a name or baptize them. They are said to have the ability to turn into white moths to hide from unsuspecting adults. Spunkies wander the earth until Judgment Day, though on Halloween they gather at churches and graveyards to meet the spirits of the recently departed and try to follow them into heaven.

Animals have ghosts too. Demon hounds, huge black dogs with glowing red eyes, haunt many areas around England. They are known as Barquists in Yorkshire, Shucks in Suffolk, or Strikers in Lancashire, and are most often sighted near ancient ruins or on prehistoric pathways. In Wales, the "derwyn corph" (corpse bird) is the phantom of a bird that sits on a windowsill and taps on the glass when someone is about to die. The most frightening of the animal ghosts is the "werewolf." King John was said to have returned to life as a werewolf, and the areas of Cumbria and Northumbria seem to be favorite grounds for werewolves. Werewolves are supernatural spirits on the borderline between life and death and have the ability to change from human to animal form, although they are said to be detectable in either form by their strong odor and reddish eyes.

"Gook" is the general Cornish term for a ghost, and "knockers" are Cornish ghosts who live in tin mines. They are supposed to be the spirits of the Jews who crucified Christ and were sent to the underground chambers for all eternity. For that reason, miners never make the sign of the cross for fear of alienating the ghosts, which help miners by knocking on the walls of mines to show where ore is located. "Kobolds" are similar spirits to the knockers, though not nearly as helpful. They cause accidents and rock falls, and generally hinder the miners' work.

"Elementals" are nature spirits, the ghosts of preternatural animals, or the spirits of supernatural beings such as fairies or elves. Elemental spirits, sometimes referred to as "sprites," are archetypal entities composed of pure energy, even if they have never existed in reality. Elementals usually take the form of some type of light phenomenon, such as balls of light or glowing mists, but they can also momentarily take the shape of birds or other animals. "Will-o'-wisp" is the name for the ghostly lights seen hovering over graves or marshes. Also known as miasmic lights, corpse fire, fairy fire, *ignis fatuus* (Fool's Fire), or jack-o'-lanterns, they are associated with the souls of people or animals at the transition between life and death. People foolish enough to follow such lights are led to an early death in isolated marshes or deserted graveyards.

Ireland has developed its own vocabulary for hauntings, and "tash" is the general Irish term for ghost. The tash can be the spirit of a human, animal, or even insect. The "phouka," on the other hand, is the Irish term for a human ghost that takes the form of an animal such as a horse or goat to trick people. The Irish believe that the dead should not be mourned for too long, since that only encourages their spirits to hang around. The "banshee" is the infamous Gray Lady of Death who haunts certain Irish families. She appears in a gray cloak and always has long, flowing hair, and she can be either young and comely or old and haggard. In either case, her wailing announces a family member's imminent death, even if that person is thousands of miles away from home.

The Scottish have also developed their own ghostly vocabulary. Their form of the banshee is called "bean nighe" ("little washer by the ford"), a woman who is seen washing the funeral clothes of those who are about to die. She is said to be the ghost of a very ugly woman who died in childbirth, and she can be identified by her buckteeth, enlarged single nostril, and elongated breasts. The "silky" is another female Scottish ghost. Known for wearing silk clothing, silkies love to work and do household chores after the family has retired for the evening. The only people silkies harm are lazy servants or malingerers. The "kelpie" is an invisible water spirit that haunts rivers and river crossings in Scotland, although it can appear as a wild man or horse that tricks people into coming into the river and drowning. The terrifying cries of kelpies can sometimes be heard during violent storms. The "nuggle" is a kelpie spirit native to the Shetland Isles. It always appears as a tiny horse, similar to a Shetland pony but with a distinctive curled tail. It has the same purpose as a kelpie, which is to lure unsuspecting people into dangerous stretches of water. "Water wraiths" in Scotland are thin old hags wearing green dresses who also try to lure people to their death by drowning.

In Scandinavia, the "fosse-grim" is a much more friendly water spirit. (The general term for ghost in Scandinavian countries is "grim," and "fosse" is the word for water.) The harmless fosse-grim usually takes on the form of a naked boy sitting in the middle of a stream or river while playing a harp. The "undine" is another harmless Scandinavian ghost that haunts rivers. The ghost is said to be a young woman who committed suicide by drowning herself after her lover rebuked her. The "kirk-grim" is a shapeshifting animal phantom that haunts old churches. It is thought to be the ghost of an animal buried alive in a churchyard as part of an old-time blessing ritual. It usually appears as a lamb, pig, or horse. In Denmark, the kirk-grim lives in the church steeple and protects the building.

The "liekkio" (flaming one) is a Finnish ghost of a child secretly buried in the woods, as was the case in unwanted pregnancies or children who died from abuse. It appears as a flame that dances on the ground to announce an impending death. The Finnish "lepke" is an apparition that appears to be a living person, until you go up to it to talk or touch it, and then it vanishes into thin air. The ghosts are also very lifelike in Iceland. In fact, nearly every jailhouse is haunted in Iceland—and with good reason. There was actually a law on the statute books for many years that enabled people to legally summon a troublesome ghost to court and have it bound over to authorities for incarceration.

In the Netherlands, the ghosts tend to be more physical than Scandinavian spirits. The "wolhaar-hond" is a large, phantom dog that emits a red glow and can be seen approaching from a distance late at night. The "tokolosh" is a ghoulish ghost of Holland and South Africa that can take on physical or spiritual form. The hairy, humanoid creature lives in rivers, though it can become invisible and is blamed for poltergeist activity.

"Doppelganger" is the German word for the co-walker of Great Britain. This apparition is considered the double of a person who is still alive, and its presence suggests that something terrible is about to befall that person. The German "poltergeist" (noisy ghost) refers to an invisible presence that makes knocking sounds or moves objects. There are hundreds of well-documented cases of poltergeists on record, and generally they tend to be destructive and sometimes violent. Recent research shows that poltergeists are almost always associated with adolescent children and possibly represent a kind of psychokinetic activity. "Nixies" are German water spirits such as the famous Lorelei that haunts a section of the Rhine. Nixies can change shape and are generally harmless, although they are said to require at least one human sacrifice per year.

The "blau kopf" (blue cap) is a ghostly sprite that haunts German mines. It takes the form of a bluish flame and can bring untold disaster if not treated with respect. The "Bergmonck" is the phantom of a giant monk that guards treasures in caves and abandoned mines. The "kneck" is a German water spirit similar to the Scandinavian fosse-grim in that it takes the form of a boy sitting in the middle of a stream playing a harp. Still, some superstitious people used to carry a knife when they went out in a boat on the river to protect themselves from the kneck should it decide to change into something more threatening.

In Romania, besides vampires and werewolves, the locals have to worry about "strigoi," soulless creatures that exist at the borderline between the living and the dead. "Chagrin" (or "harginn") is a Gypsy word for a mischievous ghost that most often takes the form of a large yellow hedgehog, which always foretells some impending disaster. In Greece, the "harpy" is a giant, ghostly bird with the face of a woman. According to tradition, the harpy is a spirit of the wind that must be kept happy or else it will possess people's souls. For that reason, the Greeks regularly sacrificed sheep to keep the harpies appeased.

"Kikimora" is an ancient Slavic term for household ghosts. Treated with respect, the kikimora protect the family and might even help with the housework. Household ghosts are so common in Russia that they have developed distinct classifications for them. "Domovoi" are domestic ghosts that tend to be nuisances or poltergeists but help out with chores if treated with respect. "Domovikha" are more quiet household spirits whose presence you can sense in certain rooms. "Pokoiniks" are relatives that refuse to leave even after they have died. The "kikimora" in Russia is a female goblin that lives near swamps and steals babies, while the "leshiy" is a wood sprite that plays tricks on people to get them lost in forests. Two Russian ghosts that haunt bodies of water are the water sprite "vodyanoi" and the mermaid "rusalka." However, Russian mermaids are not nearly as comely as those in other countries. Rusalka are hair-covered creatures with the faces of monkeys.

In France, even the ghosts are amorous. The "mara" is a mistlike presence in northern France that settles over people in their beds at night and gives them erotic nightmares. It is similar to the "succubus," the ghost of a beautiful woman who seduces men in their dreams. The "incubus" is the ghost of a handsome man who has his way with sleeping women. Sometimes this demon lover succeeds in impregnating sleeping women, who then give birth to deformed creatures like elves, trolls, and gnomes. Many medieval women hung garlic or herbs such as St. John's Wort around their beds to protect them from the advances of the incubus.

"White Lady" ghosts are also common in France, but they are found more often near bridges than in stately homes. According to tradition, these are the spirits of women sacrificed to river gods in pagan times. The "ankou" is the spirit of a person buried alive as part of a Dark Ages ceremony to consecrate the ground of new graveyards. The spirit of the victim was thought to serve as a ghostly protector for the grounds. Today these ghoulish ghosts appear to anyone who desecrates a plot or is disrespectful to the dead.

"Manes" was how the Romans described ghosts in general, and they divided them into two basic types. "Lares" were the ghosts of respectable people, while the "lemurs" were the ghosts of criminals, misfits, and vengeful relatives. The Romans sought to rid themselves of intrusive lemurs by making offerings to the gods, beating loud drums to scare them off, or burning black beans to create a stench that even repulsed the dead. Roman household ghosts ("lares domestici") tended to be very mischievous and engaged in poltergeist activity. "Larvae" was what the Romans called spirits who tormented their descendants. The larvae were thought to be most active during the month of May and many festivals were created to try to distract them from bothering families.

Such is the amazingly varied yet unique vocabulary that has developed in European countries to describe encounters with ghosts. The breadth and exactitude of these paranormal definitions is evidence of just how deeply the idea of spiritual afterlife is embedded in our Western culture and traditions. Most Europeans, even today, offer due respect to the dead, and are much more comfortable talking seriously about the supernatural than any other people in the world. Armed with their specialized terminology, we are ready to take a closer look at the ancient and modern spirits that haunt Europe to this day.

GREAT BRITAIN

Great Britain covers an area only about the size of the state of Oregon in the United States, yet the nation has had an impact on world culture and history that belies its size and population. Britain was not even considered part of the civilized world until the Roman conquest in the first century A.D. and did not become recognizable as a country until the Saxon migrations around A.D. 500. The island of Great Britain, made up of England, Wales, and Scotland is part of an archipelago, an outcropping of rock that is really part of the European continent; Ireland is a further westward extension of this same land mass. Before 5,000 B.C., these areas were connected by land links and settled by roving bands of hunters from many different lands.

Britain's cloudy past lends an air of mystery that is accentuated by its widely varied and surreal landscape. In fact, it is best to think of the island as two broad zones, the Highlands to the north and Lowlands to the south. These two zones are delineated by an imaginary line running from the mouth of the Tee River in the northeast to the mouth of the Exe River in the southwest. Another, more cultural division exists between the fertile lands of southeast England, which have closer ties to continental Europe,

and the less-accessible hill areas of the southwest and north England. Within these geographical divisions have developed unique peoples, each with their own history, beliefs, folklore—and ghosts.

As far as ghosthunting is concerned, Great Britain can be divided into ten regions: East England, Southeast England, Southwest England, London, Central England, Wales, Northeast England, Northwest England, Scotland, and Ireland. While Ireland and Northern Ireland are not part of the United Kingdom, they share geographical and cultural connections, and for convenience, are included in this section.

EAST ENGLAND (ANGLIA)

We begin our search for British ghosts in east England, an area that includes the east Midlands counties of Nottinghamshire, Derbyshire, Leicestershire, Lincolnshire, and Northamptonshire, as well as the East Anglia counties of Essex, Suffolk, Norfolk, and Cambridgeshire. This area was the first part of England to be settled by Europeans from the continent, and that long and sometimes violent history has generated lots of ghosts.

Borley Rectory, Borley, Great Britain (Vince O'Neil, Borley Ghost Club)

ESSEX

Borley

BORLEY RECTORY If you want to escape the hustle and bustle of the city of London and find a peaceful place in the country, take the A12 highway northwest out of the city into Essex County. Before long, the gray buildings will give way to green pastures, rolling hills, and sleepy little villages. By the time you reach Colchester, however, you will have to turn north toward Sudbury to stay in the country setting. Just before you reach Sudbury, you cross the Stour River into Suffolk County, but if you go west along the river on the Essex side, you will stumble onto the tiny village of Borley, location of "the most haunted house in England."

Yet you will find no souvenir shops selling Borley T-shirts and plastic ghosts, no bus tours of the haunted property. In fact, the hundred-or-so people who live in the town must travel to Long Melford or Sudbury to do their shopping and socializing, and very few are interested in talking about the scary things that still go on at the haunted site. But in the 1940s and 1950s, nearly anyone in the English-speaking world could tell you about Borley and the strange happenings there.

The publicity blitz started with the publication of newspaper articles and books about the investigation of a Borley landmark by the flamboyant occult researcher, Harry Price. Price was actually better known as a debunker rather than as a supporter of paranormal activity. In a number of cases, he had exposed the sleight-of-hand or mechanical devices behind illusions of ghostly events, and he put more than one London medium out of business. The son of a wealthy industrialist, Harry Price was born on January 17, 1881, and attended the best schools in England. Price became a tireless researcher of psychic phenomena, and his library of books on magic and psychic phenomena, now housed at the University of London, is still a primary source for scholars. In 1925, Price founded the National Laboratory of Psychical Research, the first such institution to be devoted to the scientific examination of paranormal occurrences.

But the highly regarded ghost hunter met his match in the form of an ugly redbrick building known as the Borley Rectory. Erected in 1863 across the road from a beautiful twelfth-century church, the rectory was built over the ruins of a thirteenth-century Benedictine monastery, though some evidence suggests a sixteenth-century convent also existed at the site. The gloomy twenty-three-room building served as home to Reverend Henry Bull, his wife, and their fourteen children. Immediately behind the rectory was a small servants' cottage, and in 1875, an extra wing was added to the rectory that resulted in a small courtyard between the house and cottage. The Bull family lived in the house for sixty-five years. When Henry Bull died in 1892, his son Harry took over as rector and lived in the house with his siblings until his death in 1927.

A new rector, Reverend G. Eric Smith, arrived on the scene with his wife in 1928. Smith soon found out that many of his parishioners refused to come to the rectory for meetings because they believed the building was haunted. According to legend, one of the monks from the monastery that once stood on the property eloped with a nun from a convent at Bures, a tiny community located eight miles from Borley. However, church authorities quickly apprehended the pair, as well as the coachman who drove the carriage in which they escaped. The monk was hanged, the coachman beheaded, and the nun was entombed in the walls of the convent while still alive. Afterwards, all three apparitions were sighted wandering in the area, and when the rectory was built, their forlorn spirits seemed to have taken up residence there.

Several members of the Bull family and their servants reported seeing the ghost of the woman along a path on the property that became known as the Nun's Walk, while the ghost of the monk was blamed for strange manifestations inside the house. Oddly, the Nun's Walk follows an underground stream, along which the nun meanders until the stream emerges into a creek, and then the ghost abruptly disappears. Henry Bull had a dining room window walled shut because he kept seeing a ghostly figure peering in at him, and his son, Harry, often reported seeing the nun and other apparitions while resting in an octagonal gazebo in the garden. Harry Bull suffered from narcolepsy and spent many hours languishing in a relaxed, hypnagogic state there, which might account for his increased sensitivity to the phenomena. In any case, Harry described seeing the nun, the phantom coach in which she eloped, and a long-dead family servant named Amos, who apparently slipped over from the Other Side with the other ghosts. Sometimes the phantom coach driven by a headless coachman was seen in the garden.

Hundreds of witnesses have reported hearing the murmuring voice of the nun or seeing her apparition walking slowly down the path. The nun is the most frequently sighted apparition at Borley. In fact, her ghost is said to appear regularly each year on the 28th of July, though the massive crowds that gather to witness the phenomenon seem to frighten her away. In 1988, so many people showed up that the police were called out for emergency crowd control. Everyone was disappointed, although a flurry of well-documented encounters followed in the early 1990s.

In any case, by the time the Smiths arrived, Borley Rectory had a solid reputation for being haunted. In an effort to dispel the stories, Reverend Smith wrote to the editor of London's *Daily Mirror* asking for the address of a psychical research society that could launch a scientific investigation to find some rational explanation for the sightings. Aware of his reputation as a scientific investigator and debunker, the editor dispatched Harry Price, but as soon as Price set foot on the premises, all hell broke loose. A flying stone smashed through the front window, an ornament exploded in the hallway, keys flew out of their locks, and a shower of pebbles, coins, medals, and other small objects rained down the main stairway. An astounded Price immediately set up a séance in the Blue Room, a large bedroom overlooking the garden and the Nun's Walk. At the séance, Price, his secretary, a reporter from the *Daily News*, the Smiths, and two of the Bull sisters who were visiting the house witnessed the spirit of Harry Bull make coded rapping sounds from a wall mirror.

Price began an in-depth investigation and returned to Borley many times to track down explanations for the activity. Rats eating wiring insulation in the attic could have caused the bell ringing. Lights that appeared in the windows of the empty rectory could have been reflections from the headlights of railroad engines that passed through the valley below. At one séance in the Blue Room, heavy footsteps and the low voice of a man were heard, just as the spirit of Harry Bull was being called forth. Then the sound of shutters being drawn rumbled through the room. "Are you the spirit of Harry Bull?" asked a stunned Price. In a guttural dialect, the handyman replied, "He's dead, and you're daft!"

Nonetheless, when the *Daily News* started reporting all the strange things happening at Borley, the tiny town was overrun with curious visitors, amateur investigators, eager reporters, and high-society types traveling in coach parties from London. The Smiths found themselves under siege in their own home and were forced to abandon the rectory in April 1930. Five months later, the new rector, Lionel Foyster, moved in with his wife and daughter. Foyster was Harry Bull's cousin, and their family connection seemed to escalate the ghostly activity considerably. In the first fourteen months the Foysters lived in the house, investigators documented nearly two thousand separate paranormal events. The unexplainable incidents included disembodied voices, moving and flying objects, apported objects that materialized out of thin air, and mysterious fires. Scrawled messages also started appearing on the walls that piteously pleaded for prayers of forgiveness and the saying of Mass, as if written by some tormented soul.

The Foysters put up with all the ghostly activity until 1935, when Lionel quit the church and took an office job in London. Afterwards, no other rector would agree to stay at Borley Rectory, and the house fell into disrepair. By that time, however, Harry Price had become obsessed with the place. He spent all his time trying to understand what was happening, and finally concluded that the events at Borley were true supernatural manifestations. In May 1937, he rented the rectory for one year, then moved in and launched an intensive investigation of the premises with forty-eight volunteers who monitored activity around the clock. Their work resulted in two books documenting in meticulous detail all the paranormal events. Price was working on a third volume on Borley in 1948, when he died from a sudden heart attack.

After Price moved out of the rectory in June 1938, entrepreneur William Hart Gregson, who planned to organize tours of the haunted site, purchased the property. But at a séance conducted by one of Price's volunteers in March of that year, an entity named Sunex Amures communicated that he planned to burn down the rectory to end its misery. At midnight on February 27, 1939, a mysterious fire completely gutted Borley Rectory. Both townspeople and police officers reported seeing strange figures inside the house moving around within the flames, and one constable witnessed a "lady in gray" cross the courtyard.

At another séance just before the fire, the spirit of a nun named Marie Lairre communicated that she had had an illicit love affair in the seventeenth century with Henry Waldegrave, whose manor house stood on the property. In the cellar of a convent that once stood on the spot where the rectory was located, the man strangled her and buried her body in the earthen floor. According to the spirit, it happened in May 1667. In 1943, when it was obvious the rectory was not going to be rebuilt, Price used the opportunity to excavate the cellar to search for the woman's body. He did

indeed discover the bones of a young woman, along with some religious pendants worn by nuns. He buried the bones and relics with due ceremony in the church graveyard. In 1955, a team of ghost hunters uncovered a three hundred-year-old secret tunnel underneath the rectory that connected it to the garden area, possibly to the cellar of the Waldegrave manor house. At the same time, archeologists found more evidence that a Tudor-era convent had once existed at the site.

During the demolition of the remaining walls and chimneys of the rectory in 1944, a photographer from *Life* magazine caught a picture of a "levitating brick" in the arch of the old doorway. Harry Price called it "Borley's final phenomenon," but the ghosts of Borley were hardly ready to give up. Where the rectory once stood there is now an orchard, and in recent years, several people have witnessed apparitions there. From some bushes near the Nun's Path, the murmuring voice of a woman is sometimes heard. The nun's apparition, dressed in a gray habit and cowl, is seen walking along the path, right through a modern garage built on the property, out the other side of the garage, and over the dry ditch that used to be a creek. In the former garden area, a four-wheeled coach drawn by two bay horses materializes and then disappears into the bushes, always at the same location. Sometimes a headless coachman can be seen at the reins.

Across the street, in the courtyard of Borley Church, are the graves of Harry Bull and his family. Ectoplasmic apparitions have been seen and photographed floating over their graves. Inside the church, unexplainable ghostly voices, sighs, and the sounds of an old, squeaky door opening and closing have been recorded near the altar and halfway down the aisle. Hundreds of mysterious knockings, rappings, footsteps, and the clatter of objects being tossed have been recorded in the locked-down church by several teams of researchers. Photographs of kneeling figures and hovering lights have also been taken inside the church, and near the Waldegrave family tomb, both psychics and electronic measuring devices have detected an intense, whirling column of ice-cold energy.

The best time to witness the ghostly activity at

Borley Church, the Waldegrave tomb, and in the orchard where the rectory stood is during the month of August. Paranormal occurrences recorded over the last fifty years clearly indicate that August is the peak for such activity. For more information on current investigations at Borley, visit the Borley Rectory Web site at www.borleyrectory.com or the Borley Family History Pages at www.elmroy.demon.co.uk/pages/genealogy4.html.

Holland Marches

TREASURE HOLT Another house with a lot of haunted history in Essex is known as Treasure Holt. Treasure Holt is a private residence that stands in lonely country on the edge of Holland Marshes. A long driveway leads to the house from a little-traveled road, and one could easily pass by it without knowing that it is there. But this house has a history that goes back before 1138, and it is well known as the most haunted house in the district. In the 1920s, Treasure Holt was investigated by the Society for Psychical Research, and in 1972, B.B.C. television did a broadcast from there in their Haunted East Anglican Houses series. Numerous newspaper articles have been written about the house. All agree that the house has numerous ghosts.

In earlier days Treasure Holt was called Perles Farm, and for many years it was an old coaching inn. King Charles and a band of his followers came to the isolated inn to hide from Oliver Cromwell's Roundheads. However, in less than a week, a monk was sent from the St. Osyth Priory to warn Charles that one of Cromwell's commanders found out he was staying at the inn and was gathering forces to surprise him. The king took heed of the warning and left immediately for a safer place. Many witnesses have seen the monk on the grounds, usually walking about a foot or so above the ground on the level of the old path. The phantom monk has also been seen, carrying a box under his arm, in the main room in the house. He disappears into the wall next to a fireplace that used to be an entry to an underground tunnel. It is thought that he hid stolen property from the priory in the house, though none has ever been found. The only unusual property found here was in 1928, when a brick floor was being relaid, and some human bones, leather buckles, and a token dated "1793" was discovered.

Treasure Holt was a favorite resting place for King Charles' Cavaliers and many times Roundheads and Cavaliers have been seen in ghostly battles on the property. The ghost of a lone Cavalier has also been seen in the former lounge area of the inn. Other ghosts are also seen here. There is the apparition of a lady with long blonde hair riding a white horse that rides up to the house and vanishes completely near the entrance. It is very similar to a phantom horse and rider seen in Pork Lane, Great Holland, crossing the road and then riding across the fields in the direction of Treasure Holt. A lady dressed in a crinoline gown has also been spotted inside the house in the old lounge area. Here is a statement by Charles Ambridge, present owner of Treasure Holt:

"I bought the house in January 1980, it was in a terrible condition, having fallen into disrepair over many years, the sightings started as we set about restoring the house. A carpenter was working in a back bedroom, repairing the stairs when he came down shaking like a leaf and saying that he had just seen a figure of a Cavalier, just standing on the stairs looking at him, he went to say something to the Cavalier and he just vanished into thin air. We made two of the rooms upstairs fairly habitable and we moved into them, as they were in the process of being repaired there were no doors on the rooms, one night my wife woke me and said look at our daughter she is sleepwalking, at which I looked into the children's room and saw a young girl walk across the room towards the window, I rushed to the room but the girl had vanished, but my daughter was fast asleep on the other side of the room from where the apparition had vanished, we realized then that we had just seen the 'Crinoline Lady.' In July 1995 we had some friends over for dinner, it was during the day, it was a lovely warm summer's day, we were all in the lounge having a few drinks and a chat, my wife myself and the wife of my friend went to the kitchen to bring in the food, leaving the husband in the main room on his own, he suddenly cried out and we all rushed into the room where he was sitting, he then told us that as he was sitting there he saw the apparition of a big man, dressed in a gray suit, come through the front wall, cross the room and vanished on the stairs. I told this story to a member of the local ghost society, who in turn told the local newspaper who ran the story in the local, shortly after the article appeared I received a phone call from a woman who said that the ghost that was seen was the ghost of her Uncle Percy, she was his niece and she went on to describe the apparition, she said he was a big man, dressed in a gray suit, with a red beard, now as my friend said the ghost had a red beard it was not mentioned in any of the reports, so it would appear that it was the same ghost as seen by all the other people, she also said that her uncle Percy liked to have a drink or two at the local pub, and so as not to disturb anyone when he came home late he had an entrance fitted to the back stairs, when repairing the stairway a short time later we discovered, behind the wall coverings an old doorway exactly where my friend said that uncle Percy had vanished, we have left the doorway uncovered."

Treasure Holt is located on the edge of the Holland Marshes on the east coast of England, 70 miles east of London. Treasure Holt, Burrs Road, Great Clacton, Essex, CO15 4SU England. For more information, E-mail Charlie@treasureholt. freeserve.co.uk or visit the Web site at www. treasureholt.freeserve.co.uk.

SUFFOLK

Bildeston

CROWN HOTEL There are several haunted inns where you can stay overnight in Suffolk, but only one calls itself "the most haunted public house in Britain." A fifteenth-century coaching inn, the Crown Hotel has been fully restored but kept many original features such as the exposed beams and inglenook fireplaces. Among the many ghosts here are two small Victorian children dressed in tattered clothing who stroll through the lounge, a lady in a gray dress who hanged herself, an elderly gentleman who sits in a chair in the lounge, and a man in an odd hat and gray coat seen standing in a corner of the bar.

Famed British ghosthunter Peter Underwood investigated the place and documented reports of mysterious footsteps, guests being touched by invisible hands, and loud hammering sounds at the front door when no one is there. The Crown sits along a rural road in the village of Bildeston, which is located at the midpoint of Bury St. Edmunds, Ipswich, and Colchester. The Crown Hotel is at 104 High Street in Bildeston, Suffolk. For more information, phone 1449-740510.

Blyford

QUEENS HEAD INN Moving lights, loud explosions, crackling sounds, and disembodied footsteps haunt the Queens Head Inn at Blyford in Suffolk. The manifestations did not begin until after a tunnel was discovered in the cellar that led into the nearby church, where smugglers once hid their contraband. The source of the sounds is thought to be one of the frequent gunfights between smugglers and tax collectors that took place near the old church.

Bury St. Edmunds

ABBEY OF ST. EDMUNDS The ruins of a tenth-century abbey in the oddly named market town of Bury St. Edmunds are haunted by mysterious monks, who gather around the gateway to the grounds. The abbey was home to a shrine to Saint Edmund, an Anglo-Saxon king murdered by the Danish warriors and subsequently beatified by the Catholic Church. King Henry VIII later destroyed the abbey, and the final resting place of the saint has never been found. However, the spirits of the monks appeared to a clergyman named Webling, who wrote a biography of Saint Edmund, and told the author that Edmund's body had been removed from its sarcophagus and buried deep in another part of the church to protect it from those who would defile it.

SUFFOLK HOTEL The Suffolk Hotel stands less than two hundred yards from the abbey, and its connections to the site are the source of its own ghosts. Formerly known as the Greyhound Inn, the modernized hotel became the center of the town of Bury. Today, a solitary monk haunts a tunnel that runs between the old inn and the abbey. His slightly inebriated compatriots haunt the hotel itself, although a few ghosts of drunken monks have even spilled out onto Buttermarket Square in front of the hotel. The Suffolk Hotel is at 38 Buttermarket in Bury St Edmunds, Suffolk. For bookings, phone 0284-753995 or fax 0284-750973. For more information on the ghosts of St. Edmunds, visit the White Rabbit Web site at www.afallon.com/pages/whiterabbit1.html.

Dunwich

DUNWICH BEACH If you are just interested in spending some time alone in Suffolk, you might want to take a stroll on the haunted beach at Dunwich. Dunwich was once England's sixth largest town and a very important center in medieval society. However, over the centuries, the town was destroyed by sea erosion following several large storms. Some say the city was cursed, and today, barely anything remains except the beach. But the apparition of a man in Elizabethan costume haunts the beach, and sometimes, the sounds of church bells can be heard coming from the old Dunwich Church long claimed by the sea.

Sudbury

BULL INN Built as a private dwelling for a prosperous wool merchant in 1450, the Bull became an inn in 1580. The lovely timbered building still contains a weavers' gallery, oak beams, open fireplaces, and period furniture. The ghost here is Richard Evered, a farmer stabbed to death in a hallway after an argument with a friend. The corpse was laid out in what is now the hotel lounge, but it disappeared that night and has never been found. The ghost, however, has returned and is blamed for strange noises emanating from various places in the inn, as well as moving furniture and doors that inexplicably open and close by themselves. One of the rooms above the hall in which Evered was murdered had to be locked up due to all the disturbances, and it remains sealed to this day. The Bull is on Hall Street at Long Melford, Sudbury, Suffolk. For information, phone 0787-378494 or fax 0787-880307.

ST. GREGORY'S CHURCH Simon of Sudbury haunts St. Gregory's Church in Sudbury, Suffolk. He was once Archbishop of Canterbury and was murdered by supporters of Wat Tyler in 1381. Poor Saint Gregory's head was displayed on a spike at the center of London for nearly a week, so it's no wonder his spirit has sought refuge back at the peaceful church where he spent his best years.

NORFOLK

Diss

SCOLE INN The Scole Inn is an ornate, redbrick structure, which has not changed much since it was built in 1655. The sixteen rooms of the inn would still be recognizable to seventeenth-century travelers. The inglenook fireplaces, oak beams, heavy oak doors, and opulently carved staircase are the same. The ghost is a woman named Emily, who was murdered by her jealous husband while they were staying in a room at the inn in the 1750s. Poor Emily was innocent of any infidelity, despite the amorous advances of a notorious highwayman also staying at the inn. Her pale form, wearing a long robe, is seen most frequently descending the staircase, though she has also been spotted at the entryway and in the hotel bars. The Scole Inn is near Diss in Norfolk County. For information, call 0379-740481.

King's Lynn

DUKE'S HEAD HOTEL The Duke's Head is an imposing pinkish building on the main square in the town of King's Lynn that has been the center of activity in this agricultural region for over three hundred years. The inn dates from 1683, and in the eighteenth century it became famous as an elegant coaching inn, with stages leaving for Yarmouth, Norwich, and London. The ghost who haunts the inn is a maidservant executed in the square in the eighteenth century. Her nebulous form sneaks about in the hallways, and encountering her is said to be a very unpleasant experience. The woman poisoned her mistress in their hotel room, but her motives have never been discovered. The Duke's Head Hotel is located in the Tuesday Market Place in King's Lynn, Norfolk. For more information, phone 0553-774996 or fax 0553-763556.

RAYNHAM HALL Raynham Hall in Norfolk, about twenty miles from Kings Lynn and five miles from the hamlet of Fakenham, is a sixteenth-century estate haunted by the famous Brown Lady apparition, which has appeared on the great oak staircase there for the last three hundred years. She is described as wearing a brown brocade dress and being normal in all respects, except where her eyes

Raynham Hall, Norfolk, Great Britain (*Country Life*)

should be are deep, dark holes. Her frightening ghost has been seen by scores of credible witnesses, including visiting government dignitaries. In 1787, she appeared at the foot of the bed of King George IV, who was spending the night at Raynham Hall. "I will not stay another hour in this accursed house," said King George on vacating the premises in the middle of the night, "for tonight I have seen that which I hope to God I may never see again." Guards were even posted in the house to capture the ghost, but when she appeared to them, they froze where they stood, and she walked right through them. On another occasion, on Christmas Day 1835, Raynham Hall was full of important people come from London to spend the holidays, but the Brown Lady completely disrupted the festive mood by appearing in the hallways, on the staircase, and in her former room.

The Brown Lady became so notorious that in the early 1900s, an author named Captain Frederick Marryat set out to expose the ghost as a hoax. When her apparition confronted him late at night in an upstairs hallway and refused to identify herself, Captain Marryat fired his gun at point blank range. The bullet passed through the entity and lodged in a heavy oak door, and the incredulous man instantly became a believer in spirits. In 1926, the Brown Lady was seen again, descending the main staircase in broad daylight.

Then, on September 19, 1936, a photographer for *Country Life* magazine and his assistant were at Raynham Hall taking pictures of the house. All of a sudden, the photographer saw a misty vapor appear at the top of the main staircase. As he watched, the mist coalesced into the form of a lady in a long gown who began walking down the stairs toward him. The assistant was busy setting up the camera and did not see the apparition. When the photographer hollered at him to expose the plate, the man immediately snapped the picture. As soon as the flash went off, the ghost disappeared, but her image was still captured on the film. Several experts deemed the photographic plate genuine, and the amazing photograph has been examined rigorously over the years.

The Brown Lady of Raynham Hall is Dorothy Walpole, who died in 1726. Witnesses identified her from a portrait that hung in an upstairs bedroom. In fact, the painting was removed from the house in 1904, on the mistaken belief that it would stop the haunting. Dorothy was the wife of Charles Townshend, the Second Marquis of Townshend and original owner of Raynham Hall. She was also the sister of Sir Robert Walpole, England's first Prime Minister, and her apparition has also been seen at his former residence. Dorothy's many years of blissful marriage to Charles ended when stories started to circulate about her lewd behavior when she was younger and living in Paris. She confessed that the rumors were true, and her husband never forgave her. He banished her to her room in the mansion and they rarely spoke. After she died suddenly of smallpox, more rumors began circulating that in fact her husband had pushed her down the main staircase at Raynham and she died of a broken neck. Whether the rumors originated with servants or a coroner is uncertain, and whether or not they are true will also never be known. But, then again, maybe the Brown Lady of Raynham Hall is trying to tell us something by her dramatic appearances on the staircase.

Dorothy's ghost has also been seen at Houghton Hall, the former home of her brother, Sir Robert Walpole, and at Sandringham Palace, which is also in Norfolk. Sandringham Palace is haunted by another spirit who manifests as a poltergeist that is most active on Christmas Eve. The

Sandringham Palace, Norfolk, Great Britain (John Mason)

unseen presence throws Christmas cards all over the floor of the servants' quarters on the second floor, pulls blankets off beds, walks through the corridors late at night, and breathes down the necks of maids to frighten them. The apparition of a short male lamplighter has been seen on the property, and he might be responsible for the poltergeist pranks. But the most famous ghost here is Dorothy Walpole. Prince Philip's uncle, Prince Christopher of Greece, once saw the head and shoulders of Dorothy reflected in a mirror in a bedroom in which he was staying at Sandringham.

Norfolk County

BIRCHAM NEWTON AIRBASE The former Bircham Newton Airbase in Norfolk is a modern military airfield full of ghosts. There is a phantom automobile packed with men that crashes, over and over again, into a metal hangar. Three airmen haunt the Squash Court at the airfield, and two ghostly men engaged in a fencing match have also been seen. In the 1960s, Reverend Aubrey Aitken, vicar of St. Margaret's in King's Lynn, attempted an exorcism of the lost souls. During the exorcism, a medium contacted the spirits, who explained they had all died in an airplane crash during World War II but kept returning to the airfield, reliving past scenes in their lives there. They also complained of being wet all the time, since the plane had crashed in water and their bodies never recovered. Apparently, the exorcism did not work, because many employees of the Construction Industry Training Board, which now occupies the site, have reported seeing the apparitions.

CASTLE RISING Castle Rising in Norfolk County is a massive Norman castle haunted by the screaming ghost of Queen Isabella, known as the "She-Wolf of France" for her immoral ways. She plotted with her lover, Roger Mortimer, to murder her husband, King Edward II. Isabella was forced to marry when she was only twelve, but she soon discovered that her new husband had no interest in her as he was a homosexual. He only needed her to produce an heir to the throne. Isabella and her followers succeeded in defeating the

Castle Rising, Norfolk, Great Britain (John Mason)

king and eventually had him tortured to death. But her son, King Edward III, imprisoned Isabella in Castle Rising in 1358. She soon went completely mad and died there twenty-seven years later. The queen's demented laughter and horrific screams are still heard on the castle grounds, and her wailing spirit is also said to haunt her former home, Nottingham Castle in Nottinghamshire.

FREIBRIGG HALL For over 170 years, a man who loved books more than life itself has haunted the library of stately Freibrigg Hall in the Norfolk countryside. William Windham III, an eighteenth-century scholar and close friend of lexicographer Samuel Johnson, died in London trying to save books from a fire in a friend's library. Afterwards, his spirit returned to the library he loved at his own estate. For many years, it was the duty of the butler to set out books on the table for the ghost to read. The National Trust now owns the estate, and workers there have witnessed Windham's ghost on many occasions. The apparition is usually seen sitting in an armchair near the library fireplace reading a book. Just before he fades into oblivion, the ghost calmly lays down the book on a table.

Norwich

CURAT HOUSE In Norwich County, Curat House is haunted by the sounds of disembodied footsteps walking the hallways. The haunting began after the remains of a woman's skeleton were found in the cellar of the Tudor mansion. The body dates back to a synagogue that stood on this spot but burned down in a great fire that scorched most of the town.

Stow Bardolph

HARE ARMS The Hare Arms Hotel in the town of Stow Bardolph in Norfolk is haunted by one of the landlords, nicknamed "Capon." His wife baked him a pie in which she supposedly put some psychedelic mold (ergot). The LSD-like compound caused the man to lose his mind, and he eventually committed suicide. Today, his crazed spirit is responsible for loud noises, moving objects, shuffling footsteps going around in a circle, and insane cries.

Thetford

THE BELL HOTEL The Bell is a timbered, fifteenth-century inn located in the center of one of East Anglia's original market towns, a picturesque community on the banks of the Ouse River. The hotel is haunted by a former owner from the nineteenth century. Her name is Betty Radcliff, and her restless spirit walks through her inn at night, wringing her hands, head bowed in despair. After falling in love with a stable boy at the inn and being rejected by him, Betty hanged herself from a balcony outside Room 12. The balcony is gone now, but Betty's anguished spirit remains, still suffering the pangs of unrequited love. Her unmarked grave is in the cemetery across from the hotel. The Bell Hotel is located on King Street in Thetford, Norfolk. For information, call 0842-754455 or fax 0842-755552.

CAMBRIDGESHIRE

Balsham

WRATTING ROAD Wratting Road in Balsham, Cambridgeshire, is haunted by a unique phantom known as the "Shuck Monkey." The terrifying apparition is of a large black dog with a pale, monkey's face. North of the village of Wicken Fen, the phantom of a large black dog is also seen on the grounds of Spinney Abbey, and ghostly black dogs have been seen roaming near the Wandlebury Hillfort on the Gog Magog Hills.

Barnwell

OLD ABBEY HOUSE The Old Abbey House in Barnwell, Cambridgeshire, has numerous spirits haunting its premises. The apparitions of a black nun, a man wearing chain mail armor, the disembodied head of a woman, and a huge jovial ghost known as the "Giant Squire," have all been witnessed here. The Squire lived in the house in the eighteenth century and seems to be spending most of his otherworldly existence chasing his small phantom dog, which he dearly loved in life.

Cambridge

CAMBRIDGE-TO-BEDFORD ROAD A section of road is located near the intersection of the Cambridge-to-Bedford Road and Ermine Street. An old gallows (gibbet) is all that marks the location of an old inn called the Caxton Gibbet. But the son of a landlord of the inn still haunts the area. He was accused of murdering and robbing three guests at the inn and was hanged at the gallows across from it. Some say the lad protests his innocence to this day, and his apparition is reported approaching strangers who stop at the historical marker there.

CAMBRIDGE UNIVERSITY Cambridgeshire is best known as the home of Cambridge University, which is haunted by many strange presences. A ghostly Roman centurion has been seen at several locations on the Girton College campus, and Peterhouse College can be considered as officially haunted. The senior bursar, Andrew Murison, two butlers, and several students have seen the figure of Francis Dawes, a former student who attended the college in the nineteenth century. In 1998, the college dean, Reverend Graham Ward, admitted there was a ghost at Peterhouse and said he was investigating the possibility of having the presence exorcised.

Caxton Gibbet, Cambridge, Great Britain (John Mason)

At Sidney Sussex College, two separate apparitions have appeared in the south wing of Chapel Court. In 1967, two students witnessed a "floating, pale-yellow head," and in the room directly over their room, another student observed a "large blue and purple eye" manifest in a corner. Seven years earlier, the head of Oliver Cromwell was interred in the college, and it has been suggested that that is the source of the haunting. The rest of Cromwell's body haunts Ghost Hill at Murrow in Cambridgeshire.

Cambridgeshire County

KIMBOLTON CASTLE The apparition of Catherine of Aragon haunts the Queen's Chamber at Kimbolton Castle in Cambridgeshire. She was imprisoned in her room at the castle for the final two years of her life. The unidentified ghost of a small child has also been seen on the ramparts of the castle.

MADINGLY HALL At Madingly Hall in the Cambridgeshire farmlands, a young man in Tudor dress haunts the upper floors. The unidentified apparition has a green face and carries a scowling expression. The ghost of the mansion's first owner, Lady Ursula Hyde, haunts the passageway between the house and the church. When the house was built in 1543, her husband furnished it with items taken from monasteries. Lady Hyde was very religious and never forgave her husband for what she considered a sacrilegious act.

SAWSTON HALL At Sawston Hall in the Cambridgeshire countryside, an unidentified Gray Lady haunts the hall and knocks three times at the front door whenever she appears. The ghost of Mary, Queen of Scots, appears in the Tapestry Room, where the sound of a non-existent spinet piano being played is sometimes heard. Followers of Lady Jane Grey burned down the house after Mary, Queen of Scots, stayed there while visiting. However, the gracious queen had the house rebuilt at her own expense.

Great Wibraham

CARPENTERS ARMS Another haunted hotel in Cambridgeshire is the Carpenters Arms in Great Wilbraham. It is haunted by the recurring sound of footsteps in the upstairs hallway that seem to echo from a long distance, although they can be traced as they move down the corridor and always end at the same point.

Holywell

YE OLDE FERRYBOAT INN Ye Olde Ferryboat Inn in Holywell, Cambridgeshire, is one of England's oldest inns. It sits on the Great Ouse River and is named for a ferryboat that used to cross there. The pub at the inn is haunted by the White Lady, who appears in the middle of the room, points at

a gravestone on the floor, then walks out of the pub down to the river and vanishes. She is the young lady buried on the spot where the pub now sits, and her gravestone is still in the barroom. Her name is Juliet Tewsley, and she committed suicide by hanging herself in a room at the inn, after her lover rejected her for another. Juliet is said to appear each March 17 on the anniversary of her death.

Huntington

GOLDEN LION HOTEL If you want to meet a Cambridgeshire ghost, you might consider checking into the Golden Lion Hotel in St. Ives, near Huntingdon, which has ghosts in two of its rooms. The beautiful medieval coach inn has a white Georgian façade and is located not far from the Ouse River. The inn was used by Oliver Cromwell as his local headquarters at the time of the English Civil War. It is his ghost that haunts his former bedroom here.

The ghost of the young nurse to his children also manifests here. Her likeness can be seen in a portrait on a wall in the restaurant. Because of her shimmering green ghost, she is known as the Green Lady and has been nicknamed "Ivy" by the staff. She became the mistress to Cromwell and ended up hanging herself out of despair of never being able to be truly part of his family. Records say she hanged herself from a roof beam in Room 13, though later owners of the inn eliminated the room number so as not to discourage guests from staying there. Something pulls at bedcovers, makes gasping sounds, and opens then slams doors in the room. The Golden Lion Hotel is on Market Hill in St. Ives near Huntingdon in Cambridgeshire County. The phone number is 0480-492100.

Tydd St. Giles

HANNATH HALL The unquiet dead also roam Hannath Hall in Tydd St. Giles, Cambridgeshire. The ghosts of a woman, a maid, and a fair-haired boy are seen in the corridors late at night. The woman is the wife of former owner Joseph Hannath. Joseph refused to bury his wife after her death and kept her body in the house. Finally, after nearly two months, he gave her a proper burial, though it was all too much for the maidservant who committed suicide not long afterwards. The boy was murdered in the house and is now apparently afraid to leave it.

Wansford

YARWELL TUNNEL The century-old Yarwell Tunnel at Wansford is haunted by a pet cat named "Snowy," which belonged to the stationmaster at Wansford. The man was deaf and was hit and killed by a train while looking for his cat in the tunnel. Their white ghosts are seen emerging from the mists at the entrance to the tunnel.

Wisbech

BOWLING GREEN TAP If you are seeking a little relaxation from the ghost scene in Cambridgeshire, stay away from the Bowling Green Tap in Wisbech. It is haunted by the active presence of a Quaker ghost, a male apparition, who is also blamed for poltergeist activity in the pub.

Wittering

ROYAL AIR FORCE BASE Another of Britain's haunted airfields is the Royal Air Force Base at Wittering in Cambridgeshire. The field is plagued by a phantom bomber that swoops down towards the runway with only a whistling sound. An airman wearing a World War II uniform has also been seen in the Control Tower. The manifestations date back to a 1940s accident in which a bomber hit by enemy fire attempted to land without engines. The out-of-control plane hit the Control Tower, and the accident claimed many victims.

NOTTINGHAMSHIRE

Arnold

BONNINGTON THEATRE The Bonnington Theatre in Arnold, Nottinghamshire, opened in 1982, but most of the employees there are already convinced the place is haunted. Disembodied footsteps are heard, an icy presence haunts the front landing and lighting control room above it, lights in the theater are switched on and off by some unseen force, and people get a very discomforting feeling that someone is watching them when no one is there. Two independent surveys of the theater by mediums have both concluded that the presence haunting the place is a female spirit that spends most of its time in the toilets on the front landing—probably near where she is buried. According to records, a 1700s Quaker cemetery existed on the location where the theater now sits, and construction workers building the Arnold Leisure Centre, of which the theater is a part, found human bones and a skull, presumably from the former graveyard.

BESTWOOD HOTEL The sounds of a child crying haunt the site of an old hunting lodge in Sherwood Forest built by King Edward III in 1363. In the 1680s, King Charles II and his mistress, Nell Gwynn, used it as a love nest. Nell was an orange seller before becoming an actress and meeting the king. He later gave the lodge to her as a token of his love and she spent the rest of her life there. A hotel named the Bestwood was built over the ancient stone foundation of the lodge in 1865, and ever since lodgers and employees have complained of the overpowering odor of oranges, loud footsteps late at night, and the eerie sounds of children sobbing in the hallways.

Staff members report seeing apparitions dressed in medieval clothing roaming the halls, and once a barman was changing a barrel in the basement when the lights went dim and a disembodied voice asked, "Can I help you, Sir?" The man went running up the stairs screaming and eventually quit. Other employees have also given up their jobs rather than work at the haunted lodge. Chambermaid Glennis Cuddeford reported that whenever young children stayed at the lodge, the smell of fresh oranges was almost too strong to bear. "I finally left in 1985, after two years working there," she said. "The place scared me to death!" The Bestwood Lodge Hotel is located in Bestwood County Park in Arnold, Nottinghamshire. For more information, phone 1159-203011.

Nottingham

NOTTINGHAM CASTLE Nottingham Castle is one of England's most haunted places, although many visitors are disappointed by its un-castle-like appearance. The original Norman castle was built in 1068 high on an outcropping of land that gave it a natural defensive advantage. Nonetheless, the castle was destroyed twice, and only parts of the gatehouse and foundation remain of the original structure. But the castle grounds and deep tunnels in the sandstone bluff on which it sits are what hold the spirits of Nottingham Castle today.

The most haunted tunnel is a section known as Mortimer's Hole, where the ghost of Sir Roger Mortimer tries to keep people from entering the castle. He was the illicit lover of Queen Isabel and was her accomplice in the murder of her husband, Edward II. However, the king's son, Edward III, suspected Mortimer and his mother of the crime and snuck into the castle via the network of secret tunnels one October night in 1330. He burst into the queen's Bedroom to find his mother and Mortimer making love. The unfortunate Mortimer was hanged, drawn, and quartered in London the following month, and his remains left to rot on Tyburn Gate. You can try your luck at passing through Mortimer's Hole yourself, since the Nottingham tunnels and passageways under the city are open to the public.

On the castle grounds, one of the cruelest acts by an English king replays itself over and over. In 1212, King John took twenty-eight boys from the families of Welsh noblemen hostage and kept them sequestered in the castle. The boys were allowed their freedom within the castle walls, and after some time, got used to living there. Then, suddenly one day, the King gave the order to execute all the hostages. The boys, some as young as twelve, were taken up to the castle ramparts and hanged in a row over the side. The boys' pitiful cries for mercy, as they were dragged up the ram-

parts, still echo here. All the way up until the 1920s, there were reports of the apparitions of unidentified boys showing up in the private residences of Nottingham, as if their innocent souls were still looking for decent homes. The two-hour Nottingham Ghost Walk, led by psychic mediums Jenny Bright and David Cross, begins at the Nottingham Castle gatehouse and ends in a cave beneath a fifteenth-century pub called Ye Old Salutation Inn.

Southwell

ADMIRAL RODNEY HOTEL PUB The pub at the Admiral Rodney Hotel in Southwell is haunted. The ghost of a bearded man whom the employees have named "Charlie" is most often glimpsed in the glass doors to an old ballroom located behind the pub. His face can be seen staring back at you through the glass. Recently, Charlie has taken to leaving the ballroom and playing little poltergeist tricks on customers, and, in recognition of the increased activity, the latest owner, Joe Chiarella, has renamed the pub "Charlie's Bar."

BRAMLEY APPLE PUB The Bramley Apple pub in Southwell was originally called the George and Dragon, but the name was changed after it changed hands in the 1970s. Sarah Johnson-Cooper and her husband had owned the pub since World War I, and it is Sarah's spirit that remained behind when the new owners bought it. Though she ran the pub, Sarah was a teetotaler and never touched a drink nor allowed anyone in her family to imbibe. Now, in the afterlife, she wants to stop everyone from drinking in her former establishment.

Glasses and liquor bottles crash to pieces on the floor of the basement storeroom for no apparent reason. Fairly often, the draft beer will suddenly stop flowing at the bar, and the proprietors blame Sarah's ghost for sealing up the beer barrels in the basement, which forms a vacuum and stops the pumps from working properly. The owners have monitored the situation and are convinced there is no way the large wooden pegs can get shoved in the barrel spouts except by some super-natural agency. Other ghostly reminders of the Johnson-Cooper family are present at the pub. Several members of that family played musical in-struments, and sometimes violin and piano music is heard in the pub, although no source for the sounds has ever been found. Likewise, heavy stomping footsteps are heard on the stairs and in the hallway when there is no one there.

SARACEN'S HEAD HOTEL The Saracen's Head Hotel at the center of the town of Southwell in Nottinghamshire is full of history. Parts of the building date back to the 1400s, and during reno-vations in 1986, beautiful painted murals were discovered under the wallpaper that date back to the 1500s. The Saracen's Head restaurant is haunted by a petite girl in nineteenth-century attire, possibly a former waitress, and the laun-dry room is said to be haunted by no other a presence than Lord Byron, who stayed at the Saracen's Head on occasion. While his appari-tion has never been seen, female employees are convinced it is his uneasy spirit that is still look-ing for earthly delights. A decidedly different presence haunts a storeroom near the laundry. There the apparition of a knight in a suit of armor floats precariously above the floor.

The most haunted room at the hotel, however, is Room 1, King Charles's Room. King Charles I spent his last night of freedom here in 1646, and his spirit seems to have returned there. Icy cold spots move about the room and even wake people up from sound sleep, and a restless presence is felt immediately on entering the room. Sometimes blue balls of light emerge from the wall and dance about the room. King Charles arrived at the hotel disguised as a priest and stayed in the room occu-pied by his emissary, who was negotiating a separate peace settlement with invading Scottish forces. But the Scottish emissary learned of the king's presence and had him turned over to English Parliamentar-ian forces, who beheaded him in 1649. After his capture, the owners of the hotel judiciously changed the name of their establishment from the "King's Arms" to the "Saracen's Head." Good thing too,

for Oliver Cromwell, victorious leader of the Par-liamentarians, stayed in Room 1 at the hotel when he came to Southwell in 1648.

Retford

LITTLE THEATRE One of Nottinghamshire's most haunted playhouses is the Little Theatre in Retford, which was built a decade ago on the site of another theater that dated back to World War I. The former theater was haunted by a very pow-erful presence responsible for all sorts of polter-geist activity that terrified actors and employees. On many occasions, the apparition of a man in black evening dress was seen moving through the empty rows, and sometimes he could even be heard whistling a tune. That same presence now haunts the new theater building.

Worksop

PRIORY GATEHOUSE The thirteenth-century Priory Gatehouse at Worksop in Notting-hamshire seems to be a portal to the Other Side. One ghost is seen along the Church Walk, a path that leads along the river to the Priory Gatehouse Worksop Priory. The apparition wears gray clothing with a shawl over its head. Some say it is a woman, while others believe it is a monk. The facts seem to suggest the ghost is a woman, since the body of a female was pulled from the river after being submerged for two weeks in the early 1900s. Also, the monks at the Worksop Priory are Augustinian friars and wear black habits not gray.

Another ghost, known as the Blue Lady, walks the path that runs between the Priory Gatehouse and the Priory Church entrance. Sometimes she is spotted sitting contentedly on an odd-shaped bench next to one of the trees along the path. Several private residences on Potter Street, a thir-teenth-century road that connects the Priory Gatehouse to the marketplace at Radford, have ghosts and other paranormal activity, such as un-explainable footsteps, knocking within the walls, and appliances going on and off by themselves.

One apparition is a Peeping Tom, who floats up to second floor windows on houses on Potter Street to have a look in.

DERBYSHIRE

Brimington

RINGWOOD HALL One of the more interesting hotel hauntings in Derbyshire takes place at the Ringwood Hall Hotel in Brimington. Ringwood Hall has a hidden tunnel that once lead to the town's churchyard. At the end of the tunnel, several ghosts are engaged in a passionate snooker game! They appear to be former hotel guests and employees engaged in a passionate game of pool, totally oblivious to the fact that they are dead.

Castleton

CASTLE HOTEL Derbyshire's most haunted inn is located in Castleton. The Castle Hotel is a seventeenth-century coaching inn situated in the heart of the Peak District in the town of Castleton. The hotel is within walking distance of the Castleton caverns and the ancient Peverill Castle. The forlorn ghost of the Lady in Gray haunts it. Nicknamed "Rose," she is thought to be a young bride jilted on her wedding day, following which there was to have been a reception at the Castle Hotel. Instead, she committed suicide in Room 4. Ever since, her ghost has haunted the premises, and over the centuries, she has been seen regularly, even by skeptical new owners who never believed in such things. In May 1999, a séance was organized that successfully contacted Rose's spirit, which manifested a number of unusual effects, such as gasping sounds and footsteps.

Other ghosts are also present in the hotel. One is the spirit of a chambermaid named Agnes, who haunts the upstairs hallways and laundries. She is a short, plump woman in her sixties who wears her gray hair in a tight bun and wears round glasses. Another ghost dates from the time of Charles II, who used nearby Peverill Castle as a hunting lodge. The angry ghost is one of his sentries. The soldier appears only from the knees up,

Castle Hotel, Castleton Peak District, Great Britain (Castle Hotel)

probably due to a change in floor level since that time. Another ghost here is that of a woman murdered in the hotel and buried under the front steps in 1603.

Yet another apparition at the Castle Hotel is of an elderly gentleman in a blue pinstriped suit who is sometimes accompanied by the phantom of an Old English sheepdog. He is most often seen in the Blue Room, next to the massive fireplace in the bar, or near a former side entrance to the bar that is now a ladies room. Dubbed "Mr. Cooper," he is said to be the ghost of a tin miner who loved Cooper ale and would spend hours in the bar trying to hide from his wife, who did not approve of his drinking. He died one Sunday in 1905, wearing his church suit, and apparently kept the same attire in spirit.

More information on the Castle Hotel and the surrounding area can be found on the Internet at www.afallon.com/pages/whiterabbit1.html. The Castle Hotel is on Castle Street in Castleton, Derbyshire. For booking information, call 1433-620578 or fax 1433-622902.

Chesterfield

ROYAL OAK PUB AND HOTEL The Royal Oak Pub in the middle of Derbyshire in Chesterfied is typical of the haunted hotels in this county. It was used by the Knights Templar as a rest house in the Middle Ages and became a public house in

1772. It has a colorful past and the premises are visited by the spirits of Foreign Legion soldiers as well as those of an elderly man and woman and an "unknown entity." The pub is located in the Marketplace Square in Chesterfield.

Derby

Derbyshire's most haunted city is Derby itself. In fact, the city claims to be the ghost capital of all of England, and there do seem to be an awful lot of hauntings going on here. In fact, in order to keep track of all the paranormal activity, the city has set up a Web site (www.derbycity.com/ghosts/ghosts.html) under the auspices of author Wayne Anthony and local historian Richard Felix. There is also a Ghost Walk in town that originates from the Heritage Centre. Two separate tours start at 7:00 P.M. and include a late supper afterwards. Phone 1332-255802 for more information or to make reservations.

D. LAFFERTY & SON D. Lafferty & Son in Derby is the former George Inn, which dates from 1693. The presence haunting the building has never been identified, but disembodied groaning is heard in the cellar and poltergeist activity, such as the shattering of bowls and earthen pots, breaks out in the former bar area. A female skull with a broken cranium was found in a four-foot-deep pit in the cellar along with scraps of animal skin and bones, and forensic testing showed the bones date back at least 100 years.

DERBY CATHEDRAL The front landing of Derby Cathedral is haunted by the ghost of the ever-popular Prince Charles Edward Stuart ("Bonnie Prince Charlie"), who is dressed in his best Jacobite attire. Charles came to the church with his troops in December 1745 to give thanks for his easy victories in the previous months. There is also the ghost of a White Lady seen coming down the back stairs of the church, and on the side of the church, the ghost of Derbyshire's executioner, John Crossland, is seen. Formerly a criminal himself, he was given a pardon if he would personally execute his brother and father. That he did and

went on to become one of England's busiest executioners. However, his guilt-bound spirit now seeks entry into the old cathedral to find forgiveness.

JACOBEAN HOUSE Derby's first brick building, Jacobean House, was a private mansion constructed in 1611. Today, it has at least fourteen ghosts. Among the most frequently sighted is a phantom coach and horses seen waiting in front of the house. To the left of the building, under the arched driveway, a headless coachman is seen. At the Warwick Street entrance, the dark apparition of a man appears to be standing, waiting to be let in. Inside the house, a ghostly Lady in Blue haunts the main staircase and has been observed by many servants and visitors to the house.

ST. HELEN'S HOUSE St. Helen's House in Derby, a Georgian townhouse built in 1767 on the site of a twelfth-century Augustinian monastery, is haunted by the powerful presence of a monk who lived there. In 1992, an adult student at St. Helen's witnessed a hooded human figure enter from the ceiling and pass through a wall in front of him, and other students and employees over the years have reported similar manifestations. Sometimes the presence speaks softly in people's ears—often calling them by name—and the staff has nicknamed the presence the "Whisperer." Another apparition is that of a young woman, who runs down the stairs as if something is chasing her. Some say she is running away from the monk.

Glossop

DEVIL'S ELBOW Longdendale Valley in Derbyshire has a strange feeling to it. The valley is located not far from the town of Glossop and just a thirty-minute drive from either Sheffield or Manchester. The valley is bounded by Bleaklow Mountain to the south and Black Hill to the north. In recent times, there have been many rumors of farm families who continue to practice pagan earth religions here. The valley forests are known for their strange creatures, such as the huge animal ("as big as a whale") that has been reported crossing a stretch of the B Road that parallels the main highway connecting Sheffield and Manchester. The haunted area is known as the Devil's Elbow, and many locals avoid it at night.

It is from Devil's Elbow where you can get the best view of the ghostly lights that have been dubbed the "Devil's Bonfires." Most of the sightings originate from a mysterious archeological site near the top of the two thousand-foot peak of Bleaklow Mountain. The site is known as Torside Castle, a Bronze Age rock-and-mud fortress. The ghost lights around the "castle" are best seen from Woodhead Pass at the foot of the mountain, although sometimes the glowing balls of light make the journey down the hillside and can be seen close-up. Woodhead Pass residents of Bleak House, the Woodhead Chapel, and the Crowden Youth Hostel have all reported seeing the mysterious balls of light hover over their dwellings. Sometimes, the lights string together and move about in ghostly daisy chains. There is a live Webcam of the valley called the "Haunted Valley Webcam" at www.hauntedvalley.com/webcam.htm.

Stanton Moor

NINE LADIES STONE CIRCLE The Nine Ladies Stone Circle is located about three miles (5 kilometers) northwest of the town of Matlock, above Darley Dale on Stanton Moor. The Bronze Age burial site has been considered haunted for centuries, and locals make a point of staying away after dark. The apparition of an unidentified man dressed all in black is seen standing just outside the stone circle. According to legend, the nine stones are witches caught dancing on the Sabbath to the sounds of the Devil's fiddle playing. In this view, the man in black is the Devil admiring his handiwork.

LEICESTERSHIRE

Leicester

BELGRAVE HALL Belgrave Hall is a haunted Victorian mansion near the heart of the bustling city of Leicester, and currently the most haunted place in Leicestershire. Constructed between 1709 and 1713 by Edward Cradock, it became a museum in 1937, but was known as haunted for many decades before that. John Ellis, a Member of Parliament, bought the house in 1847 and lived there with his six daughters until his death. Ellis's apparition usually appears inside the building on the stairway, and in the kitchen and dining room. His daughters are also thought to appear at his side on occasion.

Belgrave Hall, Leicester, Great Britain (BBC 1999)

Paranormal activity has been increasing in the last twenty years, and in 1987, the museum curator arranged for two mediums to investigate the premises. They found an intense spiritual presence they believed to be John Ellis. Then, in December 1998, security cameras captured two ghostly fig-

Nine Ladies Stone Circle, Stanton Moor, Great Britain (John Mason)

ures walking outside, along the back of the building. The apparitions appeared at 4:50 A.M. then disappeared into thin air, leaving behind only a swirling mist. International Society for Paranormal Research (ISPR), a research group from Los Angeles, organized an on-site investigation in March 1999. The team included paranormal researcher Dr. Larry Montz, psychics Peter James, Linda MacKenzie, Derek Acorah, and several others. Information on their investigation is contained at the ISPR Web site at www.ISPR.net.

Curator Stuart Warburton believes the security film and subsequent investigation provides proof that the museum is indeed haunted. Others working at the museum also believe it is really haunted. One who saw the ghost is the gardener, Michael Snuggs. "I was standing in the house entryway," he told reporters, "and from the top of the stairs, this figure appeared and walked down the stairs. At the bottom, she looked through the window at the garden, and then just turned and smiled, and walked through to the kitchen."

Narborough

NARBOROUGH ARMS A ghostly figure in a shroud sometimes walks through solid walls at the Narborough Arms inn in Narborough. The inn dates back to 1600, and at least once in its long history it was used as a church. The Narborough Arms is located at 6 Coventry Road in Narborough, Leicestershire. Not far away, at the Battle of Bosworth Field outside Sutton Cheney in Leicestershire, two victims of the famous battle where Richard III lost his life still walk the battleground.

Rothley

ROTHLEY RAILWAY STATION The railroad station at Rothley in Leceistershire is haunted by a former stationmaster, as well as a farmer, who lived nearby. Both men were killed when they were hit by a troop train coming into the station during World War II. Their apparitions are so lifelike that people faint when the ghosts are "struck" by oncoming trains.

Stoke Dry

STOKE DRY ANGLICAN CHURCH The church in Stoke Dry, Leicestershire, is haunted by the ghost of a woman who was accused of being a witch by a rector there. The man locked her up in a small room above the front door to the church, where she eventually starved to death. Her apparition, with cavernous eyes and sunken cheeks, is sometimes seen in the back of the church and in the tiny room where she died.

Twycross

OLD GIBBET At the old gibbet (gallows) alongside the A444 highway at Twycross in Leicestershire, the ghosts of a young girl standing next to her distraught mother are seen. They are both dripping wet. In 1800, a famous wrestler named John Massey murdered his wife and daughter by throwing them into the millrace on a nearby river. Massey was executed for the crime here. The daughter survived the experience, but now her ghost has joined her poor mother trying to make sense of it all.

LINCOLNSHIRE

Bailgate

WHITE HART HOTEL The White Hart Hotel in the town of Bailgate in Lincolnshire has a ghost on the third floor known as the "Ginger Jar Ghost." The distraught spirit is anxiously searching for his stolen ginger jar, and the odds are slim that he will ever find it. The ghost is blamed for a number of highly unusual things that happen at the hotel. The ghost of a child murdered by a hired rat catcher is seen in the older part of the hotel, while the apparition of a former highwayman haunts the orange grove on the property. For more information, phone the hotel at 1522-526222 or fax 1522-531798.

Branston

BRANSTON HALL HOTEL The Branston Hall Hotel in the town of Branston in Lincolnshire is haunted by the sounds of another era. Jazz music from the 1920s is heard, while the sounds of muffled sobbing are detected on the spiral staircase.

Cammeringham

B1398 Road On the B1398 Road at Cammeringham in Lincolnshire, the phantom of a chariot driven by a woman wearing a long robe appears in the mists. Her chariot is drawn by one black and one white horse. According to legend, she is an early Celtic queen of England known as Queen Boadicea. Her kingdom reached into the area, where she fought the Romans for control. Ermine Street in Cammeringham is known to have been a road originally made by the Romans.

Grantham

Angel and Royal Inn Lincolnshire's Angel and Royal is probably England's oldest inn, built eight hundred years ago as a hostel for the crusading knights of the fabled Knights Templar. King John liked it so much that he established his court here in 1213, and the inn remained a favorite stopover with journeying kings and nobles for centuries. An angel carrying a crown, the emblem of King Edward III, stands over the main entrance. The White Lady ghost has appeared many times in the hallways and bedrooms of the second and third floors in the Georgian part of the hotel. There is a room on one of those floors where the presence is especially likely to appear, but the management will not publicize that fact because they are afraid they might have a hard time renting it out. The Angel and Royal Hotel is located on High Street in Grantham, Lincolnshire. For information, call 0476-65816 or fax 0476-67149.

Lincolnshire County

East Kirby Airfield A more modern apparition is seen on the tarmac at East Kirkby Airfield in the Lincolnshire countryside. The ghost of a pilot is seen walking towards the control tower with his parachute trailing on the ground behind him. The haunting originated when a pilot died in the crash of a B17. Apparently, his ghost still thinks he parachuted to safety.

Lovedon

Stagglethorpe Hall Stragglethorpe Hall in Lovedon once belonged to a monastery, and for some reason, the attic is haunted by the sounds of dragging chains and metal being hammered. No psychic has been able to determine the significance of the ghostly sounds. However, on the road outside the hotel, the phantom coach that rattles by is more easily dismissed as "normal."

NORTHAMPTONSHIRE

Northampton

Church of St. Mary the Virgin One of Northamptonshire's haunted churches is the Church of St. Mary the Virgin in Woodford near Northampton. The presence of a mysterious monk has been sensed by parishioners for nearly a century. In 1964, a photograph taken in the deserted church by Gordon Carroll of Northampton clearly shows a monk kneeling at the altar, although no one was visible when he took the picture.

Church of St. Mary the Virgin, Woodford, Great Britain (Gordon Carroll)

Oundle

TALBOT INN One of the most haunted locations in Northhamptonshire is the Talbot Inn at Oundle. In 1626, the Talbot Inn was remodeled using materials from nearby Fotheringhay Castle, the site of the execution of Mary, Queen of Scots. Apparently the salvaged materials contained some remnant of the trauma, for the ghost of Mary started to be seen regularly in a particular room at the inn. Recent phenomena includes Mary's ghost getting her fingers trapped in the door, as she attempts to leave the room, and on two occasions when occupants have tried to take photographs of the room, the pictures have failed to develop at all. The Talbot Inn is located on New Street in Oundle, Northamptonshire.

Wakefield

FOTHERINGHAY CHURCH Fotheringhay Church in Northamptonshire is haunted by the sounds of ghostly dirges and music associated with a funeral that took place over five hundred years ago. The sad singing originates from the funeral of Richard, Duke of York, and his son Edmund, who were both killed at the Battle of Wakefield in 1460. Their bodies are still interred in the church.

SOUTHEAST ENGLAND

Southeast England comprises the counties of Sussex, Surrey, Kent, Hampshire, and the Isle of Wright. It is a more rural setting than Anglia and might be considered England's agricultural "breadbasket."

SUSSEX

Arundel

AMBERLY CASTLE A medieval stone wall surrounds the nine hundred-year-old Amberly Castle, located not far from the Arun River near Arundel

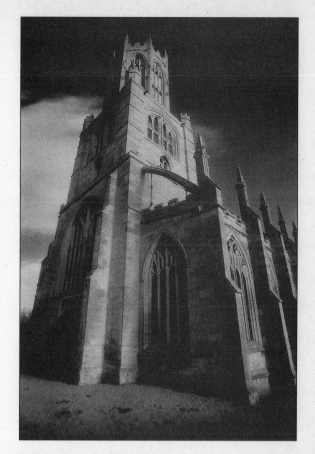

Fotheringhay Church, Northamptonshire, Great Britain (Dennis William Hauck)

in West Sussex. The wall was constructed to keep undesirables away from the privileged bishops and royalty who frequented the place. Only in the last twelve years has it been open to "commoners." That was when it was turned into a hotel. Now all you have to do is pay for lodging to pass through the imposing gatehouse and enter the elegant courtyard that leads to your room.

The castle also comes with its own ghost, a fourteenth-century servant girl named Emily. Poor Emily was seduced by one of the bishops who owned the house. Most agree the culprit was Bishop Rede, who built the great wall surrounding the castle, and that Emily died giving birth to his illegitimate child. Now her forlorn spirit is said to frequent the site where she spent most of her time, the former kitchens, which were just along the present north wall. To contact Amberly Castle, phone 7988-31992 or fax 7988-31998.

Cuckfield

KING'S HEAD PUB A ghost nicknamed "Geranium Jane," who appears only to men engaged in extramarital affairs, haunts the King's Head Pub in Cuckfield. She is said to be a woman who was killed by a plant pot falling from the roof, and it is further alleged that the pot was dropped by the landlord, whose child she was carrying. Most witnesses are understandably reluctant to speak of their encounters.

Lewes

SHELLEY'S HOTEL The oldest part of Shelley's Hotel in Sussex dates from 1526, when it was an inn called The Vine. It was later the home of the Shelley family and finally was turned into a hotel. Poltergeist activity and two different apparitions have been reported here. Shelley's Hotel is on High Street in Lewes, Sussex.

Northiam

HAYES ARMS HOTEL Originally a farmhouse dating from the fifteenth century, the Hayes Arms Hotel still lies in a tranquil setting next to the Village Green in Northam, Sussex. Even the ghost here is peaceful and well behaved. It is the apparition of an elderly lady sitting at a spinning wheel, working away quietly in the present bar area of the hotel.

Rye

MERMAID HOTEL The Mermaid, a five hundred-year-old, half-timbered hotel with leaded windows and narrow corridors, was once a notorious smugglers den. It is located in the middle of the medieval, cobblestoned streets of the village of Rye. The two ghosts of the Mermaid are engaged in eternal battle and their swashbuckling spirits have been fighting a duel in one of the bedrooms for as long as anyone can remember. But their sword fight always ends the same way. The same man is mercilessly impaled, and his body dumped down a nonexistent chute in the corner of the room.

Dressed in eighteenth-century attire, the men are thought to be members of the Hawkshurst Gang, a group of ruthless smugglers who made the hotel their headquarters. There were several murders at the hotel, and at one time there was a panel door in the room that led to an oubliette. The Mermaid Hotel is on Mermaid Street in Rye, Sussex. The phone number is 1797-223432.

Chanctobury Ring, Sussex, Great Britain (John Mason)

Sussex County

CHANCTOBURY RING The mysterious Chanctobury Ring is said to be one of the most powerful sites in Sussex. A Celtic sacred place and former Roman temple are thought to be the source of supernatural energies perceived at the ring. Today, a circle of beech trees marks the spot of the ancient site. According to legend, if you count aloud the correct number of trees in the ring, the ghosts of Julius Caesar and his army will appear.

HASTINGS CASTLE Built by Robert the Count of Eu in 1069, much of Hastings Castle in East Sussex has fallen into the sea, but what remains is haunted by the sounds of dirges, rattling chains, and agonizing screams. Some say the sea is not destroying the castle but rebuilding it, for the most frequent apparition here is of the castle itself—hovering out over the ocean, restored and renewed with "standards fluttering in the breeze." Nearby Hastings Caves contains ghosts from the Battle of Hastings. Paranormal researcher Richard Senate investigated the site in 1998 and obtained evidence of continuing activity, including photographs of unexplainable energy patterns taken inside the caves.

PEVENSEY CASTLE Pevensey Castle, an eerie place surrounded by marshes in rural Sussex, is haunted by the loyal Lady Pelham, who was killed here in the fourteenth century defending the castle while her husband was away. Sometimes the sounds of battle are also heard. Not far away, the Michelham Priory is also haunted by an ancient spirit. The ghost there is King Harold, who heads off towards Battle Abbey from the courtyard. There are plenty more ghosts too, including a Gray Lady who just stares into the moat where she drowned, a mysterious Blue Lady, a wandering monk, and even a white stallion.

SURREY

Crawley

GEORGE HOTEL The George Hotel has stood on its present site since early in the seventeenth century but its ghost dates from the modern era. The ghost here is a night watchman, Mark Hurston, who still patrols the hotel corridors. The former employee might be a little too loyal for the current managers, but guests and employees at the hotel believe he is a beneficent presence. The George Hotel is on High Street in Crawley, Surrey.

Croydon

CROYDON AIRPORT Ghosts seem to gravitate to the control tower at the Croydon Airport, just outside London in Surrey. The haunting began in the 1930s, when a Dutch pilot was killed when his plane crashed taking off in a dense fog. Now he warns pilots of approaching foggy conditions by appearing to them as they file their flight plans in the control tower. In the 1960s, after a house was built on the spot in the western portion of the airfield in which his plane crashed, the dead pilot began appearing to the new owners. The private residence in the Roundshaw Estate became internationally famous for its haunting and was investigated by the British Society for Psychical Research.

The ghosts of three nuns who were burned alive in a crash at the airport during a blizzard in January 1947 have also been reported, as well as a ghostly wartime pilot on a motorcycle on nearby Foresters Drive. People at the airport also report hearing ghostly singing coming from off in the distance where a perfume factory used to stand. More than sixty people died when the factory was bombed during World War II. To allay their fears during the bombing, the workers had begun singing. According to psychics who have visited Croydon Airport, the facility sits on a vortex of energy that is connected to the Other Side.

SELSDON PARK HOTEL Selsdon Park Hotel is a close second for Surrey's most active haunted hotel (after Oatlands Park in Weybridge). The hotel is an impressive Jacobean mansion that sits on over two hundred acres of land yet is only thirteen miles from central London in Surrey. An older building stood on the site that was given to the Knights Templar by the Archbishop of Canterbury in the middle 1100s. Most of the present building was built in 1670, and the house was re-built into a Gothic mansion in 1809. The oldest part of the present hotel is the Tudor Corridor on the second floor, which is also the most haunted part of the building.

The most frequently seen apparition is another Gray Lady, who is usually seen carrying a lit candle on the second floor. According to one story, she is a servant who killed herself in the 1930s. Another version says she is an Elizabethan resident of the house. In any case, she is a very active spirit that has lately taken to wandering through the Phoenix Bar and occasionally the Cambridge Bar. She has also been witnessed walking through Room 235, where her ghostly figure passes right through furniture and sleeping people. Selsdon Park Hotel is on Addington Road in Sanderstead near Croydon in Surrey. For more information, call 0181-657-8811 or fax 0181-668-3118.

Guildford

ANGEL POSTING HOUSE AND LIVERY A comfortable inn known as the Angel Posting House and Livery retains much of its historical character with a few added attractions that include a thirteenth-century crypt and a wooden gallery supported by great oak timbers that were salvaged from old ships at Portsmouth. It seems to be the old mirrors in the building that carry the paranormal energy and guests and employees see many ghostly images in them. The Angel Posting House and Livery is at 91 High Street in Guildford, Surrey.

Thames Ditton

HOME OF COMPASSION The apparition of a nun in a gray habit haunts the Home of Compassion nursing home in Thames Ditton, Surrey. She is seen in the hallways, kitchen, and chapel. The building used to be a residence for an order of Benedictine nuns, but the last nun died there in 1976. It became a nursing home in 1977, and almost immediately staff and residents started reporting the apparition, which sometimes walks right through witnesses' bodies. The nun appears to be unaware that she is dead and continues her former duties for her order.

Weybridge

OATLANDS PARK HOTEL The Oatlands Park Hotel in Weybridge is currently the most active haunted place in Surrey. In fact, things are so bad there that the owners appealed for help from any local clairvoyants or mediums in finding out why there are so many sightings of ghosts in recent years. The most often seen apparition is of a Gray Lady, who usually appears late in the evening. She is seen wearing a crinoline dress from the seventeenth century while moving a few inches above the floor in the Broadwater Restaurant. The apparition finally vanishes through a west wall, where at one time stood large bay window doors that opened into the garden.

Psychics believe the ghost could be a former Queen of England. The story goes back to 1538, when King Henry VIII acquired Oatlands Manor for Anne of Cleves, his latest bride. She lived there many years, and afterwards the estate served as the residence of many queens, including Queen Elizabeth I. The original house was demolished in 1649, and another house built on the foundation burned down in 1794 and was rebuilt. The hotel did not open until 1856, and extensive remodeling has been done since.

Another presence manifests in Room 1313, a third-floor room in the Tudor Wing. Extreme and sudden drops in temperature have been recorded there, as well as poltergeist phenomena like drawers opening by themselves, electrical appliances going on and off by themselves, and furniture moving of its own accord. There is also a strange buildup of electrostatic energy in the room, which makes guests feel as if someone else is in the room; sometimes guests report someone invisible sitting on the edge of the bed. Some guests in the room experience the "Old Hag" effect, which is a sleep paralysis that feels like someone is sitting on your chest, keeping you from moving or taking a full breath. More paranormal activity takes place just below the room, outside under the bell tower. It is known that in the nineteenth century, a maid got in an argument with her lover, also a hotel employee, and barricaded herself in the bell tower, which sits just above Room 1313. Out of desperation, she leapt to her death from the front tower window. Members of the Ghost Club have investigated the Oatlands. For more information, visit the Oatlands Web site at http://dspace.dial.pipex.com/town/lane/xmo85/oatlands.htm.

QUEEN'S HEAD PUB The Queen's Head Pub in Weybridge was constructed in the 1730s but became a pub only about twenty years ago. Recent investigations by the Ghost Club have documented a variety of poltergeist activity, strange sounds, and the sightings of apparitions. Most of the ghosts appear around Christmas time and after hours in the bar. They include a woman in old-fashioned dress wearing a large skirt with an apron sighted in the downstairs area and an elderly gentleman sitting on a bench wearing a "Puritan's hat," and another gentleman wearing a black jacket with a white scarf and hobnail boots.

KENT

Maidstone

BLUE BELL HILL Blue Bell Hill, located four miles north of Maidstone in Kent, is haunted by the ghost of a girl who appears in the middle of the road and is often struck by oncoming drivers. When the drivers pull over to try to help the victim, no one can be found. The ghost is thought to be a bride on the way to her wedding who died in an accident that also took the lives of two of her bridesmaids on November 19, 1965. The ladies' Ford Cortina collided with a Jaguar at 11:00 that night. Ever since, the young bride has haunted the spot where she died. In November 1992, three different drivers reported striking her phantom, which stood in the middle of the road and gazed intently into the eyes of the driver just before being hit. In January 1993, a family got a good look at the ghost as it crossed the road just a few feet in front of them. The witnesses insisted that the apparition was truly horrifying, with black beady eyes and a weathered face and mouth open

in a ghastly, silent scream. At other times, the phantom appears normal and actually engages the driver in conversation.

LARKFIELD PRIORY HOTEL Situated in the so-called "garden of England" area, this centuries-old country home has grown over the years into a fifty-four-room elegant hotel called the Larkfield Priory Hotel. There is at least one ghost here and possibly more. In the old wing of the hotel, a ghost named Charlotte has been sighted repeatedly. She is said to be a servant of the house when the surrounding land belonged to the Archbishop of Canterbury. For some reason, Charlotte hates the kitchen area and is blamed for several poltergeist effects that have occurred there. Once she threw all the pots, pans, and dishes all over the floor, and then turned on all the water faucets to the sinks. The Larkfield Priory Hotel is located on London Road in Larkfield near Maidstone in Kent. For more information, phone 7328-46858 or fax 7328-46786.

Pluckley

FRIGHT CORNER The Kent County town of Pluckley in southeast England has at least a dozen ghosts currently haunting residents there. The longest haunting is the ghost of a highwayman who haunts the spot where he was ambushed and run through with a sword that pinned him to a tree. The spot and the area around it is now known as Fright Corner. The grisly ghost of a Gypsy woman burned to death there by townspeople haunts the bridge near the crossroads, and the ghost of a miller appears only during thunderstorms at the nearby Pinnock House.

DERING HOUSE The apparition of the White Lady glides though the library of Dering House. Also at Dering House is a Red Lady ghost, a lovely woman who died in the twelfth century. She was buried in a beautiful red gown with a red rose in her hands and is sometimes seen in the church graveyard. A former owner who committed suicide by eating poison berries haunts Rose Court. Her phantom is said to appear only between 4:00

and 5:00 P.M.—the hour she died. She died by a window staring out at Greystones, a house across the way haunted by a forlorn monk, and many believe the two spirits are somehow connected. Sometimes they are even seen together, walking the grounds between the two houses. A phantom coach and several other ghosts—some recently deceased residents—also haunt the town.

Smarden

CHEQUERS INN The Chequers Inn is fourteenth-century weatherboard inn with oak beams in many of the rooms that has witnessed many poltergeist-type events, though the cause of the paranormal activity has never been determined. There have been no known traumatic events at the inn, nor do the events seem tied to any particular individual.

Stourmouth

RISING SUN INN A four hundred-year-old building, which was formerly used as a ferry house and a bakery, finally established itself as a popular hostelry known as the Rising Sun. There have been ghostly encounters with a gentleman on the premises, witnessed by the landlord, guests, and locals. Sometimes his apparition is seen, while at other times only his invisible presence is sensed. The Rising Sun is located on "The Street" in Stourmouth, Kent.

HAMPSHIRE

Andover

WHITE HART HOTEL One of the most well known of haunted Hampshire hotels is the White Hart in Andover. The seventeenth-century coaching inn has a number of apparitions floating through the corridors. The most active is a tall "Green Lady" repeatedly seen gliding along an upstairs passage. Footsteps were heard also. Another less frequently sighted ghost is a proper young lady, usually accompanied by her handsome male companion. The White Hart Hotel is on Bridge Street in Andover, Hampshire.

Hampshire County

ODIHAM CASTLE Odiham Castle is Hampshire's spookiest castle, and it has lots of history. The dark, dank stone castle is also known as King John's Castle because he stayed here the night before he signed the Magna Carta in 1215. The old castle is still haunted by a melancholy minstrel whose tranquil singing is heard on still nights, setting to song the timeless mood of this place.

Odiham Castle, Hamphire, Great Britain (John Mason)

Romsey

THE WHITE HORSE The White Horse is a serene Elizabethan hotel, next to a tenth-century abbey on the banks of the Test River. However, the playful ghost who haunts the place likes to disturb the decorum. The former stable boy likes to move or hide personal objects, make strange noises, and appear momentarily to startle guests. It is said the boy got a little too cocky with some older mates, and they ended up murdering him over a gambling debt. Apparently, he still has not learned to respect his elders. The White Horse Hotel is on the Market Place in Romsey, Hampshire.

Southampton

DOLPHIN INN The Dolphin stands on the site of a thirteenth-century inn, and the current building is a landmark of Southampton and has been for centuries. Subject of extensive renovation in 1751, the splendid Georgian facade hotel has had numerous distinguished guests over the years, including King William IV, Queen Victoria, and authors William Thackeray and Jane Austen, but its ghost is that of a commoner. The friendly spirit is called "Molly," a humble room-cleaner from days gone by, who now floats through rooms at two o'clock in the morning sweeping the floors or dusting the furniture. The Dolphin Hotel is on High Street in Southampton, Hampshire. For information, phone 0703-339955 or fax 0703-333650.

ISLE OF WIGHT

East Cowes

HEADLESS PARACHUTIST The Isle of Wight has a surreal landscape, which is just the type of decorating ghosts seem to prefer. At East Cowes on the island, the phantom of a headless soldier from World War II parachutes silently towards the ground, over and over again. Dozens of independent witnesses have reported seeing his parachute open and then watch as the trooper disappears just before he touches ground.

Freshwater

GOLDEN HILL FORT At Golden Hill Fort near Freshwater another soldier's ghost is seen. The fort was built in the early 1800s as an outpost against invasion by Napoleon, but the ghost here wears the uniform of a World War I sailor. The curious Casper likes to watch people work. Freshwater got its name as a watering hole for ships to replenish their stock of fresh water. Some of those ships never made it to port. One of those lost ships is still seen off Dunnose Point. The phantom is thought to be the *HMS Eurydice*, which sank in heavy seas on March 24, 1878, with the loss of over three hundred lives.

Quarr

QUARR ABBEY The apparition of Eleanor of Aquitaine, the wife of King Henry II, haunts the ruins of Quarr Abbey on the Isle of Wight. The woman was exiled to Quarr by her husband, but escaped and died in France in 1204. But her spirit returns to the simple and confined life she led on this lonely island.

Ventnor

ROYAL HOTEL Overlooking the English Channel, amidst peaceful gardens, the Royal Hotel is a remnant of an era gone by. In fact, the whole Isle of Wight is said to be a miniature England of a hundred years ago. The ghost here is also of a bygone era, an apparition called the Green Lady, who dates back before the hotel was built and wears clothing from the time of King Charles I. Her story, however, is unknown; only her presence is felt. Today she wanders the first two floors of the hotel, and guests sometimes sense her as a lingering cold spot on the staircase to the second floor. The Royal Hotel is located on Belgrave Road in Ventnor on the Isle of Wight. The phone number is 0983-852186. The island can only be reached by ferry from the mainland.

SOUTHWEST ENGLAND

Southwest England is made up of Cornwall, Somerset, Devonshire, Wiltshire, Dorset, and Avon counties. It is an area known for its dark sunken roads, mist-covered moors, and eerie stone circles, and is certainly one of the most mysterious and haunted areas in all of Britain.

CORNWALL

Bodmin

JAMAICA INN At the Jamaica Inn at Bolventor, near Bodmin, the ghost of a murdered sailor returns to finish his last drink, and he has also been seen sitting on a wall outside the inn. The inn was made famous by the Daphne Du Maurier novel of the same name. Cornish ghosts are often associated with the sea, from which many Cornish people made their livelihoods—either as fishermen, salvagers, or smugglers.

Boscastle

WELLINGTON HOTEL Cornwall's most haunted hotel is the Wellington Hotel in Boscastle. The lifelike apparition of a man drifts silently through the lobby of the old coaching inn, then exits right through a wall. He is described as an eighteenth-century coachman wearing leather gaiters and boots and a frock coat. Another ghost here also likes to walk through walls. She is the figure of a young girl in a cloak seen on the second floor landing. Consumed by a hopeless love affair, she threw herself from the top of the hotel's tower.

Still another unidentified presence is the dark shadowy form that floats down the cellar stairs and disappears into the darkness at night. There is also the presence of a murdered man in the building, as well as a strange "elemental spirit" that is pursued by dogs in the building.

Camelford

ROUGHTOR MOUNTAIN Cornwall's most famous ghost was written about in Charles Causley's "The Ballad of Charlotte Dymond." Charlotte's body was found on the slopes of Roughtor, near Camelford, on April 14, 1844. Her former lover, an unpopular, crippled farmhand named Matthew Weeks, was hanged for the deed at Bodmin Goal. It is widely believed he was innocent of the crime, and Charlotte's ghost started appearing soon after he was executed. Quite frequently on the anniversary of her death, Charlotte's ghost, wearing a red shawl and a silk bonnet, is seen walking near a memorial on Roughtor that marks the spot she was murdered. Some Old Volunteers guardsmen stationed in Roughtor asked not to stand watch because they feared seeing her ghostly form there.

Duporth

DUPORTH HOLIDAY VILLAGE The ghost of an eighteenth-century nun known affectionately as "Flo" haunts the Duporth Holiday Village at Du-

porth. She was a nurse in a manor house that was torn down to make way for the Holiday Village, but Flo's steadfast spirit remained behind. Employees blame a wide variety of poltergeist phenomena on her ghost. Once a sewing machine came on all by itself, and a worker, experienced in Flo's antics, politely said "No thanks, Flo. I don't need you today." The machine stopped immediately. Her apparition is seen by children near the Old Farm House. Sometimes children will carry on conversations with a "nice old lady in a black dress" that no adult can see.

Mullion

BOCHYN MANOR The Pink Lady, a short apparition less than five feet tall, haunts Bochyn Manor in Mullion, Cornwall. Whenever she appears, a phantom duel begins in the adjoining field. According to legend, the scene replays the trauma this site suffered when the father of a young woman killed her passionate suitor after a quarrel.

Penryn

ST. GLUVIAS'S CHURCH St. Gluvias's Church in Penryn is haunted by a former bell ringer, Captain Martin, a sailor who died in the 1880s after a shipwreck. A black carriage drawn by headless horses haunts the streets of Penryn. The phantom carriage appears in the days before Christmas, and it is said to have been sent by the sea to reclaim sailors who narrowly missed dying there.

Penzance

DOLPHIN INN Customers at the Dolphin Inn in Penzance have witnessed the apparition of an old sea captain, dressed in his tricorn hat and coat with laced ruffles. He is believed to have been a smuggler returning to claim his booty, but before he could claim it, he fell victim to Cornwall's infamous "Hanging Judge," Judge Jeffreys (1648–1689). Casks of brandy have recently been found hidden behind a false wall in the cellar, so it is possible more treasure is secreted away somewhere on the property.

GODOLPHIN HOUSE At an estate just east of Penzance, a ghostly funeral procession walks from Godolphin House to the chapel on the grounds. The apparition of a woman in white is sometimes seen along the same path. The woman is Margaret de Godolphin, wife of the first earl of Godolphin. She died in September 1678 but has yet to accept her own burial.

KENEGIE HOTEL At the Kenegie Hotel in Penzance, Cornwall, can be found the ghost of a housekeeper in the former mansion who traverses the hallways carrying a ring of keys.

St. Ives

ST. IVES BAY On stormy nights, a woman in white holding a lamp is seen around the bay at St. Ives in Cornwall. A phantom ship also appears far out in the bay. Local tradition says that the ghost ship is the *Neptune*. During foggy seas she tried to assist another ship in trouble, but as the crew was about to throw lines, the other ship vanished in thin air, only to be replaced seconds later by another, real vessel that collided with the *Neptune*. All hands were lost, and the ghost of the woman appears to be some terrified wife or lover of a member of the crew that died that night.

Just up the coast, the ghost of a woman is sometimes seen clinging to the rocks off Sennan. She was onboard a shipwrecked vessel and managed to make it to shore and climb onto the rocks. She hung on for hours, while rescuers tried frantically to save her, but she finally lost her grip and slipped into the raging sea.

Stratton

BINHAMY CASTLE The ruins of Binhamy Castle in Stratton are haunted by a former owner, Sir Ralph de Blanc-Minster, who died in the Crusades. For some reason, the phantom of a white rabbit is sometimes seen at the castle too. Not far away a more threatening presence is sensed. The ghost of the Evil Crusader, Henry de Pengersick, who was excommunicated for his dastardly deeds in the thirteenth century, haunts his former home, Pengersick Castle.

Talland

TALLAND CHURCH One of Cornwall's first ghosthunters and exorcists found the area around Talland, a village on the east coast between the fishing hamlets of Lope and Polperro, so full of lost evil spirits that he made it his life's duty to protect citizens from them. At least that is what Parson Richard Dodge told his parishioners. He said God gave him the power to drive out demons, and he was well known for his dramatic exorcisms. Dodge served as the vicar of Talland Church from 1713 to 1747, but he was really the head of a smuggling ring. One area possessed by the Devil, he told his parishioners, was Bridle Lane, a path that led down to the beach where the illegal trade entered England. He advised people to stay away from the area after dark or risk being possessed and their souls taken by Satan. The rouse worked for many years, until some brave person decided to have a look-see at the bottom of Bridle Lane.

Trebarwith Strand

BACKWAYS COVE Backways Cove, a north Cornwall inlet just up the coast from Trebarwith Strand, is haunted by many unidentified presences who are thought to be the spirits of shipwrecked sailors whose bodies washed up here after they drown. Numerous ships were torn apart on the jagged rocks offshore, and the shadowy spirits of their crews are still trying to make it to shore.

Wadebridge

MOLESWORTH ARMS HOTEL The sixteenth-century Molesworth Arms Hotel is a comfortable and tranquil place to rest up, unless you happen to enter the courtyard around midnight, when a phantom coach with four horses and a headless coachman drives wildly and comes to a stop in front of the hotel. The Molesworth Arms Hotel is on Molesworth Street in Wadebridge, Cornwall.

Whitesand Bay

FINNYGOOK INN If you happen to be driving along the south Cornish coast at Whitesand Bay, and you come across a quaint little pink-colored inn, keep a look out for the ghost of a smuggler named Finny. Finny used the bar at the inn as his center of operations and spent untold time planning his dastardly deeds there. During storms, he lit lanterns along shore to lure ships into the deadly rocks, then he murdered the survivors and stole their cargo. Finny stored his booty in tunnels he dug underneath the inn, and it was there he died when one of the tunnels collapsed on him over three hundred years ago. But his bearded apparition, dressed in raingear and high boots, is often seen sallying up to the bar at the inn. In fact, they named the Finnygook after his ghost. "Gook" is Cornish for ghost. The Finnygook Inn is in the hamlet of Crafthole at Whitesand Bay in Cornwall. The inn's phone number is 0503-30338.

Zennor

TINNERS ARMS HOTEL Just before thunderstorms hit Cornwall, a sudden outbreak of poltergeist activity occurs at the Tinners Arms Hotel in Zennor. The road near the hotel that leads up to Foage Farm is also haunted by the ghost of a nineteenth-century tin miner riding a bike. His face is spattered in blood, and psychics say the man was injured in an accident at the mine and was riding home on his bike to care for his wounds, which proved more serious than he thought. The man died on the road outside the hotel, and his confused soul took up residence there.

SOMERSET

Bristol

LLANDOGER TROW INN The Llandoger Trow Inn on King Street in Bristol was once the drinking bar of Daniel Defoe and Robert Louis Stevenson, but it is the ghost of a forsaken lame boy, who limps around the establishment carrying a white enamel pail that haunts the place. The boy's presence is also sensed in the kitchen and maintenance rooms.

Brockley Combe

BROCKLEY CHURCH Brockley Combe (a combe is a deep, narrow valley) is another haunted area of Somerset. The apparition of an old cleaning woman wearing a brown dress haunts Brockley Church, as well as a former priest by the name of Hibbetson. The priest killed a squire for his money. And in the valley, a phantom coach with a headless horseman appears surrounded by a greenish-yellow ball of light. A female apparition appears somewhere in the village every twenty-six years, and she is due to reappear in 2016. But beware: seeing her ghost drives people insane.

BROCKLEY COURT Brockley Court is haunted by a menacing man with a rapier at his side who walks through doors to bedrooms. The manor house was built in the mid-1600s and remained in the Pigot family until the beginning of the twentieth century. It was mostly members of the Pigot family who saw the ghost.

Chard

CHOUGH HOTEL The hanging judge, Judge Jeffreys, has been seen in this hotel, although an even more frequent presence at the Chough is the apparition of a man in a suit of armor that appears to startled guests. And then there is the tombstone behind the fireplace in the lounge. It is said that it has never been photographed no matter what kind of camera is used.

Glastonbury

GEORGE & PILGRIMS The George & Pilgrims was founded to meet the needs of pilgrims to the sacred sites of Glastonbury. It also offers a few sacred relics of its own, including the apparitions of a jovial monk and a grinning man in a modern sports coat, who is surrounded in a halo of beautiful blue light. Built in 1475, it is from his room at this hotel that King Henry VIII watched the demolition of Glastonbury Abbey during the dissolution of the church. The George & Pilgrims Hotel & Restaurant is at 1 High Street in Glastonbury, Somerset. For bookings, call 14588-31146.

GLASTONBURY TOR Glastonbury Tor in Somerset is the most magical place in all of England. It has long been a focal point of angel, fairy, and even UFO sightings, and the ten-mile area around the town contains landscaped outlines of astrological figures that researcher Katherine Maltwood has dubbed the "Temple of the Stars." According to legend, this was where Jesus lived as a boy and possibly even where he took his name, since long before his arrival, the Druids worshipped a god named Yesu or Esus. It is said Jesus built a shelter on the sacred ground where the abbey now stands and several locations commemorate his presence there, such as the Jesus Well at St. Minver in Cornwall and the Chalice Well at the foot of Glastonbury Tor (a "tor" is a tall rounded hill or mountain). Apparently it was known among his disciples that Jesus had lived in Glastonbury, for Joseph of Arimathea traveled here in A.D 63. with Jesus' cup from the Last Supper in which he had collected Christ's blood from the Crucifixion. When he arrived, Joseph drove his staff into the ground on top of Wearyall Hill. The staff grew into the Holy Thorn (hawthorn), which blossomed every Christmas until 1643, when a Puritan zealot cut it down. However, a descendent of the original Holy Thorn in front of St. John's Church (on High Street) still blooms every December. The plant is a rare variety with white flowers that is native to Palestine.

Christ's cup, said to be imbued with supernatural powers, became the basis for British legends of the Knights of the Round Table and their search for the Holy Grail. The location of King Arthur's home, the Isle of Avalon, is thought to be the Glastonbury Tor on which Glastonbury Abbey was built. The Tor is an abrupt outcropping of land that rises five hundred feet above

Glastonbury Abbey, Somerset, Great Britain (John Mason)

sea level and was once completely surrounded by water. In 1190, during rebuilding of the abbey, monks are said to have discovered the tomb of King Arthur and his wife, Guinevere. Modern excavations have confirmed the existence of the burial site, and a plague now marks the spot where Arthur's bones were discovered. Ghostly monks haunt the abbey, but the most powerful presence is King Arthur himself. According to legend, Glastonbury is where King Arthur sleeps waiting to return to life when he is needed again. Every Christmas eve, however, Arthur's spirit rises for a bit of fresh air, and he is usually seen riding a horse into the abbey courtyard.

South Cadbury Hill Fort in Somerset is an

South Cadbury Hill Fort, Somerset, Great Britain (John Mason)

Iron Age fortress that archeologists agree was part of Camelot. King Arthur and his Knights of the Round Table are said to be buried here. On Midsummer's Eve, their spirits supposedly rise and head down the hill to Glastonbury Tor.

The last Abbot of Glastonbury, Saint Dunstan, was hanged by King Henry VIII for his allegiance to the pope, and that brought an end to the abbey. However, Dunstan was also an alchemist and had allegedly discovered how to transmute base metals using the supernatural secrets he uncovered at Glastonbury. In the late 1570s, grave robbers opened Dunstan's tomb and discovered two vials of powder and a "book of symbols" in his coffin. The famed alchemists Edward Kelly and John Dee obtained these items, and they used them to uncover the secrets of transmutation. In December 1579, using the two powders and following the instructions in the book, the two men successfully transmuted large quantities of silver from lead and gold from tin. The process, Dee wrote later, was one that involved not only knowledge of chemistry but also demanded metaphysical changes in the two alchemists themselves. Apparently, they were all too successful. In 1583, the British government issued an attachment on all their possessions that accused them of illegally minting gold coins. The men fled with their families to the continent where they demonstrated their gold-making abilities to heads of state in several countries. Kelly ended up making gold for Emperor Maximilian II, and Dee returned to England where Queen Elizabeth granted him a license to make alchemical gold in return for his "mystical services" to the country. For more information on Glastonbury, write the Tribunal Tourist Centre, 9 High Street, Glastonbury, Somerset, BA6 9DP England. Their phone number is 01458-832954.

Kilve

HOOD ARMS The Hood Arms in Kilve, Somerset, is a seventeenth-century coaching inn situated at the foot of the Quantock Hills. The ghost here is a previous landlord's mother, who sits in a corner of the Old World bar in a rocking chair. She quietly watches over the old inn from the Other Side.

Nunney

GEORGE INN The George Inn in the town of Nunney is haunted by a decidedly macabre sound—the unmistakable sound of bodies swinging from nooses. They are the invisible ghosts of rebels executed after being captured in the Battle of Sedgemoor in 1685. On the roads near the inn, the more visible apparition of a phantom hitchhiker is seen.

Taunton

CASTLE HOTEL The Castle Hotel in Taunton, Somerset, is an imposing building that was once part of a Norman fortress. It has been welcoming royal travelers to Taunton since the twelfth century. Now an elegant, thirty-five-room hotel, it is home to a most beguiling spirit that is never seen, only heard. Sometimes, from somewhere in the depths of the castle, unexplainable violin music issues forth. Several phantom violins play melancholy music of a time gone by. The Castle Hotel is located on Castle Green in Taunton, Somerset. For more information, phone 0823-272671 or fax 0823-336066. Not far from Castle Green, Somerset's famous hanging judge, Judge Jeffreys, returns in spirit to the old Tudor Tavern.

Wedmore

GEORGE INN The ghost of a lady in Edwardian dress haunts the George Inn in Wedmore, near Glastonbury. There is also an angry presence at the inn that holds guests down in their beds against their will. Sometimes the manifestation telegraphs its presence by an icy wind that penetrates the comforters of the person in bed.

DEVONSHIRE

Coleford

NEW INN A monk haunts the New Inn at Coleford, a thirteenth-century, thatched country inn that was once a monks' retreat. Sebastian the Monk, the resident ghost, roams guests' rooms and is responsible for chilling breezes and doors opening by themselves.

Exeter

EXETER CATHEDRAL A nun who appears regularly during July, around seven in the evening, haunts the cloisters of Exeter Cathedral. A monk haunts the cathedral's close year round.

LORD HALDON HOTEL The Lord Haldon Hotel in Exeter consists of the surviving wing of the original Haldon House. The ghost of a sad young maidservant wanders around the top floors in soaking-wet, eighteenth-century clothes. She was seduced by Lord Haldon, and when she fell pregnant, drowned herself in a nearby lake.

Kentisbeare

BRADFIELD HALL An outdoor spirit can be found at the Bradfield Hall estate in Kentisbeare. It is home to the strange ghost of a laborer driving a horse-drawn roller. He is said to make an appearance every night at midnight.

Lewtrenchard

MANOR HOTEL A couple of "old" spirits can be found in the Manor Hotel in Lewtrenchard, Devonshire. The inside of the hotel is haunted by a ghost nicknamed "Old Madam," who walks the long gallery in the building. The apparition of a White Lady, though, wanders around outside the building.

Lydford

LYDFORD CASTLE At the west edge of Dartmoor lie the ruins of Lydford Castle, which Henry VIII called "one of the most detestable places in the realm." Nonetheless, the damp, cramped stone fortress did find use as a prison all the way into the nineteenth century. The castle is haunted by the infamous Judge Jeffreys, who is said to be doomed to haunt the heinous spot for all of eternity in the form of a black pig. His company in

Lydford Castle, Devonshire, Great Britain (John Mason)

the spectral realm is Lady Howard (see Okehampton Castle below), who appears here as a black hound.

Milton Combe

WHO'D HAVE THOUGHT IT INN The pub at the Who'd Have Thought It Inn at Milton Combe in Buckland Monachorum is haunted by a former landlord and a ghostly Cavalier who keeps ringing for service.

Newton Abbot

OLD INN AT WIDECOMBE The Old Inn at Widecombe in the Moor in Newton Abbot is haunted by "Old Harry," a friendly ghost who potters around the hotel. Sometimes the ghostly cries of a child are heard from a particular room at the inn.

Okehampton

OKEHAMPTON CASTLE The ruins of Okehampton Castle in southwest Devon near Dartmoor are protected by the ghost of a vicious black dog, but even more threatening is an encounter with Wicked Lady Howard, who rides past the castle every night in a coach made from the bones of her four husbands, all of whom she is said to have murdered. As part of an exorcism performed centuries ago, Lady Howard is committed to plucking one blade of grass from Okehampton Park and bringing it to her home in Fitzford every night

Okehampton Castle, Devonshire, Great Britain (John Mason)

throughout all eternity. Lady Howard also haunts Lydford Castle.

WHITE HART HOTEL White Hart Hotel in downtown Okehampton is home to the friendlier though mischievous spirit of a small boy named Peter. He is known for opening doors in the hotel to people he likes and slamming them in their faces if he does not care for them. Children staying at the hotel sometimes play with the ghost without realizing he is not among the living. He has even been known to steal their toys.

Plymouth

BEDFORD HOTEL The Bedford, an ornate hotel near Plymouth, was built in the fifteenth century on top of a tenth-century Benedictine abbey. The present stone porch and gateway were part of the original abbey. The Bedford's ghost originates from that era. She is a young girl who was raped and murdered by a monk. Now her frequently sighted apparition walks through the corridors and bedrooms of the hotel and has even appeared to startled guests in the hotel restaurant. The Bedford Hotel is at 1 Plymouth Road in Tavistock, Devonshire. For information, call 0822-613221 or fax 0822-618034.

Dartmouth

ROYAL CASTLE HOTEL The ghost of Queen Mary, wife of King William III, haunts the Royal Castle Hotel in Dartmouth. She spent her first night in England here and loved the place. In the autumn, though, her carriage is sometimes seen and heard rumbling around the courtyard outside.

Postbridge

B3212 HIGHWAY If you are motorcycling on the B3212 Highway between Postbridge and Two Bridges in Devonshire, watch out for a dangerous ghost. A pair of hands covered in thick hair have materialized over motorcyclists hands, trying to force them off the road. The hands have also been seen clawing at windshields of cars and trucks.

The only recorded fatality on the road was a prison doctor who died in a motorbike crash there in 1921, but no one knows if his death is the source or the result of the haunting.

Shebbear

DEVIL'S STONE PUB The Devil's Stone Pub in Shebbear, Devonshire, takes its name from a megalithic stone that stands outside the churchyard. But the pub has its own ghosts, a little girl accompanied by a gray-bearded man. They are a father and daughter murdered in their room at the inn.

South Zeal

OXENHAM ARMS The Oxenham Arms in South Zeal, Devonshire, was originally built as a monastery in the twelfth century then rebuilt as a manor house in the fourteenth century. For some reason, one of the rooms has a granite monolith in it similar to the many to be seen standing on the high moors, and it is thought to be the source of the haunting here. Heavy footsteps in the corridor and the sound of something being dragged along the ground are reported.

Torquay

PALACE HOTEL Former servants haunt the Palace Hotel in Torquay. It was once the home of the Bishop of Exeter, but only the ghosts of his faithful servants, chambermaids, porters, and vicars remain behind.

Wistman's Woods

THIRTEEN OAKS Some outdoor ghosts in Devonshire can be found among thirteen twisted oak trees of Wistman's Woods. The line of trees marks the path where monks once carried corpses for burial. The ghosts of the silent monks are still seen, as well as a phantom pack of red-eyed hounds from hell said to be hunting the souls of the unbaptized.

Wistman's Woods, Devonshire, Great Britain (John Mason)

WILTSHIRE

Salisbury

STONEHENGE Stonehenge is located on the Salisbury Plain eighty miles southwest of London in Wiltshire. The world's most famous megalithic monument, Stonehenge was built as a religious temple and astronomical observatory over five thousand years ago, though the origins of the sacred site itself could be even older than that. Theories about who built Stonehenge include Merlin and King Arthur, the Druids, Greeks, Egyptians and Phoenicians, Atlanteans, and even extraterrestrials. While the Druids used the structure for ceremonial purposes, construction was begun long before the Druids arrived in England. Nonetheless, it is the ghosts of Druid priests who haunt

Stonehenge, Salisbury Plain, Great Britain (Pamela Heath)

the site. They are witnessed just outside the entrance, at the huge Heelstone, which weighs several tons, and along the Avenue that leads to the site. Druid apparitions are also witnessed at the Altar Stone, which is set in the center of the circle of blue standing stones, and within the one hundred-foot-diameter Sarsen Sandstone Circle, whose rocks carry Druid carvings.

In order to protect Stonehenge for future generations, it was put into the care of the English Heritage Trust in 1918. Ever increasing amounts of visitors had caused damage to the stones and prehistoric carvings. Visitors are no longer permitted to walk among the stones, and since 1978, they have been asked to keep to the path around the outside stone circle. Modern Druids still lay claim to the site, which was closed to them in 1988 after four thousand people showed up to participate in a Summer Solstice celebration. Finally, in 1998, the English Heritage Trust, which now owns over 1500 acres of land around Stonehenge, allowed 150 white-robed Druids to participate in Summer Solstice rituals at the site. However, the ceremonies were once again mobbed by Neo-Pagans, who go to the site to "party" during the solstice. Some of the unauthorized revelers ended up dancing naked on top of the stones. Over four hundred of them were evicted by police, which resulted in several injuries and twenty-three arrests.

Wiltshire Downs

AVEBURY CIRCLE At Wiltshire Downs, just west of Marlborough, in Wiltshire, lies another mysterious circle of stones known as Avebury Circle that is haunted by small figures dancing in the moonlight. Sometimes strange music can be heard coming from the center of the circle. The ghosts of hooded Druid priests have also been seen walking with their heads bent down along West Kennet Avenue in Wiltshire Downs. The ancient road once connected Avebury with a smaller stone circle located on top of Overton Hill. The stones were erected about the same time as Stonehenge—over five thousand years ago.

Today, the twenty-eight-acre Neolithic site consists of a thirty-foot-deep moat located between a circular dirt mound and an inner circle formed of tweny-seven standing stones. Originally, there were a hundred stones in this inner circle. Within that inner circle at one time were two smaller circles of twenty-nine stones each. Inside the north circle, a ritual site was erected using three giant stones fifteen feet high and eight feet wide. Inside the south circle, there stood a sacred obelisk twenty-one feet high.

It is the stones themselves that seem to carry the paranormal energy at Avebury, and each has its own "story" to tell. For instance, the Barbers Stone carries a ghost from the fourteenth century.

Avebury Circle, Wiltshire Downs, Great Britain (John Mason)

The Catholic Church had ordered all the Avebury stones buried in an effort to purge the site of its pagan ties, although it proved a daunting task that was never completed. At least one man was killed when one of the giant stones fell on him. He was the town barber, actually a physician of sorts, and his ghost started appearing near the stone that killed him. Centuries later, the man's skeleton was discovered still buried beneath the stone. The Church also encouraged people to build houses out of the stones, though it soon became obvious that anyone who built their homes of Avebury stones would be visited by a terrifying ghoul known simply as "the Haunt."

AVEBURY MANOR This is the case with Avebury Manor, whose own "Haunt" seems to have opened a doorway to the Other Side. The house was built using Avebury stones in the northwest corner of the circle. This section is known for a variety of paranormal phenomena, including mysterious crop circles that form overnight. Some of the crop circles are 150 feet in diameter and most are generated using an eight-fold pattern. Among the more traditional spirits at the stately Tudor mansion is Sir John Stawell, a former owner who lost his beloved home after the English Civil War. The gentleman's presence is presaged by the overpowering odor of roses. A Royalist apparition is seen in the Cavalier Room (formerly the Crimson Room), and the ghost of the White Lady is seen both inside the house and on the grounds. She is a former servant girl who was in love with a Cavalier killed during the conflict. She killed herself by leaping out an upper window and now likes to accompany visitors from the yard to the front door of the house. Tours of Avebury Manor include guides dressed in period costumes and an Elizabethan Torture Chamber in the basement.

DORSET

Beaminster

ST. MARY'S CHURCH A child's ghost haunts St. Mary's Church in Beaminster. A boy, who returns with some regularity on June 27 of each year, haunts the church gallery. The boy is John Daniel, who was murdered here in 1728. The gallery of the church was once used as a schoolroom, and he first appeared here before his schoolmates not long after he died. When they starting throwing stones at his apparition, he promptly disappeared. Because of the frequent appearances of his ghost, his coffin was exhumed, and blessed. They also discovered that the boy had been strangled to death and had not died from a fit, as had been previously thought.

Evershot

ACORN INN Another haunted hotel in Dorset is the Acorn Inn, an authentic sixteenth-century inn with beamed ceilings and stone walls that is haunted by the ghost of a murdered highwayman. The Acorn Inn is at 28 Fore Street in Evershot, Dorset.

Lyme Regis

ROYAL INN The Royal Lion is a sixteenth-century former coaching inn located close to the sea in the town of Lyme Regis. The hotel stands next to the Old Town Gallows, and that is the explanation given for all the disembodied footsteps, chilly sensations, and sheets of ectoplasmic mist that appear in the corridors here. Lyme Regis is the setting for John Fowle's novel *The French Lieutenant's Woman*. The Royal Lion Hotel is at 57 Broad Street in Lyme Regis, Dorset.

BOVEY HOUSE The Bovey House was originally a medieval manor. Charles I retreated to this town after his defeat at the Battle of Worcester in 1651. Charles's lavender water perfume waifs through the hotel, and its odor presages his ghost's appearance to jostle with the phantom of a headless man. A phantom army haunts the streets around the Black Dog Pub in nearby Uplyme from that same battle. The pub, incidentally, was named for one of the phantom dogs that also haunt the neighborhood.

Poole

CROWN HOTEL The Crown Hotel in Poole is haunted by the distinctive sound of a body being dragged and the accompanying noises of running feet and high-pitched screams. These are the ghosts of a former landlord's abused children. He said he kept them locked away because they were deformed.

Shaftesbury

GROSVENOR HOTEL Located right in the center of Shaftesbury's Market Place in Dorset, the Georgian hotel called the Grosvenor has a history that goes back over four hundred years. For most of that time the Grosvenor has served the needs of traveling merchants, monks, and commoners. The ghosts of monks are often seen in the cellar passageways, which at one time led out to a nearby monastery. But the most active presence is the Lady in Gray, who walks the corridors and likes to hang around the Chevy Chase sideboard in the upstairs lounge. When she passes you in the hall, she leaves behind a chilling wind. Yet the Lady of the Grosvenor is given to common tastes, for whenever her ghost is spotted, beer stocks at the hotel unaccountably dwindle. No amount of investigation and accounting has yet been able to explain where all the beer is going. The Grosvenor Hotel is located on the Commons in Shaftsbury, Dorset. For more information, phone 0747-52282 or fax 0747-54755.

West Lulworth

CASTLE INN Built in the sixteenth century, the Castle Inn has a distinctive creeper-covered thatched roof and a one-of-a-kind ghost that lets its feelings be known about changes to the place. The ghost is an elderly lady, who met her death in the inn's garden. Now she objects to the fact that the inn has expanded into part of the former garden and expresses her displeasure with little poltergeist tricks. The Castle Inn is located on Main Street in West Lulworth, Dorset.

AVON

Bath

The town of Bath in the English Midlands is famous for its ancient Roman baths and other Roman structures, and many spirits from that era are said to haunt them. Visitors often report seeing strange figures resembling Roman legionnaires or unexplainable streaks of light showing up in photographs taken in the area.

Roman Baths, Bath, Great Britain (Pam Heath)

GARRICK'S HEAD PUB The most active paranormal hotspot in Bath is not haunted by Romans. The area around the Garrick's Head Pub in central Bath is teeming with spirits. The shadowy figure that haunts the entryway to the pub, just off the gently sloping street, is the ghost of Beau Nash, who owned the building when it was a gambling hall. The pub also shares a ghost with the theater next door, and the two buildings are said to be linked by a secret passageway. The theater ghost is known as the Gray Lady, whose presence is indicated by the smell of jasmine. She is believed to be a beautiful young lady who fell in love with an actor who was killed by her jealous husband in a duel. On learning of her lover's death, she committed suicide by hanging herself, and her spirit continues to haunt the theater where he worked and the pub where they relaxed together. Often her spirit manifests as an icy cold spot in one of the balcony boxes at the New Theatre

Royal or near the bar in the pub. During renovations at the pub, her apparition was seen in the nearby Bath Bingo Hall. Ghost Walks tours start from the Garrick's Head Pub, next door to the New Theatre Royal in downtown Bath.

Bristol

ALL SAINTS CHURCH In Bristol, Avon, All Saints Church is a serene sanctuary planted firmly on the corner of Corn Street and High Street. However, looks are deceiving, for the church and vicarage have been haunted since at least the 1840s by the figure of a black-robed monk, who opens locked doors, shakes beds in the middle of the night, and gestures for people to follow him before disappearing into a wall. The church was indeed once a monastery, but when King Henry VIII dissolved the Catholic monasteries and ordered that they surrender all their wealth, the prior had all the valuable objects hidden away. Despite all the king's efforts, the treasure cache was never found, and the ghostly monk is said to guard its whereabouts even to this day.

LONDON

In sheer number of cases, London is the ghost capitol of England, and no visit to the country would be complete without a few nights' stay in the heart of England. The city is over two thousand years old and almost every building carries centuries of history. Oddly, there are very few haunted hotel rooms in London, but that is more than compensated for by the large number of haunted prison cells.

There are also over a dozen separate Ghost Walks in this very haunted city. The Original London Ghost Walk conducts most of the ghost walks. The two-hour walk begins at 8:15 P.M. every Sunday (or 8:00 P.M. on Mondays, Tuesdays, Fridays, and Saturdays) from Blackfriars Underground Station. Other ghost walks include Ghosts of the West End (from Embankment Underground Station at 7:30 P.M.), Ghosts of the Old City (from St. Paul's Underground at 7:30 P.M.), Ghosts, Gaslight & Guinness (from Holborn Underground at 7:30 P.M.), and the Dracula Walk (from Embankment Underground at 7:45 P.M.). For reservations contact the Original London Ghost Walk, 67 Chancery Lane, London, WC2A 1AF England. Phone: 0181-5308443. The City Ghost Walk Tour, "Apparitions, Graveyards, and Alleyways," leaves every Sunday at 7:30 P.M. from Blackfriars Tube Ticket Hall. The Jack the Ripper Walk is conducted by Ripping Yarns Ltd. and leaves every night at 6:45 P.M. from the Tower Hill Underground Station. For information on train connections in London, call 0345-484950. For bus schedules, call 0181-6687261.

BAKER STREET Baker Street is London's most haunted street. The ghost of actress Sarah Siddons, whose house once stood on the spot, haunts the electrical substation at 228 Baker Street in London. The Volunteer Pub in the Baker Street area is haunted by a member of the Nevill family, who owned a manor house at the same location that burned down in 1654. The apparition of Rupert Nevill, dressed in breeches and fancy stockings, is seen in the cellar of the pub. The two-hundred-year old Kenwood House Hotel, also in the Baker Street area, is haunted by the apparition of a Cavalier gentleman, and a certain piece of furniture with a mirrored window seems possessed by a poltergeist, for its doors open and close by themselves.

BALMORAL CASTLE Several royal palaces in London are haunted, but none have such a prestigious living witness as Balmoral. The present queen of England, Queen Elizabeth, is reported to have seen the ghost of John Brown, consort and lover of Queen Victoria, walking the corridors of Balmoral Castle late at night.

BANK OF ENGLAND The small garden in the center of the Bank of England building in London is haunted by the ghost of a very tall man and a mentally unbalanced woman. The man was an eight-foot-tall cashier at the bank, who was terrified that after he died, his body would be stolen by a cult of resurrectionists for one of their rituals. Somehow, he got permission from his superiors to be buried inside the bank. During alterations on the building, his lead coffin, wrapped in iron chains, was found. The female apparition is Sarah Whitehead, whose brother worked at the bank and was executed for forgery in 1811. The distraught woman eventually lost her mind and went to the bank every day asking for her brother, until her own death in 1836.

BERKELEY SQUARE The house at 50 Berkeley Square in London was renowned for its hauntings for many decades. It was finally abandoned when no one would live there, though the ghost attacked homeless people attempting to spend the night there. Some of them were brutally killed and thrown out the window by an unseen and lethal presence. Recently, the place was successfully exorcised of its demons, and people are once again living there. Ghostbusters have since moved on to Charles Dickens's former home at 29 Dougherty Street in the Clerkenwell section of London, which is said to be haunted by his ghost.

BLACK SWAN PUB The Black Swan pub on Bow Road in London is another spooky pub. The two daughters of a previous owner haunt it. They were pretty but mischievous young women named Cissie and Sylvia Reynolds, and their ghosts seem to stay confined to the cellar. They died with their mother, when the building was destroyed in a German zeppelin air attack on September 23, 1916. Both girls were in their twenties at the time of their deaths.

BLACKWELL TUNNEL Not all London ghosts stay indoors, however. For instance, the apparition of a motorcyclist in leathers haunts the Blackwall Tunnel in Greenwich. The man was killed in an accident there in 1972. Another example is the phantom coach, which floats some six feet above the ground, bobbing down Bell Lane in the Enfield section of London. It is thought the scene dates from the time the area was flooded when the Lea River ran over its banks, trapping coaches in torrents of water and sweeping them away.

BLOOMS HOTEL One of London's few haunted hotels has to borrow its ghosts from the British Museum. The Blooms Hotel is part of an eighteenth-century terrace adjoining the British Museum, and it suffers from a plethora of spirits that drift in from its famous next-door neighbor. Psychic Paul Hughes investigated the hotel and concluded it was "crowded with spirits," many of whom came from the British Museum. His theory is that the building "acts as an exit point for all the spirits of the people and artifacts, Egyptian, Greek, Assyrian, that fill the Museum next door."

One modern presence is the ghost of the "Man in Room 1," of whom most people perceive as a great thinker. Some feel that he is sitting in a chair in the room, although a few feel he is sitting outdoors in the sunshine. Actually, Room 1 is a new addition to the hotel and was built over part of the garden. Many buildings near the museum in the Bloomsbury district where the hotel sits are considered haunted by strange or intellectual presences. The oldest haunting in the area is the Atlantis Bookshop on Museum Street. Founded in 1922, it has had its own resident bookworm ghost almost from the beginning. The Blooms Hotel is at 7 Montague Square in London. For bookings, phone 0171-323-1717 or fax 0171-636-6498. For more information, visit the White Rabbit Web site at www.afallon.com/pages/whiterabbit1.html.

BRITISH MUSEUM The prestigious British Museum is haunted by an Egyptian mummy case that carries a curse. The mummy case in Exhibit 22542 is blamed for causing thirteen deaths so far. It belonged to a beautiful young girl who was a singer to the god Amon Ra. The mummy case is covered in hieroglyphs and has a portrait of the girl. English tourists visiting Thebes in Egypt purchased the case in the 1880s. The new owner was injured in a hunting accident the very next day, and had to have his arm amputated after the accident. After a member of his party mysteriously disappeared and was never found, the man was convinced of the curse and sold the case to a dealer in Cairo.

Three people bought it after that and all of them died shortly afterwards, yet not before it found its way to London. It was bought by a collector, but a friend of the collector was psychic and felt great evil emanating from the coffin. He warned the man to get rid of it or it would kill him. The collector took heed and sold it immediately. The new owner decided to have it photographed professionally, but the photographer unexpectedly died the day afterwards. Once the pictures were developed, instead of the beautiful girl on the case, they showed an ugly old hag—her eyes filled with evil. The owner then sold it to a rich widow, and on its first night in the house, all of her pet animals died and every piece of glass in the house was smashed. She fell into a strange sleeping sickness that no one could diagnose, but as soon as she gave the case away, she recovered.

The British Museum obtained the case in 1889, and as the porters carried it in, one of them fell and broke his leg, and the other died a few days afterwards from a fatal cut he got from the case, even though no sharp edges were found that could have caused such a wound. The mummy case gained certain notoriety, but nobody was able to sketch it or photograph it accurately. Burly security guards were terrified to patrol the room at night, claiming they were followed by an invisible, horrible presence. Then one of the security guards saw an apparition rise from the coffin, "a thing with a wrinkled yellow-green face." A photographer for the museum allegedly killed himself after seeing some of his photographs of the mummy case develop. A secret exorcism was performed in the museum in 1921, and the two men taking part said the source of the curse was a protective spirit evoked by the magical hieroglyphics on the case. They confronted this demonic force and said that it "had the face of a glowing jellyfish." In actual fact, ghostly activity at the exhibit substantially declined after their exorcism ritual.

BUCKINGHAM PALACE Buckingham Palace is haunted by Major John Gwynne, a private secretary to King Edward VII. Thinking that his divorce case would bring dishonor to the Royal Family, he shot himself at his desk in his first floor office at the palace, and that is where his presence is sensed and from where a single unexplainable

Buckingham Palace, London, Great Britain (Bruce Schaffenberger)

gunshot emanates late at night. The other ghost of the palace is the stubborn ghost of a monk bound up in chains, who most often appears on Christmas Day as a reminder of Christian cruelty. A priory once stood on the site of Buckingham Palace and the monk died in his cell after enduring much punishment.

CLEOPATRA'S NEEDLE Another Egyptian artifact that brought trouble to Londoners is Cleopatra's Needle along the Thames River. The "needle" is a large Egyptian obelisk that is more than three thousand years old. Something about the obelisk, however, drives people to commit suicide near it. Over the years, the site has gained notoriety for the number of suicides, and some of those lost souls still cling to the spot. One of the strangest apparitions seen here is a tall, naked man that leaps into the Thames River near Cleopatra's Needle and disappears under the water to the sounds of far-off laughter.

DARTMOOR PRISON The old Dartmoor Prison in London is haunted by a former prisoner, David Davis. Imprisoned here in 1869, Davis spent much of the next fifty years behind bars. He was assigned the job of looking after the prison's sheep and soon grew to love his job. He called each one by name and would even stay with them during illness or birthing. After he was released, he committed petty crimes to make sure he could return to his beloved sheep. After his death at the prison in 1929, his ghost following the flock of sheep was reported by guards and prisoners alike. The graveyard at the back of Dartmoor Prison is haunted by the apparition of a short man with long, black hair, who is seen gliding over the lawn late at night.

GRENADIER PUB The Grenadier Pub on Wilton Row is one of the most famous haunted bars in the world. The ghost of a young military officer from the nineteenth century appears regularly in September, on the anniversary of his death. The man was caught cheating at cards and in the scuffle that followed, he fell downstairs and broke his neck. Sometimes, the ghost manifests as poltergeist activity, while at other times he takes the form of a shapeless blob of light or as swirls of "hot smoke."

GUN INN PUB The ghost of Horatio Nelson is said to haunt the Gun Inn Pub at Coldharbour in the Docklands. He is seen late at night waiting in the pub or "sneaking" through the corridors of the inn. It is a historical fact that the good admiral often rendezvoused with Lady Hamilton at this inn.

HAMPTON COURT PALACE Of all the royal residences in London, none is more haunted than Hampton Court Palace. Located in Middlesex along the Thames River, it lies on sixty wonderfully landscaped acres that include its famous maze. The palace has been open to the public since 1838, and today, authentically costumed guides lead tours, with Tudor music playing in the background. You enter the grounds through the Outer Green Court and then cross the bridge over the moat through the Great Gate House. Continuing through the inner gatehouse, Anne Boleyn's Gateway, you enter the Great Hall, whose finely carved ceiling soars up to the building's hammer beam roof. You can visit the Royal Chapel and great galleries of art, as well as the

Hampton Court Palace, London, Great Britain
(Richard Senate)

lavish kitchens, drawing rooms, antechambers, and bedrooms.

It is an experience that can take you back in time, and there's even a possibility that you might meet one of the palace's owners or residents from those bygone eras. The palace was built in 1514 for Cardinal Thomas Wolsey, the chief minister of Henry VIII, but the ambitious cardinal soon fell out of favor with the king, who acquired it himself in 1528 and set it up as the residence for five of his six wives. King Henry was a capricious man, who had the nasty habit of accusing his wife of adultery and having her arrested when he grew tired of her. That was the fate of his second wife, Anne Boleyn, who was executed in 1536 on charges of adultery. Her saddened spirit, clad in a blue dress, is seen floating through the palace hallways, as if she is still looking for a way to regain her privileged palace life. The Renaissance Picture Gallery is home to the screaming apparition of Catherine Howard, the eighteen-year-old fifth wife of Henry. One evening in 1541, within a year after her marriage, she was arrested on charges of "harlotry and adultery" and bound by her captors in a small room near the Queen's Great Staircase. But Catherine escaped her captors and ran shrieking down the gallery corridor to the chapel, where the king was in prayer. She pleaded for mercy, but the king would not interrupt his prayers to hear her, and she ended up imprisoned in the Tower of London, where she was beheaded the following year. Her frantic ghost is said to return to the gallery (now known as the Haunted Gallery) each November 4, the anniversary of the date she sought her freedom from the heartless monarch. Once, an artist sketching a wall tapestry in the gallery saw a hand materialize in front of it. He hurriedly sketched what he had seen and was able to draw in some detail a ring on one of the fingers of the phantom hand. The jewel was later identified as having belonged to Catherine.

Another female ghost in the Haunted Gallery, as well as in the Clock Court, is that of Queen Jane Seymour, Henry's third wife. She died here on October 12, 1537, after bearing him a son, and her apparition is seen carrying a tall, lighted candle back and forth between a doorway in the Queens' Old Apartments and the Silver Stick Gallery. Several servants have quit after seeing the queen gliding along the stairway connecting the two rooms, and her ghost is one of the most active. In 1999, paranormal investigators Richard and Debbie Senate encountered her apparition near the place where she died. Another active ghost is the Lady in Gray, a tall woman in a long gray robe with a hood over her head. She is usually sighted in the hallways on the second floor. Psychics have identified her as Sybil Penn, the nurse of Edward VI, Jane Seymour's child and King Henry's only legitimate son. Sybil died of smallpox in her room in the southwest wing, which is still haunted by sounds of voices, footsteps, and an old-time spinning wheel. Many irrefutable witnesses, including Queen Elizabeth I and Princess Frederica of Hanover, have seen her apparition.

There is also a haunting at Hampton Court involving children. It started in 1887, when the three-year-old son of a nobleman drowned in the small lake on the property. Then in 1927, a young couple visiting the palace watched in horror as their three-year-old girl ran straight into the lake and "sank like a stone." Again in 1967, the lake claimed a child, when a single mother taking her four-year-old son for a walk around the lake, watched helplessly as he suddenly ran off toward the water, fell in, and went under. Fortunately, this time, a man saw it happen and leapt into the lake to save the boy. When the boy was asked why he ran into the lake, he said calmly, "to play with the other children." The Hampton Court Lake is next due to claim a child in the year 2007.

Some of the ghosts here have been laid to rest. Two young Cavaliers haunted the Fountain Court, until a sewer worker found their bodies buried about two feet under the pavement. In 1917, a policeman opened the front gate for a group of two men and seven women wearing old-fashioned clothing, but as they walked past him, they all vanished into thin air. The ghost of a page-boy, about eight years old and dressed in a black-and-white costume, once made his way through startled guests at a garden party and walked calmly up the stairs into the back of the house. Having performed his spectral duties, he was never seen again. For more information, visit the official British Ghosts Web Page at www.buckinghamgate.com/events/features/ghosts/ghosts.html.

HORNS PUB The Horns Pub on Crucifix Lane near London Bridge sits under the arches of the railroad. The ghost is a harmless elderly lady who just likes to visit the old place. For many years, the ghost of a little girl seeking its mother at the pub was seen, but she has not appeared recently. Whether the two hauntings are related is unknown. Ye Old Gate House on Highgate Hill in London is an old drovers pub built in 1306. The ghost is poor Mother Marnes, murdered for her money. She is sometimes seen dressed in black, but the kind woman never shows up if children or animals are on the premises. It is assumed she does not want to scare them.

KENSINGTON PALACE Kensington Palace is haunted by a man wearing white breeches who strolls about in the courtyard. The ghost of an aunt of Queen Victoria has also been seen at the palace, sitting at her spinning wheel. But the most famous ghost of Kensington is King George II, who has been seen on the roof of the palace, staring at the weather vane. Sometimes he is heard to ask, "Why don't they come?" The king died on October 25, 1760, at the palace, waiting desperately for news from his homeland.

LANGHAM HILTON HOTEL A building owned by the British Broadcasting Corporation (B.B.C.) contains many ghosts seen by broadcasters and employees. The Langham opened in 1865 and was London's first Grand Hotel, then in the 1950s it was purchased by the B.B.C. for corporate use. Recently it has been refurbished to its original Victorian style and reopened as a Hilton hotel. At last count, there were five ghosts at the Langham, and many of these presences originate from the time the hotel was occupied by the B.B.C. A gray-haired Victorian gentleman haunts one of the old B.B.C. dormitory areas. He is dressed in a cloak and cravat, and he is known for his blank staring eyes. The man was a doctor, who killed himself after murdering his bride on their honeymoon night in the hotel.

But the most famous of the Langham's ghosts is the one that haunts Room 333. In 1973, a B.B.C. radio announcer stayed overnight because he had to do an early morning show. During the night, he awoke to observe a luminescent, floating ball that slowly took on the shape of a man wearing Victorian eveningwear. The announcer asked the ghost what it wanted, and it began to float towards him, with its legs cut off some two feet below the ground, arms outstretched, eyes staring emptily ahead. At this point the announcer got up and fled, but when he came back a bit later, the ghost was still there. This time it was not as "visible" and much less threatening. Other B.B.C. staff reported seeing the same apparition in the same room, although it only seems to appear during the month of October. All witnesses agreed that the apparition's legs seemed to be cut off. The ghost apparently walks on the original level of the Victorian hotel, before central heating ducts were installed and the floorboards had to be raised.

Another of the rooms was used by the B.B.C. as a reference library, and employees occasionally felt a cold presence and sometimes reported seeing the figure of an eighteenth-century footman dressed in a blue livery uniform. One B.B.C. announcer claimed to have seen the form of a large Germanic-looking man in military style dress. The apparition was standing at a fourth floor window, the same window out of which a German prince threw himself just before the outbreak of the First World War. For some reason, the exiled French emperor Napoleon III returns from his last resting place to haunt the Langham's basement. The Langham Hilton Hotel is at 1 Portland Place on Regent Street in London. For bookings, call 0171-636-1000 or fax 0171-323-2340. For more information, visit the White Rabbit Web site at www.afallon.com/pages/whiterabbit1.html.

NATIONAL GALLERY The National Gallery in London is haunted by a group of apparitions attracted to a particular painting. Late at night, the ghosts show up in Gallery 16 in front of a painting by the seventeenth-century artist Jan Vermeer. Between one and three apparitions seem to be admiring the painting. Guards have seen the ghosts on security cameras as well as in person on their night patrols. Gallery officials admit that at least three guards working different shifts have reported witnessing the phenomena.

OLD QUEENS HEAD PUB An unidentified lady in Tudor dress accompanied by a sad little girl haunts the Old Queens Head pub on Essex Road in Canonbury, a suburb of London. On the first Sunday of the month the doors are opened and closed by unseen hands and the sound of footsteps is heard. For more information, visit the White Rabbit Web site at www.afallon.com/pages/whiterabbit1.html. For information on bookings, E-mail afallon@fallon.com.

ROYAL ALBERT HALL Royal Albert Hall, London's most prestigious performance venue, is haunted by surprisingly uncultured presences. The ghosts of former prostitutes and their clients are seen roaming about. The hall was constructed on the site of Gore House, which was a popular high-class brothel in the nineteenth century. Count D'Orsay (1801–1857) owned the house and kept a bevy of prostitutes in his basement. While the count's ghost has never been seen in the building, the apparitions of flirtatious young Victorian girls are seen flitting about, as well as a pale-faced Victorian "john" who passes through walls at Royal Albert Hall. Recently the theater's management has called in noted ghostbuster Andrew Green to deal with their little "problem."

ROYAL ARSENAL The cries of prisoners being tortured can still be heard in the hall leading to the office of the Duke of Wellington at the Royal Arsenal in southeast London. Parts of the main building housed prisoners during the Napoleonic wars, and not a few Frenchmen were taken to this office for brutal "attitude adjustments." There were so many prisoners taken that those that could not be housed in the arsenal were kept in barges docked on the Thames at the rear of the building. Other sounds that haunt the building date from the last forty years. They include the coughs of a young secretary who died of tuberculosis while at work and the distinctive creaking sounds of the rope from which a senior civil servant hanged himself after being caught stealing supplies. Near the guardhouse, the footsteps of a nineteen-year-old still patrol late at night. He shot himself after being informed he was going to be shipped off to the front in France during World War I.

The apparition of an old lady who haunts Building 2 has been seen in broad daylight and late at night. Multiple witnesses have seen her ghost in the corridors or walking down the stairways. Sometimes only her footsteps are heard. She is thought to be a secretary, who worked for the Navy during World War II. She was killed in a freak accident when a bullet somehow got mixed in with some firewood. When the wood was burnt in the office fireplace, the bullet went off and struck her. Building 11 is haunted by the ghost of a soldier from World War I. The apparition wears the uniform of an Army major, and he seems to be associated with a collection of military models on display in the building. His apparition is seen carrying a stick or whip tucked under his arm. Guards in the building have also reported some poltergeist activity, including flying fluorescent bulbs that detached from their fixtures and crashed through windows on the upper two floors.

ROYAL GEOGRAPHICAL SOCIETY The Royal Geographical Society in Kensington is haunted by the ghostly figures of monks walking the premises late at night. A former telephone operator at the society, Cicely Blaylock, described her encounter with one of the monks: "He was a tall thin man, quite nasty looking and he was wearing a dirty white canvas gown. He had a cap on one shoulder that hung down over one shoulder and had a tassel on the end. He had piercing blue eyes and was pointing a bony finger straight at me; I could even see the dirt under the nail."

The employee apartments, which used to be stables, are haunted by the apparitions of a small man in a jockey's satin uniform and a taller, bearded man wearing canvas boots, blue shorts, and an Australian cowboy hat. The apparition of polar explorer Captain Robert Scott is seen riding his dog-driven sled in the snow in the middle of summer on the grounds. His original sled is kept on display at the society. For more information, visit White Rabbit's Haunted Britain Web site at www.afallon.com/pages/whiterabbit1.html.

ST. JOSEPH'S COLLEGE St. Joseph's College in Norwood is haunted by a man who committed suicide in the private house that serves as the administration center at the center of the campus. In 1864, a man who bred racehorses owned the house, and his groom, Daniel Philpot, bet all he owned on one of the horses. The horse lost, and Philpot was suddenly bankrupt. The desperate man hanged himself in the Oak Room of his master's home, and his ghost is said to appear there regularly every five years. He is next scheduled to appear in 2003.

TOWER OF LONDON Just about every former or present prison in London is haunted, but the most haunted of all is the Tower of London. When touring the Tower of London, however, never question the Beefeater tour guides about the ghosts there. They will immediately change the subject or ignore the question, for according to tradition, mentioning ghosts in the Tower of London is bad luck and will cause the ghosts to stir. Sentries on duty at the Tower have reported

Tower of London, London, Great Britain (Dorothy O'Donnell, Gryphon)

feet above the green. Tourists, caretakers, and even Welsh Guardsmen have seen her white shapeless ghost. The Duke of Northumberland haunts the halls in the aristocrats' section of the Tower, and an unidentified woman's ghost also walks the corridors here. She is the beautiful Veiled Lady, who has a black void where her face should be.

Many other London jailhouses are haunted. The ghoulish phantom of a famous criminal known as Crippen is seen standing over his grave at Pentonville Jail in London. The apparition, with an obviously distended and crooked neck, hovers over his patch of lawn in the graveyard that has been dubbed "Crippen's Grass." The House of Detention at Clerkenwell in London dates back over three centuries. In 1845, it was completely rebuilt and became the biggest prison in London, able to hold over 10,000 prisoners. The site was abandoned in 1890 and stood in crumbling ruin until it was remodeled in 1983 and opened as a tourist attraction. Today, many ghosts from those bygone, traumatic days roam the premises, and sensitive people are sometimes overcome with anguish on visiting the site.

Apparitions include assorted guards and many former prisoners, such as an elderly woman who is frantically searching for something, another younger woman with her blonde hair parted in

seeing ghostly figures carrying decapitated bodies on stretchers, phantom funeral carriages, and other ghastly visions. In fact, several soldiers have refused duty at the Tower, many have fled their posts or passed out from shock after an encounter, and one even died of fright after seeing a ghost in 1816.

One of the gruesome ghosts here is the headless form of Anne Boleyn, the second wife of Henry VIII, who was beheaded at the Tower in 1536 on charges of adultery. (See Hampton Court Palace, London.) The ghost of Jane Grey, Queen of England for only nine days, was executed on the Tower lawn in 1554, but her ghost is still seen there and walking on the roof of Salt Tower forty

Clerkenwell Jail, London, Great Britain (John Fraser, Ghost Club)

the middle, and a lost, sobbing little girl, one of many children who were imprisoned here. An investigation by England's Ghost Club in 1995 produced a sighting of the woman with her hair parted in the middle, as well as unexplainable drops in temperature in the same area as the sighting. Another investigation by the group in 1998 documented further unexplainable drops in temperature at locations inhabited by spirits, as well as disembodied footsteps, the bolting and unbolting of doors with no one around, and untraceable problems with electrical apparatus. When a ten-member Ghost Club team returned in 1999, they were greeted with unusually intense paranormal encounters. Vice Chair of Investigations John Fraser summed up the group's experiences: "The ghost of a Prison Overseer, who was graphically described as being cadaverous, skinny and emaciated, with a strong and unhygienic body odor, would perhaps give some flavor of the night's proceedings. In fact, the intensity of the experiences and feelings of nausea and intense sadness picked up by Club members were so strong that two sessions in areas of the prison had to be curtailed." More information is available at the Ghost Club Web site http:/dspace.dial.pipex.com/town/lane/xmo85/gc_fr.htm. At another London jailhouse, the old Wandsworth Jail, both guards and prisoners frequently witness the apparition of a middle-aged woman wearing a gray, wool dress. They have nicknamed her "Wandsworth Annie." Most believe she is the ghost of a woman who used to work at the jail in the middle of the nineteenth century.

WIMBLETON COMMON WINDMILL Wimbleton Common Windmill in London is now a popular tourist museum, but it was the scene of some violent act that has left its imprint. Bloodstains in the living quarters underneath the windmill keep reappearing dripping wet no matter how thoroughly they are cleaned, and the sounds of clanging chains and unexplained footsteps fill the night. A recent exorcism by a priest did not placate the restless spirit.

Wimbleton Common Windmill, London, Great Britain (John Mason)

CENTRAL ENGLAND (MIDLANDS)

Central England is the Midlands region and consists of Gloucestershire, Berkshire, Buckinghamshire, Oxfordshire, Warwickshire, Hertfordshire, Bedfordshire, Shropshire, the West Midlands, part of Hereford and Worcester, and Staffordshire.

GLOUCESTERSHIRE

Cotswold Hills

SNOWSHILL MANOR At Snowshill Manor, located in the gentle Cotswold Hills in Gloucestershire, the ghostly monk who walks the halls is named Brother Geoffrey. At one time Snowshill was part of a monastery that was disbanded by Henry VIII. The ghost seems to have developed an ongoing relationship with a frequent visitor to the manor that has lasted over seven years. Judy Farncombe first visited Snowshill with her husband to admire the extensive collection of Japanese armor and swords there assembled by Charles Paget Wade, the eccentric man who owned the manor before bequeathing it to the National Trust.

While touring the kitchen, Judy, who is a gifted psychic, noticed the presence of a large man dressed in a monk's robe in the far corner. Despite the crowd of people, Judy tried to communicate with the powerful presence, because it seemed so

Snowshill Manor, Glouscestershire, Great Britain
(Judy Farncombe)

angry and upset. "He was a very angry monk," Judy recalled. "He felt that his beautiful religious house was being desecrated by the visitors walking up and down, disturbing the meditation of the monks. He was furious that it was no longer a religious house, and he was especially annoyed about the heathen collections housed within it. The last owner had a small collection of Islamic artifacts housed in the room next to the kitchen, and Geoffrey hated them as much as he loved the children's toys up in the attic. I tried to impart to him how much all these visitors appreciated the beauty of his home. The home he was trying to protect."

Eighteen months later, when Judy and her husband returned to Snowshill, she found Geoffrey in a very different mood. "This time Geoffrey was moving about the crowds enjoying himself," Judy recalled. "Geoffrey came with me up to the attic to look at the toy collections. He loved them the best of all the bric-a-brac collected by the last owner, although he took great pleasure in gazing at the Christian artifacts. Geoffrey came with me to the garden, and we talked about the peace of the garden and how he was free to leave if he wished to. He was reluctant to go; it had been his home for too long."

Judy went back to visit her new otherworldly companion on several occasions. On one of these, Geoffrey seemed concerned about the spirit of the previous owner. He was still tied to the Priest's House in the stable block, where he had lived for the months before he died. Geoffrey confessed that he had driven the owner out of the main house because the man attempted to exorcize Geoffrey by placing non-Christian religious artifacts throughout the building. Judy's attempts to help the man failed, however. He was, in Judy's terms, "incommunicable."

Judy returned to Snowshill Manor in September 1999 to take photographs for a Web site on hauntings she was developing. "Geoffrey welcomed me at once," she said. "First by touching my left hand with warm energy and then by draping his arm across my shoulders. The house was undergoing roof repairs, so we could not go up to the attic to see the children's toys; instead we concentrated on the other rooms. Geoffrey pointed out the Christian relics as we went, but some of the items made Geoffrey sad, as they were no longer on consecrated land. He also sniffed with his usual disgust at the 'heathen' items, like the small Buddha in the Japanese Armor room. These items are an irritant to Geoffrey."

Currently, Judy is trying to open a channel of communication with the spirit of the last owner, Charles Paget Wade, and she hopes to let him know that the ghost he tried to exorcize from his home really lived there long before he bought the place. "Perhaps they ought to spend some time together," notes Judy. Snowshill Manor is near the town of Broadway in Gloucestershire.

Chalford

RAGGED COT INN There are not a lot of haunted places to stay in Gloucester, but among those that are, the loveliest is the unique Ragged Cot Inn at Hyde near Chalford. The Ragged Cot is a seventeenth-century stone inn next to over six hundred acres of pristine countryside under control of the National Trust. The unpaid guests at the inn are said to be the wife and child of the first landlord, whom he murdered.

Dean

LITTLEDEAN HALL The countryside along the Severn River near the Welsh border in Gloucestershire is dominated by dark-green medieval forests, but the forested landscape around the town of Dean comes to an abrupt halt at a desolate hilltop on which sits a stark, three-storied brick house known as Littledean Hall. You would not suspect that the *Guinness Book of Records* has named this the oldest occupied house in England. Most of this boxlike manor house was constructed in the thirteenth century, but sections of it date back to fifth-century Saxons. Another distinction of this house is that it has also been called the most haunted house in England, though unfortunately, most of the spirits stem

Littledean Hall, Dean, Glousestershire, Great Britain (Randy Liebeck)

from violent deaths that have taken place here. Paranormal manifestations include sounds such as screams, clashing swords, slamming noises, and pistol shots, as well as cold spots, moving objects, glowing orbs, animated mists, and recognizable apparitions.

The most active apparition is a black servant boy who murdered his master and was executed in 1744. His hapless ghost is seen walking along the second floor landing holding a dim candle. Another powerful presence is a woman in a blue dress who stands by an upstairs window in the Oak Bedroom. She is thought to be the mother of an illegitimate baby whose corpse was found stuffed in a secret panel in the room. Other frequently encountered ghosts are the lonely figure of a monk, two brothers who killed each other in a duel over a woman, and several Royalist soldiers. Outside in the walled garden, more ghosts roam. Apparitions of two girls wearing Edwardian dresses, a man in a cap and cowl, and a Roman priestess have all been reported there. A heavy atmosphere permeates the property, and residents and visitors have been punched and shoved by unseen presences.

The current owner, Donald Macer-Wright, believes that the malevolent forces are growing stronger and has called in several paranormal investigators in recent years to try to stop it. In 1996, a team of investigators under the direction of Randy Liebeck of the Ghost Research Society conducted three separate investigations that confirmed unusual electrical vortexes in the house, even when all the electricity was turned off. Fortunately, recent exorcisms and clearing ceremonies seemed to have helped rid the house of some its negative influences.

Gloucestershire County

BERKELEY CASTLE Gloucestershire's most ancient ghost is King Edward II, who haunts Berkeley Castle. Built in 1153, Berkeley is the oldest continuously inhabited castle in all of England. Edward II was imprisoned in the castle for some time, and then he was sadistically murdered in the dungeon. That

Berkeley Castle, Gloucesterhire, Great Britain (John Mason)

is where his presence is felt the strongest, and sometimes his agonizing screams can still be heard echoing through the stone hallways.

Tewesbury

TUDOR HOUSE HOTEL The Tudor House Hotel in the lovely town of Tewesbury was founded in 1540 and has lots of history. It stands on the tranquil banks of the Avon River. The ghost here is equally tranquil, a gentle White Lady ghost. However, the peaceful atmosphere is sometimes broken by a ferocious Black Dog phantom, which is seen on the grounds.

BERKSHIRE

Arborfield

ST. BARTHOLOMEW'S CHURCH The apparition of a young bride is seen near the larger of two yew trees next to St. Bartholomew's Church in Arborfield, Berkshire. The woman was about to marry the young gardener of Arborfield Hall but was murdered by the jealous butler. The apparition is seen most often on January 1 of each year. Before it was demolished, Arborfield Hall was itself haunted by a Gray Lady who carried a baby in her arms while walking down the main staircase.

Ascot

BERYSTEDE HOTEL The Berystede is a distinguished hotel that stands with nine acres of beautiful, wooded grounds. The turreted Victorian building is decorated in keeping with the elegance of that period and is noted for its fine cuisine and luxury. The only thing the management is a little embarrassed about is the ghost of the maid of a former owner still searching for her lost jewels in certain rooms of the present hotel. A family of Berkshire aristocrats built the house in the 1870s. The Standish family had estates in England and France and had close ties to the British Royal Family. Henry Standish married a French noblewoman and built the house to entertain family friends.

However, on October 27, 1886, disaster struck when the house caught fire and everything went up in flames. Mrs. Standish's fifty-year-old French maid, Eliza Kleininger, died in the fire. She had gotten out of the house in time to escape injury but returned to fetch her jewelry and was burned to death. Her bones were found at the foot of the servants' stairs, surrounded by the jewels she had been trying to save. After the turn of the century, the ruins were rebuilt into a fashionable hotel. Today, Rooms 306, 361, and 362 are afflicted by a strange presence. Room cleaners refuse to go into the rooms or insist on working in pairs. Other haunted areas are the attic and a linen cupboard on the third floor that always seems unnaturally cold. The Berystede Hotel is located near the Ascot Racecourse on Bagshot Road, Sunninghill, Ascot. The phone number is 1344-623311 and the fax is 1344-872301. For more information, visit the White Rabbit Web site at www.afallom.com/pages/whiterabbit1.html.

Barkham

BARKHAM ROAD The "Phantom of Barkham" is a headless soldier, who is seen walking along Barkham Road in Barkham, a small town in Berkshire. The unidentified ghost is most often seen in the autumn months. Not surprisingly, most witnesses have a difficult time recalling any details of the soldier's uniform except for the missing head.

Bracknell

QUELM LANE A man riding a white horse haunts Quelm Lane in Bracknell, Berkshire. The phantom supposedly grabs small children, which is the oldest legend associated with the haunting. Apparently, the haunting has been going on for some time, since "Quelm" is Old English for "death" or "execution."

Berkshire County

BISHAM ABBEY Bisham Abbey is located in the Berkshire countryside on the Thames River near Marlow. Now home to the National Sports Centre and training grounds for the English football team, the building is haunted by a ghost that emerges from a portrait that hangs there and walks the hallways. Sometimes she appears like a photographic negative image with her face and hands white and her dress black. At other times, her apparition walks the building, constantly washing her hands in a bowl that floats eerily in front of her. The ghost is Lady Elizabeth Hoby, wife of Sir Thomas Hoby, who owned the abbey during the reign of Queen Mary. Lady Hoby was a cousin of Queen Elizabeth and a very educated woman for her time, known for her poetry, which she wrote in Greek and Latin.

Lady Hoby was sorely disappointed in her firstborn son, William, who was something of a dullard. Instead of reading books and doing his lessons, the child drew pictures in them or blotched his work with water, and his mother grew increasingly violent towards the child. One day, she lost her temper and beat him to death with a piece of wood, and her mournful spirit pays the price to this day. Dozens of witnesses, many in recent years, claim to have seen her apparition, sometimes emerging from the portrait of Lady Hoby in the main hall. During renovations in 1840, workers discovered a cache of William's workbooks hidden behind a shutter in the window casing. On the messy, crumpled pages, the ink was blotched in places by his tears.

NEWSTEAD ABBEY Newstead Abbey in the Berkshire countryside near Abbotsford was built in the twelfth century, and became the home of the Byron family in 1540. George Gordon Byron, the famous poet, was born in London in 1788 and lived at the abbey for several years. Not long after his marriage in 1815, Byron encountered the abbey's frightening "Goblin Friar" ghost in the gallery of the house late one evening. He described the apparition as a dark, hooded figure wearing beads around its neck. Seeing the threatening ghost convinced Byron that rumors of a treasure hidden in the abbey during the era when Henry VIII claimed all the holdings of the Catholic Church might be true. He frantically searched for many months, but no treasure was ever found. Byron did uncover the skull of one of the monks, and he had it made into a gilded goblet that became a macabre family heirloom.

Another ghost started appearing at Newstead Abbey in the mid-1800s, after the Byron estate was sold to another family. The apparition of a White Lady was seen walking among the trees and inside the house. The owners identified the ghost as a frail woman they had taken in out of pity, after finding her wandering around in the woods on the estate. Her name was Sophia Hyatt, and she died after being struck by a coach on the road to Nottingham. She was a great fan of the poet Lord Byron, and after he died, she started visiting his former home, spending hours roaming the estate and even carving her name on the bark of trees. Some say her spirit has never left the property she loved so dearly. For more information, visit David Haslam's Web site at www.geocities.com/Area51/Station/9814/ghostmain.html.

QUEEN ELIZABETH'S WELL The ghost of Bisham Abbey, Lady Hoby, is also seen at Queen Elizabeth's Well, which is within walking distance of the abbey. The well is really an ancient spring located at the bottom of Bisham Hill near highway A404 in Berkshire. In the fourteenth century, so many pilgrims came here to be healed by the well's allegedly miraculous waters that the local bishop declared the spring was the work of the devil, and he had it blocked off. He threatened anyone who visited the well with excommunication. However, within a few years, people cleared the spring and were once again visiting the well to be cured or encounter supernatural visions. Even Queen Elizabeth visited the well, probably while she visited her cousin Lady Hoby, and that is how it came to be known as Queen Elizabeth's Well.

WINDSOR CASTLE Windsor Castle, the oldest castle in England and traditional retreat of the royal family, is located twenty-three miles (37 kilometers) from London in Berkshire. More than two dozen ghosts, including such famous monarchs as King George III, King Charles I, King Henry VIII, and Queen Elizabeth I, haunt it. The queen was one of the world's true psychics and believers in spiritual phenomena. She had a vision of her own her death in her bedroom at Windsor, and within days after her death in 1603, her figure wearing a black mantilla was seen in the Queen's Library and walking on the castle ramparts. Over the years many members of the royal family have seen her ghost—most recently Princess Margaret. Another prominent ghost at Windsor is King George III, who went mad in 1810 and had to be kept locked up in a room at Windsor. His presence still lingers in that room, and sometimes his insane ranting can be heard there. King Charles I has been reported many times standing next to a table in the Library, and King Henry VIII is seen walking through a wall along the battlements of the castle where a door once stood.

Perhaps the most active ghost at Windsor is a lands warden called Herne the Hunter. In the last 250 years, his ghost has been seen hundreds of times. Usually, it is an unforgettable sight: Herne's apparition is described as wearing deerskins and a helmet with antlers on it. Sometimes a pack of phantom dogs is seen by his side. Herne was chief gamekeeper for King Richard II in the fourteenth century, until a few members of the King's court accused him of practicing witchcraft. Rather than face trial, Herne hanged himself from a large oak tree in the Great Park.

The oak tree was cut down and burned in 1868 to try to prevent Herne's ghost from reappearing, but where the tree once stood on the East Terrace, his apparition still materializes. His ghost is also reported along the Long Walk and even on the Royal Golf Course. Just after World War II, a young Grenadier Guard committed suicide by shooting himself on the Long Walk near where Herne had killed himself a century earlier, and the guard's ghost also haunts that spot. In 1976, one of the prestigious Coldstream Guards saw Herne the Hunter and was discovered unconscious in the Great Park.

Eton

ETON SCHOOL Eton School, the famous aristocratic prep school, is haunted by the ghost of a Gray Lady. She is believed to be Jane Shore, dedicated mistress of Edward IV. When Edward became king and wanted to dissolve the school, she dissuaded him, much to the gratitude of the fellows of the college. Later, when she was imprisoned, they won her freedom and gave her free quarters in the school until she died in 1526.

Warfield

FOREST ROAD On October 28, a procession of ghosts marches along Forest Road in Warfield, Berkshire. On that date in 1874, the villagers rallied against Lord Ormathwaite of the Warfield Park estate for mistreating his wife. Lady Ormathwaite was very kind to the people of the village, and when they learned of how cruel her husband was to her, they marched on the house to voice their displeasure.

Wickham

FIVE BELLS INN Five Bells Inn in Wickham, near Newbury in Berkshire, is a delightful four hundred-year-old inn made up of two buildings, joined together. The unidentified apparition of a young lady dressed in white has been seen in one of the bedrooms, an event accompanied by a sharp drop in room temperature.

BUCKINGHAMSHIRE

St. Leonards

DUNDRIDGE MANOR Dundridge Manor in St. Leonards is haunted by the apparition of former owner Margaret Pole, who was executed for treason at the Tower of London. Her ghost is seen in broad daylight walking through the manor corridors, and sometimes the swishing of her skirts can also be heard. Panicked footsteps are also heard on the stairway, echoing a fight between two boys, one of whom was killed with a ploughshare. Nearby, the old Ostrich Inn in the Buckinghamshire countryside is haunted by a man named Jarman, a medieval innkeeper who used to rob and murder guests.

West Wycombe

GEORGE & DRAGON INN The George & Dragon Inn in West Wycombe was built in 1720 on the site of an older inn dating from the 1400s. The leaden signboard outside shows Saint George fighting the dragon, and a large door gives way from the higher street in front to a wide courtyard. This is the area where a White Lady haunts the garden. Inside, the footsteps of an unseen man are heard going up and down the wide central staircase. But the most active presence here is the ghost of a sixteen-year-old servant girl nicknamed "Sukie." She is blamed for an uncommon cold in one of the rooms, as well as small items disappearing within the building. Sukie was a very pretty girl who caught the attention of three young men, but her charms were directed toward a handsome and wealthy traveler who occasionally stayed at the inn. As a prank, the three boys sent Sukie a note, allegedly from the rich traveler, asking her to meet him at a local cave. She duly kept her appointment but was enraged when she did not find the man there. In her fury she began to throw rocks at the three young men, and in the fray, she fell and cracked her head against the cave's stony wall. They carried her body back to the pub where she finally died in the room now unnaturally cold.

Many people staying in the room have reported seeing her apparition, sometimes with a pink bandage on her head. In 1967, an American author felt her fingers touch his face as he lay in bed, and other guests have reported seeing her sitting at a dressing table, gazing into a mirror. Her ghostly form is also seen coming down the stairs or out of a cupboard in the kitchen. For more information, visit the White Rabbit Web site at www.afallon.com/pages/whiterabbit1.html. The George & Dragon Inn is on High Street in West Wycombe. For reservations, phone 1494-464414 or fax 1494-462432.

ST. LAWRENCE CHURCH At the top of a hill behind West Wycombe Hall (see entry below) is the St. Lawrence Church, where the mausoleum of the Dashwood family is located, and below the mausoleum on the hill is the entrance to the West Wycombe caves. The entrance has been fashioned to look like the doorway to a Gothic church, when Sir Francis Dashwood enlarged the ancient caves in the 1750s. Sir Francis had the caves cut in labyrinthic patterns that supposedly carried alchemical significance in the way they were laid out. The caves crossed a stream of water known as the River Styx, which also had symbolic meaning for Dashwood and the freethinking members of the Hell Fire Club who assembled there. Participants included members of Parliament, philosophers, and famous revolutionary thinkers such as Benjamin Franklin. Rumors circulated of pagan ceremonies, orgies, and black magic being practiced in the caves, and many believe that to this day it is an area where the realm of magic meets the mundane world. The Wycombe Caves are open to the public. For further information, call 1494-533739.

WEST WYCOMBE HALL To find ghosts in Buckinghamshire, just say "West Wycombe" three times. West Wycombe Hall, a Palladian mansion located in West Wycombe Park in the middle of the city of West Wycombe, was built by the notorious devil-worshipper Sir Francis Dashwood. He created the infamous "Hell Fire Club" (officially called the Order of the Knights of St. Francis of Wycombe) in 1755, and many investigators blame the current hauntings there on those activities. The ghost of at least one former member of the club, its steward Paul Whitehead, has been seen on the grounds numerous times. One guest at the house once saw eleven ghosts sitting around the table in the Dining Room. Two decidedly pleasant spirits haunt the Music Room in the house. The first, a monk, was witnessed by composer Noel Coward. He described the specter as "an amiable smiling monk" who appeared leaning against the piano as Coward played. Famed clairvoyant Tom Corbertt saw the second ghost in 1962. He described her as a beautiful woman, very gentle and non-threatening. West Wycome Hall is managed by the National Trust and open to the public.

OXFORDSHIRE

Dorchester-on-the-Thames

GEORGE HOTEL The George Hotel in Oxfordshire is a gabled, fifteenth-century inn on the Thames River that is haunted by the spirit of a previous landlord's daughter, who saw her lover murdered and has never gotten over the trauma. She most often is seen wearing a white dress in the Teardrop Room at the inn. The George Hotel is on High Street in Dorchester-on-the-Thames at Wallingford in Oxfordshire.

Oxford

OXFORD UNIVERSITY Oxford University has its share of ghosts. The most famous is from Merton College at the university. The former manor house is haunted by the apparition of Colonel Francis Windebank, who was shot and killed here after surrendering to Oliver Cromwell in 1645. Students, professors, and visitors have reported seeing his surprised ghost walking in the Fellows Garden.

Thames

BIRD CAGE To find the most haunted place in all of Oxfordshire, you have to travel to the Aylesbury Valley to the picturesque little town of Thames. The Bird Cage in Thames is so named because it used to be a prison during the Napoleonic wars. There are a variety of poltergeist effects reported on the property, but the resident ghost is a poor leper, who was stoned to death by a mob at the site.

His angry spirit still likes to upset people who have a lot more going for them than he did.

NOBLE EDDEN The ghost of Noble Edden is the town of Thames's favorite visitor from the Other Side. His apparition appears on the spot where he was murdered on the Thames-to-Aylesbury Road, near Gibraltar. He is said to still appear on the road to warn travelers of dangers ahead. His spirit is also thought to manifest at Close Court Pond, where the men who murdered him washed his blood off themselves. Edden was killed in 1828 walking home from the market one evening, but his wife had a psychic vision of him lying dead in a ditch and told everyone that he would not return home that night. His wife even saw the face of her husband's killer in her vision, whom she identified as a friend of the family named Benjamin Tyler. Tyler denied the accusation, but he and an accomplice were executed for the murder in 1830, based largely on Edden's wife's testimony. Noble Edden's gravesite can be seen in the St. Mary's churchyard.

ST. MARY'S CHURCH A ghoul with "horns like a ram's head that goes down to the river to drink at midnight" is said to haunt the graveyard of St. Mary's Church. Inside the church, many witnesses have seen the apparition of the Gray Lady over the years. Thames has a phantom knight in shining armor too. He can be seen walking over Whiteleaf Cross at midnight.

Towersey

TOLL GATE HOUSE In the city of Towersey, a headless horseman has been seen so many times that the local team adopted the headless horseman as a logo. The apparition is of a soldier from England's civil war, who hid from his pursuers in a barn near Church Farm but his horse neighed loudly at precisely the wrong moment, and he was captured and executed in the churchyard. And the apparition of a burly man in a heavy green coat walks down the middle of the road near the Toll Gate House. He has been blamed for several accidents.

Weston-on-the-Green

WESTON MANOR HOTEL Oxfordshire is Shakespeare country, and the Weston Manor Hotel is a magnificent old country house that could have been a prop in any of his plays. The house dates from the eleventh century, although the main part of the building was added in the fourteenth and sixteenth. It was originally a private manor home, but the owner turned it over to the Church and it became an abbey. A ghost named Mad Maude was actually a beautiful young nun who was caught in improprieties with several monks. For those indiscretions, she was burned at the stake in the mid-1400s.

Wearing a blue habit, her apparition appears in and around Room 7, the Tudor Room, which is noted for its huge four-poster bed. Sometimes her laughter can be heard throughout that section of the hotel. In the 1980s, a manager of the hotel saw the ghost of a young and foppish Cavalier, who is thought to be Prince Rupert, the younger brother of King Charles I. Meanwhile, a phantom coach and horses sometimes drives through the courtyard at the rear of the hotel and then disappears into thin air. The Weston Manor Hotel is in the center of Weston-on-the-Green in Oxfordshire. For more information, phone 0869-50621 or fax 08621-50901.

Woodstock

BEAR HOTEL Oxfordshire also has a few haunted inns. One of the most active is the Bear Hotel, a former coaching inn that retains parts of the original structure and staircase from the sixteenth century. There is a haunted bedroom there, where footsteps and other unexplainable sounds have been heard in the dead of night. The Bear Hotel is on Park Street in Woodstock, Oxfordshire.

WARWICKSHIRE

Warwickshire is the location of Stratford-upon-Avon, the birthplace of William Shakespeare. The city holds a theatrical walking tour of Stratford's darker side called Grimm's Ghostly Tour. The tours begin at 3:30 P.M., 5:30 P.M., and 7:30 P.M. from the Country Artists Fountain, Waterside, next to the Royal Shakespeare Theatre. Phone: 01789-551702.

Baginton

OLD MILL HOTEL There are a few haunted places to stay overnight in Warwickshire, and one of the nicest is the Old Mill Hotel. The hotel, not surprisingly, was once a mill, and many of its features have been preserved, like the eighteen-foot-diameter iron mill wheel that can still be seen in the restaurant area. That is also the area that is haunted by an unidentified Gray Lady, whose apparition and voice have been witnessed by diners in the restaurant. The Old Mill Hotel is on Mill Lane in Baginton, Warwickshire.

Brailes

BRAILES CATHOLIC CHURCH The Brailes Catholic Church is the home of a ghost nun, who had her baby taken from her to avoid a scandal. And the bridge on the Shipton Road is haunted by a headless man seen only at dawn.

HIGHWAY A45 Near the town of Brailes, highway A45 is haunted by a phantom truck that comes head-on at drivers then disappears. It has been blamed for several near-accidents and is thought to be from a true incident in which a lorry entered the wrong way onto the expressway. The highway is one of Britain's first freeways. The phantom truck is always seen on the section of A45 that crosses the Dunsmore Heath in Warwickshire.

QUAKER MEETINGHOUSE Despite the lack of ghost tours, the town of Brailes is probably the most haunted town in Warwickshire. George Fox, the famous Quaker, walks past the old Meetinghouse in Brailes. Not far away in the center of town, there is the ghost of Granny Austin, a legless witch who appears on New Year's Eve.

Leamington Spa

MANOR HOUSE HOTEL The Manor House Hotel is a grand, red brick mansion that became a hotel in 1847 to cater to visitors to the royal spa situated in the town. Behind its plush appearances, however, hides the ghost of a housekeeper in a long gray uniform, who has been seen wandering the hallways. An extreme and sudden drop in temperature usually marks her appearance. She is said to be a former employee who dearly loved her job but was forced to take an early retirement. Now she returns to finish her work. The Manor House Hotel is on Avenue Road in Leamington Spa, Warwickshire. For more information, phone 0926-423251 or fax 0926-425933.

HERTFORDSHIRE

Bishop's Stortford

GEORGE HOTEL Built in the fourteenth century, the George Hotel is the oldest coaching inn in the town of Bishop's Stortford. It seems as if any place named the "George Hotel" in Britain is haunted. This particular George Hotel has an unidentified ghost that has been described as a woman "in swirling gray mist." The George Hotel is on North Street in Bishop's Stortford, Hertfordshire.

Dover

DOVER HARBOR The main city in Hertfordshire is Dover, which is located in a strategic harbor that marks the shortest sea route to mainland Europe (just twenty-one miles). On a clear day, you can see France from the White Cliffs here, and this was where the Romans, Angles, Saxons, and Normans entered England. A few miles east of Dover lies the treacherous Goodwin Sands, where many ships have run up aground. Sightings of phantom sailing ships in the area continue to this day, yet no one has been able to connect the sightings with any particular ship. The legendary phantom ship *Lady Luvibund*, which supposedly wrecked on Goodwin Sands on Valentine's Day, 1748, and returns every fifty years thereafter, has

recently been ruled false. No ship by that name was ever registered.

DOVER CASTLE It seems the real ghosts of Dover have taken up residence in the massive, twelfth-century Dover Castle that overlooks the harbor. The ghost of a drummer boy, killed during the Napoleonic Wars, is the principal presence, and is most often seen during the full moon walking alone on the ramparts. While carrying money for the garrison, the boy was attacked by thieves who mutilated and beheaded his body. The apparitions of a person in Royalist dress and a pikeman have been reported in the castle proper.

Dover Castle, Dover, Great Britain (John Mason)

At the west end of the castle is a Roman lighthouse, where the ghosts of a Roman soldier and a hooded monk have been witnessed. A 1991 investigation detected unexplainable noises like doors slamming in a passageway called the Spur, violently vibrating doors in the Keep area, and a shadowy apparition in the lower St. Johns Tower. In the maze of tunnels underneath the castle, many mysterious presences, some dating back to Napoleonic times, have been sensed. In 1993, several tourists and a tour guide encountered a more modern ghost in a section of the tunnels that housed a powerful telecommunications center during World War II. In four separate sightings that year, witnesses reported seeing and sometimes speaking with the apparition of a young man who was accidentally killed while assembling an amplifier rack in what was then known as the Hellfire Corner station.

Markyate

The ghost of a famous female robber known as Lady Ferrers haunts the roadways around Markyate. She used to drop from trees onto passing coaches and rob passengers, but the adventurous woman was eventually shot and killed by one of them.

Hertfordshire County

HINXWORTH PLACE During stormy weather in the autumn months, strange noise and unexplainable electrical disturbances plague Hinxworth Place in the Hertfordshire countryside. The effects seem to be connected with the spirit of a mischievous boy. The lad dressed up as a ghost to frighten his nurse, but she was so scared that she struck and killed him. The boy has been playing the part ever since. It is as if the boy's spirit taps into the electrical energy from storms to manifest.

WADESMILL INN Wadesmill Inn in Hertforshire is haunted by the ghost of a frail, fair-haired girl, who was run over by a London-bound stagecoach that stopped here centuries ago. Built in 1615, it was originally known as the Prince's Arms, though the inn changed its name in 1670 and became one of the busiest coaching inns in the area.

BEDFORDSHIRE

Aspley Guise

DICK TURBIN'S HOUSE On Weathercock Lane in the town of Aspley Guise, Bedfordshire, the ghost of a man on horseback rides up to a particular manor house, where he dismounts and walks through a hedge into the front door of the house. Sometimes just the sound of the galloping horse is heard, and the hedge rustles as the invisible presence pushes through. At other times, the horse rider is plainly seen wearing a dark cloak.

The ghostly rider is thought to be Dick Turpin, an infamous highwayman, on his horse Black Bess. Legend says the daughter of the owner of the manor house had fallen in love with a man her father despised, and one night they were together when the father returned home unexpectedly. The two lovers hid in a cupboard in the kitchen; however, her father had already spotted them through a window. On entering the house, the cruel man moved furniture in front of the tiny room, leaving them there to starve to death in each other's arms. Soon afterwards, Dick Turpin broke into the house to rob the owner and found the two corpses. The brash highwayman waited calmly for the owner to return and blackmailed him into letting him use the house as a hideout and base of operations, while Turpin robbed the countryside.

Bedfordshire County

WILLESDEN-RAVENSDEN ROAD The road connecting the towns of Willesden and Ravensden in Bedfordshire is haunted by the ghost of a woman wearing black clothes. Encounters with the angry woman are always unpleasant, and she has even appeared in broad daylight to startled witnesses. Psychics say she is the spirit of a witch who used to practice the black arts in a cottage in the area. On Station Road in Stanbridge, a phantom hitchhiker is seen. The sightings began in 1979, and no one has figured out what the ghost wants, unless it is just a ride out of here.

WOBURN ABBEY Several ghosts haunt Woburn Abbey in the Bedfordshire countryside. The most frequently sighted specter is a man in a top hat who has been seen walking through a wall in the old marketplace. Other often reported manifestations are a monk in a brown habit and a manservant who appears in the Masquerade Room. Doors open and close by themselves, and invisible hands tap people on the shoulder or touch them gently from behind. The abbey has a long history dating back to the twelfth century when Hugh de Bolebec founded a Cistercian abbey here. It is known that an abbot was beheaded on the grounds for speaking out against Henry VIII's marriage to

Anne Boleyn, and it is perhaps his ghost that has been sighted. The manservant was murdered in the room he still haunts, and it has been suggested that the figure in the top hat may be a previous duke of Bedford, though his exact identity is still unknown.

SHROPSHIRE

Ironbridge

TONTINE HOTEL Shropshire is England's most tranquil county, and it seems that very few ghosts seem to end up here. But Room 5 at the Tontine Hotel at Ironbridge in Shropshire still suffers from the violent emotions of long ago. The room is haunted by the ghost of a man who was arrested there after murdering his wife. Nearby, on the Thames River, a barge piled with dead bodies with a hooded figure at the helm is seen floating by. The phantom barge dates back to the days of the plague, when boats would carry the dead down to the enormous Plague Pits for burial.

Ludlow

THE FEATHERS INN The Feathers, another Shropshire inn, was built in 1603 as a private residence but later opened as an inn. Curiously, the ghost at the Feathers is reputed to be a young girl in modern dress who has never been identified. The Feathers Inn is on Bull Ring in Ludlow, Shropshire.

WALES

Wales is composed of Clwyd, Glamorgan, Powys, Dyfed, Gwent, and Gwynedd counties. However, County Clwyd seems to have captured the majority of Welsh ghosts for some reason.

CLWYD

Abergele

THE GWENNON GORN Other ghosts haunting Clwyd include a ghost ship that has been reported many times off the coast of the resort town of Abergele and a haunted road. The ship is Prince Madoc's *Gwennon Gorn*, a vessel that sailed from here and was lost at sea.

Abergwili

BRYN MYDDIN The ghost of Merlin, King Arthur's fabled sorcerer, has been reported on a hill near Abergwili, Wales. Bryn Myrddin (Merlin's Hill) is also said to have a concealed cave where Merlin spent his final days and is buried. His ghost has been seen in Alltfyrddin (Merlin's Grove) on the hill and sitting on a carved rock known as Merlin's Chair. The grove of trees had to be sealed off to the public in the 1950s because so many people, especially children, were being injured in freak accidents there. A historical poem from 1673 is one of many to reference the site: "That mighty prophet when on earth; Who in Alltfyrddin formed a cave; Which served him for his house and grave." According to some legends, this hill is also where Merlin found King Arthur and his knights frozen in time, ready to rise again should England need defending.

Clywd County

GWRYCH CASTLE Other castles in County Clwyd are haunted. Two lady ghosts haunt Gwrych Castle in Clwyd. According to tradition, the one dressed in white died a natural death, while the one dressed in red was killed in a hunting accident.

PLAS PREN RUINS The castle ruins at Plas Pren in Clwyd are haunted by a skeleton phantom, while the ghost of a Roman soldier haunts the old bridge nearby. Those who see the soldier's apparition are said to be close to death themselves.

PLAS TEG ESTATE Several ghosts haunt the beautiful manor house and estate at Plas Teg in Clwyd. It was built in 1610 by Sir John Trevor and remained in his family for centuries. The White Lady of Plas Teg is a young woman in love with one of the Trevor boys who was killed in a duel.

Overcome by grief, she jumped down the well on the property and died of a broken neck. The apparition of a man dressed in Regency costume is a later descendent of John Trevor who committed suicide because he was despondent over the recent death of his wife. He intentionally drove his carriage into a tree. On the old road in front of the estate, the phantoms of three men on horses suddenly appear and pursue anyone who happens to be on the road at the time.

Corwen

OWAIN GLYDWR HOTEL The Owain Glyndwr Hotel in the north Wales town of Corwen was originally a monastery built in 1329. The ghost here is a young woman who snuck into the monastery late at night for secret trysts with one of the monks. After their clandestine meetings were discovered, the monk was quietly sent out of the area, and the woman never heard from him again. The woman went to her deathbed still wondering why the monk stopped coming, but her spirit still returns to the old monastery, looking anxiously for her lost lover. The Owain Glyndwr Hotel is at the center of Corwen in Clywd, Wales.

Cwn

BLUE LION INN The Blue Lion Inn in the town of Cwn in County Clwyd is home to the ghost of a farm worker who was murdered in the building, when it was still a farmer's cottage. The man's name was John Henry, and his powerful presence produces apparitions as well as poltergeist activity at the inn.

Denbigh

DENBIGH CASTLE Denbigh Castle in the town of Denbigh in Clwyd has a Gray Lady apparition that walks the corridors at night. The small Goblin Tower at the castle is haunted by the sad ghost of a boy who died in an accident during the construction of the tower. His forlorn face is seen peering out the windows in the tower in which his spirit is trapped.

Henllan

LLINDIR INN A sexually ambiguous apparition haunts the Llindir Inn in Henllan, Clwyd. Some reports describe it as a female ghost; others say it is male. In any case, the spirit is thought to have originated with an incident at the inn in which a jealous husband murdered his wife, and some have suggested their two spirits have merged for all eternity into one ghostly presence.

Nannerch

NANNERCH-AFONWECH ROAD A Lady in Black, who crosses the road in front of traffic and causes accidents, haunts the road between Nannerch and Afonwech in Clwyd. She is the apparition of a Victorian woman, who died on the way to church in an accident on the road. Clwyd also is home to many haunted inns and hotels.

Rossett

LLYNDIR HALL HOTEL The Llyndir Hall Hotel in Rossett, near Chester in Clwyd, dates back to the 1400s, but an apparition that dates from the English Civil War haunts it. She is a young girl named Henrietta, who committed suicide at the hotel after learning that her lover was killed in the battle of Rowton Moor in 1645.

GOLDEN LION INN PUB The pub at the Golden Lion Inn is haunted by "Old Jeffrey," who was hanged for murder in the town of Ruthin. Afterwards, his body was sent to Rossett to be hanged from a gibbet on public display. The spirit is thought to have arrived at the Golden Lion via a wooden palette from the gibbet that was salvaged and used in the construction of the inn.

GLAMORGAN

Gower Peninsula

LLANRHIDIAN After victims of a shipwreck were welcomed into the homes of villagers from nearby Llanellan, the entire town was wiped out by the plague the stranded people brought with them.

Ghosts still haunt the area near Llanrhidian where the town once stood.

RHOSILLI BEACH Rhosilli Beach is located on the western tip of Gower Peninsula, west of Swansea, in West Glamorgan. A phantom coach is seen racing across the beach toward the ocean here. It is a replay of an emotional scene in which a treasure ship wrecked on the beach and townspeople raced to retrieve the plunder.

Margam Abbey, Wales, Great Britain (John Mason)

Rhosilli Beach, Wales, Great Britain (John Mason)

RHOSILLI RECTORY At Rhosilli Rectory, the only structure still remaining near the beach, an evil presence sneaks up behind people and whispers in their ear, "Why don't you turn around and look at me?" No one has yet had the courage to do that. All they do is tell stories about "something very unpleasant indeed" that lurks in the former rectory.

Port Talbot

MARGAM ABBEY Margam Abbey in Port Talbot, Wales, is haunted by at least two ghosts and also carries an ancient curse. The present deserted castle at Margam was built in 1840 on the ruins of a Cistercian abbey founded in 1147. The monks were forced out of their abbey when the property was inherited by a member of the Mansel family, and the displaced monks placed a curse on the property, saying that if the original stone pillars

at the gateway were ever dismantled, the owner's family would soon die out. In the early 1700s, when a member of the Mansel family ignored the curse and tore down the pillars, the family name died out within five years.

The next owners, the Talbot family, were careful to find the original pillar stones and re-erect them. They were spared from the curse, but not the persistent haunting by a monk that is still seen roaming through the ruins. In recent years, he has been joined by the apparition of a White Lady, thought to be the wife of one of the former owners who dearly loved the castle—of which only the shell survives. The chapel of the original abbey survived and is still used as a parish church.

DYFED

Haverfordwest

ROCH CASTLE Roch Castle, which is located west of Haverfordwest in Dyfed, Wales, was built by Lord Roch, who died from a venomous snakebite, just as a local witch had predicted. Though Roch refused to leave his castle because of the prophecy, the poisonous snake was concealed in some kindling branches brought in to start a fire in his bedroom fireplace. The castle, however, is haunted by the ghost of Lucy Walters, who was born there in 1630. Lucy grew into a beautiful woman and became the mistress of Charles II. Her footsteps are still heard running through

Roch Castle, Wales, Great Britain (John Mason)

the house, and her apparition, clad in an elegant, white gown, is seen floating through the solid stone walls.

Llangadog

RED LION HOTEL A mother and child haunt the Red Lion Hotel at Llangadog in south Wales. The Red Lion is an old coaching inn that dates from the early 1500s and the mother and child apparitions date from Victorian times. The Red Lion Hotel is in Llangadog, which is near Carmarthen in Dyfed.

Pembroke

MANOBRIER CASTLE Manobrier Castle outside Pembroke in Dyfed, Wales, is an ancient Welsh castle that is haunted by a White Lady. During the First World War, a sentry fired his rifle at the approaching apparition, only to see her disappear into thin air.

GWENT

Chepstow

ST. PIERRE HOTEL The St. Pierre Hotel in Chepstow in south Wales dates from the fourteenth century, when it was a manor house. Today, the hotel is a resort consisting of over four hundred acres of grounds. A Gray Lady, who died

Manobrier Castle, Wales, Great Britain (Andrew Hayden)

on her wedding night in a freak accident, haunts the hotel building. The St. Pierre Hotel Country Club Resort is in Chepstow, which is near Monmouth in Gwent, Wales.

GWYNEDD

Conwy

CASTLE HOTEL The Castle Hotel is next to Conwy's magnificent castle, but it is the ghost of a former employee who haunts the hotel. The staff nicknamed the friendly spirit "George" and credits him with helping with the cleaning. The Castle Hotel is on High Street in the town of Conwy in Gwynedd, Wales.

NORTHEAST ENGLAND

Northeast England is composed of Yorkshire, Durham, Tyne & Wear, Northumberland, Humberside, and Cleveland counties. There are lots of Ghost Walks in Yorkshire that attest to its haunted history. The Ghost Walk out of Whitby is one of the longest running tours of its kind. There are two different walks on alternate nights that begin at 8:00 P.M. in the Market Place on Church Street in Whitby. The Whitby Dracula Walk starts from outside the Royal Hotel in West Cliff. Call Harry Collett at 01947-602138. Fax: 01947-821734. E-mail: fcoll@globalnet.co.uk. The Ghost Walk of York is one of the first such tours in the world and leaves nightly from King's Arms Pub. Phone: 01759-373090. Mad Alice Ghost Tours leave at 7:30 P.M. every night except Mondays from Clifford's Tower in York. Meet at the phone box opposite the Stakis Hotel. The Haunted Walk of York is a ninety-minute tour that leaves at varying times. Phone: 01904-621003. The Ghost Hunt of York leaves at 7:30 P.M. from the Shambles, every night no matter what the weather. Telephone or fax: 01904-608700. The Victorian Ghost Walk led by Jayne Phillips leaves from the James Tea Rooms at 75 Petergate in York. Phone: 1904-640031.

YORKSHIRE

Clifton

KIRKLESS HALL The ghost of the legendary Robin Hood haunts his gravesite at Kirkless Hall in the Yorkshire woods at Clifton, near Brighouse. The stone farmhouse rests on the foundation of a Cistercian priory built in 1098, and it was the Prioress Elizabeth de Staynton, who was responsible for his death. Elizabeth was Robin's cousin, and he went to her for a bloodletting, a common practice in the Middle Ages for a variety of ailments. For some unknown reason, the woman bled Robin to death, buried him in the nearby woods, and marked his grave with a simple stone marker. According to legend, Elizabeth was actually a vampire who preyed on anyone who came near the priory, although her ghost and those of nuns have also been seen on the property. In the 1700s, the grave was dug up to confirm that Robin Hood was buried there, and the gravediggers reported that they left his remains "undisturbed."

The crumbling gatehouse where Robin died and his gravestone can still be found on the property. The gravesite is surrounded by an iron fence erected in the nineteenth century to keep trespassers from chipping pieces of the headstone for souvenirs. The present owner, Lady Margerete Armytage, keeps the exact location of the grave secret to prevent desecration, though she sometimes grants personal viewings of the site. In recent years, psychics and others have performed blessings and exorcisms at the grave. They report that Robin's spirit is still active, still seeking justice for his gruesome murder.

Dorcester

CROWN HOTEL AND POSTING HOUSE The Crown is a seventeenth-century inn that was a regular stop on the stagecoach routes between York and the rest of England. It entertained many famous guests, including such diverse types as Daniel Defoe (creator of Robinson Crusoe) and the deadly highwayman Dick Turpin. Among the ghosts who stayed on at the inn are a waitress murdered by her jealous lover; an elderly monk who succumbed to a heart attack in the old stables; and a Crinoline Lady who perished in a fire and has since been sighted wearing wide skirts, floating down the corridors of the old wing. The Crown Hotel and Posting House is on High Street at Bawtry, Dorcester, South Yorkshire. For information, phone 030-710341 or fax 0302-71198.

Kirby Lonsdale

ROYAL HOTEL The Royal Hotel at the Kirkby Market Place in Kirby Lonsdale, Yorkshire was originally called the Rose and Crown, but the name was changed by permission of Queen Adelaide, because she was so happy with the accom-

Royal Hotel, Kirby Lonsdale, Yorkshire (Royal Hotel)

modations during her stay in 1840. The most active ghost today is a female apparition the staff has nicknamed "Catherine." Recently, she has been seen in 1995 by landlord Pay May and in 1997 by housekeeper Olive Barker and her colleague. Catherine manifests as the misty form of a short woman (about five-foot four inches) with short blonde hair wearing a traditional black and white maid's uniform. She has been spotted in the lobby and even in the women's toilets, but most often she appears in Room 20 or Room 21 or on the landing between those two rooms.

The ghost everyone now calls "Catherine" was one of five maids at the inn, who were burned to death in a fire at the hotel on December 6, 1820. The women were trapped in their rooms on the third floor, which today are rooms 7–10. There is an obelisk monument to the horrible fire that can still be visited at St. Mary's Church. Some guests in the area smell burnt wood in the area of the 1820 fire, but it seems Catherine does not like to return to that spot in the hotel and would rather spend her time in places of which she has fonder memories.

Another ghost of the Royal Hotel is a middle-aged man dressed in formal attire, complete with a top hat, cape and cane. His apparition is seen on the stairway and in the area between the lounge and the dining room. Numerous guests and employees have encountered the ghost, the most recent being the barman, Jamie Allen, who saw the ghostly figure near the glass door that separates the lounge and dining room. The cellar of the hotel, on the other hand, seems haunted by a more plebian ghost. The spirit there is a man who likes to play tricks like disconnecting the pumps for the draft beer, stealing keys, and other typical poltergeist pranks. Mostly, however, the ghostly hanger-on just likes to sleep in the cellar, and a half-dozen or more witnesses have heard his distinctive snoring sounds over the years. For more information, visit the White Rabbit Web site at www.afallon.com/pages/whiterabbit1.html. For information on bookings, E-mail afallon@fallon.com.

Mosborough

MOSBOROUGH HOTEL A South Yorkshire hotel known as Mosborough Hall in the town of Mosborough, near Sheffield, has a secret network of tunnels that run under the former estate that are said to be haunted by an invisible presence who reaches out to people in unfamiliar ways. A murdered maid still haunts the inside of the hotel.

Newby

NEWBY CHURCH Much more threatening than most church apparitions is the shadowy hooded figure that has been seen and photographed near the altar of the Newby Church in Yorkshire. In 1963, Reverend Jack Lord took a photograph of the inside of the church and the strange apparition showed up standing next to the altar. Every expert who examined the photo, including analysts from the British government, has declared it genuine.

Pocklington

FEATHERS HOTEL Yorkshire has a number of old haunted inns and hotels, and a few have had modern additions made that are not haunted. One of these is the Feathers Hotel, a former coaching inn located in the center of the town of Pocklington in East Yorkshire. There is a modern chalet and the older inn, but the ghosts are sensed only in the older section. The Feathers Hotel is at 56 Market Place in Pocklington, East Yorkshire.

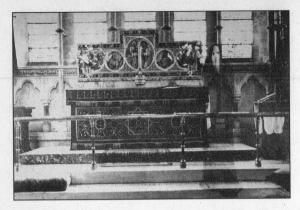

Newby Church, Yorkshire, Great Britain (Jack Lord)

Pontrefract

ROGERTHORPE MANOR A variety of other spirits haunt the shire lands outside of York. The ghosts of pale-faced children rattle doorknobs at the Rogerthorpe Manor at Pontrefract in West Yorkshire. The apparitions of a Cavalier and old women also appear there.

Rotherham

HELLABY HALL A South Yorkshire haunted place that only recently became haunted is Hellaby Hall in Rotherham. After Hellaby Hall was gutted by fire in 1980 and renovated, the ghosts started appearing. So far, the apparitions of an elderly lady and a little boy have been seen, and some unknown presence has started to manifest poltergeist effects.

Sheffield

HOWDEN MOORS Howden Moors in the Peak District northwest of Sheffield in South Yorkshire is haunted by phantom airplanes that crashed in the area. Fifty planes have crashed in the region bounded by the moors and the Ladybower Reservoir to the south, and over three hundred people have died because of the crashes. Many of the accidents date from World War II. In 1945 alone, the moors claimed the crews of a B29, a Royal Canadian Lancaster bomber, and a U.S. Dakota fighter. More recently, a B-29 Superfortress and a Hawker Hunter crashed during storms. Ever since the 1950s, people living in the area report seeing the shadows of airplanes on the ground without anything being in the sky above. Sometimes witnesses see propellers but hear no sounds, or watch an airplane go down in the moors but find no wreckage.

So many sightings of phantom aircraft are reported that a local group under the direction of Ron Collier has been formed to study the phenomenon. One reason for the ghostly activity is thought to be the fact that very few bodies have been recovered from the bogs. For instance, the wreckage of the Hawker Hunter that crashed in 1993 marks the grave of pilot Walter Cubitt. It is estimated that his body is entombed at least thirty feet below ground. A group of psychics who attempted to contact some of the lost pilots determined that their souls are not at rest where they were buried.

Staithes

BURTON AGNES HALL At Burton Agnes Hall at Boulby Cliff in Staithes, Yorkshire, the apparition of a Lady in Blue is seen. She is Anne Griffith, who was murdered for a valuable ring she always wore. Her dying wish was that her head be buried inside the house she loved, but her husband could not bear the thought, and she was interred intact. However, the violent poltergeist activity that followed her burial convinced her husband otherwise, and she was exhumed so her final request could be fulfilled. Afterwards, her apparition started showing up in the evening hours, walking silently through her beloved home. Boulby Cliff is best known in paranormal circles for the ghost of a schoolgirl who died when part of the cliff fell off and she fell into the sea. Her apparition is usually seen suspended in midair, where the cliff used to project.

Whitby

WHITBY ABEY Whitby Abbey in north Yorkshire overlooks the harbor on a cliff three hundred feet above the town of Whitby. Two ghosts haunt the dark ruins of the abbey. One was the niece of the King of Northumbria, later named Saint Hilda, who founded the abbey in A.D. 657, and is credited with ridding the district of serpents by cutting off their heads and driving them over cliffs with her whip. Hilda's shrouded ghost stares out of the highest window in the castle. The other presence here is Constance de Beverley, a nun who broke her vows and gave herself to a faithless knight. She was walled up alive (immured) in the dungeon, though her ghost is most often encountered on the winding stairway trying to run away from her captors. The abbey was destroyed by the Vikings in A.D. 850, and then rebuilt by the Normans in 1067. That building survived until 1539 and now sits an abandoned ghost itself.

Whitby Abbey, Yorkshire, Great Britain (John Mason)

ST. MARY'S CHURCH Just up the road from the ruins at Whitby Abbey at the parish church of St.

Mary, a ghostly coach sometimes races up Green Lane and stops next to the cemetery. Drawn by six headless horses, the coach then continues down Henrietta Street towards the cliff and disappears over the edge into the churning waters. Locals believe it is the sea reclaiming the souls of sailors that rightly belong to her. Mortals can descend the cliff via a stairway of 199 steps that leads from the churchyard into the town below.

WHITBY STREETS The streets of Whitby are haunted by the "Barguest," a demonic black dog who roams the streets looking for victims out after midnight. Another ghost that roams the streets here is a mysterious figure in a black cape who walks right through people on the sidewalk. Some say it might be the ghost of explorer Captain Cook, who was born in Whitby, while others insist it is a remnant of the early 1930s, when filmmakers came to the foreboding area to bring Bram Stoker's classic novel *Dracula* to the screen. For travel information, contact the Tourist Information Centre, Langborne Road, Whitby, North Yorkshire, YO21 1YN England. Phone: 01947-602674. For more information on the ghosts of Whitby, visit the Web site www.fortunecity.com/roswell/shaman/282/supernatural.html.

York

The city of York has been called the most haunted city in Europe, and paranormal researchers have catalogued over two hundred ghosts here, although skeptics go to great pains to point out that there are also over four hundred pubs in the city.

BLACK SWAN There are undoubtedly a lot of pubs in York, and many of them are haunted, including the oldest pub in town. The sixteenth-century Black Swan on Peasholme Green in York has a pair of Victorian ghosts. One is the glowing apparition of a young lady with long hair in a white dress who stands at the bar gazing into the fireplace. The other is the restless apparition of a working-class man wearing a bowler hat who appears to be waiting for someone. Neither ghost has ever been identified.

CLIFFORD'S TOWER Clifford's Tower is all that is left of the Roman fortifications that founded the city of York. The old lookout tower is now only a mound of earth and white limestone in the center of the old town, but it still stands well above all the surrounding buildings. The ghost of Lord Clifford, after whom the Clifford Tower is named, has been spotted hanging from chains above the gate, his body in a decomposed state. The apparition dates from the fourteenth century, when Clifford was executed for high treason. But the most persistent presences at Clifford Tower originated from a period of anti-Jewish frenzy that struck England during the reign of Richard the Lionheart. In A.D. 1190, during a gruesome slaughter of Jews that was actually encouraged by the Governor of York, many Jews fled to a wooden fortress that stood on top of the tower mound. A local friar set fire to the tower to flush them out, but rather than surrender, the Jews committed mass suicide and hundreds died.

During the subsequent rebuilding of the destroyed fort white stone blocks were used, and some of these developed mysterious and persistent red stains, which were dubbed "Jew's blood" by locals. Some of the red staining is still visible on the gatehouse, and visitors sometimes report scenes of blood pouring down the walls of the tower. Many report hearing the cries of children coming from inside the stones. An excavation of the tower uncovered an ancient well, at the bottom of which were found the bodies of forty young children and babies. Scientific dating showed they died in the same time frame as the riots, and after the tests were complete the bodies were given proper burial. Apparently, the parents had dropped their children down the well rather than allow them to fall into the hands of the mob.

COCK AND BOTTLE PUB The ghost of poet and Parliament member George Villiers haunts the Cock and Bottle pub in York. His heavyset apparition with shoulder-length hair is usually seen sitting at a particular table near the fireplace, though he has been known to appear to women taking showers or touching them while they are dressing. He died in 1687 and is buried at Westminster Abbey. George Villiers is the subject of the political nursery rhyme "Georgie Porgie" and was known for his licentious behavior. Not surprisingly, his ghost only appears to women.

COLLEGE STREET The house at Number 5 College Street in York is haunted by the sad spirit of a little girl, who is heard and seen crying. Her apparition was first seen in the early twentieth century. Residents of the building have described her as about seven years old, and she is usually seen on the top floor. Eventually, a medium was called in to try to placate the spirit. According to the medium, the child dates back to the time when the plague struck York and all the houses on College Street were quarantined and sealed off from the rest of the city. The disease claimed her parents, but the little girl survived, only to die from starvation.

Another building on College Street is also haunted. The ghost is a former student at St. William's College who sent his younger brother to the gallows for a murder the boy did not commit. He framed his brother in a robbery in which they both took part, though it was the older brother who ended up stabbing their victim to death. The horrific scene sent the younger brother into a nervous breakdown, unable to defend himself to authorities, so the older boy took advantage of his brother's condition and turned him in for the deed. The student ended up tortured by guilt at what he had done, and spent the rest of his days pacing back and forth in the hallways at the college, unable to eat or sleep until he finally died in his room. Those tortured footsteps, first laid to the floorboards in the era of King Charles I, are still heard to this day.

COPPERGATE On the site of the former Craven's Sweets Factory at Coppergate in York, the current row of stores is haunted by a powerful presence that used to haunt downstairs workrooms at the factory. Fagin's Bookshop, the Body Shoppe, Olympus Sports, and other shops are bothered by a variety of poltergeist phenomena, such as breaking glass, fire alarms, electrical disturbances, moving objects, and disheveling clothes.

HOLY TRINITY CHURCH A ghost from the Middle Ages haunts Holy Trinity Church in York. The pathetic presence there is a medieval woman buried with her husband in the cemetery. Her ghost searches for her lost child, who died from the plague and was buried outside the city walls somewhere. Also, in the Holy Trinity churchyard, the headless ghost of Thomas Percy, seventh earl of Northumberland, searches for his head buried somewhere among the graves. He was beheaded in 1572 for plotting to overthrow Queen Elizabeth, and his head spiked at Micklegate Bar for public display, but one of his followers stole it and secretly buried it at the church.

JUDGE'S COURT The narrow streets in the city of York, called "snickleways" because just two people have trouble passing each other, are haunted by the sinister presence of the Barguist, Yorkshire's infamous phantom black dog with glowing red eyes that searches for his prey among those walking in the narrow passages. Judge's Court, a narrow passageway off Coney Street in York, is haunted by an unidentified presence first witnessed in the nineteenth century. The apparition is of a large man in heavy riding boots that make a tingling sound as he walks. He seems like a real person, recently appearing to a guide and group of tourists walking through Judge's Court. When renovations took place in the passageway, workers discovered an old well, and in the bottom of the well was a large male skeleton wearing old leather riding boots with broken spurs.

KING'S MANOR The ancient King's Manor in York is haunted by a lady in a green Tudor costume, sometimes seen carrying a bunch of roses. Some say she is the ghost of Anne Boleyn, who stayed here during her brief marriage to Henry VIII. A gray apparition is frequently seen on the Huntington Room staircase in the North Wing of the house. Psychics say the shadowy presence is Henry Hastings, who had the staircase built. Whenever the Hastings ghost is seen, a portrait of a Stuart dignitary falls off the wall, though no one has yet explained the connection. In the main courtyard of the manor, the groaning and screams

of Roundhead soldiers, taken here for medical treatment during the Civil War, can still be heard. Roundhead troops are also present at the Old Starre Inn at Stonegate in York. Their apparitions are seen gorging their mouths with food in the kitchens, while their less fortunate colleagues scream in agony from their wounds. The inn is also haunted by an unidentified elderly lady, who is seen climbing the stairs, and two spectral cats, whom living dogs like to chase through the pub.

MICKLEGATE BAR Micklegate Bar is part of the old wall around the city, and inside the dwelling there, another ghost also searches for something through all eternity. Young Sarah Brocklebank was the daughter of the city's gatekeeper, and in 1797, while playing on her birthday, she lost the keys to the city. Because her father could not lock the city gate at dusk, the Lord Mayor fired him. The family ended out living on the street, and her father never spoke to her again. Poor Sarah went to her grave fixated on finding the keys. Today, visitors to the Micklegate Bar Museum still see the small shadow of a little girl flitting around the rooms, and sometimes feel a gentle, invisible hand touching their backs.

PETERGATE BAR PUB Another haunted pub in York, at the ancient Petergate Bar (or fortress wall), is haunted by the apparition of a Lady in Gray, a former nun who was bricked up in the cellar of the building. Her crime was giving birth to an illegitimate child, and her ghost is frequently seen at the Petergate, as well as the York Arms pub nearby. She has even been known to appear in the men's restrooms. The powerful presence is both seen and felt, and is blamed for poltergeist activity that ranges from opening locked doors to throwing cutlery around in the kitchens.

ST. MARY'S CHURCH A woman named Jane Evans, who was regressed under hypnosis to her past life as a Jewish girl in York at the time of the oppression of Jews, recalled escaping Clifford Tower that infamous day in 1190 (see Clifford's Tower, above) with her family and running to nearby Castlegate, where they hid in a crypt in

St. Mary's Churchyard, York, Great Britain (John Mason)

St. Mary's churchyard. However, members of the mob followed them, broke into the crypt, and butchered her entire family. No such crypt existed at the church, however, and many people dismissed her testimony as fantasy. Then, in 1975, workmen uncovered a hidden burial vault in the churchyard that exactly matched Jane's description. The ruins of St. Mary's Abbey, located nearby in the Museum Gardens, are haunted by a monk, who moves rapidly among the fallen stones. Some believe he is the apparition of the Black Abbot, a notorious former abbot of St. Mary's.

TREASURER'S HOUSE The most ancient ghost in the city of York can be found in the Treasurer's House, which sits behind York Minster in York. The house was built in 1648 at the location of the earlier Treasurer's House that dated back to the late fifteenth century. The sounds of trumpet blasts are heard in the cellar of the house, then a procession of twenty or so helmeted men dressed in grimy kilts and carrying lances and swords comes marching through the one wall in the cellar and out through the opposite wall. But they appear from only their knees upwards, and even the lead horseman is partially sunk into the floor.

According to the curator, the house lies right in the middle of an ancient road that used to exist a foot or so below the current level of the cellar floor, and in some places, as much as twenty feet below the modern road. The Romans are seen emerging at places where the ancient level meets the modern grade, but their cadence and footsteps can be heard all along the route. The Roman road was used by the Ninth Roman Legion, which disappeared mysteriously when called back to Rome. A ghost dating the first Treasurer's House at the same site also lingers behind. He started appearing in the 1960s, after major renovations to the building. The activity seemed to elicit the ghost of a stonemason who worked on the original house. In fact, the craftsman even told one visitor that he had carved one of the intricate sculptures by the west door.

DURHAM

Consett

LORD CREWE ARMS The Lord Crewe Arms is a six hundred-year-old stone manor house that became part of a nearby monastery built in 1165 by the Premonstratensian Order. In the 1720s, the entire complex was turned into an inn. It is named after Lord Crewe, a Jacobite sympathizer who lived in the house during the uprising of 1715. Today, the building maintains its medieval character and is located in the unspoiled village of Blanchland in the heart of the North Pennines Mountains. The ghost is an eighteenth-century relative of Lord Crewe named Dorothy Forster, whose hazy form is most often witnessed in the Bamburgh Bedroom. Phantom monks from the earlier era are also seen walking up the stairs to the Bamburgh Bedroom, and white-robed monks kneeling in prayer haunt other bedrooms at the inn. The Lord Crewe Arms is in Blanchard near Consett in Durham County. For bookings, call 0434-675251 or fax 0434-675337.

Cradlewell

NEVILLE'S CROSS At Neville's Cross on the way to Cradlewell in County Durham, the apparition of woman holding a child is sometimes seen. The ghost is most often reported on December 20, the day when a woman was murdered at the spot.

Darlington

SWALLOW KING'S HEAD HOTEL Refurbishing and enlarging the Swallow King's Head Hotel in Priestgate has led to an increased number of sightings of their resident ghost. Dubbed "Albert the Butler," he appears most frequently in Room 419 or Room 426. After many harmless encounters with the ghost, people still were unwilling to stay in the haunted rooms, so management had to offer some incentives. Guests willing to stay in those rooms receive free room service, including a whisky nightcap, breakfast in bed, and complimentary wine with dinner. The Swallow King's Head Hotel is at Priestgate, near Darlington in Durham.

CIVIC THEATRE The Civic Theatre in Darlington, County Durham, is haunted by the original owner, Rino Repi. The flamboyant vaudevillian called the place the "Darlington Hippodrome" and has had a very hard time turning it over to the new owners. Psychics have also detected the presence of a stagehand who committed suicide in the building.

Durham

DURHAM PRISON In December 1947, an inmate in the Main Wing of Durham Prison used a table knife he stole from the dining room to murder a fellow prisoner. The cell in which the killing took place became haunted by the incident, which was replayed to horrified inmates who were placed there. After numerous encounters that left hardened criminals blabbering in the corner of the cell, the authorities had no choice but to turn it into a storeroom.

LUMLEY CASTLE Lumley Castle in Durham was built in 1392 by Sir Ralph Lumley, and it is full of hidden rooms and secret passageways. It has been transformed into a medieval fantasy hotel with lots to see and do while staying here. You might even get a chance to see the castle's ghost, the tragic figure of "the Lily of Lumley," wife of Sir Ralph. She was murdered by a visiting priest determined not to let her forsake her Catholic faith by following heretic John Wycliffe. The priest disposed of her body by dumping it down a well on the property.

That well is now located underneath the shower stall in Room 45, and when the river rises, Lady Lumley arises from her watery grave and walks again through the corridors of her former home. Almost everyone notices the exceptionally cold spot located in the corridor between Rooms 45 and 46 that presages her appearance. Another well in the lobby near the bar is also said to be the source of "something nasty" that leaves the well and roams the surrounding area. Still another ghost, that of a murdered child, is said to manifest in the second floor rooms. The Lumley Castle Hotel is on Chester Street in Durham. The phone number is 91-389-1111; the fax is 91-387-1437.

Newton Aycliffe

REDWORTH HALL Redworth Hall is an old Jacobean house that was turned into a public school and is now a one hundred-room hotel. It is also home to a dozen ghosts or more. The most active phantom is the infamous Lady In Gray of Redworth, who is thought to be Lady Catherine, who leapt to her death from the tower roof in the mid-1800s. But she is a benign spirit who looks over children and seeks to soothe people's problems. Her favorite haunt is Room 26. Other rooms here are also haunted. China dishes vibrate mysteriously in Rooms 5 and 9, and poltergeist effects like doors opening and closing by themselves or appliances turning themselves on and off have been reported in Rooms 11 and 12. In the other rooms, hazy figures are sometimes seen, and disembodied coughing and crying is heard. Occasionally, there are noises from a ghostly party underway after midnight. But the patience of hotel management is growing thin. The manager got so tired of employees refusing to go into certain rooms that he recently offered a five thousand-pound reward to anyone who could prove any of Redworth's rooms was haunted. So far, no one has collected the reward money. The Redworth Hall Hotel is in Redworth near Newton Aycliffe in Durham County. For more information, phone 0388-772442 or fax 0388-775112.

Rushyford

EDEN ARMS SWALLOW Room 19 at the Eden Arms Swallow in Rushyford is haunted by a Gray Lady and ghostly children who roam the corridors at night. They are revenants from the family that first owned the old mansion.

Seahouses

BEADNELL HOUSE Beadnell House in the town of Seahouses is a Victorian mansion set near the Northumberland coast. The place is haunted by a naval officer, who just wanders around in full dress uniform.

Tantonbie

OAK TREE INN A popular haunted inn in Durham County is the Oak Tree Inn. The old red brick building is located in the village of Tantonbie near Stanley. It has some odd ghosts, including an eternally inebriated ghost in the bar and a playful invisible presence that locks men in the toilet.

TYNE & WEAR

Barlow

SELBY'S STILE The figure of a man in distinctive Quaker dress has haunted the road connecting Barlow and Winlaton in Tyne & Wear County for many decades. The ghost in a black frock coat and breeches has been seen numerous times on this stretch of road. The ghost emerges from the hawthorn hedges and appears on the side of the road near a bus depot at the end of Barlow Lane and Cromwell Road. The site is called Selby's Stile and is named for a Quaker man who was one of the judges who sentenced King Charles I to death. The king's supporters eventually tracked the man down this road and hanged him from a tree in the woods. Local residents, not understanding why the man was executed, cut him down, drove a wooden stake through his heart, and buried him at the crossroads.

Ever since, his ghost has been seen there. Most witnesses are amazed at the how real the ghost seems until it disappears in front of them. Jim Ross, a construction worker, saw the ghost while traveling on foot along the haunted section of road near the village of High Spen. "I told my friends in the pub that night," he confessed, "and they said 'Jim, you've been drinking that Newcastle Ale again,' which is a potent local brew. But I know what I saw. The Quaker did not even notice me, like he was a thought projection into our reality. Ghosts are not wispy vague things but are solid to look upon and gone the next moment."

Newcastle-Upon-Tyne

STENG CROSS At an ancient crossroad known as Steng Cross near Newcastle-Upon-Tyne, east of the village of Elsdon on Morpeth Road, stands a macabre sight. It is a timber gibbet (gallows) where the body of an executed man was hanged in chains as a "warning to evildoers until the end of time." That is exactly what is taking place at the site, for the gruesome ghost of William Wynter is still seen hanging from the gibbet. William was hanged in 1791 for the beating death of an elderly woman living on the outskirts of Eldson. The evidence that convicted him was the distinctive impression of the hobnails in his boots left in the mud at the murder scene.

Tynemouth

TYNE PRIORY RUINS The apparition of a Viking is seen walking in the ruins of the ancient priory on the Tyne River at Tynemouth. Sometimes he is seen crossing the river with his ghostly dog waiting on shore. The apparition is Olaf the Viking, who converted to Christianity, became a monk, and then was assigned as prior of Tynemouth. In performing his duties, Olaf crossed the Tyne everyday, and his dog followed him to wait for his return on the shore. One day Olaf did not return, but the dog remained at the site until it died several years later. Locals have nicknamed the phantom dog "Wandering Willie."

NORTHUMBERLAND

Alnwick

DUNSTANBURGH CASTLE It is Northumberland's castles that are haunted. Dunstanburgh Castle, north of Alnwick in northeastern Northumberland, is not accessible by car. The only way to get to this awe-inspiring, cliff-top castle ruins is along a grassy footpath from the coastal village of Craster. The castle was built in 1314 to protect the harbor below, however, the harbor was never developed and the huge fortress now sits out in the middle of nowhere.

The extensive ruins are haunted by the gro-

Dunstanburgh Castle, Northumberland, Great Britain (John Mason)

tesquely deformed apparition of the Earl of Lancaster. Everything went wrong at this execution, and it took eleven blows from an axe to remove his head. His spirit has not forgotten his tortuous demise. A more romantic tale involves the ghost of a wandering knight named Sir Guy. According to legend, he entered the castle shortly after it was built and discovered a beautiful maiden, the White Lady, whose spirit is tied to the castle through a large crystal. At that moment a disembodied hand offered him a golden sword to smash the crystal open or a golden horn to summon help. He chose the horn, which as it turned out was the wrong choice, and the maiden's spirit remains trapped in the castle to this day. Sir Guy's spirit walks the ruins, still trying to free her. Meanwhile, the spirit of the White Lady has been spotted on stormy nights walking the ramparts, a beautiful maiden trying to project her spirit to the wind and freedom from her leaden existence in the castle.

Northumberland County

DILSTON CASTLE Dilston Castle, in the Northumberland moors, is haunted by the ghost of the wife of James Radcliffe, who was executed in 1716 for his part in the Jacobite Rebellion. Most often, she is seen wringing her hands in anguish.

THIRLWALL CASTLE Thirlwall Castle is a thirteenth-century edifice in Northumberland that has been abandoned for over four centuries. The ruins are haunted by the figure of a frightening dwarf, who is said to be protecting a golden table hidden in a deep well on the property. The strange legend says that only the son of a widow can claim the table.

HUMBERSIDE

Hull

YE OLDE BLACK BOY PUB Ye Olde Black Boy Pub in the city of Hull in Humberside County dates from the 1730s. Originally a coffee house, it served as a pipe shop, tobacconist, and merchandise store before it became a pub. In the last two

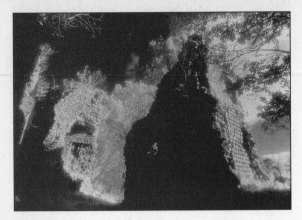

Thirlwall Castle, Northumberland, Great Britain (John Mason)

decades, the pub has been the site of unexplainable poltergeist activity. Employees and guests have seen glasses shake and dance on tables and liquor bottles burst, and when the staff tries to rearrange tables and chairs in new positions, they find them returned to their original positions the next morning. Not long ago, a distinguished gentleman sitting at a table in the front room of the bar saw two arms reach out of the oak paneling behind him and try to grab him. He ran from the pub never to return again.

NORTHWEST ENGLAND

Northwest England is composed of Cumbria, Lancashire, Cheshire, Merseyside, and Manchester counties.

CUMBRIA

Barrock Fell

HIGHWAY A6 The pleading cries of someone dying of exposure are heard along Highway A6 near Barrock Fell in Cumbria. A highwayman was strung up on a gibbet and left to starve to death, but after a few days, a coach driver showed mercy and shot him.

Bassenthwaite

OVERWATER HALL Overwater Hall is an inn near Bassenthwaite in Cumbria's lake district. Built in 1811, the house was in the Gillibanks family for many years before it became an inn. Today, the apparition of an armless black girl in a high headdress or bonnet is frequently seen. She is seen most often at the beginning of a new year and sometimes presages her appearance inside the house by tapping on an outside window. Her apparition is also seen walking through the door to Room 3, where guests see her linger at the window, looking out at Lake Tarn. The ghost is a young black girl who followed her former lover to England from Jamaica.

Overwater Hall, Bassenthwaite, Cumbria (Overwater Hall)

Joseph Gillibanks was a merchant who made his fortune in Jamaica, and married the daughter of the Chief Justice there. However, he kept up an illicit love affair with a young black girl even while married. Joseph returned to England with his wife and settled down at Overwater Hall in 1814 to become a magistrate and highly respected member of the community. However, his past came to haunt him when the black girl showed up on his doorstep one day. Pretending to still care for her, he rowed her out into the middle of Lake Tarn and pushed her into the icy cold water to drown. When she clung to the boat, he took a sword and hacked off her arms. Locals say that after that, the lake never froze over again. Whenever ice covers the lake, a black hand cracks through the ice and breaks it open.

Carlisle

DALSTON HALL HOTEL Dalston Hall Hotel is a fifteenth-century mansion located on highway B5299, three miles south of the village of Carlisle in Cumbria. As you drive up to Dalston Hall, keep a lookout for the ghost of a handyman from Victorian times who haunts the driveway and grounds. But do not let your guard down when you enter the hotel. The gallery in the Manorial Hall is home to the oldest ghost in the hotel, Lady Jane, a member of the Dalston family who is seen wearing Tudor clothing. The cellar is home to a shadowy male presence that is associated with the sounds of wooden barrels rolling around. Wooden barrels are no longer used at Dalston Hall. A maid who leapt to her death from the tower haunts room 4, and several guests have asked to be moved into an "unhaunted" room. Room 12 has a more benevolent presence. Guests there report hearing the giggly whispering of two invisible girls. The Dalston Hall Country House Hotel is in Carlisle, Cumbria. For information, phone 1228-710271 or fax 1228-711273. The E-mail address is info@dalston-hotel.co.uk, and the Web site is at www.dalston-hall-hotel.co.uk.

Dalston Hall Hotel, Cumbria, Great Britain (Dalston Hall Hotel)

WARDREW HOUSE Wardrew House is a bed and breakfast inn that was originally built as a watchtower against raids from nearby Scotland. It is thought the ghost of a Green Lady seen there dates from those earlier times. Sometimes she is experienced as a sudden whirlwind that picks up green curtains or clothes and throws them around, while at other times just her melancholy voice is heard. Wardrew House is in the village of Gilsland near Carlisle in Cumbria.

Cartmel

FOREST LADY The apparition of the Forest Lady is seen in the woods around the town of Cartmel in Cumbria, and sometimes her voice cries out. She calls for her lover, a charcoal burner who was struck by lightning. She refused to leave his hut and eventually died of exposure.

Cumbria County

HAWKESDALE HALL Do not be overly concerned if you see a boy carrying a lantern walk calmly into the river near Hawkesdale Hall in the Cumbria countryside. There is nothing you can do. He is the ghost of a boy who committed suicide on Halloween many years ago, but his spirit still walks out of the front door of Hawkesdale Hall, carrying the lantern, heading down the path to the river.

PENDRAGON CASTLE Cumbria has its share of haunted castles too. At Pendragon Castle in Cumbria, the ghost of King Arthur's father, Uther Pendragon, is seen. He built the castle, and his ghost patrols the property on horseback, leading some to suspect that there might be a hidden coffer of treasure somewhere on the land.

Eden River Valley

EDENHALL HOTEL The Edenhall Hotel is situated in the lovely Eden River Valley in Cumbria. It was first known as Woodbine Cottage, an eight-bedroom private residence, although parts of the building date back to the middle of the seven-

Pendragon Castle, Cumbria, Great Britain (John Mason)

teenth century. There are three ghosts in the present inn. Room 38 is haunted by the figure of an unidentified man, a dignified ghost that sometimes sneaks down to the bar. In the attic, the spirit of an old lady in a long Edwardian dress walks about, though her apparition is also seen ascending the stairs into the attic and sitting in an armchair in a corner of the lounge. Room 25 is haunted by the apparition of a woman, who steps out of a large mirror behind a sunken bathtub. Sometimes the ghost shows up staring at guests from the foot of their beds in the middle of the night.

The ghost became so famous that people started staying in the room just to see the apparition form in the mirror. In the 1980s, an aid for Member of Parliament Lord William Whitelaw always wanted Room 25, when he accompanied Lord Whitelaw there, just to see the ghost again. Oddly, the mirror marks the dividing line between the old and new parts of the building. Because of all the hysteria about the room, it is now reserved for use only by staff members.

FOX & PHEASANT INN Also located in the beautiful Eden River Valley is the Fox & Pheasant Inn in Armathwaite, which is haunted by the apparition of a woman in old-fashioned brown clothing who strolls into the bar and then walks though a door to another room. She seems like a normal person, until you realize she has walked through the door without opening it. Psychics say she is a

woman whose two children were run over by a coach in front of the inn. The other ghost can most often be found in Room 3 of the inn. A notorious highwayman was hanged from the window in that room after being apprehended nearby. Now his nasty ghost plays poltergeist tricks on guests staying in the room.

LONG MEG AND HER DAUGHTERS One of the spookiest spots in the Eden River Valley is a megalithic circle of stones known as Long Meg and Her Daughters. To this day, witches hold nighttime ceremonies at the site, and the ghosts

Long Meg and Her Daughters, Cumbria, Great Britain (Andrew Hayden)

of ancient Druid priests still haunt the place. In the 1990s, a dark, shadowy apparition was seen moving rapidly around the site and even passed right through one witness, who felt instantly cold and frightened. In fact, one legend states that the megaliths themselves were formed when a wizard turned a coven of witches to stone. The 300-by-360-foot site consists of a lone twelve-foot-high megalith (Long Meg) surrounded by fifty-nine stones in a circle (her Daughters). According to folklore, it is not possible to count the same number of stones in the circle twice, and if you do, bad luck will follow you from the site. The "cup and ring" carvings on Meg are secret glyphs relating to certain vortexes of energy seen by shamans in altered states of consciousness. Similar markings are found at many other stone circles in Britain, and some people visiting the sites also report seeing the psychic vortexes. To get there from Penrith, take Highway A686 to Langwathby, then turn left onto the road to Little Salkeld. Go through the village and follow the signs to the "Druids' Temple." For more information, visit the Megalith Web site at www.henge.demon.co.uk/cumbria/meg.html.

Esk Valley

MUNCASTER CASTLE   Muncaster Castle in the Esk Valley is one of the scariest and most haunted castles in all of England. The Muncaster Castle estate has been owned by the Pennington family for many centuries and the family still lives there, although the castle is open for tours. There is a headless ghost of a local carpenter looking for his head at the castle. The man was suspected of having sexual trysts with the young daughter of Sir Ferdinand Pennington, who had the man's head chopped off. There is also the ghost of the castle jester, Thomas Skelton or "Tom the Fool," who provided our term "tomfoolery" and from whom comedian Red Skelton took his stage name. On instructions from Pennington, Tom killed the carpenter, removed the head, and took it into the castle as proof of his deed. Tom was an amoral man, who used to trick people by giving them directions that would take them through quick-

Muncaster Castle, Esk Valley, Great Britain (John Fraser, Ghost Club)

sand in the marshes. Very funny indeed. Tom the Fool died in 1600 and soon joined the carpenter haunting the castle.

There seem to be a few other ghosts in the castle. Something grabs onto the door to the King's Room and refuses to let anyone in, and then suddenly disappears into thin air as the door falls open. Ghostly footsteps tread the stairway and halls. But by far the most haunted room in the castle is the Tapestry Room, a gallery of stern family portraits that has a cold and some say evil atmosphere. One of the ghosts who has been seen walking in the room is the apparition of the mother of Sir William Pennington. The room had been a nursery in the mid-1900s, and the sounds of a baby crying and a light female voice singing lullabies have been heard. The room is also haunted by the sounds of footsteps walking on stone, though the room is carpeted, and rustling noises from old-fashioned skirts.

But there are other, more sinister presences. People who sleep in the Tapestry Room's four-poster bed sometimes feel a heavy presence on top of them in the middle of the night or catch a glimpse of a hooded figure at the foot of the bed. During an investigation in 1994 by a team from the Association for the Scientific Study of Anomalous Phenomena led by Jason Braithwaite, team member Ian Topham reported an incident around 3:00 A.M. in the Tapestry Room. "Slowly," he recalled, "a figure walked through the open wooden door and paused. It was three-dimensional but very dark; you couldn't see any features on it. When it got within a couple of feet of me, it sort of vanished." A teammate entering at that moment from the King's Room confirmed his sighting.

The ghost of Mary Bragg, a former maid, is the most often seen apparition in the castle. In 1805, Mary fell in love with the handsome footman at the castle, but one of her rivals, another maid, arranged for two male employees of the castle to lure Mary from her home in Ravenglass on the ruse that the footman was gravely injured and requested her presence at Muncaster. However, the two men stopped at a remote turnoff on the road to the castle and clubbed Mary until she died. Two boys found her body the next morning, but the family used their influence to avoid a scandal. The body was thrown in the Esk River, hopefully to be forgotten forever. A few weeks later, her corpse was found floating downstream in the river. According to the coroner's report, her head was smashed in so badly that eels had eaten away much of her brain. Nobody was ever convicted of the crime, but Mary's spirit is said to have gotten her revenge. Everyone associated with the murder and its cover-up died within a few months, and not long afterwards, Mary's ghost started being seen by members of the remaining staff and family. The sightings have continued up to this day. For more information on Muncaster Castle, visit the Web site at www.afallon.com/pages/whiterabbit1.html or E-mail information@muncastercastle.co.uk.

Kirkby Stephen

RAVENSTONEDALE ROAD A blind man stumbling along the side of the road haunts Ravenstonedale Road near Kirkby Stephen in eastern Cumbria. But do not stop to help. He is the evil ghost of Lord Wharton, said to have been struck blind for his wickedness.

Kirkstone Pass

KIRKSTONE PASS INN The highest pub in Cumbria is the Kirkstone Pass Inn. The tiny inn stands at the very top of the pass in the Cumbria Lake District, just before the road forks off for Windermere or Ambleside. Built in 1496, the inn used to be very difficult to reach in winter, though many died trying. One of these was a woman named Ruth Ray, who walked up from Patterdale to see her sick father at the inn. She took her young child with her, but when the weather turned bad, she was forced to huddle with the child under her shawl to keep it from freezing. That is how they found her frozen body in the morning, but the child had somehow survived. Ruth's indomitable spirit made it to the inn, however, and that is where her apparition is seen to this day. In 1840, when the inn was completely remodeled, a new road up the mountain was built, and the trip to Kirkstone Pass became much less life threatening.

Another apparition seen at the inn is a man in a black tricorn hat, who is most often seen in the bar area, though in April 1993 he showed up in the background in a photo taken in the doorway to the inn. His ghost has also been known to touch people and even leave his finger marks on their skin. Yet another ghost seen at the inn is a young fell runner who died on the slopes. As is a common practice among the runners, he had a small stone in his mouth to keep it from getting too dry in the frigid air. Apparently, he somehow swallowed the rock and suffocated. His apparition has been seen in his former room, Room 2.

Stainton

BARON'S HILL A man on horseback haunts Baron's Hill that overlooks the town of Stainton in Cumbria. He was the local baron at the time of the Dissolution, and he ordered the destruction of the monastery, so he could use the materials to build his manor house. Before his house could be completed, he was killed when his horse threw him going up Baron's Hill, and he broke his neck.

Thirlmere

DALE HEAD HALL The ghost at Dale Head Hall in the village of Thirlmere in the Cumbria Lake District is a young girl who visits guests staying in rooms 6, 7, or 8. The unidentified apparition comes out of the inglenooks on the side of the chimneys. These recessed areas next to fireplaces were used for drying clothes, diapers, etc., and Room 7 served as a nursery for some time. The ghost of an accused murderer haunts the driveway to Dale Head Hall. After a man was murdered on his way home from the King's Head Inn, the villagers accused one of his drinking buddies, who steadfastly proclaimed that he killed no one. The man was forced to flee the town and live in caves near Patterdale until his death. His apparition is seen at the spot of the murder protesting his innocence and seeking the real killer. Dale Head Park is haunted by the "Park Boggle," a mysterious spirit that moves through the park in a whirlwind of sparks and fire and leaves behind large mounds of dirt. To book stays at the Dale Head, phone 17687-72478.

Dale Head Hall, Thirlmere, Cumbria (Dale Head Hall)

Wasdale

SCREES INN The Screes Inn in Wasdale in Cumbria's lake district has a lot of ghosts in its walls. Room 4 is haunted by a presence that just wants to be alone. The invisible ghost pushes against the door to keep people from entering, bangs on the door at night if people are staying in the room, and shuts off the television to get guests to leave the room. Room 3 has also witnessed some minor poltergeist activity, though the strongest presence at the Screes haunts the bar. In the 1920s, the place was a temperance hotel, where liquor was never served, and the haunting in the bar did not begin until the establishment got its liquor license.

The apparition is described as a man with dark hair who wears an old-fashioned white shirt with a large collar and black, silver-buckled shoes. He is blamed for thwarting the efforts of bartenders and generally perpetrating chaos in the bar. The temperate spirit locks the men's toilet in the bar to prevent patrons from using it, tosses cutlery around in the kitchen next to the bar, and slams cupboards shut in front of customers. Another trick seems designed to scare patrons away. As recently as 1997, beer mugs float up from their drawer underneath the bar, turn in circles in mid-air, and then come to rest gently on the floor. Needless to say, many who have seen that spectacle have not returned to see what is next. For discounted booking rates at haunted Cumbria inns, E-mail wcti@btinternet.com or consult Tony Walker's *Ghostly Guide to the Lake District*. For more information on Cumbria's haunted places, visit the White Rabbit Web site at www.afallon.com/pages/whiterabbit1.html. The Screes Hotel is in Nether Wasdale, Seascale, Cumbria. The phone number is 19467-26262.

LANCASHIRE

Colne

WYCOLLER HALL During thunderstorms in the area east of Colne in Lancashire, a horseman riding a steed that "breathes fire through its nostrils" can sometimes be seen. The phantom rider continues through the village to the Wycoller Hall, where he enters the front door and climbs stairs that no longer exist. Upstairs the brutal murder in the Cunliffe family is reenacted, as a husband kills his wife, while she screams for help. Another phantom, that of a large, black dog locals call the Guytrash Lightfoot, haunts the woods near Wycoller Hall.

Goosnargh

CHINGLE HALL At the center of the tiny village of Goosnargh, north of Preston in Lancashire, is the oldest brick house in England, although the plain-looking building is even more widely recognized as the most haunted house in a country of

Chingle Hall, Lancashire, Great Britain (Andrew Bennett, Ghost Club)

haunted houses. Without doubt, Chingle Hall has witnessed unspeakable violence, torture, and murder, and at last count, there were twenty-one ghosts here. The house is hidden away at the end of a long driveway, over a small bridge that once spanned a moat. Built by Adam of Singleton in 1260, the house has always had strong religious overtones. It is the birthplace of the Catholic martyr, Saint John Wall, and the house is constructed in the shape of a cross with its own chapel in the west corner. This Priests' Room contains a secret panel in the floor and another in the fireplace chimney where priests hid their relics and sacred items, since practicing Mass was forbidden during the Catholic Counter-Revolution. The original Sanctuary Knocker, a Y-shaped iron hammer symbolizing the Holy Trinity, is still attached to the oaken front door, and there is a Witches Window set into the front wall in which a candle was burnt indicating it was safe to approach the house. According to the owner, if you call "Jesus Christ" and bang on a wall three times, three more bangs will follow from "inside" the wall.

The John Wall Room is situated above the main entrance and at one time housed a large winch that raised and lowered the drawbridge. The only trace of this mechanism is two alcove-type cupboards in the stone wall, through which heavy chains once passed. Sometimes people hear the drawbridge operating. These sounds, like a

giant metal ratchet operating, have actually been recorded on tape by investigators. An upstairs bedroom is haunted by the melancholy presence of a young woman, and visitors often feel overwhelming sadness there. Several people have collapsed in the room after seeing the woman's apparition or being touched by the ghost. A feeling of dizziness, as if one is entering another dimension, is reported by many people on a landing not far from the room. Bone-numbing cold spots are also felt in this area of the house, and sensitive people entering the upstairs bathroom are overcome with the urge to jump out the window!

Other ghosts here include the kitchen poltergeist, which throws dishes and stacks up pots and pans to the ceiling. Once, two witnesses observed a wooden plaque on the kitchen wall above the fireplace float across the room and land in the middle of the floor. There is also a fire spirit that starts logs in the fireplace and is held responsible for a roof support beam that broke into spontaneous combustion in front of several witnesses. Fire investigators were at a loss to explain how the wood caught fire, since it burnt from the inside out. The beams in the house carry strange markings, and scientists have recently shown that the wood actually comes from an old Viking longboat apparently salvaged to help build the house. There are also numerous phantom monks who wander the grounds, especially in the garden and on the south lawn. Two praying monks are sometimes seen in a downstairs room, and a long-haired monk has been observed walking through a second-floor window, even though it is twelve feet above ground. One monk in a dark cowl who peers through windows is especially frightening and has been described as "hardly human."

Chingle Hall is open to the public from April through October, and overnight stays can be arranged by appointment. The current owners, Judy and Trevor Kirkham, keep an incident book of visitors' experiences. Scores of photographs have also been taken at Chingle Hall that capture mysterious spiraling energy vortexes moving through the house. The Web site, www.tomcat.clara.co.uk/chingle. html, contains paranormal photos and sound files made during an investigation of Chingle Hall in 1999. The photo shown was taken by this group and shows a spiraling column of energy to the far right in the picture that cannot be explained by camera malfunction, developing flaw, or obstructed lens. The group returned several times and encountered many strange events. "Around 4:00 A.M.," noted one of the investigators, "two of our group were sitting in the darkened John Wall Room with the door closed waiting for something to happen. Just as one of them complained that nothing was happening, some footsteps were heard walking *away* from the door. Minutes later there was a loud bang on the door! When they opened it, no one was there. The unexplainable loud banging on the door to this room has been experienced by others." Another group conducting ongoing investigations at the house is the Tameside and Oldham Paranormal Research Association (TOPRA). For more information, visit Chingle Hall Web sites at www.phenomena. ndirect.co.uk/phenomena/chinglesept98.html, www. ghostweb.com/chingle.html, www.geocities.com/ Area51/8911/chingle.html, and www.fortunecity. com/roswell/shelly/43/chingle.html.

Lancaster

GRAND THEATRE The Grand Theatre in Lancaster is haunted by actress Sarah Siddon, whose brother once managed the theater. Apparently, the ghost likes to keep it in the family, because her brother's spirit is also sensed in the old theater. Recently, they have been joined by an unidentified Gray Lady. An aunt, perhaps?

Lancashire County

RUFFORD OLD HALL A stubborn woman in a gray bridal gown haunts Rufford Old Hall in the countryside of Lancashire. When her new husband went off to fight in Scotland, she promised him she would never change her dress until he returned. He never did, so she never did. Her apparition is still seen waiting for him in the same dress.

Littleborough

STUBLEY OLD HALL Stubley Old Hall is a fifteenth-century manor house in Littleborough, just outside Rochdale, Lancashire, that has long had a reputation for being haunted. The most active of the three presences that have been detected there is the ghost of a Saracen girl named Fatima, who is seen by newlyweds who visit the Stubley Old Hall Restaurant. In the twelfth century, Fatima set off to find her fiancé, Ralph de Stobbeley, who failed to return from the Crusades. Soon after she left, her beloved returned, but the Black Death had taken her. Today, her spirit still tries to make it back to the place they were to celebrate their marriage, though the jealous girl is blamed for ripping off brides' headdresses or scaring female members of wedding parties trying to put on makeup in the restroom.

Activity in the building increased dramatically during recent renovations. Several workers refused to work alone in the building because of strange "electricity in the air" and overpowering feelings of being watched. In January 1998, owners Peter and Helen Garner reported that the ghost showed up in the restaurant and appeared to many startled guests. The attraction apparently was a female patron who had just gotten married and was wearing her wedding gown. A local investigative group known as the Tameside and Oldham Paranormal Research Association (TOPRA) conducted an overnight vigil at the old hotel and restaurant in September 1998 that was carried live on the Internet and broadcast on the B.B.C. Eerie whistling sounds were recorded, the unexplained odor of pipe smoke, and a glass that inexplicably materialized on a wooden beam were all documented. This was the first ever live Internet coverage of a paranormal investigation and attracted thousands of visitors to the Web site at www.hauntedvalley. com/stubleyoldhall.htm.

Milton

MILTON HALL For some unknown reason, a Cavalier gentleman haunts Mitton Hall. No historical or traumatic incident connects the building with a Cavalier personage, although the estate existed at the time of the Cavaliers. The old manor house is located in the town of Milton in Whalley, Clitheroe, Lancashire.

CHESHIRE

Alderly Edge

PEEPING TOM PHANTOM A naked ghost is seen walking the streets of the Cheshire town Alderly Edge. The long-haired male apparition sometimes peeks in the windows of residents, but he promptly disappears if someone screams or speaks to him. The streaker specter never stays around for witnesses to get a good look at his face.

Cheshire County

COMBERMERE ABBEY The translucent ghost of Lord Combermere was photographed seated in his favorite chair in the library at Combermere Abbey in Cheshire. The photo was taken on December 5, 1891, by Sybell Corbet, a family acquaintance staying at the manor. At the time the photo was taken (2:00 P.M.), Lord Combermere was being buried four miles away. The Combermere family had a history of dealing with ghostly phenomena. Another Lord Combermere served as Governor of Barbados in the early 1800s, and was the first person to scientifically investigate the mystery of the moving coffins of the Chase family vault (see Christ Church, Barbados, Central America).

Chester

The city of Chester in Cheshire is situated on a strategic outcropping of land along the Dee River. Chester was originally a military camp founded in A.D. 77 by the Twentieth Roman Legion on the border of Wales. It has plenty of history and lots of ghosts. To see for yourself, take the Chester Ghost Walk, which starts from the Chester Visitor Centre at 6:30 P.M., Wednesday through Saturday during the months between May and

Combermere Abbey, Cheshire, Great Britain (Sybell Corbet)

October. For more information, call Mo Parker at 1244-402445.

NORTHGATE The original Roman entrances to the city of Chester are well marked even today. At the north end of the city lies Northgate. This is the location of the Roman-built gates that led in and out of the city, and the canal there marks the spot of the original moat around the city wall. This was the most attacked entry to the original settlement, and it is here that people report seeing the apparition of a lone Roman sentry from the fourth century. He is the last soldier of the empty fortification, left behind by the Roman legion, so their commander could say he had not deserted the fort. Welsh tribesmen viciously mutilated and murdered the man, but his spirit never gave up his post and the town was not destroyed. Chester continued to be a frontline defense for the Roman Empire until it fell in the fourth century.

ST. JOHN'S CHURCH St. John's Church in Chester is an ancient edifice built in the eighth century. Part of the structure is in ruins, and the other is still in use. Among the ruins and at the mined steeple at the south part of the active church is seen the hooded figure of a monk, who sometimes is uttering words in the Anglo-Saxon tongue and seems so real that people go up to him to say hello. The apparition has also been reported walking through the church, then through a wall or window down towards the river and the Anchorite Cell, a church hermitage. Stories passed down through the ages say the ghostly monk dates from 1066, when the Normans defeated King Harold at the Battle of Hastings. After the defeat, his wife, Queen Ealdgyth, hid at the Anchorite Cell and spent the rest of her life in seclusion. The monk spent most of his time with the deposed queen, supposedly in prayer, though the gossip was that they were lovers.

THORNOTON'S CHOCOLATES SHOP Thornoton's Chocolates Shop on Bridge Street in Chester is haunted by the mischievous spirit of a girl named Sarah. Sarah's fiancé never showed up on the day of her wedding, and she ended up hanging herself out of humiliation. Now she takes out her revenge on symbols of romantic love and is especially active during the Valentine's Day season. Her poltergeist is responsible for strewing heart-shaped chocolate boxes about the store and destroying displays depicting young lovers. Sometimes she even attacks young gentlemen in the store, and most recently pushed an American down the stairs. She is also credited with scaring off a young man who burglarized the store late one night.

YE OLDE KING'S HEAD PUB If you prefer liquor to chocolates, you can find your spirits at Ye Olde King's Head in Chester. The hotel pub is haunted by a presence that communicates by writing messages on the bathroom mirror. The hotel's unregistered "guests" also include a child, and the ghost of a man that has some connection with a sword found hidden under the floorboards of Room 4. You can contact Ye Olde King's Head Pub by calling 1244-324855 or faxing 1244-315693.

Congleton

LION & SWAN INN The Lion & Swan Inn at Congleton in Cheshire, founded in 1496, has the appealing ghost of a beautiful woman, wearing only a pair of togs, who appears most often next to an intricately carved fireplace in the lounge.

Knutsford

ROYAL GEORGE HOTEL Royal George Hotel at the center of the town of Knutsford is a thirty-one-room hotel that dates from the fourteenth century. It was rebuilt as a coaching inn in the eighteenth century, and that era is from where its ghost originates. Edward Higgins was a reckless highwayman of the time that still haunts the place. He played the role of a refined gentleman during the day, but at night he put pads on his horse's hooves to muffle their sounds and took to the roads to rob travelers. One evening in 1767, he broke into the Royal George ballroom to rob a noblewoman of her jewels, but he was caught in the act and chained up in the cellar. The next morning, he was hanged from a tree.

It appears Higgins is still looking for victims at the inn, for strange footsteps are still heard in the ballroom at night, and the Round Room, a powder room off the ballroom, is still haunted by his sinister presence. Small children entering the room are known to burst into tears. The cellar had to be locked up because of all the paranormal manifestations there. When Higgins's was locked up there, he chalked a picture of himself on a dirty, barred window there. Sometimes the picture he drew is visible on the old glass, despite all efforts to erase it. The picture shows Higgins's face and hands holding onto the bars of the very window he drew it on. Another more benign presence haunts the Clarford Suite at the hotel. Guests and staffers see the luminous apparition of Victorian author Elizabeth Gaskell sitting in one of the chairs there. The woman wrote *North and South*, and the suite is named after another of her novels. The Royal George Hotel is on King Street in Knutsford, Cheshire. For information, phone 0565-634151 or fax 0565-634955.

Nantwich

RED CROW PUB Ghostly activity in Cheshire is plentiful outside the city of Chester too. At the Red Cow Pub in Nantwich, Cheshire, the ghost of a woman and her baby appear. They died from the plague in the 1730s, and sometimes manifest as pacing footsteps or as poltergeist effects, such as doors rattling. The haunting at the Heathercliffe Country House in Frodsham, Cheshire, did not begin until an owner started experimenting with a Ouija board in the 1970s. Now a poltergeist haunts the place, throwing food from the dessert cart and moving objects in the kitchen.

Prestbry

HAUNTED VILLAGE Prestbry is a very haunted village in Cheshire. There is the ghostly Black Abbott who walks out of the Prestbury Church every Christmas, Easter, and All Saints' Day. At Cleeve Corner, an inn near the church where a young bride was murdered, visitors are strangled in bed by an unseen presence. A ghost known as "Old Moses" haunts Walnut Cottage, while in Sundial Cottage, the sounds of a nonexistent spinet piano are heard. On the streets, a long-dead knight in armor rides merrily onward, while a ghostly Cavalier on horseback relives a scene in which he was killed by a rope strung across the road. An old woman peers through windows in residences on the main street in town, and over on Swindo Lane, a phantom shepherd and his herd tie up traffic.

Rosset

LLYNDIR HALL HOTEL The fifteenth-century Llyndir Hall Hotel at Rosset, near Chester, is haunted by the ghost of a young girl name Henrietta, whose lover was killed in the civil war Battle of Rowton Moor in 1645. The devoted woman still awaits his return.

MERSEYSIDE

Bebington

BEBINGTON CHURCH In the town of Bebington, in Merseyside, the apparition of a gray monk is seen in the churchyard, floating a foot over the ground. The monk walks on the original level of the ground before natural erosion and modern construction lowered the grade.

Liverpool

ABERCROMBY SQUARE Most of Merseyside's ghosts seem attracted to the lights of Liverpool. Around the corner from Mulberry Street in Liverpool's Abercromby Square, there stands a house that has a long reputation for being haunted. The Old Bickerstaffe House, now owned by the University of Liverpool, was owned by the Bickerstaffe family in the mid-1800s. One day, Mr. Bickerstaffe's first wife, Eve, heard her newborn baby choking in the second floor nursery and ran up the stairs to see what was the matter. By the time she reached the room, the baby was blue-colored and had stopped breathing. In a moment of utter panic, she opened the window and jumped out, breaking her neck on the sidewalk below. Both mother and baby died that day. Not long afterwards, the doorbell would ring when no one was there. On opening the door, however, the apparition of a tall woman dressed in black entered the house, rushed up the stairs, shouting "The baby!" Next, witnesses heard the distinctive sound of a window being opened, and then a sickening thud was heard on the pavement outside. Today, university staffers and security guards still hear the front doorbell ringing when there is no one on the doorstep. For more information on Liverpool hauntings, visit author Tom Slemen's Web site at www.ghostcity19.freeserve.co.uk.

ADELPHI HOTEL Several hotels in Liverpool are considered haunted, but only the Adelphi Hotel will admit to being haunted. The hotel's ghostly guest is the apparition of a man, whom staffers have dubbed "George." The unidentified presence haunts several of the hotel bedrooms.

MERSEY TUNNEL The Mersey Tunnel just outside Liverpool might be a portal to the Other Side. The tunnel itself is haunted by the phantom of a young girl riding on a motorbike. She was killed in an accident inside the tunnel in the late 1960s. But the motorcycle ghost is no match for the rapidly spinning phantom lady that drifts across the dunes along the coastline on the other side of the tunnel. She is capable of reaching speeds up to forty miles per hour, but will instantly disappear if approached or called to. A strange and frightening apparition haunts Formby Point, located on the ocean fifteen miles north of Liverpool. A large black dog also haunts the beach, and at a medieval stone house on Formby Point, a ghostly monk has been seen for many decades. During renovations, a man's skeleton was found in the wall, and it is surmised he was a monk who starved to death when he got caught in a priest's hole, a severe penance and spiritual practice.

PENNY LANE Liverpool's Penny Lane is known for more than being immortalized by the Beatles. Among paranormal researchers, the persistent poltergeist at Number 44 Penny Lane is far more interesting. The first reports come from the First World War, when witnesses told of loud noises, thudding footsteps, and a strange voice emanating from the unoccupied house at Number 44. In 1930, the noises were so loud and annoying that the occupants of the house next door had to move out. The same sounds started being reported in 1945, after the house was converted into a shop that was damaged by bombs in World War II and never reopened. Neighbors complained of heavy treading sounds and a loud, unearthly voice. Finally, neighbors on both sides just gave up and moved away.

The bombed-out building was eventually remodeled and used as a commercial storefront. When a print shop opened there in 1971, the owners suddenly had to deal with the complaints of neighbors about the weird sounds coming from their vacant shop at night. Police were called several times and never turned up any clues as to where the noises were coming from. An investigation by the owners revealed a long history of hauntings in the house, including the sighting of the apparition of a young woman. The owners were finally able to capture the ghostly sounds on tape, and the case made headlines around the country. The activity eventually lessoned and finally ceased altogether within a few more months. Today, Number 44 Penny Lane is a pottery shop, and researchers are waiting with a wide array of modern electronic equipment for the poltergeist to return.

WALTON JAIL Liverpool's Walton Jail also has a haunted prison cell. In the late 1920s it housed William Kennedy, who had an accomplice named Guy Frederick Browne. Together, they murdered a police constable and shot out both his eyes. Both were hanged for their crimes in 1927, but prisoners staying in that cell have reported seeing a black figure standing at the foot of their beds. Some prisoners would even go into solitary rather than occupy the haunted cell.

MANCHESTER

Manchester

GREAT WESTERN HOTEL The Great Western Hotel in the city of Manchester is haunted by a man in a gray sweater, who is most often seen in the cellar. He is thought to be a former custodian, who loved his job and worked there for many years.

SHAKESPEARE HOTEL Another haunted Manchester hotel is the Shakespeare Hotel. A former maid, who died at the hotel about fifty years ago, still haunts the place. She is sometimes seen in the halls sweeping or in the rooms making beds, but she has never been glimpsed doing windows or toilets.

Oldham

COLISEUM THEATRE The ghost of actor Harold Norman haunts the Coliseum Theatre in nearby Oldham. He was killed in 1947 during a sword fight in a production of *Macbeth*. He appears most often on Thursdays, the day he died. So many people have been killed or injured playing parts in *Macbeth* that it is considered Shakespeare's cursed work, and some actors refuse roles in the production for just that reason.

SCOTLAND

Scotland is comprised of the counties of Highlands, Strathclyde, Dumfries & Galloway, Grampian, Borders, Lothian, Tayside, Fife, Central, and the Western Isles. Edinburgh is the most popular tourist destination in Scotland, and several tours of haunted locations are available there. One of the better ones is the Witchery Tours, which conducts a variety of entertaining tours of Edinburgh's dark side. The Tours meet outside the Witchery Restaurant, 352 Castlehill, Royal Mile, in Edinburgh. For more information, E-mail lyal @witcherytours.demon.co.uk or phone 0131-225-6745.

HIGHLANDS

Inverness

CASTLE STUART Castle Stuart is located near Inverness in the Highlands, about five miles east of Aberdeen, which is across the county border in Grampian. Originally built by members of the Stuart family, the place has a long history of violence. The construction of the castle was begun by the first earl of Moray, half-brother of Mary Queen of Scots, in 1561, but he was brutally murdered before he could finish, and the castle was not completed until the third earl of Moray laid the final stone in 1625. Unfortunately, not long afterwards, the Clan McIntosh attacked the castle and the Stuart family abandoned the castle. It was not until after the Battle of Culloden, when the clans were defeated by the noblemen, that the Stuarts returned to the castle. By then, it had already gained a reputation as being haunted.

During an amazingly violent storm in 1798, the roof of the East Tower was destroyed and the entire tower wing was sealed. The Stuarts once again abandoned the castle, and it was held by a variety of owners. In the 1930s, a Canadian named John Cameron bought the property and attempted to repair the damages and renovate the castle. During his work, he found a doorway hidden behind plaster in a wall. Behind the doorway was a stairway down to another wall. As he punched through this second wall, he heard a ghastly voice cry out "No!" Thinking it was his imagination, he struck again, only to be pushed backwards off his ladder by some unseen force. At the same time,

his blow made a hole that released a foul odor. He ran out of the castle but got enough gumption to return for his tools. Still frightened, he wedged the front door open and walked towards the newly discovered chamber. Suddenly all the lights went out and he heard the front door slam shut. As he stumbled towards the door, invisible, ice-cold hands grabbed him and tried to pull him back into the chamber. With all his strength, he broke away, yanked open the door and got into his car and never came back. The castle sat vacant for many years, until another family of Stuarts purchased it in 1977.

Another haunted spot in the castle is the three-turret room at the very top of the cursed East Tower. Today it is simply known as the Haunted Room. One of the earls of Moray, wanting to give up his life in London and return to the peacefulness of the Highlands, returned to live in the abandoned family castle. However, he found no peace at Castle Stuart and soon became convinced the place was haunted by some very upset presences. He returned to London and offered a large reward to anyone who could discover what was going on at his castle.

A Presbyterian minister and two other fearless souls took up the offer. Their plan was that each of them would spend several nights in the Haunted Room and then compare stories to uncover common elements that might hold some truth about what was behind the haunting. The minister took the first series of sleepovers. On the first night, he had nightmares of a huge man covered in blood that came into the room and sat next to him. On the second night, the minister had trouble falling asleep and stayed up late reading the Bible. Suddenly the apparition of the blood-spattered man walked through a wall and entered his room. Behind the ghost, the wall seemed to turn into a shimmering mirror, which contained the reflection of a skeleton. The ghost asked "What are you doing?" and the minister passed out cold. It took many weeks for him to fully recover from the encounter.

That did not dissuade the others, however, who each took their turn in the room. The first man saw the nonexistent "mirror" form on the wall and a figure resembling the Devil walk in through the door. The demonic form took a seat in a chair across from him, and the frightened man promptly passed out and was found unconscious the next morning. The second man entered the room the next night. The following day he had disappeared and the room was in complete disarray, as if a violent struggle had taken place. They soon found his crushed body on the castle lawn, with an expression of terror frozen on his face. He had either jumped or been pushed from the Haunted Room.

If you would like to try your luck in the Haunted Room, you can rent the entire castle for just £1,200 per night. Write to Castle Stuart, Petty Parish, Inverness, Scotland, IV1 2JH Great Britain. You can also phone them at 01463-790745 or fax them at 01463-792604. For more information, visit the Castle Stuart Web sites at www.castlestuart.com or www.highlanderweb.co.uk/haunted/haunt3.htm.

STRATHCLYDE

Biggar

SHIELDHILL COUNTRY HOUSE HOTEL In an isolated spot in the rolling farmlands of the Scottish Lowlands sits a very old granite manor house, which dates from 1199. It was originally a castle but was turned into a home and then the Shieldhill Country House Hotel. The haunting here originates in the fourteenth century, when the daughter of the Chancellor household became pregnant out of wedlock. One story is that she had a love affair with the gamekeeper's son; another version says passing soldiers raped her. In any case, the family abandoned the baby in a field where it eventually died.

Today, the distraught girl's ghost is seen walking towards the burial place on the grounds, or walking through the wall between the honeymoon suite and the Culloden Room where there used to be a hallway. Her footsteps are also heard on the roof above the honeymoon suite, as if she were scanning the horizon to find some sign of her dying baby. The Shieldhill Hotel is located at Quothquan in Biggar, Lanarkshire, Strathclyde. For information, phone 0899-20035 or fax 0899-21092.

Girvan

CARLETON CASTLE Another of Strathclyde's haunted castles is Carleton Castle, located northwest of the hamlet of Poulton, six miles south of the city of Girvan. The castle was originally built as part of the string of Kennedy Watchtowers along Scotland's coast, but the ghosts there date from a powerful baron who lived there much later. He was a male chauvinist who simply pushed his wives over the cliff when he got tired of them. That is how he got rid of seven of his wives, but their spirits came back and warned his eighth wife, Mary Culean. She took matters into her own hands (so to speak) and sent the baron tumulting over the cliffside. Now the murderous baron haunts the ruins of his earthly castle, occasionally visited by the shining spirits of his former wives.

Carleton Castle, Strathclyde, Scotland (John Mason)

Kilmarnock

DEAN CASTLE Dean Castle in Kilmarnock, Strathclyde, sits on land given to the Boyd family by Robert the Bruce in appreciation for the family's support at the Battle of Bannockburn. In 1350 the family started work on a castle keep on the property, then in the 1460s, a palace was built after Thomas Boyd's marriage to Princess Mary.

The estate remained in the Boyd family for the next four hundred years. William Boyd, the fourth earl of Kilmarnock, was the last member of the Boyd family to live in the castle. Apparently, his ghost has never given up the place.

William Boyd was captured at the Battle of Culloden, where he was fighting for Scotland as a Jacobite, in an ambush arranged by his own son. Betrayed and hopeless, William went willingly to his beheading and asked only that his head be caught in a large cloth. The proud man could not stand the thought of his bloody head rolling around in the dirt. Ever since, witnesses have reported seeing the gruesome sight of William Boyd's severed head rolling slowly along the floor of the castle corridors, as if someone were using it for a bowling ball.

In 1975, the castle was turned over to the city of Kilmarnock, which opened it as a public museum. Since then there have been many reports of ghosts by guides and visitors. The most frequently reported apparition is of an elderly woman wearing a long black dress that reaches down to her ankles with her head covered in a plaid shawl. The ghost most often appears on the walkway overlooking the courtyard, but she has also been seen in the kitchen. In 1992, one of the guides followed when the apparition waved to her and was led to a small office. There she seems to have become possessed by something that left her unconscious and violently ill. She kept hollering for something to "get out" of her and experienced such violent vomiting that she projected it to the ceilings. One witness said that the woman also appeared to be oozing some vile substance from her pores. The guard recovered and still works at the castle.

The ghostly sounds of medieval chamber music is reported in the Minstrels' Gallery and a portrait of William Boyd in the study has a habit of popping off the wall. The windowless Castle Dungeon is shaped like a funnel with the narrowest part at the doorway. It was designed that way so prisoners could simply be pushed through the door and slide down into the dungeon pit. This also made escape from the room impossible. At the very bottom of the dungeon floor is a sunken-brick box known as an oubliette (French for "cast aside"). People were placed in the tiny airtight box and left to suffocate after a stone slab sealed it. Prisoners were never washed, nor were they given food or water. They were simply thrown down into the dungeon and left to eventually die. The ghost of the last woman to die in the oubliette, a Coventers sympathizer, is sometimes felt in the Castle Dungeon, and many visitors report being overcome by feelings of constriction and difficult breathing there. For more information on Dean Castle, visit the Highlander Ghost Page at www.highlanderweb.co.uk/haunted/haunt3.htm.

DUMFRIES & GALLOWAY

Clarencefield

COMLONGON CASTLE Rising high above the Solway Firth, Comlongon Castle was built by Sir Cuthbeert Murray in the fifteenth century as a border outpost. The thirteen-feet-thick walls enclose a chapel, great hall, and master bedroom. The teenage ghost of Marian Carruthers still roams the castle. She had lived with her father at nearby Borthwick Castle until September 1564, when her father ordered her to enter into an arranged marriage. The romantic woman could not stand the thought of spending her life with someone whom she did not love, and ran away to Comlongon where she was taken in by Sir Charles Murray. In gratitude, she awarded Murray half her inherited estate. Some say she leapt to her death from the tower's highest window after her father filed a legal case to have her fulfill the marriage arrangements. Others say she was pushed from the window by Sir Charles, who wanted her estate. In any case, her spiteful father refused to give her a funeral and buried her body in unconsecrated ground in the nearby woods. Today, on the spot where she landed, nothing will grow. And on every September 30, the date of her death, her ghost walks the garden area. There is a Gothic-styled house adjacent to the castle that has been turned into an eight-room inn, and the owners have met Marian's pathetic ghost on several occasions. Comlongon Castle is in the town of Clarencefield in Dumfries County. For information, call 038787-283 or fax 038787-266.

Deeside

CRATHES CASTLE On the Loch of Leys in the county of Dumfries & Galloway, stands Crathes Castle. Located at the town of Deeside, near Banchory, the picturesque Jacobean castle owned by National Trust for Scotland is a favorite tourist destination. Work on the turreted castle was begun in 1550 by Alexander Burnett of Leys and not completed until 1590. A surprising number of tourists, and even royal dignitaries such as Queen Victoria, have encountered its revenant spirit, the Green Lady of Crathes.

For many centuries, even before the present castle was built, this spot has been haunted by the beneficent presence of the Green Lady. She is a revenant from an older castle that stood here before the current one was built. More than likely, many of the stones and materials in the old castle were salvaged to build the new one. She appears in a particular room, now called the Green Lady's Room, where her apparition is seen gliding gracefully across the floor to a massive fireplace and then lifts a small baby out of thin air. During renovations in this room, the skeleton of a baby was discovered under the hearthstone of the fireplace. Some believe the Green Lady used to live

in the castle and had a child out of wedlock that was murdered by her husband or father. Others think the Green Lady is a benevolent spirit that came to nurture the tortured souls here and just decided to stay. It is known that the Green Lady will even appear to members of the Burnett family to warn them of impending disaster or death.

GRAMPIAN

Aberdeen

BRAEMAR CASTLE Braemar Castle in Aberdeen, Grampian County, is haunted by at least two ghosts. Residents of this still-occupied castle are haunted by the ghost of a young bride. She awoke in bed one morning to find herself alone with no

Braemar Castle, Aberdeen, Scotland (John Mason)

Crathes Castle, Deeside, Scotland (John Mason)

sign of her husband. Wrongly assuming he had deserted her, the dejected woman committed suicide. Her spirit remains tied to the place of her desperate act. Another persistent ghost here is John Farquharson, the "Black Colonel of Inverey," who tried to burn down the castle in the eighteenth century.

Fyvie

GIGHT CASTLE Gight Castle sits along the Ythan River to the east of the town of Fyvie in Grampian. It was built around 1560 by members of the Gordon family and was plagued throughout its history by murder, hardship, and unexpected deaths. Even the castle itself met its demise, and all that remains are its skeletal ruins. The family lost the castle in 1787, when Catherine Gordon, mother of the famous poet Lord Byron, had to sell the entire estate to pay for the gambling debts of her husband. Near the castle is the Hagberry Pot, a near-bottomless natural well where the seventh laird of Gight hid his treasure to protect it during the Covenanters Rebellion. But when the greedy man tried to reclaim his riches after the rebellion was over, he was in for a surprise. A diver he sent down to retrieve the treasure scurried back to the surface saying the Devil himself was protecting it. When he insisted the diver try again, the diver's lifeless body floated back up to the surface after a few minutes. Something had severed the body into four pieces. The castle can only be reached by a footpath off the B9005 highway between Fyvie and Methlick that starts at a building named the "Old Smiddy at Gight." For more information on Clan Gordon, visit their Web site at www.tartans.com/clans/Gordon/gordon.html.

Grampian County

LEITH HALL Leith Hall in the Grampian countryside is a manor house built in the 1650s that is haunted by several ghosts. For over three hundred years it was in the Leith family. Unidentified noises and odors also plague residents here. A large, bearded man with bandages around his head is the most frequently encountered apparition. It is probably John Leith, who was shot in the head at a dinner party in Aberdeen in 1763, though it could also be Colonel Alexander Leith May, who was shot at the Battle of Balaclava in 1900. The apparition of an unidentified woman in Victorian dress has also been seen. Other spirits are the ghosts of a governess and a young child.

BORDERS

St. Mary's Loch

TIBBIE SHIELDS INN Tibbie Shields is the name of the strict landlady who ran this place in the nineteenth century and who haunts it to this day. After her husband died, Tibbie turned their farmhouse into one of the most popular inns in the region, and stuffed as many as thirty-five guests into a tiny inn that comfortably accommodates only eight. Even today, her ghost is felt nudging its way through the hallways and lounge. Tibbie died here in 1878 at the age of ninety-four, though she still keeps a benevolent eye over her former home. The other ghost here is that of a dog left tied up in a room while his master went to a nearby village on business. Unfortunately, the man had a heart attack and died that day, and the dog eventually starved to death. That was over eighty years ago, but the dog still shows up in the bar and kitchen looking for something to eat. The Tibbie Shields Inn is at St. Mary's Loch in Sel-

Gight Castle, Grampian, Scotland (John Mason)

kirkshire, Borders County. The telephone number is 0750-42231.

LOTHIAN

Edinburgh

EDINBURGH CASTLE Edinburgh Castle is an ancient fortress with a violent history. A military outpost since the seventh century, the site was re-fortified as a castle in 1337. King Henry II took it in 1174; Edward I conquered it in 1296; the earl of Moray captured it in 1313; and Cromwell's troops successfully stormed it in 1650. All that violence has left behind a few spiritual remnants, and many psychics visiting the site are overwhelmed by their impressions. Even a soldier on guard at the castle passed out after seeing one of the ghosts that linger here. The most frequent apparition is a headless sentry. The ghost of a drummer is also seen, though most investigators agree they are manifestations of the same presence. For more information, visit the Witchery Web site at www.witcherytours.com.

Edinburgh Castle, Scotland (Martin Houston, Witchery Tours)

ROSSLYN CHAPEL The ghosts of Knights Templar have been sensed guarding some secret source of esoteric knowledge in this mysterious chapel. Visitors often report feeling something curious and compelling, as if some wonderful message were hidden in the chapel's enigmatic carvings. Built between 1450 and 1480 by Sir William St. Clair III, the chapel soon became a focus for the Knights Templar and later for the Freemasons. The Knights Templar, once the most powerful Christian sect in the world, fled to Scotland after being banished by the Catholic Church for practicing unsanctioned rituals. In fact, the Knights were preservers of a pre-Christian tradition of individual spiritual perfection that had its roots in ancient Egypt.

The outside of the chapel is adorned with a prominent sculpture of Hermes, while the inside is covered with a bewildering variety of Egyptian, Celtic, Islamic, and pagan symbols. Sir William said that he built the chapel to the "greater glory of God" and dedicated it to the one true God beyond all religions. Sir William planned to build a full-size replica of Solomon's Temple, the Templars' headquarters in the Holy Land, but he died before his goal was realized. Tombs in the chapel include that of the first William St. Clair, who died in Spain in 1330 while escorting the heart of Scottish leader Robert the Bruce to the Holy Land. Rosslyn Chapel is located near the town of Roslin. Take the Edinburgh Bypass (A720) to the Straiton exit and follow A701 south.

WESTERN ISLES

Isle of Arran

BRODICK CASTLE Brodick Castle is located on the Isle of Arran in the Western Isles of Scotland. It has stood here since Viking times, though the oldest part of the present building dates back only to the fourteenth century. Cromwell garrisoned his army here and enlarged the castle considerably. The apparition of a White Lady is the most frequently sighted. She is seen at the back of the castle. The library is haunted by a man in a wig wearing a green coat and breeches. The apparition of a woman is seen walking the corridors, though she always ends her strolls in the servants' quarters, where she disappears into thin air.

She is thought to be a former servant girl, one of three women who died from the plague brought to the island by Cromwell's soldiers.

Their bodies were buried in unmarked graves within the castle itself. To herald the death of the head of the Hamilton family, the phantom of a white deer appears in the front of the house. This is an unusual from of an apparition known as the banshee, a spirit that warns of impending disaster and death.

IRELAND

Ireland is composed of the provinces of Ulster, Munster, Connacht, and Leinster.

MUNSTER

Glin

GLIN CASTLE Glin Castle has been in the Fitzgerald family for over seven hundred years. It stands on five hundred acres along the Shannon River in County Clare near the village of Glin. The castle is surrounded by beautiful formal gardens. The Fitzgeralds produced a long line of knights and noblemen, and it is their spirits that still haunt the castle. Lights flicker and dim in ghostly rhythm, drawers open and close rapidly by themselves, footsteps are heard when no one is there. Many feel their unseen presences. An odd apparition, the phantom of a rope, is sometimes seen dangling from the ceiling above the main staircase. The frayed rope is all that remains behind of an accident that occurred here in the late nineteenth century. A hired worker fell to his death on the stairs when his safety line broke.

LEINSTER

Drogheda

NEWGRANGE Newgrange is the oldest intact building in the world, older than Stonehenge or the pyramids of Egypt, and the spirits sensed here are also among the earth's oldest. Built over 5,200 years ago, the structure is a large stone temple dedicated to immortality and a higher spiritual reality. The entrance to the chamber is covered in five hundred pure, white quartz stones. Inside, the walls have strange spiral carvings symbolic of the evolving soul. At sunrise on the Winter Solstice, a shaft of light pinpoints a triple spiral carved in the rear wall. The triple spiral symbolizes the soul traveling through eternity. Newgrange is north of Dublin near Drogheda on a high hill overlooking the Boyne River Valley.

NORTHERN IRELAND

The counties of Northern Ireland are Derry, Antrim, Tyrone, Fermanagh, Armagh, and Down.

DOWN

Belfast

BELFAST FLAXWORKS The Belfast Flaxworks, a former linen mill in the historical preservation district in Belfast, is haunted by the powerful presence of Helena Blunden, a woman who spent her life working there. Born in 1892, Helena was sixteen years old when she started working in the spinning room at the mill. She lived in a small house on Raphael Street close by and walked to work every day. Helena was an exuberant, loud girl, full of life and laughter, who loved to sing and hoped to become an opera star one day. However, life at the mill was harsh, and the girl worked long, sixty-hour weeks. Late one evening, after an especially hard day, Helena was coming down the broad stairway to the fourth floor, when she tripped over a mop left on the upper stairs by the cleaning crew. Propelled over the banister, she hit the cement floor below with a sickening thud. Helena died at the age of sixteen, just a few months after starting at the mill, but her irrepressible spirit lingers on.

Employees of the print shop that now occupies the old mill site where Helena died have not only heard her screams as she fell to her death but have also heard her pleasant humming as she worked. Materializations of her apparition are accompanied by a "cozy" warm spot and a flowery scent. Her apparition is most often encountered in a hallway connecting a storeroom at the back of the building with a studio office. She is also sensed in an elevator installed in 1912, the year of her death. Helena is blamed for moving objects and rifling through files, and her image has been caught by a Webcam installed in the storeroom. An online Ghostwatch of the linen mill began in 1998 and has resulted in several spectacular sightings. The live Webcam of the haunted site can be found at www.irelandseye.com/ghost/index.shtm.

ANTRIM

Carrickfergus

DOBBINS INN HOTEL The Dobbins Inn Hotel is a seventeenth-century inn at the center of the town of Carrickfergus in County Antrim. The inn sits not far from the Carrickfergus Castle, which dates from the twelfth century. Many secret passageways were built under the inn, one of the largest of which connected the inn to the castle. It is in this tunnel the ghost of the inn, nicknamed "Maud," can most often be found. She is a friendly and humble spirit, who is said to have been a sad loser in both her station in life and her success in love. Psychics say she seems much happier on the Other Side.

BALLYGALLY CASTLE Ballygally Castle sits overlooking the sea at the head of Ballycastle Bay in the county of Antrim. Scotsman James Shaw built it in 1625, and its five-foot-thick walls were constructed with local stone in the Scottish Baronial style. Now the castle is a thirty-room hotel, complete with a restaurant and dungeon bar. It is also one of the most haunted places in Ireland. In fact, it has been noted that on some nights, this hotel can have more ghosts than guests! The most active ghost is reputed to be a former resident, Lady Isobel Shaw, who keeps knocking at the doors of different rooms and disappearing. The poor lady was locked up in her room and starved by her husband, only to end up leaping to her death from a window.

She is still seen and heard walking frantically through the halls and near the basement bar, as if looking for someone. Another ghost who likes to knock on doors is Madame Nixon, a nineteenth-century resident who can sometimes be heard rustling about in her silk dress. The castle's turret guest rooms are haunted by an unidentified presence that likes to bang doors. One guest witnessed "unseen hands" rifling through a newspaper. A whole party of seventeenth-century ghosts that seem to be having a raucous time have been seen in Room 1625. The Ballygally Castle Hotel is on the Antrim Coast Road at 274 Coast Road, Ballygally, Antrim. For bookings, phone 1574-83212 or fax 1574-83681.

CONTINENTAL EUROPE
AND AFRICA

AUSTRIA

Austria has a rich and sometimes tragic history, and for that reason the country has been called the "soul" of Europe. It was inhabited by Celtic tribes before being conquered by Rome in 14 B.C. It became part of the Holy Roman Empire in A.D. 955. The Austro-Hungarian Empire was one of the most powerful monarchies in the world in the late 1800s and included Austria, Hungary, Bohemia, Moravia, Bukavina, Transylvania, Carniola, Kustenland, Dalmatia, Croatia, Flume, and Galicia. Today, Austria is composed of the states of Burgenland, Carinthia, Lower Austria, Salzburg, Styria, Tyrol, Upper Austria, Vienna, and Voralberg.

BURGENLAND

Burgenland Province

SCHLOSS BERNSTEIN Schloss (Castle) Bernstein is in Burgenland, the easternmost province of Austria that was once part of Hungary and became part of the Federal Republic of Austria after World War I. The apparition of a White Lady has been observed there several times and has even been photographed. Experts have scrutinized these photos, and a scientific paper on this topic was published in 1925. An impressive painting of the White Lady is located in the Main Hall of the castle. Schloss Bernstein is now a hotel.

LOWER AUSTRIA

Warth

STEYERSBERG CASTLE From the outside, Steyersberg Castle is one of the most beautiful in all of Austria. Located on a tall hilltop not far from Vienna near the town of Warth in Niederosterreich (Lower Austria), the one hundred-room castle is an imposing sight. For centuries, the castle has been owned by descendents of the original Count von Wurmbrand. Today, the deeds of the Wurmbrand family haunt the castle. The souls of men tortured in the castle's dungeon haunt the rooms above the dungeon and roam about touching people or chilling them with their icy presence. One of the prisoners cast a curse on the Wurmbrand name, saying that no male family member would die naturally until the family name died out. The curse seemed to hold true right up until the last

Count Wurmbrand died a few years ago, but that did not placate at least three other dungeon ghosts who still haunt the castle.

SALZBURG

Salzburg

SALZBURG CASTLE The ghost of the famous alchemist Paracelsus has been sensed in recent years by tourists visiting Salzburg's imposing castle. Born in 1498 in Switzerland, his real name was Theophrastus Bombastus von Hohenheim. He moved to Austria when he was nine years old and was trained in a mining school near Villach, but at the age of fourteen, decided to become a doctor and left home to attend medical school. During the next five years Paracelsus attended seven prestigious universities throughout Europe yet found no teacher he respected. He was an independent and stubborn thinker whose revolutionary ideas became the basis for modern medicine. He was known for his argumentative and arrogant way of conversing, and our word "bombastic" comes from his name. Paracelsus made a lot of enemies among the traditional bloodletting physicians of his time by suggesting that herbal tinctures, minerals, and drugs could cure people. He was expelled from every major university in Europe for his ideas.

In 1541, Paracelsus was offered asylum by his former enemy, the Prince Bishop of Salzburg. Paracelsus was destitute and had no choice but to accept the invitation, even though he was once expelled from Salzburg for "subversive activities." Shortly after he arrived, he was severely beaten by assassins hired by the medical faculty of the University of Vienna. On September 24, 1541, he died alone in his small room at the White Horse Inn. No reason for his death was recorded, and he was hastily buried in the graveyard of Salzburg's St. Sebastian Church. To this day, many ill and crippled people visit his gravesite hoping for a miraculous cure from the spirit of the greatest doctor of all time.

Psychics say his ghost roams the castle grounds

Salzburg Castle Ghost, Salzburg, Austria (Deb Dupre)

searching for his many manuscripts that were taken from his room after his death and hidden away by the Prince Bishop. American tourist Deb Dupre was one of many to feel the presence of Paracelsus in the castle. Her encounter during a visit in 1986 changed her life, causing her to become more unconventional and creative and open to the deeper symbolism of alchemy. She even started painting dramatic and colorful depictions of alchemical forces in her own life. Dupre also picked up paranormal energy in several photographs of the castle, including the spiraling mist that followed her around.

STYRIA

Hitzendorf

SCHLOSS ALTENBERG A bed-and-breakfast inn known as Schloss Altenberg, in the village of Hitzendorf near Graz, is haunted by the valet of a former owner who was responsible for his master's murder. The guilty ghost is most often detected in the livery near a closet that contains a secret passageway to outside the house. In the first part of the nineteenth century, the owner of Altenberg treated his farmers and laborers very badly, and they revolted against him. When the angry mob broke into his house, he hid behind the secret door in the closet. But the man's valet told the mob where the owner was hiding, and they murdered him on the spot.

Styria Province

GLEICHENBERG CASTLE Gleichenberg Castle is a fourteenth-century fortress in the Austrian province of Styria that has been the scene of both miracles and a dreadful curse in its long history. The castle was and still is home to the Trauttmansdorff family and their descendents. However, the family name was almost lost when the only son of the original Count Trauttmansdorff was near death from lung disease. Then one day, a mysterious Gypsy came to the count's court and revealed the location of a hidden spring on his property whose water would heal the boy. The count uncovered the spring and the boy became strong and healthy drinking from it. The count rewarded the Gypsy handsomely, and the spring became the source of many other healings over the years and flows to this day.

However, during the trial of twenty local women accused of being witches, Count Trauttmansdorff was forced by Catholic authorities to find them guilty and execute all of them. Before they died, they issued a curse on the count and his family that has been blamed for many tragedies and deaths. Not long afterwards, the Turks murdered all of the sons and nephews of the count, and delivered all twenty-one corpses to the feet of his hysterical wife. Then, fiendish phantoms started appearing that seemed to be trying to deliberately scare everyone from the estate. For centuries, the castle was plagued by violent poltergeist effects such as windows shattering, doors slamming hard, and loud crashing sounds that reverberated through the hallways at night. In an effort to stop the haunting, one family member had the courtyard dug up and moved the twenty female skeletons to a pit in the forest and had it covered in concrete. It did not help. Soon, mysterious fires broke out periodically until nothing was left of the interior of the castle but burnt timbers. Today, the once proud castle lies in ruins, the witches' curse fulfilled. However, if you do plan to visit this place, be forewarned not to stay overnight on the castle grounds. No one is certain whether of not the property still carries the curse.

UPPER AUSTRIA

Stein am Forst

ERNEGG CASTLE Ernegg Castle is an elegant Renaissance structure near the hamlet of Stein am Forst, which is located just off the main highway between Vienna and Ybbs in Oberosterreich (Upper Austria). Still owned by the family of the original builders (the Auersbergs), the castle is now a bed-and-breakfast inn that offers comfortable amenities along with a ghost from the family closet. The ghost is a former servant who fell in love with a daughter of the family and was caught sneaking into her room one evening. The girl's father, Prince Auerberg, had the man arrested and executed, but the servant's love-struck spirit still returns to seek the girl.

VIENNA

FLAKTURMS They stand in the neighborhoods of Vienna like giant gray ghosts of the past that no one knows how to get rid of. The massive, windowless, concrete "Flakturms" scattered throughout the city are much taller than any of the surrounding buildings for a reason. The towering monoliths were constructed as gigantic ammunition bunkers and anti-aircraft turrets during World War II, and they were built to survive direct bombing hits. On top of each, resting on protruding "ears" at the corners, were 8.8-caliber AA guns, the heaviest anti-aircraft weapon used by the Germans in the war. Most had concrete ramps running along the top perimeter that were big enough to drive huge ammo trucks on. The bunkers themselves are so massive that it is impossible to demolish them. Any attempt to dynamite or implode them would destroy most of the neighboring buildings.

So they still stand, ghostly reminders of the death and destruction of war, the only part of the Thousand Year Reich that just might last a thousand years. To make matters worse for Viennese authorities, several are haunted. Austria Army soldiers and even a few World War II-era vehicles have been seen on top of the towers, and unexplainable footsteps, loud banging sounds, and shouted orders are heard coming from the tightly secured and deserted structures. Paranormal events have been reported at the Radetzky Flakturm, the Apollo Flakturm, the twin Neulig Flakturms, and the two different Augustiner Flakturms.

Radetzky Flakturm, Vienna, Austria (Bruce Schaffenberger)

HAPSBURG CURSE Austria's infamous Hapsburg Curse started in the sixteenth century when Count Hermann of Hapsburg looted the Temple of Rama in Burma. After Count Hermann and his men forcibly took everything of value from the temple, the high priest entered a weeklong period of constant meditation. At dawn on the eighth day, the priest began his pronouncement of the curse and did not end until noon. The curse laid every kind of misfortune imaginable on anyone who ever came in contact with the stolen sacred items and temple jewels. The priest's vengeful presence has stayed with his temple's treasure ever since.

Count Hermann was the first to suffer his fate. When he took the treasure back to Vienna, his own royal relatives confiscated it, and he was committed to an insane asylum. He was not insane when he entered the asylum, but he died there a raving lunatic. Afterwards, every member of the House of Hapsburg who shared in the Burmese booty met a violent death or suffered undreamed of tragedies, and the name Hapsburg became synonymous in the German language with "bad luck." Some of the artifacts were considered "possessed" by strange spirits and were given away or destroyed. Several family members gave up all their money and titles to become poor commoners in an effort to break the curse.

Others, such as Emperor Franz Joseph, did not believe in the curse. Yet, from almost the day he received his $5,000,000 inheritance of temple bounty, his life took a downward spiral. Almost overnight, he became the most hated man in Europe and there were many violent attempts to bring down the Hapsburg dynasty. His beautiful wife, Queen Elizabeth of Bavaria, was murdered by the royal shoemaker, who attacked her with an awl. His son Rudolph committed suicide with his lover (see Imperial Palace, Vienna). Many other similar tragedies plagued the family, and Franz Joseph finally came to believe the Burmese wealth was indeed cursed. To the amazement of the world, he gave nearly every penny of his $5,000,000 share of the temple treasure to his political foe, Archduke Maximillian. Maximillian at first refused the cursed wealth, but his wife Charlotte was tempted by the beautiful jewelry and made her husband accept it.

As for Franz Joseph, his efforts to end the curse came too late. In 1914, his nephew, Archduke Franz Ferdinand, was assassinated by a young fanatic at Sarajevo. The war precipitated by the assassination of Archduke Ferdinand took the lives of over twenty million people, and the Hapsburg family was decimated by death and destruction, and the great Austrian empire collapsed. Franz Joseph watched it all happen, and ended up a broken-hearted, feeble old man.

The limousine in which the archduke and his wife were touring was a brand-new, blood-red, open-seat touring car, and it apparently assimilated the Hapsburg curse. The Governor of Yugoslavia took possession of the car but gave it up after four accidents and the loss of his arm. He insisted that the haunted car be destroyed, but a skeptical physician friend took the car anyway and was crushed to death when it overturned on him. A Swiss racecar driver then thought he could tame the vehicle, but he was killed when the car threw him over a stone wall. A rich farmer then bought the car. He and a friend were killed when the car suddenly lunged forward while they were attempting to tow it. Then, a fearless man bought the fancy car, had it repainted a festive blue color, and used it to go to a wedding. He and four companions were killed in a head-on crash. The fame of the haunted car grew so great that it was put on display in a Vienna museum, yet no one was ever allowed to sit in it again. It proved a popular exhibit until World War II broke out and the museum was reduced to a pile of rubble by bombing. The car has never been seen since, though there are rumors that a museum attendant by the name of Karl Brunner, who had become obsessed with the car, was somehow able to salvage it.

The man to whom Franz Joseph presented the Buddhist treasure, Maximillian, was made emperor of Mexico by Napoleon. Maximillian's wife Charlotte, empress of Mexico, was wearing the cursed jewelry the day they arrived at their palace in Mexico City. Her imperial glory did not last long, however. A civil war soon broke out and her husband was executed at the palace. Charlotte was in Europe at the time, trying to get her royal relatives to come to their aid. When she heard the news, she collapsed and lost her mind. She spent the rest of her life confined to the Castle of Bouchout, where she pretended her husband was still alive and she was still the empress living in Mexico City. The next ruler of Mexico, President Porfirio Diaz, expropriated all of the Burmese treasure from the palace and claimed it for his own. When things became too politically dangerous for him, he loaded the treasure onto the chartered steamer *Merida* and headed for France. For some strange reason, the steamer got lost at sea and ended up at the mouth to the Chesapeake Bay, where it

sunk with the loss of everyone on board. In the last ninety years, every attempt to salvage the vessel has ended in disaster. But if you would like to try your luck against the Hapsburg curse, the ship is located forty-five miles off the Virginia Capes in only 192 feet of water at latitude 37° 20' North and longitude 74° 47' West.

IMPERIAL CASTLE Vienna's Imperial Castle is haunted by the ghost of Countess Mary Vetsera, illicit lover of Prince Rudolf. She met the thirty-year-old prince in Vienna's Prater Park in November 1888 and promptly agreed to start seeing him in private. Rudolf never loved his wife, who was picked for him for political reasons, but he fell madly in love with Mary at first sight. Frequently, she snuck into the Imperial Palace and the two spent days together at his hunting lodge in Mayerling, about an hour outside of Vienna. The two lovers became increasingly despondent over the prospects of their ever living together. On the morning of January 30, 1889, in bed together in Rudolph's room at Mayerling, the two lovers committed suicide. He shot her first and then put the gun to his head and pulled the trigger. A note from Rudolph demanded that he be buried next to Mary; a letter from Mary to her mother asked that she be buried next to him. To this date, their dying wishes have not been granted. Rudolph was given a state funeral and Mary's dumped in a hastily dug, unmarked grave at the Cistercian monastery. Later she was given a proper burial at the Heiligenkreuz Cemetery in Vienna. Even in eternity, they seem to be separated, for Mary's apparition is seen gliding up the stairway at Mayerling and then moving down the hallway into the prince's former room. She has also been observed in the Amalienburg Wing of the Imperial Palace.

The Imperial Palace has at least one other ghost. A Capuchin monk haunts an older section of the castle known as the Swiss Court, which dates from the late 1200s. This part of the castle originally housed a small monastery, and the friar's apparition is seen in the hallway connecting the old section with the newer one. Parts of the castle date back to the time of the Holy Roman Emperors, but most of it was built after 1400.

BELGIUM

The name Belgium comes from "Belgae," the name of an ancient Celtic tribe that first settled here. The land was conquered by Julius Caesar in 57 B.C. At one time it was also part of the Spanish Empire, the Austria Empire, the Netherlands, France, and Germany, the Belgium people have usually resorted to open rebellion to free themselves of other countries' control.

Ghent

CASTLE OF ST. BAVON The fourteenth-century-old Castle of St. Bavon in the city of Ghent, Belgium, is haunted by the horrifying apparition of a butchered woman carrying the body of a young man in her arms. In 1310, the castle was ruled by Count Alard. His first wife bore him three sons, and he had yet another boy by his second wife. From the beginning the boys were tended by a devoted nurse named Blanfar, who had brought her own teenaged son, Nold, to live in the castle. Nold was a simple lad who could not control himself around the comely maids of the household, though he was warned repeatedly to stay away from them. One night Count Alard caught the boy in bed with a serving maid, and in a fit of rage, beat him to death. Blanfar never forgave the man. She was a large and powerful woman, and in the course of the next few months, murdered all four of the count's sons and made the deaths look like accidents. When the count realized what she had done, he ordered her taken into the courtyard and "hacked into quarters by the axman." Her body parts were buried in separate, unmarked graves in the St. Wandrille Forest, but Blanfar was not to be gotten rid of so easily. By 1350, residents of the castle were reporting her ghastly apparition, dripping rot and decomposing flesh. The distinctive ghost of the large woman has been seen many times since, always covered in dried blood, and sometimes carrying the body of her teenaged son in her arms.

CZECH REPUBLIC

The former country of Czechoslavakia lasted from 1918 to 1992 and is now known as the Czech Republic. The land shares its early history with Bohemia and Moravia.

Kolodeje

HOSTY STREET HAUNTING An unusual domestic haunting is at a home on Hosty Street in the town of Kolodeje in the Czech Republic. The apparitions of dwarves have been reported there for the last thirty years. The unappealing apparitions walk through walls, chase pets in the household, and sometimes just appear next to the beds of sleeping residents, staring them in the face. Several tenants have been forced to move because of the unexplainable phenomena, and the house is becoming harder and harder to rent out as word of the haunting spreads.

Kutna Hora

HOLY VIRGIN CHURCH From the street, the Holy Virgin Church in the village of Kutna Hora appears to be a lovely Gothic church with a walled churchyard. But the church was built in front of a smaller, older church to hide it from public view. The inside of the older church (called Charnel House and later, All Saints' Church) is a grotesque and horrifying sight for most people. It is built from the bones and skulls of over ten thousand people. Almost everything in the church, from the chandeliers to the altars, is built of human bones. The church was erected in 1280 on holy soil brought from Calvary, and for that reason, everyone wanted to be buried there in hopes of resurrection. Then, in just a few months in 1318, when the plague hit this area, over thirty thousand people were buried in the already crowded churchyard. More tragedy stuck the area in the Thirty Years' War in the 1600s, during which time Hus-

Holy Virgin Church, Kutna Hora, Czech Republic
(Andrew Hayden)

site soldiers ransacked the church and stole everything of value. The sacrilegious soldiers replaced
their bounty with macabre decorations made from
the plentiful supply of bones in the churchyard.
Later, villagers added the bones and skulls of Hus-
site soldiers killed in battle, and afterwards the
bones remained the church's only decorations.
Many apparitions have been reported inside the
church, which is open to visitors. The church is
open for worship on only one day of the year—
Easter—a time to reflect on the fate of the body
and the supremacy of spirit.

Prague

Kozna Street Kozna Street is a narrow street
where tanners once worked. "Kozna" means
"skins" in the Czech language, and it is the ghost
of one of those fourteenth-century tanners who
haunts the street. His great misdeed that ties his
spirit to this place is that he disliked stray dogs

and had the habit of killing them with poisoned
meat. Though not such a terrible deed in itself,
the dogs were the city's rat patrol and kept the
rodent population in check. Without the dogs, the
rat population grew rapidly, which also brought
the Black Death, bubonic plague, to the city and
thousands died. Ghost Tours of Prague can be
arranged at the Visitor's Center in Old Town
Square. They leave at 8:15 P.M. from the City Hall
clock tower.

Podskalska Street Another haunted avenue in
Prague is Podskalska Street, where the pathetic
apparitions of innocent little children congregate.
Life for poor children in seventeenth-century
Prague was very hard, but one man, a monk
named Nicholas, did all he could to comfort them.
He gave food, shelter, and fatherly support to any
child who needed him, and even to this day, the
ghosts of lost children find their way to the doorstep of the house where he once lived. Many have
caught sight of the fleeting apparitions, and in the
winter, have seen their tiny footprints in the snow.

Ungelt Alley Ungelt Alley near the Old Town
Square is haunted by the "Turk of Ungelt." He
was a traveling merchant who fell in love with a
young woman he met in Prague. The two agreed
to marry on his return from his travels, but after
many years, the woman gave up hope and married
another. When the Turkish merchant finally
showed up, he was enraged that the woman had
violated her vow. He chased her into this alleyway,
and with one blow from his curved saber, severed
her head from her body. The merchant took the
head in a wicker casket back to Istanbul, but he
was so haunted by her ghost that he returned with
his trophy to Prague to give it a proper burial.
But he was not rid of his guilt so easily, and his
turbaned apparition holding a head by its long
blonde hair still returns to the place of his dastardly deed.

Tyne Church The north portal of the Tyne
Church on Prague's Old Town Square has been
haunted since the fifteenth century by a priest
known as Uhlrich. The man was tutored in the

black arts by his mother who was a witch, and then attended a monastery to learn Catholicism. Sometimes, in the middle of church service, he would ask his parishioners if they wanted him to contact any dead family spirits, then he would proceed to raise the ghost of that person outside in the cemetery that night. As his powers and fame grew, Uhlrich became more daring and started raising the ghosts of the dead right on the steps of the church. One evening, he conjured up so many apparitions that the sight frightened even him, and the ghosts, apparently sensing their power over him, attacked. He ran down toward the Vltava River, but the phantoms caught up with him and literally tore him to pieces. His decapitated torso is depicted in a carving on the stone portal that can be seen to this day.

Two phantoms, known to locals simply as the "Whore and the Priest," haunt Celetna Street in Prague. The two crossed each other's paths on the cobblestone street one summer night, and the whore brazenly exposed her breast in an attempt to seduce the priest. The outraged priest struck her with a heavy iron cross he carried and killed her. A crowd gathered round the murder scene and the mortified priest had a heart attack and died on the spot. Today, both their apparitions are seen reliving that horrendous day. Over and over again, the whore emerges into the light to approach the priest, who runs away from her back into the shadows.

Vltava River

KRUMLOV CASTLE An apparition called the White Lady haunts Krumlov Castle on the banks of the Vltava River in Bohemia. She has been seen on the stairway, in the halls, and roaming the bedrooms of the castle for over a century, yet no one is quite sure who she is. Most assume she is the wife of the first owner.

DENMARK

Denmark was settled by the Danes, Scandinavians of Teutonic descent, in the fifth century A.D. The Danes participated in the Viking invasions of England and France beginning in the eighth century and were feared throughout Europe for centuries. Denmark did not become a united country with a constitution until 1282. For many years, Denmark, Greenland, and Iceland were part of a single commonwealth, and the countries still have close ties.

Helsingor

GURRE WOOD A ghost of King Valdemar IV, the "psychic king," appears in Gurre Wood near Helsingor, Denmark. Valdemar was known a clairvoyant who foresaw many events and even counseled those close to him. He drew his powers "naturally" from the outdoors and was known to spend many hours relaxing in Gurre Wood.

Slewig

POOLE Another Danish monarch, King Abel, appears at Poole near the city of Slewig whenever some crucial event is about to happen. He is rarely seen but did appear before the bombardment of Copenhagen in 1807, in 1864 before the country lost a war with Austria, and before the German occupation in 1940.

Tisvilde

TIBIRKE 5 The small coastal town of Tisvilde is one of the most mysterious in Denmark. There are many prehistoric gravesites, as well as Viking burial grounds. The town's church is built on top of an ancient pagan site known as "Tibirke 5," and there is a Holy Spring nearby. The town even has its own saint, Saint Helena, whose body was found on the beach. Tisvilde's Troll Forest has been considered haunted by "little people" for many centuries, and over the nearby bogs, strange balls of lights dart around at night. The apparition of a White Lady is seen in the woods around Tisvilde, and she seems to be made out of moonlight. The stronger the moonlight, the more real she seems. Locals believe the unidentified apparition could be the so-called Snow Queen, Holle, Frue

Holle. According to Norse pagan tradition, she is the goddess of the dead, protector of the souls of the dead and the unborn souls of children.

Paul Rinehart, who owns a summer cottage in the town, described his recent encounter: "There was a full moon out, a harvest moon I think they call it, when the moon is unusually big and has a reddish tint to it. At any rate, the power went off in the whole village; the strange thing was that the lightbulbs still glowed, a light reddish hue to them. I looked out my living room window and I saw it. Faint, but I could see her plain as day, dressed in a white shroud staring at me with one black hole of an eye. To give you an idea of how far from her I was, it was only a matter of perhaps ten feet. My curiosity got the better of me and I ran outside, but by the time I got out there, she was gone."

EGYPT

Egypt is an ancient civilization that developed in thirty dynasties of pharaoh kings from 3000 B.C. to 332 B.C., when the outsider Alexander the Great was made pharaoh. Napoleon invaded but withdrew quickly in 1798. Egypt was basically part of the Ottoman Empire until 1914, when it became a British protectorate. Egypt became independent in 1922.

Cairo

ST. MARY'S COPTIC CHURCH An Egyptian government investigation concluded "without doubt" that some sort of paranormal phenomena took place in the Cairo suburb of Zeitoun and lasted for fourteen months. On the night of April 2, 1968, three Muslim mechanics stopped on the street and started pointing at the brilliant white apparition of a woman on top of the center dome of St. Mary's Coptic Church. Soon a crowd gathered, and hundreds of people witnessed the phenomena. Thinking it might be a nun about to commit suicide, the mechanics procured a ladder and started climbing up to rescue the woman. At that moment, the apparition formed a ball of

golden light and shot up vertically into the dark blue sky. Before the apparition completely disappeared, however, someone identified it as the Mother Mary. At that moment, the figure seemed to bow to the crowd in acknowledgment.

Over a hundred witnesses reported spontaneous healings as a result of witnessing the apparition, including one of the mechanics who was cured of a gangrenous finger that was to be amputated the next morning. The apparition continued to reappear above the church for the next ten days. Various apparitions continued to appear in the vicinity of the church until the end of 1969, and a dozen different figures were reported. The longest appearance of an apparition took place on June 8, 1968, and lasted for over seven hours. Other phenomena included silvery winged objects, colored doves manifesting out of thin air, phantom crosses, and large red, perfume-scented clouds that appeared and disappeared within seconds. The total number of witnesses to the phenomena at Zeitoun is estimated as high as 500,000.

FINLAND

Finland was widely settled by the eighth century A.D., and then it was invaded and "Christianized" by Sweden in the twelfth century. It was ceded to Russia by Sweden in 1809. After a revolt and with help from the Germans, Finland gained independence from Russia in 1920. Finland is known among paranormal researchers for its many poltergeist cases.

Haapavesi

LESKELA Typical of Finnish poltergeist cases is the "Devil of Haronen," which occurred in 1873 on the Haronen family farm near the village of Leskela in the parish of Haapavesi. As is the rule with poltergeist activity, the activity seemed to center around an adolescent, in this case a daughter in the family. An invisible presence started teasing the girl, tugging at her hair and pushing her. It escalated to untraceable scratching sounds, then mysterious fires were started, and finally objects were thrown about the farmhouse. Any visitors who mocked the phenomena found themselves attacked or shouted at by the "devil."

Researcher Heikki Tikkala collected over fifty such cases, which are summarized at the Finnish Poltergeist Web site at personal.inet.fi/tiede/poltergeist/kansi.htm. "The profile of the poltergeist in Finland," notes Tikkala, "is much the same as elsewhere. Finnish ghosts move objects, knock and scratch on walls, throw stones, light fires, imitate sounds, and sometimes even speak. The trajectory of the thrown objects is often unnaturally tortuous and the objects fly unnaturally slowly. And as elsewhere, the most impressive thing about the Finnish poltergeist is, that the same unbelievable phenomena are described over and over again, although the events have no historical connection."

Kuivaniemi

OIJARVI ELEMENTARY SCHOOL A powerful poltergeist plagued the Oijarvi Elementary School in the parish of Kuivaniemi in 1946. Both students and adults witnessed mysterious sounds such as knocking and scratching, and more blatant manifestations such as the poking and teasing of children and throwing of objects about the classroom. Another poltergeist was associated with a young worker at the Jyvaskyla Stoneworks in the city of Jyvaskyla. In 1954, an invisible presence smashed stones and threw them and other objects about the factory. It also made a mysterious whistling sound.

Parkano

NERKOO Sometimes in poltergeist cases, the entity will actually begin speaking to witnesses from inside the walls. This was the case at the Hemmila family farm outside the village of Nerkoo in Parkano parish. A "Speaking Devil" visited the family for several months and would respond to questions from witnesses in a booming male voice. The poltergeist was associated with a young servant girl and was observed throwing stones and other objects. In a case known as the Ghost of Makisalo that took place in 1936, the presence would actually strike anyone who mocked it, as well as make loud knocking sounds, start fires, and throw objects. The poltergeist was associated with the teenaged son at the Makisalo farm near the village of Leppikylä in the parish of Isojoki.

Puulavesi

LAHTI For over six months in 1974, a young married girl was attacked by a poltergeist at her home in the city of Lahti. It all started with knocking sounds at the windows, as if something wanted to get in the house, then the unidentified presence moved inside the house and started making weird noises in the kitchen and bedrooms. The sounds got louder and louder until, finally, objects started moving by themselves. Investigators documented many strange events, as objects were propelled about the rooms, sometimes striking witnesses. Visit the Finnish Poltergeists Web site at personal.inet.fi/tiede/poltergeist/english.htm.

FRANCE

France, too, has many unique ghost tales to share. Celtic Gauls inhabited the region at least as far back as 700 B.C., and it became a province of Rome in 121 B.C. For the next 1,400 years it was repeatedly invaded and divided up in feudal states by Norman and Germanic warlords. It was finally reunited into a country by King Philip Augustus in the Hundred Years' War in the thirteenth century.

Ales

TORNO HOUSE In the town of Ales (formerly "Alais") northwest of the city of Nimes in the province of Gard, a private residence is haunted by the voice and figure of Guy de Torno, who continues to keep a jealous eye on his widow's ghost, also trapped in time in the home. The two ghosts have been arguing for the last fifty years, much to the dismay of tenants. Several exorcisms have failed to lead the passionate couple to the Other Side.

Brittany

ANKOU On the wind-sculpted terrain of Brittany on the northwest tip of France, a frightening phantom rides a horse-drawn cart looking for victims. He is the "Ankou," the grim reaper who takes anyone who looks him in the face. The only warning given of his approach is the roar of the solid wooden wheels on his cart. Brittany is a unique area with a Celtic heritage whose traditions blend paganism with Catholicism, and that is what the figure of the Ankou represents.

BRENNILIS Another Breton belief is that the Gates of Hades (Hell) are located near the town of Brennilis, beneath an eerie moor located at the center of the Monts d'Aree (Black Mountains), which mark the border between North and South Finistere in France. There are many old stories about people seeing the Devil himself or the Devil in the form of a large black dog emerge from the bottomless moor to wreak havoc on the world. At one time, innocent girls were thrown into the lake to appease the Devil and keep him from leaving the moor. When the French government built an experimental nuclear reactor right over the Gates of Hades in the middle of the moor, many Bretons were convinced that the misguided act would bring about the end of the world.

Burgundy

LA PYRAMID DE CAUCHARD The odd, pyramid-shaped ruin of ancient brickwork known as La Pyramid de Cauchard is haunted by a strange phantom that has been described as "neither human nor animal." The ghost "lives" in a large hole at the center of the pyramid that at one time held a funeral urn with the ashes of a powerful chieftain.

Archeologists believe that the pyramid at Autun in the province of Burgundy dates from Roman times. It was once over sixty feet high and covered in white marble with a stairway that led to the capstone, where ceremonies were performed. It is thought that the pyramid marks the burial monument to Diviciacus, a chieftain of the Gauls who was a practicing Druid priest and associate of high-ranking Romans like Cicero and Julius Caesar. It is the magical power of Diviciacus that draws certain people to this site while at the same time protecting it from others, and it is his shape-shifting apparition that people still see here.

Domremy-la-Pucelle

BASILICA OF JOAN OF ARC The ghost of Joan of Arc haunts the basilica at Domremy dedicated to her memory. She was born in the lovely village on the Meuse River in 1412 and has returned to spend eternity after her tumultuous life. The town is in the province of Vosges in northeast France.

Languedoc

MONTSEGUR CASTLE Montsegur Castle is located high on a hilltop 2,485 meters (4,000 feet) above sea level at Pays de Cathars in the Languedoc region of France, and it is not surprising that people visiting it today believe it is haunted. Montsegur Castle was the final refuge of the Cathars, a gentle group of Christians whose name means "the Pure Ones." They were persecuted in the thirteenth century because they believed that redemption of the soul could be achieved by following the example of Christ's life on earth. This was in contrast to Catholic dogma that offered salvation only for those who sought it through the Church, and in 1209, Pope Innocent III declared a crusade to exterminate the heresy. One stronghold was the city of Beziers. Since it was not possible to tell the Cathars from the Catholics, the pope's representative ordered the murder of everyone. Over twenty thousand men, women, and children died in a single day. By 1243, the last of the Cathars took refuge at Montsegur and withstood an onslaught of ten thousand crusaders for ten months. Finally, on March 1, 1244, the small remaining group was given two weeks to renounce their faith or be burned alive. On the morning of March 15, a great bonfire was lit and the crusaders prepared to storm the castle and fulfill their promise. Then, the gates of the castle opened and the final 216 Cathars walked slowly and silently down the hill, and each one stepped into the fire voluntarily. The spot is now called the Field of the Burned and many sense a purified emotional energy there. Sometimes, too, the ghosts of Cathars are seen shrouded in mist as they walk down the hill to their deaths.

It is believed that the last treasure of the Cathars was hidden at Montsegur, but no one has yet discovered its whereabouts. Some say the treasure includes the Holy Grail or documents revealing the truth of Christ's death and resurrection. Adolph Hitler believed the Grail belonged to the German race and enlisted a young medieval scholar by the name of Otto Rahn to search for it. In the mid-1930s, Hahn made two extensive excursions to Montsegur to look for the treasure. Shortly after he got back from the second trip, he committed suicide.

RENNES-LE-CHATEAU The hard-to-reach town of Rennes-le-Chateau is located on top of an isolated hill in the Languedoc district of France, but nearly thirty thousand people a year make the journey. Their goal is a small church in town, which is said to contain a profound secret uncovered by a village priest, whose ghostly presence still protects the site of his discovery. According to legend, the priest's spirit protects some wonderful artifact hidden in the church by the ancient Knights Templar that has variously been described as the ancient Emerald Tablet, the Ark of the Covenant, the treasure of the Cathars, or perhaps the Holy Grail. The Templars were a group of knights who protected Christians in Moslem lands. Their headquarters were in the Temple in Jerusalem, where they were said to have discovered many ancient secrets that could topple the Church if released. Tensions grew, and in 1307, Pope Clement ordered the arrest of the Templars everywhere. In 1314, the final Grand Master of the group, Jacques de Molay, was burned at the stake.

In 1885, a new parish priest by the name of Francois Berenger Sauniere was assigned to Mary Magdalene Church at Rennes-le-Chateau. The church, dedicated in 1059, was badly in need of repair, and Sauniere began a major rebuilding project. Not long after he started renovating the church, Sauniere discovered something that changed his life and the life of the tiny village forever. When he lifted the cover of the altar, he discovered that one of the Visigoth columns supporting it was hollow. Inside were several wooden tubes containing parchments. One parchment contained a genealogy of the villagers written in the fifteenth century and the other parchments were written in code in the nineteenth century by one of Sauniere's predecessors, Abbot Antoine Bigou. To this day, no one is certain what the coded documents said, but Sauniere suddenly became very secretive and started behaving strangely. He would leave the area for long periods on secretive journeys, and when he was in town, he spent a lot of time digging at night in the churchyard.

Suddenly, unexplainably, the penniless priest became one of the richest men in France, and he embarked on an obsessive quest to transform the whole town. In the next two decades, he would direct the spending of over thirty million francs on his pet projects. He purchased most of the land in the village and built a massive chateau he named "Villa Bethania" and surrounded his estate with elaborately landscaped gardens. Over a gaping chasm in the westernmost part of the village, he constructed a tower library (the Magdalene Tower) stocked with many rare Hermetic books and manuscripts. He furnished his house with the finest furniture and priceless collections of art, stamps, wine, and exotic animals. Then he started throwing lavish parties attended by heads of state and other famous people from all over Europe. It is also known that he opened large bank accounts throughout Europe.

Sauniere's restoration of Mary Magdalene Church was hardly in keeping with his original assignment of returning the church to its original condition, nor was he guided by the dogma of the Catholic Church. At the former Stations of the Cross, he painted eerie, nonsensical scenes, such as Mary and Joseph holding twin babies, Pontius Pilot wearing a veil, St. Roch showing his wounded thigh, as in the legend of the Grail King. Another painting shows a boy wearing a kilt, and some have suggested this refers to the body of Christ being buried in Scotland, possibly in Rosslyn Chapel. The Catholic Church was not pleased with Sauniere's handiwork and tried to transfer him to a seminary, but he refused and died at his opulent estate in 1917.

Just inside the front entryway to the church, Sauniere placed a statue of a gargoyle-like demon with horns named Asmodeus, the supernatural being who guarded King Solomon's treasure. Over the church entrance, he inscribed the Latin sentence *Terribilis est locus iste*, meaning "This is a terrible place." The statuary in the church contains many alchemical references. A statue of the demon Earth spirit supports a basin of Water on which Fire lizards (salamanders) crawl, and above, four spirits of Air (angels) bless them.

These alchemical symbols might provide a clue to the source of Sauniere's wealth, for it is known that alchemy was practiced at the Chateau des Seigneurs de Rennes, from which the village takes its name. A mysterious treasure of gold was said to have been hidden in the chateau in the twelfth century, and one crumbling edifice of the old chateau still carries the name Tower of Alchemy. The Blanchefort family, who lived at the chateau, were said to be carriers of a great secret and several members were alchemists. Abbot Bigot was the personal chaplain to family members and heard their confessions weekly.

In the last decade, Sauniere's ghost has been reported in the old churchyard, and many sensitive people detect another more mysterious and powerful presence inside the church itself. In 1996, the head of the demon statue in the front entryway of the church was severed and removed by unknown persons, probably trying to exorcise the spirit that still haunts Mary Magdalene Church.

Libourne

ENTREVOUS The small town of Entrevous, near Libourne in France, is haunted by a centuries-old apparition. At the center of town during the Mid-

dle Ages stood Vaubaughn Castle, a large fortress surrounded by a deep moat. During assaults on the castle, the townspeople took refuge inside and the drawbridge was pulled up. During one of these sieges, a young woman lagged behind because she could not find her gold locket and did not want the invaders to find it. When she finally found it, she ran to the castle, but the drawbridge was just being pulled up. She leapt for it but missed and fell to her death on the jagged rocks on the walls of the moat. Soon after, her white apparition, identified by the locket she wore, could be seen lingering near the moat—eternally locked outside of the castle. Even after the castle was removed and the moat filled in, her ghost still haunts the spot. Many modern witnesses have no idea how ancient is the spirit they encounter there.

Paris

EURO DISNEY Euro Disney (Parc Disneyland) theme park is located thirty-one kilometers (nineteen miles) southeast of Paris off the A4 Highway. Phantom Manor in Frontierland is a Gothic house-on-a-hill funhouse that is advertised to have

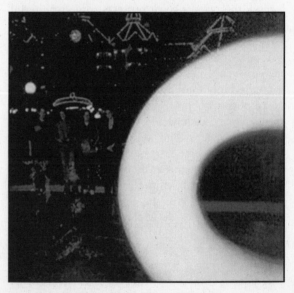

Euro Disney, Paris, France (Jodi Brockman)

999 ghosts. Apparently, a real ghost has decided to make it an even 1,000. Employees and visitors to the attraction have witnessed a variety of poltergeist phenomena, including moving exhibits when no power is on, untraceable equipment problems, screams coming from nowhere, and objects moving by themselves. The effects are real but no source has been found. Some investigators have suggested the paranormal energy arises from the genuine fright and panic felt by some teenaged visitors. Several photos taken in and near the attraction contain unexplainable vortexes of light typical of such manifestations. Most recently, an American tourist took a photo of some friends that contained the energy imprint.

NOTRE-DAME CATHEDRAL Notre-Dame Cathedral has long been considered haunted. Clerics, tourists, guides, and guards have all reported encounters with ghostly presences here. The cathedral was built on the ruins of two previous Christian basilicas, which were themselves built on the ruins of a pagan temple sacred to the Roman god Jupiter. Work on Notre-Dame was begun in 1163 by the bishop of Paris, Maurice de Sully, and not completed until 1250. Several balconies, porches, and chapels were added over the centuries. The central spire was not added until the nineteenth century. The two square towers at the front of the cathedral were also supposed to be topped by tall spires but the work was never completed.

The apparitions of robed figures with tall pointed hats have been seen outside the cathedral on the chapel's rear balcony. The figures seem to be admiring the huge rosette stained glass, and it has been suggested that they might be Rosicrucian alchemists who saw mystical significance in the colored glass patterns. Other apparitions seen here include numerous gnome-like phantoms climbing the exterior walls. Perhaps people's expectations at seeing Quasimodo, the fictitious hunchback of Notre-Dame, have focused paranormal energy at the ancient site to take these forms. The apparition of a bishop, perhaps Maurice de Sully himself, has been reported near the nave and transept areas.

Notre-Dame Cathedral, Paris, France (Bruce Schaffenberger)

Picardy

CHATEAU DE RARAY The Chateau de Raray in Picardy is a magnificent old mansion with dozens of sculptures of pagan gods decorating the manicured grounds and golf course. Today, it is an exclusive retreat for Paris businessmen, but in the seventeenth century it was the residence of the Bouteiller family, and it is from that time that the ghost originates. A servant girl had gotten pregnant by another member of the staff, and their stormy relationship ended after a few years in his leaving her for another. The girl took her child into the woods and hanged herself from a tree, but not before trying to crush and suffocate the little boy. Later, the boy was found wandering in the woods, mortally wounded, but still looking for his mother. And that is what his apparition is seen doing today, although sometimes, the remorseful ghost takes time out to play with living children visiting the grounds.

St. Germain

SEQUANA SPRINGS The springs at the headwaters of the Seine River near St. Germain in France were considered sacred for many centuries before the rise of Christianity. It is known that Paleolithic peoples migrated here, and a pagan temple dating from 300 B.C. has recently been discovered at the site. The first temple built here was Celtic, then Gallic, and later it was remodeled to suit Roman tastes. The temple was destroyed by Christian zealots in A.D. 400.

Pagans came here to worship Sequana, the Gallic goddess of abundance and healing. Many votive figurines have been discovered, each sculpted to depict a specific disease and bearing a prayer to cure it. Hundreds of figurines depict everything from leprosy to lumbago. The apparition of Sequana was said to have appeared regularly in a sacred stone basin or "piscina" to grant the wishes of supplicants. The piscina is located in the sanctuary next to a spring that flows to this day.

Versailles

VERSAILLES PALACE The apparition of Marie-Antoinette and members of her court are still seen on the grounds of Versailles Palace in Versailles, France. The ghosts were first reported in 1870, though the most documented and credible witnesses were two high school principles visiting the palace in August 1901. Eleanor Jourdain and Charlotte Moberley were walking near the Petit Trianon, a house built by Louis XV in 1774 for his queen, Marie-Antoinette. As they crossed a small bridge to the terrace in front of the house, they both felt an "extraordinary depression," as if they had entered a dream. They both agreed that "the heavy dreaminess was oppressive." Apparently, the two women were transported back in time to a scene from the late 1700s. Marie-Antoinette was on the lawn sketching a landscape, and there were out-

buildings that no longer existed. When the ladies researched their experience, they discovered old maps showing the buildings were actually there in the 1700s. The two women decided to return to Versailles in January 1902 to look for ghosts. At the Hameau, a small reproduction of a peasant village that Marie-Antoinnette loved and often visited, Miss Jourdain saw the ghosts of two workers wearing hooded capes loading sticks into a cart. The haunting at Versailles appears to recreate the last peaceful days of the royal family before they were imprisoned and Marie-Antoinnette beheaded during the French Revolution.

In October 1928, two English tourists saw the apparitions of a guard and workmen from the 1700s along the path between the Grand Trianon and the Petit Trianon. In September 1938, another tourist saw the ghosts of peasant workers pushing a wooden cart loaded with logs in the same area. In October 1949, three tourists saw the apparition of a woman in eighteenth-century clothing carrying a parasol on the steps of the Grand Trianon. In May 1955, two more tourists encountered ghosts at the Petit Trianon. This time there were three apparitions, a woman in a full yellow dress and two men in black breeches. Today, tourists still report seeing ghosts here, including the apparition of Marie-Antoinnette wearing a pink dress and large shepherdess hat, enjoying the sunshine on a splendid August day over two hundred years ago.

GERMANY

The Teutonic peoples who settled along the Rhine River and north of the Danube were never part of the Roman Empire, and became a separate political entity in A.D. 843 after the Treaty of Verdun. Religious and political rebellions within Germany after that resulted in many changes in its borders and relationships with neighboring countries right up to modern times. Germany's most famous ghost tale is the Lorelei, the mysterious singing ghost that sits on a tall rock on the right bank of the Rhine at Hesse-Nassau.

Bavaria

LAUENSTEIN CASTLE Lauenstein Castle is a picturesque, twelfth-century castle in northern Bavaria that is haunted by the tragic White Lady of Lauenstein. In the fifteenth century, the master of the castle, Otto von Orlanmunde, died in battle, leaving behind his wife and two children. Katharina von Orlanmunde was still a young and vivacious woman, and she soon fell madly in love with a handsome nobleman by the name of Albrecht of Nurnberg. For some reason, she was convinced he was not attracted to her because of her children, so she decided to do something about that. One day, alone in the castle, she took a long, sharp needle and pressed it deep into the back of the head of each child, holding it tightly as it convulsed and died in her arms. With the pinprick barely visible, no one suspected foul play, and the children were buried in the nunnery graveyard at Himmelkorn. Before long, the woman was overcome with guilt and entered the nunnery herself, after giving up all her possessions. But her haunted soul never forgot the deed, and her sad apparition haunts the castle in the early evening hours. She is most often observed on the stone stairway leading to the main tower.

SCHLOSS ALTEBAR A well-heeled German ghost appears to descendents of Count Johannes Rathenau, an Austrian noble who slaughtered the defenders of Schloss Altebar in Bavaria during the Middle Ages and set up his home there. To this day, the Baroness Russlein von Altebar seeks her revenge, first appearing as a beautiful courtesan then turning into a rotting corpse. In Vienna, she boarded the cab of Walther Rathenau, who died of fright. Major Helmut Rathenau met her in a casino in Baden Baden and died of a heart attack.

Berlin

WHITE LADY OF THE HOHENZOLLERNS The noble "Ahn Frau" or "White Lady of the Hohenzollerns" is one of the world's most mobile ghosts. She has appeared in castles all over Europe, including Neuhaus, Bechin, Tretzen, Raumleau, Trebon, Krumlov, Hradce, and the Royal Palace in Berlin. She is seen in gardens among lilac bushes, floating down palace corridors, and even on the streets, dressed all in white with a hood over her head. The White Lady is thought to be a fifteenth-century princess, Perchta von Rosenberg, who haunts the descendents of her cruel husband and has been seen many, many times over the centuries. It is said that if she wears white gloves, a female family member is about to die; if she wears black gloves, a male member will soon perish.

In 1604, she appeared wearing black gloves at the castle of Jindrichuv Hradce in Bohemia, and actually told a priest to prepare last rites for prince Jachym. When the priest checked on the sleeping prince, he found him dying of a sudden illness. In 1619, she appeared again wearing black gloves in the palace of ruler John Sigismund, and the next day he died. In 1740, she appeared to a whole palace of guests in Berlin to announce the impending death of Prince Frederick I. In 1806, she appeared a few days before Prince Louis of Prussia was killed in battle fighting against Napoleon. In 1914, the White Lady showed up a week before Archduke Francis Ferdinand was assassinated. In the 1920s, she appeared repeatedly in Berlin to foretell the fall of the Kaiser. More recently, in Munich, descendent Carl Heinz Rathenau was "turned into a mummy" after meeting the come-hither ghost on the street.

Koblenz

SCHLOSS REICHENSTEIN Schloss Reichenstein is an eleventh-century castle on the Rhine River between the towns of Bingen and Koblenz. A two-mile-long road leads up to the castle from the hamlet of Trechtingshausen. The castle was the headquarters for a band of robber knights in the late thirteenth century. When they were finally caught and brought to justice by Emperor Rudolf von Habsburg in 1282, their leader, Dietrich von Hohenfels, begged the Emperor to take his life but spare the lives of his nine sons, who had assisted their father in his illegal rampages. The Emperor decided to leave the matter in "God's hands." The criminals were brought to a clearing just below the castle and lined up in a row, where the St. Clement Chapel now stands. Then the Emperor told Dietrich that he was going to behead him, but every one of his sons that he could run past after being beheaded would be spared. With his sons lined up before him, the executioner severed Dietrich's head with one mighty blow of the sword. Dietrich's head rolled to the ground, but his bloodied torso stood erect and lunged forward, stumbling and swaying, until it passed every one of his sons. Finally, the headless body fell to its knees, a fountain of blood shooting high into the air where his head had been. Several witnesses fainted and all present beseeched the Emperor to keep his word, which he did.

In an act of repentance, the von Hohenfels family erected the St. Clement Chapel on the spot where the bizarre execution took place, and sometimes, inside the chapel, Dietrich von Hohenfels's headless apparition can be seen repeating his grotesque run to save his sons. Dietrich is buried on the property, and his red sandstone marker depicts a knight in armor with no head. The outer castle has a hotel and restaurants, and a museum. For more information, visit the Schloss Reichenstein Web site at www.caltim.com/reichenstein. Hotel Burg Reichenstein, Im Burgweg 25, Trechtingshausen am Rhein, D-55413 Germany. Phone: 011-49-6721-6101. Fax: 0011-49-6721-6198.

Munich

DACHAU CONCENTRATION CAMP This former concentration camp is located twelve miles (sixteen kilometers) north of Munich outside the town of Dachau. Built in 1933, it was the first Nazi concentration camp and also the site of gruesome medical experiments performed on unwilling prisoners. The experiments measured the effects on the human body of starvation, drinking seawater, malaria, freezing, electricity, and sudden changes in atmospheric pressure. Seven of Dachau's "doctors" were sentenced to death at the Nuremberg trials. In all, more than two hundred thousand prisoners entered Dachau and between thirty thousand and fifty thousand of them died

Dachau Ghost in Showers, Bavaria, Germany (Dave Goodwin)

there. By 1940, disposal of dead bodies became a major problem and a crematorium was built on the grounds. By 1942, mass exterminations were taking place on a daily basis and a larger "more efficient" oven had to be added.

In 1943, still another crematorium was built that incorporated a homicidal gas chamber disguised as a large meeting room. It was located in a housing area referred to as "Barracks X" in the Nazi records. Prisoners would be led into the room for a meeting, then the room was sealed and poisonous gas introduced. There were four other gas chambers at Dachau, some of which were connected directly to shower stalls. German historians insist these were used for disinfectant purposes, but the paranormal evidence seems to contradict these claims. Several reports of disembodied screaming, voices shouting "gas," and naked running apparitions originate from these shower stalls. During a recent visit to Dachau, American tourist Dave Goodwin took a photograph in the shower area that appears to show a ghostly figure running out of the showers.

Regensburg

SCHWARZENBERG FORTRESS Schwarzenberg Fortress is a medieval castle located in Bavaria on a hill northeast of the city of Regensburg and not far from the border of the Czech Republic. Built in 1300, the castle was destroyed in 1415 by Catholic armies and again in 1634 by invading Swedish forces. Today the site is abandoned, although the formidable towers, walls, and great halls still survive. The violent ghosts of marauders and robber barons, who made the ancient ruin their headquarters in the sixteenth century, as well as a few lingering Swedish ghosts from the seventeenth century, are still seen here. The most benevolent presence to have moved into the abandoned castle, however, is "Rotmantel" ("Redcoat"), a reddish apparition full of life and energy that psychics say was originally a mountain sprite or elemental spirit of nature. To reach the site by train, take the Schwandorf-Furth line and get off at Newbau.

WOLFSEGG FORTRESS Wolfsegg Fortress is a privately owned castle located not far from the Danube River outside Regensburg in the province of Upper Palatinate in Bavaria. Built in 1028, Wolfsegg is a formidable structure that has never fallen to enemies in its long history. The castle was in the Wittelsbach dynasty for centuries and is now owned by George Rauchenberger, who is restoring it. Wolfsegg is plagued by unexplainable noises such as disembodied footsteps and voices, and a glowing apparition known as the White Lady is sometimes seen in the courtyard and inside the castle. She is a former baroness, who became a pawn in a plot to gain ownership of the castle. In the fourteenth century, a group of covetous relatives arranged to have a man seduce the woman and then informed her husband of their rendezvous. When the husband discovered them making love, he killed them both. Then, in true medieval justice, the family of the woman murdered the husband, and the property was inherited by the man's relatives. Investigator Hans Holzer and medium Edith Reidl visited the castle and held a séance during which time they successfully contacted the White Lady, who they say is still trying to prove her innocence and expose the plot.

Rosenheim

KONIGSTRASSE 13 One of the most famous poltergeist cases on record started in November 1967 in the law offices of Sigmund Adam at Konigstrasse 13 in Rosenheim, Bavaria. The problems started when the telephones began dialing themselves and placing calls, and the law firm was billed for nearly six hundred calls that no human ever made. All the calls were to the recorded time phone number. Then, for no apparent reason, lightbulbs started exploding in their sockets, fluorescent tubes twisted in their fixtures and went out, pictures spun 360 degrees on the wall, chandeliers moved to impossible angles, pages were torn from a calendar by an unseen hand, drawers popped out and had to be wedged shut, and a four hundred-pound cabinet moved over a foot with no one around. Over forty witnesses observed the phenomena. Many experts were called in, but no one could figure out what was going on, although a few parapsychologists suggested that the paranormal activity emanated from Adam's intern lawyer, eighteen-year-old Annemarie Schneider.

Recording devices monitoring electromagnetic activity were normal when Annemarie was not in the building, but soared off the charts when she reported for work in the morning. According to a psychologist who interviewed her, the teenager suffered from "frustrated rage" and hated having to spend her day in the office. The ghostly phone calls to find out the current time were projected from her unconscious desire to know how much time she had left at work. When Adams fired the girl, the phenomena stopped, although the poltergeist had already done over 15,000 DM in damage to the office. Outbreaks of poltergeist activity seemed to follow the girl from job to job for the next several years.

One of the experts allowed into the law office was Viennese magician and debunker Alwin Neumann, who pretended to be a professor at the University of Vienna who was studying paranormal phenomena. Neumann ended up writing a chapter on the case in a book called *Faked Spooks and Genuine Swindlers* (Zsolnay Verlag, Vienna, 1969) that accused Adams of somehow faking the phenomena. In 1969, Adams went to the district court in Traunstein to stop distribution of Neumann's book and the defamation on his character. In his defense he assembled an impressive list of respected scientists, parapsychologists, and eyewitnesses, who all attested to the genuineness of the poltergeist activity. They all concurred with the findings of Dr. Hans Bender, of Freiburg University, who concluded that this was the "first case of scientifically-authenticated psychokinesis." Amazingly, the judge agreed that the office was haunted and that Adams had not hoaxed anything. He issued an injunction against the book, which was published with the offending remarks against Adams deleted.

Saxony

FALKENSTEIN CASTLE There is a huge, ornately carved bed in Falkenstein Castle that is so haunted it has to be kept in a sealed room. The twelfth-century castle is located in the Harz Mountains in the Saxony-Anhalt region of Germany and is well known for its haunted bed. The case has been investigated by numerous researchers from Harry Price (see Borley Rectory, Essex, Great Britain) to English ghost photographer Simon Marsden. It is thought that the ghost is a member of the von Asseburg family, who bought the castle in the mid-1400s and still holds the deed to the property. The door to the windowless Haunted Room had been kept locked for many centuries and no one remembered why.

Then, in 1839, workmen removed the door. Inside a hollow section of wall, they found the skeleton of woman still wearing the tattered remains of a dress. The bones were buried in Pansfelde Cemetery, but the new earl of Asseburg ordered the room sealed again. Finally, in 1945, occupying American soldiers broke through the door. According to official reports, they found a deserted bedroom with intricately carved furniture and a large butcher's hook hanging on a chain from a ceiling beam. Today, the castle is a national museum and the Haunted Room is open for all to see. And the mysterious ghost is free to roam the entire castle.

SCHLOSS MORITZBURG Schloss Moritzburg, in the Moritz-Dentel Forest near Dresden in Saxony, was built as a nobleman's hunting lodge around 1700. By 1750, the castle came into the possession of Count Ugo von Dentel and his wife Countess Elsa von Karman-Liechtenstein. Their marriage was an unhappy one, and when his wife could bear him no heirs, the count could see no reason to continue it. On October 19, 1756, he arranged for his wife to accompany him on a boar hunt in the nearby woods, where he strangled her and left her body to be fought over by wild boars and hunting hounds. When her mangled corpse was brought to the castle, he feigned disbelief and grief.

Soon the appalling apparition of his wife, with a shredded face and dripping in blood, began appearing at his bedside pleading for her life. Almost every night she appeared, and always, she left a trail of blood from his bedroom, down the hall and stairway, out the door, and off along the Western Corridor to the spot in the forest where she was murdered. The count finally took his own life by stabbing himself in the heart as he lay in bed one night. But the gory apparition still returns and has been seen many times over the years. And very often, on the morning of October 20, the staff at Schloss Moritzburg discovers a mysterious trail of blood leading to the upstairs bedroom.

Thuringa

ROTHENBERG CASTLE The ruins of Rothenberg Castle near the village of Kelbra in Thuringa, Germany, have been haunted for centuries by the phantom of a man in a long, dark cloak accompanied by a large, black hound. The lifelike apparition of a former countess of Rothenberg has been reported in the forest below the castle. Once the ghost approached an elderly woman in the woods and asked her if she had seen the cloaked man's phantom, and if she had, to ask him how much longer she had to wander the property as a spirit.

The phantom is blamed for at least one death. One wintery morning in the nineteenth century, a local man was found hanging from a tower window. Below the body in the snow were the footprints of a man's hobnailed boot and the paw prints of a large dog. Even today, locals avoid the castle, and visitors report seeing terrifying apparitions at the site.

Westphalia

SCHLOSS SCHWARZENRABEN Schloss Schwarzenraben is an eighteenth-century Baroque palace in Westphalia, Germany. Because it is surrounded by a moat, most people consider it a castle, although it was never really meant to be used as a fortress. The ghost here is the Blue Lady, the melancholy spirit of Maria Anna von Horde, a resident of the palace who lived here with her husband at the turn of the seventeenth century. It is known that she was a very religious woman trapped in an unhappy marriage. The apparition was first reported in the 1850s in the front entry, but it has also been seen in the salon, a gallery, and on the main staircase. The apparition is readily identifiable as Maria from a portrait hanging in the den. She hovers a few inches above the floor and seems to be imploring people to pray for her. As soon as they begin praying or acknowledge the request, the apparition disappears. The ghost developed a singular relationship with a Jesuit priest and is said to have met daily with him in a room adjoining the chapel. However, in 1928, Maria actually attacked another priest who took down her portrait and placed it under his bed, insisting that he would be able to exorcize her ghost in a single day. The priest admitted that Maria materialized sitting on his chest around 3:00 A.M. and start strangling him. The ghost did not stop until he promised to put her portrait back and leave the palace.

GREECE

Greece was settled very early in human history, sometime in the Paleolithic era. Invasions from all directions started around 2000 B.C., and the land was divided up into city-states that often fought one another. Greece was conquered by Rome in 146 B.C., and later became a pawn in the Crusades between Christian and Islam forces. It gained independence from Turkey after a war that ended in 1829. The Greeks set up a monarchy whose powers were drastically curtailed after a coup d'etat in 1967, and the monarchy was finally abolished in 1974.

Mount Olympus

MYTIKAS PEAK Do the gods still walk on Mount Olympus? Many modern visitors to the primordial mountain have experienced the presence of the otherworldly guide Hermes, felt the lustful spirit of Aphrodite, or encountered the bloodthirsty, warrior phantom of Ares. Others sense Zeus himself, the supreme god of mind and consciousness, presiding over the high, windswept landscape. Though Mount Olympus is the tallest mountain in Greece, it is only a moderately difficult hike to the top. The highest and most haunted spot on the mountain is the Mytikas Peak at 2,917 meters (9,570 feet). It is located in northern Greece, about one hundred kilometers (62 miles) southwest of the city of Thessaloniki.

Mount Parnassus

KASSOTIS SPRING Regularly, since 1500 B.C., otherworldly spirits have been contacted at a sacred spot on the side of Mount Parnassus in Greece. The site was originally dedicated to the earth goddess Gaia and named after "Pytho," a great serpent (representing the life force) that protected the spot. The apparitions of three women have been seen at the Kassotis Spring, in which female seers bathed before making contact with the oracle goddess. Traditionally, the three spirits of Kassotis are the three of the Muses, said to inspire men with creative energy.

The spot where the spirits speak was marked by a large stone known as the Omphalos (or Navel Stone), which the ancients considered the center of the world. According to mythology, the conical stone was placed at the exact spot where the sun god Apollo slew Pytho and set up his own temple. Apollo took the form of a dolphin to recruit priests, and his temple became known as "Delphi," from the Greek word for dolphin. The Greeks built the Tholos Temple at the site and dedicated it to Athena, goddess of spiritual wisdom. The oracular tradition continued at Delphi for over one thousand years, until it was discontinued by Christian reformers in the fourth century. Delphi is located on Mount Parnassus, which is 160 kilometers northwest of Athens overlooking the Gulf of Corinth.

Patmos

HORA In an ancient cave on the small Greek island of Patmos, there is a small hole in the rock wall that is considered a direct link to the Other Side and source of divine revelation. The island was first settled in 500 B.C., and a temple honoring the goddess Diana was built there, but during the Roman Empire, the island was used to house political prisoners. In A.D. 95, St. John was exiled here and lived in a small cave just below the old temple. From a fissure in the wall, he heard a voice that described the course of future events, and he recorded the information in his book of Revelations. John also wrote the Fourth Gospel while living in the cave.

The temple to Diana was destroyed in the fourth century by Christians, who built a church on the same location that was later destroyed by invading Islamic armies. Finally, a monastery was built there in 1088 and the town of Hora grew up around it. The cave turned into a chapel known as the Holy Grotto of the Revelation, which is open for visiting.

HUNGARY

The origins of Hungary lie with the Magyars in the ninth century A.D. They ruled until 1301, when the Arpad dynasty ended and the crown passed to rulers of various European countries. It became a Soviet republic in 1919, with the People's Republic of Hungary established in 1949. Hungary became an independent republic in 1989.

Bucharest

HEIDENREICH HOUSE The Heidenreich House in Bucharest has been haunted by the ghoul Bassarab for decades. Bassarab was the sole survivor of the dynasty of Walachia, which is now a province in Romania. The Vlach ruler was said to have used occult means to secure power and also to survive death.

Debrecen

PUSZTA PLAIN The ghost of Ivar Kiraly haunts the Puszta Plain in the Hortobagy region near Debrecen. The boy has been seen riding his horse along the horizon by hundreds of people over the years. A newly enlisted teenager in the Italian Army, Ivan was wounded in 1915 at the Battle of Trentino. During his convalescence at his home in Debrecen, he sought to forget the horrors of war by staring out over the great Puszta Plain. Soon, he became obsessed with the "better world" within the distant mirages rising in the dust and heat in the distance.

One day, he suddenly rose from his cot, mounted his older brother's horse, and road off into the setting sun in search of the mirages. He was never seen again, but his spirit returned as the "Mirage Chaser," the ghostly rider in search of a more perfect world at the borderline between real and unreal. Peddlers, travelers, and others crossing the Puszta Plain, not knowing the story, reported seeing the apparition of a bare-legged boy riding a gray stallion, and a separate legend of the "Golden Horseman" grew. Only recently has it been realized that they are the same apparition.

ITALY

The seat of the Roman Empire, Italy ruled most of the known world. The Empire died after barbarian (German and Ostrogoth) invasions in the fourth and fifth centuries. The independent Vatican state became the political ruler of Italy and seat of the Holy Roman Empire in A.D. 962. Italy was divided by Austrian and French rule in the sixteen century and was not reunited into one country until a popular revolution in the nineteenth century. Italy fought on the side of the Allied powers in World War I and on the side of the Axis powers in World War II. It became a republic in 1947.

Bolzano

ROVINA CASTLE Rovina Castle in the Italian Tyrol south of Bolzano is haunted by an unidentified presence that has only manifested as a pale white hand that emerges from the stone walls to grab at people. Other effects associated with the mysterious presence include icy, moving cold spots, and the sounds of footsteps when no one is around. For obvious reasons, the owners of the present bed-and-breakfast at the castle do not like to talk about their scary, resident ghost. Rovina Castle is near the village of Rovina, Merano, northern Italy.

Italian Alps

BRIXEN CASTLE Overlooking the Eisack River, about twenty miles south of the Brenner Pass near the town of Brixen in the Italian Alps, stands a crumbling castle known as the Brixen Ruins. The wooden drawbridge has long since rotted away, and the only entry to the castle is by crossing the icy, swift-flowing river. Those agile enough to find their way into the castle are rewarded for their strenuous efforts by a murderous presence that likes to push people through windows or down stairs. A man's insane laughter is also heard echoing through the empty rooms. It is the earthbound spirit of the evil Count Wolfgang, who was known for his sadistic torturing of innocent people and his use of black magic to defend himself against his enemies. He kidnapped his wife from a nobleman and never returned her after ransom was paid. When he got tired of her, he threw her from the castle tower into the river below. The same fate awaited any woman who wandered near his castle. He kidnapped them, brutally had his

way, then delighted as they pleaded for mercy before he threw them off the tower.

Lake Bracciano

CASTELLO DI BRACCIANO The Castello di Bracciano is a four-towered, medieval fortress near the town of Roccanero on Lake Bracciano. In the 1400s, the castle was ruled by a cunning and ruthless man by the name of Guidobaldo Orsini, who still rules the spectral scene along with his beloved son. Guidobaldo frequently is seen kneeling before the altar in the family crypt or sitting in front of the fireplace in the Main Hall. The one-armed apparition of his son, Attilio, also appears in the Main Hall, as well as in the hallways, bedrooms, and outside walking in the mists along the shore of the lake. He lost his arm in battling against a band of marauders, even though he was wearing a full suit of armor when he left the castle. The robbers mutilated the young man, then threw his body in the lake. His arm was never recovered, but the suit of armor he was wearing was on display in the Main Hall for many years.

Parma

LA ROCCA DI SORAGNA The La Rocca di Soragna, a former palace in the province of Parma in Italy, is haunted by the vengeful presence of Cassandra Marinoni, wife of the Marquis Diofebo di Soragna, who lived there in the sixteenth century. On June 18, 1573, Casandra was murdered along with her sister, Lucrezia, during a burglary at Lucrezia's castle. At least that is what the robbers wanted it to look like. In fact, the plan was hatched by Lucrezia's husband with the full knowledge of Diofebo. With both sisters out of the way, Lucrezia's husband would inherit a sizable fortune and split it with Diofebo. Almost immediately after her death, Cassandra's apparition, wearing a red dress, started terrorizing Diofebo and continued to harass all his descendents up to the present day. She is most often seen in the Hercules Room but is also known to appear in the galleries, bedrooms, and loggias. She also likes to celebrate the approaching death of a Soragna family member with a cacophony of noise, which sounds as if every piece of furniture in the palace is bouncing up and down on the floors.

Piedmont Mountains

DAMANHUR The underground city of Damanhur in the foothills of the Piedmont Mountains in northern Italy is full of occult energies and refined spiritual essences. Visitors return convinced of the power of spiritual forces and speak of otherworldly energies that are being mishandled by our misguided contemporary society. Located thirty meters underground near the city of Turin and the town of Baldissero Canavavese, Damanhur is a community of modern Hermeticists who seek to apply the ancient principles of alchemy to the transformation of individuals and society. Funded by a three hundred-member Council of Elders that consists of some of Italy's richest families, the grandiose, gold and marble city-state stresses individual freedom and determination. Children are taught to use both masculine intellect and feminine intuition in relating to the world, and the quality of individual consciousness is considered more important than family or national traditions. The city consists of five domed temples that represent the alchemical elements (Earth, Air, Fire, Water, and the Quintessence) in terms of light. For example, the Temple of Air is surrounded in mirrors and covered with illustrations depicting outer space and the cosmos, and the Temple of Earth contains the largest stained glass image ever created. The city-state was founded in 1975 by Oberto Airuldi and has its own coinage and government. Permission must be obtained before visiting the underground temples, although no outsider is permitted in the Temple of the Quintessence.

Rome

CATACOMBS Rome is very proud of its twenty-five miles of modern subways, but hidden ten to eighty feet beneath the city are over 120 miles of haunted catacombs. The first catacombs were built in the second century A.D. to hide the burial vaults of Christian saints from Roman desecration. Other Christians wanted to be buried with the saints, and by the fifth century, there were sixty-six separate catacombs containing thousands of bodies. Most of the bodies were simply stuffed into rectangular holes dug out of the walls. Tourists and guides have encountered many ghostly figures wandering in the tunnels, many of them early Christian souls, though six of the catacombs contain the bodies of Jews.

Catacombs Ghost, Rome, Italy (LJJ/Madison Ghost Club)

COLISEUM Rome, the eternal city, has its share of eternal residents, and the census of ghosts here is one of the highest in all of Europe. By sheer number, the ghosts of gladiators, soldiers, and spectators at the Coliseum make it the most haunted spot in the city. Tourists and workers there have been seeing their apparitions for centuries, and the aura of this place is one of brutality and voyeurism. As many as eighty thousand people showed up here to watch men slaughter each other and innocent animals. Just during opening ceremonies in A.D. 80, over five thousand terrified lions, bears, and other wild animals were killed in the arena. In the "games" held by Emperor Trajan, nine thousand gladiators fought to their

Coliseum, Rome, Italy (Ginger Hauck)

deaths in 117 days. (The Coliseum is at the end of the Via dei Fiori Imperiale in Rome.)

PANTHEON Strange balls of blue light and the apparitions of pagan priests have been seen in the Pantheon in Rome. It was built by the Emperor Hadrian in the first half of the first century A.D. as a temple dedicated to the "pantheon," the twelve most important pagan gods. There is a round hole in the roof of the temple that was intended to link the archetypal forces "above" with the world of mortals "below."

SANTA MARIO DEL POPOLO CHURCH The spot where Santa Maria del Popolo Church in Rome now stands was haunted for many centuries by the evil ghost of Emperor Nero. Nero committed suicide in A.D. 68 at that location and was buried there. After his death a great oak tree grew up from his grave and attracted his spirit back to the realm of the living. His menacing apparition was seen so many times and scared so many people, that a petition was drawn up in 1099 to beseech Pope Padschal II to exorcise the emperor's ghost.

The pope went into a period of fasting and prayer, during which time the Virgin Mary appeared and told him how to dispense with Nero's ghost. The walnut was cut down and his bones dug up; both were burned and thrown into the Tiber River. After that Nero's apparition was never seen again. To commemorate the victory, a chapel was built over Nero's former resting place. In 1472, the more majestic Santa Maria del Popolo Church was built. Bas-relief sculptures on the church ceiling retell the story of the exorcism of Nero's ghost.

TITUS LIVIUS The world's first paranormal researcher was Titus Livius, an ancient Roman who dedicated himself to "separating fact from fiction" and wrote 142 books objectively chronicling unexplainable events, as well as more mundane happenings, in the history of Rome. He described spontaneous human combustion, mind over matter, apparitions, channeling of spirits, bizarre things falling from the sky, UFO sightings, and cattle mutilations long before *The X-Files* came along.

According to Livius, paranormal happenings have surrounded the Roman rulers for over thirteen centuries. Rome's very first ruler, Romulus, disappeared into thin air when a strange storm cloud came out of nowhere and took him away. He was reviewing his troops on the Campus Martius at the time, and over three hundred witnesses told the same story of his abduction by the mysterious cloud. Another Roman ruler, Servius Tullius, became head of Rome because he was able to produce a variety of poltergeist effects. Servius was a homeless boy taken in by the Queen of Corniculum in 600 B.C. One day while he was sleeping, his head suddenly erupted in flames, and servants were rushing to fetch water to put out the spontaneous fire. But the queen intervened and ordered that the boy should be allowed to awaken on his own before anyone threw water on him. As soon as he awoke, the flames dispersed and left no trace of fire. The queen considered this a sign of divinity and the boy was raised as a prince.

Turin

CATHEDRAL OF TURIN Sealed in a roll of red silk on an altar in the Cathedral of Turin is a linen burial cloth measuring 3 ½ by 14 feet that carries the image of a naked man with the marks of being crucified. According to tradition, this is the burial cloth of Jesus Christ. It is the image itself that is of interest to ghost researchers, for it represents a manifestation of a type of radiant energy that is often associated with apparitions. The cloth carries a negative three-dimensional image made by the projection of intense light. The image becomes positive (or normal) only when photographed. The history of the shroud is known back to 1357, and scientific techniques place the origin of the shroud as possibly sometime before A.D. 800. However, researchers at Hebrew University and the Israeli Antiquities Department have analyzed the shroud's fabric and discovered several types of pollen from plants that are unique to the Jerusalem area and pollinate only in the months of March and April, the time frame in which Jesus was crucified. Today, many people consider this controversial religious artifact direct evidence of the survival of spirit through the projection of a body of light energy after death.

It is indeed an inspiring image to behold, and just being in the presence of the cloth has been credited with healing powers. The best documented case was Josephine Woollam, a ten-year-old English girl who was dying of a severe bone disease in 1955. Unable to walk, Josephine became convinced that if she could just see the shroud close up, she would be healed. After gaining the permission of King Umberto, former king of Italy and official owner of the shroud, Josephine was taken to Turin to view the artifact. Within a few days, she was completely cured and doctors could offer no explanation. In 1978, the shroud was put on public display for a short time and private viewings were arranged for sick and handicapped people, many of whom also reported miraculous cures.

Umbria

ASSISI Assisi was considered a sacred site for nearly nine centuries before the founding of Rome. An ancient settlement grew up around a healing spring in the Umbria hills, and in the first century B.C., a temple to the Roman goddess of wisdom (Minerva) was build here. The Catholic Church appropriated the temple in the twelfth century and turned it into a commune. St. Francis was born in the town in 1182, and the Basilica de San Francesco (Basilica of St. Francis) was built on the former temple in 1228.

St. Francis was born to a rich family, but repudiated all worldly connections at the age of nineteen and became a Christian mystic. In 1210, he founded the Franciscan Order of Friars, which gained a large following throughout the world for its humility, vows of poverty, and love of nature. St. Francis's apparition is seen infrequently here, usually in the forested area below the basilica. But it is his profound spirit that everyone senses. "The entire town and more particularly the Basilica," said explorer of sacred sites Martin Gray, "have a most definite atmosphere of peacefulness which awakens and stimulates that same characteristic in the human heart. In this regard, it is perhaps more fitting to call such sacred sites empowerment sites." Assisi is located about ninety miles north of Rome.

Vatican

ST. PETER'S BASILICA Some of the ghosts at Vatican date from before the Papal City even existed. In the first century A.D., the one hundred-acre site was where emperors Caligula and Nero tortured and executed undesirables and troublemakers, and their tortured souls still haunt the grounds. Among those victims was Saint Peter, who is buried here in St. Peter's Basilica. That is why the

St. Peter's Basilica, Vatican City, Italy (Ginger Hauck)

location was holy to early Christians and why they built the first Christian basilica in Europe (St. John Lateran) here. The Vatican grew up around the basilica and eventually became a whole separate country right in the middle of the bustling city of Rome.

Across from St. John Lateran, the Pope's Chapel contains the *Scala Santa* (Holy Stairs), on which the presence of Jesus himself is sensed. The stairs came from the home of Pontius Pilate, and Jesus is believed to have walked on them before his trial in Jerusalem. In deference, Christians ascend the twenty-eight stairs on their knees.

Venice

BRIDGE OF SIGHS The Ponte dei Sospiri or "Bridge of Sighs" spans a narrow channel known

Bridge of Sighs, Venice, Italy (Pam Heath)

as Rio di Palazzo in Venice, Italy. For many decades, witnesses have reported hearing disembodied voices, groans, and sighs in the area of the ornate enclosed walkway. Built in 1600 by the architect Antonio Contino, the passageway at one time connected the Doge's Palace to the prisons, and it is thought the unexplainable voices originate from that era.

MALTA

Malta is an independent country consisting of three islands in the Peloponnean chain off Sicily in the Mediterranean. It has a long and ancient history, having been settled by the Phoenicians in prehistory. It was conquered by Rome in 218 B.C., and in 1530, Holy Roman Emperor Charles V gave it to the Knights of Malta. The islands were later conquered by Napoleon and the British. It became a republic within the British Commonwealth in 1974.

Birkirkana

ADDOLORATA CEMETERY The ghost of a bewildered man with black holes where his eyes should be haunts this cemetery and often leaves it to appear on the street. Sometimes he even materializes in passing cars. Recently, a taxi driver returning from the airport late one night was shocked to

Addolorata Cemetery Chapel, Birkirkana, Malta (Raymond Finch)

find the unidentified man in the back of his cab. When he saw the two glaring black holes in the man's face, the driver screeched to a halt and ran from the cab. His frightening passenger followed him for some distance, and then disappeared through the locked front gates of the cemetery. The driver just knelt down by the curb until passing cars stopped to assist him. He had to be hospitalized and was treated for shock.

Russian Cultural Centre The ghost of a knight haunts the Russian Cultural Centre here. The spectral manifestations that workers at the center complained about consisted of the sounds of mysterious parties or ceremonies, banging sounds, black scratches on a wall that could not be covered or removed, and sudden, unexplainable gusts of spectral wind that feel as if someone is blowing on your face. The manifestations started in 1993, when staffers heard noises that sounded as though there were people partying in the building. The noises of cutlery being moved, footsteps, and murmured voices, could be heard when nobody was there. Even some of the neighbors started complaining about the late night parties. The scratch marks are on a wall that is the only part of the original house that is still standing. Scratches seem to keep appearing on the wall no matter how many times it is cleaned or repainted.

According to investigators, the ghost behind these strange happenings is Sir Oliver Starkey, a sixteenth-century English Knight who was the Latin secretary of Grand Master Jean de La Valette of the Sovereign Military Order of St. John (the Knights of Malta). The Russian Cultural Centre was formerly the home of Sir Oliver, who died in Malta in March 1588 at the age of sixty-five. He was the only Knight who was not a grand master to be buried in St. John's Cathedral, which is just a block away from the Russian Cultural Centre. Starkey was a close friend of La Valette, who is a national hero who defeated the Turkish Armada of Suliman in 1565.

According to Sir Oliver's will, which was found in the National Archives some time ago, he had left money for Catholic masses to be said for the repose of his soul. His final request was never realized, however, and that is the reason his spirit is tied to his former dwelling. The staff at the center arranged for masses to be said for the soul of Sir Oliver once every three months. After the first few masses were celebrated, the manifestations decreased in intensity, although they have not stopped entirely.

Sliema

ACHILLI MANSION Sliema is a seaside town that has become one of Malta's most popular shopping districts. Accordingly, many older buildings are being replaced by commercial structures. One of the old mansions that has survived this trend is a monastic mansion that was the headquarters for a religious sect in the nineteenth century, the Achilli Mansion. The leader of the group was a defrocked Italian priest by the name of Dott Achilli. Achilli did everything in his power to convert Maltese citizens to his own brand of Protestantism, including paying them money to attend services.

Although his mission to convert island residents failed, his ghost has not given up trying. He still walks his former residence and headquarters, scheming for ways of reaching the masses, and his presence is felt still waiting patiently in the courtyard to begin his lectures. Some say that the soul of Dott Achilli cannot rest due to the fact that he renounced his priesthood in the Roman Catholic Church.

VERDALA CASTLE Verdala Castle was built by French Grand Master HuguesLourbenx de Verdalle in 1585. The castle bears the Latin motto *Cedantcurae Loco*, which means, "let your worries surrender to this place." It is indeed a beautiful place in which to relax and center oneself. The castle is surrounded by the Buskett Gardens, the only forest-like gardens in Malta. Throughout the centuries, Verdala has served as the official residence for many rulers of Malta, as well as foreign dignitaries visiting the island. There is another guest who is always at home in the castle, for the Blue Lady of Verdala has been haunting the place for centuries.

The Blue Lady was thought to be the young

niece of Grand Master De Rohan. The elderly man offered her his love but she rejected him. In return, he kept her a prisoner in his castle, to prevent her ever falling in love with anyone else. One afternoon, the desperate girl tried to escape through one of the windows in her room and fell to her death. Since then, she has haunted the castle in the same blue gown she wore on the day of her death. Many visitors to the castle see her apparition trying to scale the walls and falling to the hard ground below. However, she always vanishes before she hits the ground. Sightings of her ghost increased at the beginning of the twentieth century and have peaked in recent years.

Valletta

ST. URSOLA STREET Valletta, the beautiful capital city of Malta, was built as a fortification on Sceberras Hill and is full of palaces and lovely homes. One of these outstanding homes is on St. Ursola Street and known locally as the "House of a Thousand Steps" because of the long stairway leading to its entrance. The young wife of the first owner died in a tragic accident, and not long afterwards, her apparition started appearing in the house. Sometimes her apparition manifested as a faintly glowing figure, while other times it was indistinguishable from a human being. The house gained a reputation for being haunted and sat abandoned for many years.

During World War II, two naval officers were walking down to the harbor on St. Ursola Street when they were approached by a beautiful young lady, who asked for their help. She had been locked out of her house and no one was home, and she wondered if they would help her get back in. There was a half-open window on the second floor, and one of the officers scurried up the trellis and into the house. Inside, the home was richly decorated with oil paintings and priceless antiques everywhere. When he opened the front door to let the woman in, he deliberately left his cigarette lighter behind so he would have an excuse to return the next day and learn more about the beautiful yet mysterious lady. When he returned, however, he found the house was not the same as

it had appeared the previous night. It was in near-ruin and looked as if it had been abandoned for years. Unable to believe his eyes, he went up to the second-floor window, which was still half open, and let himself in. The inside of the house was covered in cobwebs and most of the furniture was missing. But on a ledge in the entryway, he found the cigarette case he had left there the night before.

Marsamxett Harbor

PARISH CHURCH The small church in a tiny village on the north shore of Marsamxett Harbor is haunted by a former parish priest named Father Charles. The church was used mostly by the locality's fishermen and hunters, and for their convenience, the first mass was celebrated every morning at 5 A.M. for their convenience. Father Charles was an extremely conscientious person and he had promised to perform a large number of masses but had died before he could perform them. For many years, his apparition was seen at the altar saying one mass per night.

When the new priest, Father Simon was assigned to the parish, he immediately ran into problems. From the beginning, someone was getting into his personal belongings in the cupboard of the sacristy and rifling through them. He was certain it was the caretaker, and the two got into many arguments over who was responsible for leaving his things in such disarray. Finally, the priest changed the lock and kept the only keys, but still the invisible intruder managed to get into the priest's things. More determined than ever, the priest started spending the entire night in the church. Then, one night at 3:00 A.M., he saw a priest emerge from the sacristy and go to the altar, where he began holding mass. Father Simon followed the priest back into the sacristy after the mass, but when he opened the door, no one was there but the cupboard had again been opened.

Seeking to find the mysterious priest, Father Simon gave his description to several people who told him it fit Father Charles, the parish priest who had died of a heart attack two years earlier. Father Simon confronted the apparition again and pledged to say all the remaining masses, plus an extra mass for Father Charles too. Once that was accomplished the apparition of Father Charles was never seen again.

NETHERLANDS (HOLLAND)

The Netherlands were settled by Paleolithic peoples and strongly influenced by the Celts, Germans, Spaniards, and Romans. After a revolt that started in 1581 and lasted eighty years, the Netherlands united themselves into a union of states and won independence from Spain. Under Napoleon, it became part of the French Empire in 1794. It became the Kingdom of Holland in 1806. Today, the most haunted area of the country is the Friesland, a northern province along the Waddenzee Inlet.

Friesland

FRIESLAND CANALS Ghosts are sighted along many of the canals that crisscross Friesland. The Sminkevaart Canal is well known for its many ghostly sightings. The most frequently reported apparition is the White Lady, a friendly spirit that comes up from behind and walks alongside startled witnesses. She also is seen walking along the De Neurde path between Wyckel and the town of Sondel. A married couple walking there said the White Lady emerged from some bushes and then fell in line with them and accompanied them for some distance. Another witness on the same path said he was accosted by a misty presence that sidled up to him, and then suddenly pushed him into some shrubbery. It is probable he encountered a less sociable apparition dubbed the Black Lady that also haunts De Neurde, as well as other areas around the town of Sondel and in the forests near Nijemirdum.

GASSTERLAND Gassterland is widely considered the Netherland's most haunted area. A sandy plateau located in north Netherlands in the province of Friesland, Gassterland has a long history of hauntings. Many of the stone farmhouses here are centuries old or built on top of former manor houses that go back to feudal times. At such locations, the ghosts of prisoners and mistreated serfs are still seen. At the former residence of Baron Menno van Coehoorn in the village of Wyckel, the sounds of chains rattling in the darkened dungeon can still be heard, and at Beuckenswijk Manor in the hamlet of Sondel, the same eerie sounds of chains with the screams of tortured prisoners are heard. Residents living at the old manor houses Minnemastate and Titemastate in the town of Harich also report similar manifestations.

SPOKERSWEG The roads of Friesland are especially haunted. The phantom of an old windmill is sometimes seen along the old Spokersweg Road, which goes from the west edge of the town of Harich to the *Witte Brug*. The sightings are sometimes accompanied by the creaking sounds of the nonexistent mill machinery working. The road got its name from the ghostly mill. "Spokersweg" means Ghost Road.

Harich

FARM POLTERGEISTS The farms outside the hamlet of Harich have produced some macabre hauntings. One particular poltergeist was so punctual that it opened doors and turned off the lights at the same time every day, and many witnesses attested to the bewildering activity. An exorcist was called and found the body of a child buried in the cellar of the house. After the child was properly buried, the haunting ceased. When the same thing started happening at another farmhouse, the exorcist promptly started digging up the cellar. He found the bodies of three adult men, and when they were interred in the town cemetery, the haunting stopped there too.

Hemelum

WITTE BURCH In the village of Hemelum, there is an old tree called the *Witte Burch* located near the Gallowspool. This tall tree was the town's hanging tree and many restless souls are seen in its vicinity even today. According to psychics, some of the spirits are still protesting their innocence.

Rijs

RIJS-OUDEMIRDUM ROAD Another haunted Dutch road, which connects the villages of Rijs and Oudemirdum, is haunted by a ghoulish apparition that emerges from a hollow tree alongside the road, as well as a more benevolent ghost known as the White Woman of the Cellars. She has been known to appear to people lost in snow storms to help them find their way. And the three-forked road known as the Boegen is haunted by a poltergeist spirit that likes to play jokes on people who stop there or to farmers who live nearby. The spot is located where the roads to the villages of Oudemirdum, Kippenburg, and Nijemirdum intersect in the province. Sometimes the apparition of a man is seen hiding behind an apple tree or barn; he is thought to be a former farmhand at one of the nearby farms. A paved road behind the village of Nijemirdum is notorious for the strange phantom of a large dog with a ring of keys tied around its neck. The ghostly mongrel follows people for the length of the road, and then disappears.

Ruigahuizen

PARISH CHURCH When the old church and bell tower were torn down at the parish church in the town of Ruigahuizen, the ghosts took over the churchyard cemetery and many sightings were reported, especially in the years immediately following the demolition.

Soesterberg Air Base

MUNITIONS FLIGHT AMMO DUMP The area of this U. S. Air Force base known as the Munitions Flight (or Ammunitions Dump) is a storage area for munitions and heavily guarded by both American and Dutch military police. It is also guarded by ghostly K-9 dogs. The phantoms of three Doberman pincers have been reported several times, and all the witnesses agree that the lead dog has only three legs—and no eyes. In 1995, a guard at the

Bell Tower, Ringhuizien, Netherlands (Jolling Luinenburg)

Munitions Flight gatehouse called in for help, saying that three Dobermans were attacking the guard shack and breaking in. When relief arrived no signs of any dogs could be found, although the guard continued to insist they were there. He was adamant they were Doberman pincers, even though the dogs have been outlawed in Holland for nearly fifty years.

During World War II, a German Luftwaffe pilot died when his plane crashed on the road leading to the secured area. His name was Effy, and his ghost became a permanent fixture at the base, although he spends most of its time walking up and down the road where his plane crashed. However, he never approaches the ammunitions dump or the new constructed gatehouse. Perhaps he too is frightened of the phantom Dobermans.

Just a quarter mile away from this road is a gravesite where the heroic spirits of eight Jewish prisoners from World War II can be felt. They were forced to dig their own graves before being shot by Nazi soldiers. For a long time Queen Beatrice would come to the site in May to commemorate their souls, and many people still come the graves to pay their respects.

POLAND

Slavic tribes in Poland united under a common dynasty in the tenth century. Over the centuries, that alliance has been split asunder by invading Mongols, Swedes, Russians, Austrians, and Germans. It became part of the Soviet Union in 1947 and its own republic in 1991.

Galacia

CHATEAU DE NIEDZICA Chateau de Niedzica is a medieval fortress on the banks of the Dunajac River in the Tartar Mountains of Galicia, Poland. Now a museum run by the state, in the late eighteenth century the chateau was privately owned by the Benesh family. One of the sons, Sebastian became an adventurer who traveled to Peru, married a beautiful Incan woman, and had a daughter, Umira. Their daughter then grew up and married an Incan prince. About that time the Incans revolted against Spanish control and were savagely put down. Sebastian's wife and Umira's husband were both killed by the Spaniards, but Sebastian and Umira escaped to the family estate in Poland.

Unfortunately, Spanish assassins followed them and one day cornered the Incan princess in the courtyard of the chateau and stabbed her to death. They also searched through her belongings but left empty-handed. It was said that Umira carried a map or other information about the whereabouts of the fabled Incan treasure of gold that has yet to be found. Perhaps that is why her ghost returns to Niedzica to this day, to protect the great secret of the Incas. Her apparition appears first as a ball of light from which the figure of the princess emerges.

Warsaw

CENTER STREET A redbrick house with white siding on Center Street in Warsaw is haunted by the phantoms of dolls that seem to come to life and walk around. The dolls belonged to two young girls, who died in a tragic automobile accident. Ever since their deaths, their spirits seem to have taken up residence in their beloved dolls. Now, even when there are no dolls in the house, tenants report seeing them running playfully through the halls. The case is interesting in that it illustrates the plasticity of apparitional phenom-ena, and begs the question: Can ghosts have ghosts?

ROMANIA

Slavic settlers banded together to form early principalities, but they didn't unify as a country until 1861. Most of Romania fought with the Axis powers in World War II, but switched over to Allied forces in 1944. It was occupied by Soviet forces until 1989, when the communist regime was overthrown. The country's first free elections since 1937 were held in 1990. As far as ghostly presences are concerned, the dominant presence in Romania to this day is a Slavic prince from the fifteenth century named Vlad Tepes.

Transylvania

BONTIDA CASTLE Bontida Castle is an abandoned Baroque palace located in Transylvania about fifty miles from the city of Cluj-Napoca. This area of Romania used to be part of Hungary, and the structure was built by the Banffy family of rich Hungarian noblemen. The Nazis burned the palace as a punishment to a member of the Banffy family who disagreed with their philosophy, and it has sat empty ever since. It has a reputation for being haunted by many different presences, and even Gypsies will not take advantage of the shelter of its buildings.

The most frequently reported apparition is a young boy who is seen wandering inside and outside several of the buildings on the estate. He was a stable boy who noticed that one of the daughters of the household often snuck off late at night to rendezvous with a young nobleman at a neighboring castle. When he threatened to tell her father, she seduced the boy, and while they were making love, stabbed him to death. She buried his body near the stable, although no one has yet discovered where.

CORVIN CASTLE Corvin Castle is one of the most magnificent-looking fortresses in all of Europe, but it is suffering a slow death caused by the industrial pollution from factories in the city below it. Even its one hundred-foot deep moat has not protected it from the onslaught of modern civilization. The fourteenth-century castle is located in Hunedoara in the fabled province of Transylvania, and it has many ghosts from its tortured and barbaric past. The Knight's Hall and Main Tower are haunted by the bloodied apparition of a White Lady, who was most recently seen by janitors working late one night in 1990. She was a young lady of a fifteenth-century household who was discovered making love with a servant. Her husband had her dragged, still naked, to the Knight's Hall, where he had her tied to one of the marble pillars and drove a large iron spike into her head. Her skeleton was discovered by workmen beneath the tower stairway. A rusted spike was still wedged into her skull.

In the courtyard, a deep well is haunted by the spirits of Turkish prisoners forced to dig with their bare hands for nine years. After they finally struck water, they were mercilessly thrown from the castle ramparts into the moat. Prisoners were also forced to fight bears and lions in the outdoor amphitheater, and most ended up as animal feed. Over forty human skeletons still remain in the dungeon beneath the Main Tower, and there is also a giant swinging blade used to slowly slice up prisoners tied to a wooden table. But the castle itself has also suffered. The Main Tower was struck by lightning in 1854 and the interior of the castle destroyed in the ensuing fire. It remained abandoned for many years until restoration was begun, although today, manmade pollution is accelerating its relentless deterioration.

Wallachia

TIRGOVISTE One of the cruelest men the world has known is said to lurk on the grounds of his former palace in the city of Tirgoviste, which is located in the Carpathian foothills in the province of Wallachia. Prince Vlad Tepes, or Vlad the Impaler, earned his nickname in 1462, when the Sultan of Turkey led an army to take over the city of Tirgoviste. He was greeted with a nightmarish scene: Vlad had constructed a mile-long wall of decomposing bodies at the approach to the city consisting of twenty thousand Turkish prisoners impaled on tall wooden stakes planted firmly in the ground. The gruesome site and accompanying stench was enough for the horrified Sultan to turn his army around and head back to Turkey. On Easter Day in 1457, Vlad rounded up two hundred noblemen and their families as they were coming out of churches. He impaled the women and elderly on the city walls and chained the young men and teenagers together and marched them sixty miles to Poienari Citadel, his castle in the Arges Valley. There, he worked them to death hauling stones to renovate the structure, the ruins of which can still be visited.

In another episode, Vlad invited all the sick and poor in his province to a free banquet, where they dined on the finest food and wine. Afterwards, his men locked the doors and set the great hall on fire, burning to death everyone who showed up. The ruins of the burned-out dining hall are next to his personal chapel that still stands at his court in Tirgoviste. The only other building still standing is the Chindia Watch Tower, a guard post and observation deck from which Vlad watched the frequent public torturing and impalements that took place in the courtyard below. According to some reports, Vlad drank the blood of his victims, and he is the origin of the Count Dracula legend. Many Romanians are convinced that he actually was a vampire, and that his spirit still haunts their country. Nobody knows who killed Vlad, but when his body was found in the Vlasia forest, it was decapitated, which is an accepted method of killing vampires. His body is entombed in the floor in front of the altar at the Snagav Monastery in Wallachia and is marked with his threatening-looking portrait. The corpse was exhumed in 1935—it was well preserved and dressed in fine clothing, but the head was missing.

RUSSIA

Russia was inhabited by Slavic peoples who were overrun by numerous nomadic tribes. The Mongols controlled virtually the entire country by the thirteenth century. The first tsar was crowned in 1547, and the longest lasting dynasty was the Romanov family who ruled from 1613 to 1917. After the Bolshevik Revolution, Russia and its former provinces and possessions became the Union of Soviet Socialist Republics. The U.S.S.R. was dissolved in 1991, and Russia became a separate republic.

Bishkek

FRUNZE MUSEUM A Russian ghost apparently upset with the fall of Soviet power was that of Army Commander Mikhail Frunze, who appeared in his museum in 1993 and threw things around in a poltergeist rage. His museum was located in the capital of the Kirgizia province. The city,

Moscow Ghost, Moscow, Russia (Alex Novik)

which had been called Frunze in his honor, was changed to Bishkek after the Soviet collapse.

Moscow

KREMLIN The Kremlin is haunted by the apparition of Ivan the Terrible, the ruthless Russian tsar. He is seen carrying a large baton while flames cover his face. His appearance forebodes disaster to Russian rulers. The most sightings of Ivan took place in 1894, before the marriage of Nikolai II to Alexandra Fyodorovna. Another Kremlin ghost is Nikolai Lenin, whose apparition was first seen in his office in October 1923, a few months before he died. He was living in Gorky, but while on his deathbed, his ghost returned to his office to dig through his papers and books looking for something. Over the years, Lenin has been blamed for much poltergeist activity at the Kremlin.

In 1961, Lenin's spirit allegedly contacted a Communist heroine and medium named Darya Lazurkina. Lenin's message: He hated lying in state in his public mausoleum next to Stalin, who "caused the Party so much harm." Darya had been imprisoned by Stalin for nearly twenty years for her devotion to Lenin, and in an address before the Twenty-second Congress of the Communist Party, the frail woman revealed the wishes of her dead hero. Amazingly, the following night the body of Stalin was secretly removed from public display and interred in an obscure cemetery within the Kremlin. The next day, visitors to the mausoleum on Red Square realized that Lenin's wish had been granted. Lenin's spirit still appears in Russia. In 1993, during the collapse of communism, several reliable witnesses saw his apparition pacing back and forth in his old office and at other government buildings in Moscow and St. Petersburg.

STATE ARCHIVES The State Archives of the Russian Federation in Moscow are haunted by an unidentified woman in a white, flowing gown. Many employees have reported seeing the apparition walking among shelves housing archives from former tsars.

TUNNELS OF MOSCOW Subterranean passageways under Moscow are haunted by the ghostly figures of monks, soldiers, and even Gypsies. A network of tunnels under the city has been used for centuries by dissidents, malcontents, and other "undesirables" as hideouts and a secret transportation system. Most of the existing tunnels can be accessed through modern fallout shelters or subway stations. Under the Centralbank building, bright lights move about and the mysterious phantoms of Stalin-era soldiers are seen. Beneath the Cathedral of Christ the Savior a chest full of an evil presence was removed at the request of the dean of the church. Under Skliffasovsky Clinic, phantom monks gather around a stone altar. Many tourists taking photographs above these areas on the streets of Moscow have got strange lights and electromagnetic activity on film. For more information, visit Alex Novik's Web site at www. geocities.com/Area51/Nova/6457.

St. Petersburg

PAVLOVSK PALACE Pavlovsk Palace is located south of St. Petersburg in the city of Pavlovsk. The eighteenth-century palace is haunted by the apparition of a White Lady, who moves silently through the corridors and is also known to appear in the Cavalier Room, Queen Olga's Salon, and several of the bedrooms. She is thought to be Maria Feodorovna, Empress of Russia, a willful woman who had the palace constructed according to her own tastes and tried to rule her cantankerous family with an iron fist. Her husband, the Czar Paul, was murdered in a coup by his eldest son Alexander.

While his father was considered a tyrant, Alexander became a hero to the people. He defeated Napoleon in the War of 1812 and was known as a just ruler. He was also a wise man who never trusted Russian politics. Many years after his reported death while vacationing in the Crimea, rumors circulated that he was living as a hermit in Siberia. Lenin himself became curious as to whether Alexander was still alive, and had the czar's coffin exhumed. When opened, there was nothing but stones inside. But Alexander's whereabouts were never discovered.

PORTUGAL

A people known as the Lusitanians settled Portugal in ancient times, but they were subjugated by the Romans, Visigoths, and Moors, until the twelfth century when it became an independent country under King Alfonso. In ensuing centuries, Portugal became a powerful force and had possessions and protectorates all over the world. It became a republic in 1910 and a dictatorship following a military coup in 1926. The dictatorship was dissolved in 1933, when a constitution for a new corporative style of government was enacted.

Fatima

COVA DE IRIA North of Lisbon in central Portugal, one of the world's most witnessed apparitional events took place for six consecutive months in 1917. At Cova de Iria, an open pasture near the village of Aljustel in the parish of Fatima, the apparition of an angelic lady in white appeared to three children and announced it would return to the same place at the same time every month. The children identified the glowing figure as the Virgin Mother, who spoke to the two girls and conveyed a message of repentance, prayer, and communion to assure world peace. The third child, a boy, heard nothing.

By October 13, over sixty thousand people had shown up to witness the phenomenon. Many saw a variety of religious apparitions, including Mother Mary, Jesus, and St. Joseph, but the most commonly reported effect was the "Miracle of the Sun." The sun emerged from a break in the clouds, started rotating and emitting rays of multicolored light, and then appeared to fall to earth, giving off a penetrating heat. For the next ten minutes, the fallen "sun" created a seventy-meter-wide path of "solid light" that dried out the ground and people's clothing from earlier rain. Then, the sun returned to its proper place in the sky. People caught in the golden light felt a powerful healing energy enter their bodies, and the mysterious solar display was witnessed by others miles away. In 1927, the Catholic Church declared Fatima an official pilgrimage site and later built a basilica, hospitals, and hostels there.

SOUTH AFRICA

South Africa was settled by the Bantu people in the fourteenth century and by Dutch settlers called Boers in the 1650s. Ceded to Britain in 1814, the British annexed Transvaal in 1877 and created the Republic of South Africa. It became an independent republic in 1961.

Cape Town

CAPE TOWN CASTLE The Cape Town Castle ghost has been appearing for over three centuries. The tall, luminous figure is most often seen walking on the battlement of the castle, built in 1665. The ghost is thought to be the stubborn Dutch merchant and adventurer who built the fortified mansion.

Great Karoo Forest

SPOKEVELD Amazingly, a whole region of South Africa is considered off limits to the living. Spokeveld ("Spook Country") is along the southern edge of the Great Karoo between the Patatas River and the Southkloff, and the entire area is haunted by spectral wagons, phantom horse riders, and ghostly wanderers.

Johannesburg

STATION TUNNEL A more recent phantom is one of the men who died building the underground tunnel that runs from the Post Office to Main Railway Station in Johannesburg. Many people walking through the dark passageway encounter his frightened spirit. The man died when a section of the roof collapsed on him about halfway into the tunnel.

Kalahari Desert

KING BUSHMEN About half the adult population of the King Bushmen tribe in the Kalahari Desert enter group trances to connect with the powers of the Other Side. At irregular intervals, members of the tribe begin ritual dancing ceremonies designed to put the participants into deep trances. During these altered states of consciousness, the whole group shares experiences and objectives. Sometimes there is a need to heal someone in the group or contact the spirit of an ancestor to find out about future events relevant to the tribe's survival. Psychologists from Harvard University discovered that the unique trance state appears to create a "synergistic consciousness" to which all participants contribute.

Port Elizabeth

PORT ELIZABETH HIGHWAY In a more urban setting, Port Elizabeth Highway (between the Hex River Mountains and Drakensberg) is haunted by a phantom automobile that is blamed for causing more than one accident in recent years. The automobile dates from the 1960s, but its owners have never been identified. There have, however, been several fatal accidents along this stretch of highway.

Uniondale

BARANDAS-WILLOWMORE ROAD The Barandas-Willowmore Road near Uniondale, South Africa, is haunted by the apparition of twenty-two-year-old Maria Roux, who was killed in an accident there on April 12, 1968. Several independent witnesses have identified her as a woman seen walking or hitchhiking along the road. Witnesses include policemen, soldiers, motorcyclists, and businessmen. If the woman is given a ride, she mysteriously disappears from the vehicle. In 1976, Marie climbed into the back seat of a man's car who had stopped to give her a ride. After a few miles, he heard a scream from the back seat and turned to see the right-side door open. A witness in a following car said he observed the rear door open wide, but no one jumped out.

Zululand

INZINGOGO Among the Zulu tribe of southern Africa, snakes are holy creatures that are never harmed. They believe that it is not possible to tell the difference between a normal snake and spirit snakes. They believe that everyone's soul has a particular guardian spirit, known as an *ehlose*, which is a spirit snake. *Inzingogo* are men who refused to give up their bodies at death and retained their blood, flesh, and bones in a vegetative state. Their ghosts or spirits then take over the bodies of animals, usually baboons, and live in the forest.

However, sometimes the ghosts take on the form of a black mamba or other poisonous snake, and go after specific individuals at the request of witch doctors who have learned to control the spirit world. During the Zulu rebellion, an unusually high number of British troops died by black mamba bites, and on the average, eleven deaths per year are attributed to *inzingogo* even today. If either the *inzingogo* human or animal body is destroyed, their spirits are absorbed into the bowels of the earth. There, the *inzingogo* takes on the form of an *isikqukqumadevu*, a squatting, bloated monster.

SPAIN

Spain is one of the oldest civilized nations in Europe and evidence of Stone Age Neanderthal settlements can be found throughout the country. It was colonized around 700 B.C. by Phoenicians, and then the Greeks and Romans arrived. Around A.D. 700, it was conquered by Moorish invaders from Arabia. Spain was reunited as a Christian country in 1479 and became one of the world's greatest imperialistic powers, conquering nations both in Europe and the New World. Napoleon conquered Spain in 1809, and the first Spanish republic was set up in 1874. The Spanish Civil War in 1936–39 established the dictatorship of General Francisco Franco. When Franco died in 1974, the nation became a parliamentary monarchy.

Iberia

SANTIAGO DE COMPOSTELA New Age visitors consider the Cathedral of Santiago de Compostela in Iberia, Spain, a reservoir of powerful positive psychic energy. They sense the spiritual energy and devotion to the divine that tens of thousands of pilgrims brought to this site, and sometimes they even report seeing the apparitions of those dedicated souls making their way through the city to the holy shrine. The most famous historical apparition seen here was the "Moorslayer" Santiago Matomoro, who appeared on a white horse to lead Christians against the Arabian Moors. The church was built in A.D. 829 on the spot where the sacred relics of St. James the Elder were found by a hermit who followed a "star" and celestial music to an empty field. St. James was one of the twelve apostles who traveled widely spreading the news of Christ's resurrection.

But the ghost of St. James has never been seen here, and today, most historians agree that St. James never visited Iberia. The discovery of his relics was apparently a hoax perpetrated by the Church to attract pilgrims and take the region back from Arabian settlers. It is known that the Cathedral of Santiago sent hired "storytellers" to spread the news of miracles associated with the relics, and their tactics seemed to have worked, for by the twelfth century, this was the most popular pilgrimage site in Europe. The Church built hostels to house pilgrims, and a very profitable tourist trade was established. Nonetheless, the pilgrims came here seeking the divine in utmost humility and faith, and it is their sincere passion that permeates the site. Where the relics came from is anyone's guess, but some of the strange implements have been identified as tools used by alchemists.

San Sebastian de Garabandal

Los Pinos The small village of San Sebastian de Garabandal, Spain, was visited by an apparition of a radiant boy for several years in the 1960s, and the repercussions of his appearance are still being discussed. It all started when four girls, eating apples and walking carefree down a lane, were startled by a rumbling sound in the cloudless sky. Next, a brilliant ball of light formed above them, and projected within it was the apparition of a boy of about nine years of age. The boy was dressed in a blue robe that hung down all the way to his feet, and he had black eyes and dark skin. The most noteworthy thing about him, however, was the attitude of maturity and authority that he carried.

When the girls, all around twelve years old, told their parents about the apparition they encountered, they were greeted with disbelief. The next day, the girls returned to the spot and were enveloped in a light so tactile and brilliant that it frightened them, and the phenomenon immediately ceased. Before long, the whole village was talking about "the angel," and speculation was rife that it was of religious significance. The children were taken to the village priest, who told them about good and bad spirits and instructed them to ask the apparition its name. When once again the apparition appeared, however, it refused to disclose its name.

The religious fervor in the village was increasing, and the next time the girls visited the lane, several adults followed them and watched them pray for the "angel" to come. When nothing happened, the adults sarcastically advised the girls to "say a few more Hail Marys." This seemed to work, and the boy appeared to the girls, although none of the adults were able to see him. They were, however, able to observe the state of trance-like rapture the girls entered, and everyone present knew at once that whatever was happening, the girls were not making it up.

By now, the girls were convinced the vision was a religious visitation, and that is how things played out. The next time the boy appeared he told them he was the Archangel Michael. The boy started to appear more easily to the girls and at places anywhere in the village, though most of the visitations took place at *Los Pinos*, a clump of nine old pine trees just outside the village. When the boy appeared, the girls immediately fell to their knees, fixed their vision upwards so that their eyes rolled back in their heads, and entered a deep trance state. Investigators performed all kinds of tests while the girls were in these trances and were never able to disturb their state of ecstasy. One thing discovered was that the children became so heavy during their trances that they could not be lifted off the ground. Also, when the vision commenced, the children dropped dead to their knees, making a tremendous noise "like a wooden board breaking." As the vision continued, the children could move around and follow the apparition without seeing where they were walking. They never looked down at the ground and often walked backwards, but they never stumbled or even stepped on anything sharp or fragile.

Sometimes they remained in a trance for over four days at a time without sleep or signs of exhaustion. The girls described three "calls" that meant they were about to have a vision. The first call was a vague feeling of joy interrupting their everyday train of thought. The second call is similar but stronger and something they could not ignore. That is when they left to seek the apparition. The third call consists of overpowering, wonderful thoughts and feelings that fill them with "both agitation and happiness at the same time." At this point they are about to become one with their visions.

The adults continued to press the children for answers about what was going on and what it was the angel wanted from them. Finally, the radiant boy appeared with a tablet written in words the children could not fully comprehend. They agreed, however, that the tablet began with the words "It is . . ." or "There must be . . ." The apparition of the boy starting bringing other visions that included the Virgin Mary, Jesus Christ, and the Eye of God. It was the Virgin Mary who elucidated on the message of the tablet. Conchita Gonzales, the first girl to see the apparitions, summarized their message: "There must be many sacrifices, much penance. Above all, we must be very good. If we are not, a punishment will fall on us. Already the cup is filling. If we do not change, the punishment will be very great: The cup of wrath will be emptied on a people grown godless, uncaring, and filled with self alone." This message is basically the same as that received by other children who experienced similar apparitions at Fatima, Lourdes, or Beauring.

The children of Garabandal experienced over a thousand visitations in the period between 1961 and 1965, and their encounters became increasingly real, ending with their ability to touch and even hold the apparitions, as well as to receive "apports" or physical manifestations (such as a host wafer that materialized on Conchita's outstretched tongue in front of scores of witnesses). It all started with the radiant boy, who at other times in the world might have been called Mercury, Hermes, or Thoth, and today might be seen as a small silvery creature in a UFO—a messenger apparition that opens us up to the Other Side of reality. Typically, these kinds of experiences take on the form of a person's belief system, which "fills in the blanks" with some kind of acceptable explanation. But the message is always the same: Live in accord with the universal principles of a higher, nonmaterial reality or face destruction.

Saragossa

PALAZON HOME Across the border from Portugal in Saragossa, Spain, the Palazon family holds conversations with a voice speaking from a stovepipe that identifies itself as Duenda de Zaragoza. Investigators have confirmed that a person by that name lived in the house in the 1930s, but no one is quite sure what he wants.

Zaraus

PALACIO DE NARROS The Blue Room at the Palacio de Narros in the village of Zaraus, Spain, is haunted by a unidentified presence that makes fire come out of the walls. The first man to try to exorcize the room of its demon was Father Coloma, who stayed overnight in the room and wrote a book about his experiences called *The Blue Chamber*. According to his account, just after midnight a burning ball of reddish yellow flames bounced into the room from the ceiling, burned a gaping hole in the floor, and entered the room below. More recently, exorcist Father Pilon spent a night in the room with all kinds of electromagnetic monitoring devices and recorded a lot of anomalous activity, including the shrill babble of a woman's voice.

According to legend, the room became haunted when a shipwrecked passenger washed up on shore in front of the palace and was taken to the Blue Room to recover. It turned out the man was a fanatical Protestant heretic escaping from France, and just as he expired, a shaft of flame emerged from the wall above his head and sailed from room to room in the palace. Another, less likely, candidate for the ghost of the Blue Room is a woman named Germaine. She was a beautiful French governess who ended up marrying the Marquis de Narros, although she was rejected by jealous family members until the day she died. Her apparition has been seen walking in the patio gallery and sensed at other locations in the palace, though she does not seem to possess the fiery spirit necessary to produce the effects witnessed in the Blue Room.

SWEDEN

Sweden was settled by several independent tribes including the Vikings. It became united and Christianized in the eleventh century. Sweden lost territory in a long war against Russia from 1743 to 1809, after which it became a monarchy. It became a parliamentary monarchy in 1971.

Hialta

STAD GRIM The city of Hjalta in Sweden is haunted by the *Stad Grim*, the seminaked figure of a bald old man who is seen in public places and on the streets. The eccentric man was ostracized by the community, and he never forgot the way its "proper" citizens treated him. He still loves to cause panic throughout the old neighbohood.

Kil

APERTIN MANOR Apertin Manor guesthouse near the town of Kil in the province of Varmland is haunted by the apparition of a noblewoman who once lived there. Her ghost suddenly appears at the center of guest rooms on the second floor of the house, then floats out by passing through one of the walls. Many sleeping guests wake up in the middle of the night to see her apparition.

TOGO

Togo is a country in western Africa that was part of the German protectorate of Togoland until 1914, when it came under French jurisdiction. It became an independent republic in 1960.

Chaine de Lama Mountains

KABIYE Invisible spirits called *siou* haunt the Kabiye tribe of Togo, West Africa. Tribe members live in stone dwellings near the Chaine de Lama Mountains (north of the city of Lama-Kara) and the Djambe Mountains (on the West Africa savannah). The *siou* are intermediary spirits that exist between heaven and earth. They can be helpful, such as carrying prayers to God, or they can be vengeful and capable of killing people. Like conventional ghosts, the *siou* live in the houses with the residents, but often remain behind if the owners move, even if the dwelling is abandoned. Residents speak to the *siou* as if it were a member of the family, and some even leave food for them at dinner time. Every marketplace also has its own *siou*, which lives in a small pyramid of stones called a *hee*. When someone dies, the Jojo (holy man) takes up a collection of food from the sellers. The food is then placed at the *hee* as a goodwill offering, so the *siou* will escort the deceased's soul to heaven.

Other ghosts of the Kabiye include a phantom python called the *doo*, which inhabits a person's house and influences events for good or ill depending on its mood. The *alewa*, which come in male and female forms, can also be good or bad spirits. People seek out good *alewa* and offer to share their homes with them. Evil *alewa*, however, are like mischievous poltergeists that can reduce a household to shambles. They can even "eat the spirit" of a living person and cause that person to eventually die.

YUGOSLAVIA

Yugoslavia is a remnant of the collapse of Austria's Hapsburg dynasty in 1917. From the remnants of the former Austro-Hungarian Empire, a state called the Kingdom of Serbs, Croats, and Slovenes was created. In 1929, the name was changed to Yugoslavia. With all the bloodshed in recent years, it is becoming more obvious to the world that the united "kingdom" of Serbs, Croats, and Slovenes was one of the worst ideas ever conceived. Then again, perhaps we are simply dealing with more consequences of the infamous Hapsburg curse (see Austria).

Belgrade

DANCE OF DEATH Throughout Yugoslavia during the week of Pentecost every year, an ancient pagan sect known as the Vlachs takes to the streets of Belgrade and other Yugoslavian cities to try to conjure up the dead. The Vlachs originally inhabited the Transylvania Alps near the Romanian border, and today they number over fifteen thousand members. They celebrate Dionysian rituals and worship the goddess of fertility, but during Pomana (Festival of the Dead), they try to contact dead relatives by visiting their graves and enticing the spirits to come out with offerings of wine, cakes, candles, music, and magical charms. Many witnesses claim they are successful in their efforts and report seeing apparitions hovering over graves or conversing with relatives. At village squares, the Vlachs gather to perform the Kolo (Dance of

Death), in which groups of three girls and three young men dance long hours until one of the girls falls into a trance. Then, they all form a circle around her and start chanting, as the spirits of recently deceased persons possess the woman's body to communicate with the living.

Bosnia

SARAJEVO The trauma of modern times has created their share of wandering spirits in Yugoslavia. Vaso Miskin Street and Vojvode Putnika Boulevard (also known as "Sniper Alley") in Sarajevo, Bosnia, are haunted by the ghosts of innocent people slaughtered there. Nearby, the streets of Bijeljina are haunted by Mehmed, a Muslim killed by a Serbian strike force.

Croatia

MEDJUGORJE On the "Hill of Apparitions" outside Medjugorje in Croatia, hundreds of witnesses have observed strange apparitions emerging from the sun, while others report sensing an overpowering spiritual presence. Since the early 1980s, apparitions of the Virgin Mary have appeared on this rocky slope to Catholic believers, and the entire hill is littered with crucifixes and the remains of votive candles. The Mary apparition first appeared to six adolescents (four girls, two boys) on June 24, 1981. The teenagers began a spontaneous regimen of fasting and prayer that allowed them to become pure enough for the visions to continue. Mary appeared daily for the next eighteen months, then she started to appear on a weekly basis, and by 1987, the apparition was appearing regularly on the 25th of each month. Over three thousand sightings of Mary have been recorded, most of which take place in the Chapel of Apparitions, a former rectory behind St. James Roman Catholic Church in Medjugorje. Her message is about the need for prayer and the importance of making time for communion with Jesus.

People of other faiths also witness a variety of paranormal phenomena and apparitions. In 1981, above the Hill of Apparitions, the word "Mir" ("Peace") was written in glowing letters in the night sky. A bush caught fire on the hill in October 1981, but when the fire went out, there were no signs of burning or charring. Unnatural rays of light seem to strike the cross on the hill, and many photographs showing anomalous lights have been taken near it. Like the phenomena at Fatima (see Portugal), the sun over the hill sometimes seems to pulsate with rays of multicolored light, spin about in the heavens, or change into a pure white disc. In the church, people report that silver Rosary chains turn to gold and that they see silhouettes of Mary and Jesus moving through the pews.

ZAMBIA

Zambia is a nation of several tribal African communities that became the Congo Free State in 1884 and achieved independence from Belgium in 1960. There was a military coup in 1965 and the name changed to Zambia in 1971.

Congo Basin

NGANGA In Zambia, spirits are summoned and their supernatural energy focused in *muti* bags, which are small bags made of leaves, twigs, and feathers. They are created by a *nganga*, a tribal shaman or witch doctor, who used his connection with the Other Side to infuse the objects with power. The bags are hung at the end of sticks on top of hills, mounds, anthills, and termite mounds to protect crops, residences, or villages from thieves. The bags are taken very seriously, and whole roads have been re-engineered around them. To disturb a *muti* means certain death, and there are many cases of people dying who touched the cursed objects.

ZIMBABWE

Settled by the Bantu people in central Africa, it was known as Rhodesia when a British colony. It became an independent republic in 1970 and was renamed Zimbabwe in 1980.

Bulawayo

MEMORIAL HOSPITAL The ghost of a former physician haunts the Memorial Hospital in Bulawayo, Matabeleland, in Zimbabwe. Sometimes the spectral physician even appears to help other doctors in their diagnosis. The apparition of the good Dr. Ellis is most often encountered in the hospital's outside office building, though occasionally he wanders the hospital area.

Chizarira Hills

BANTU Bantu tribesmen refer to the spirit of a dead person as the *mudzimu*, and it can be invited back to the world of the living by its loved ones. In this way, spirits can be tied to the earthly plane to watch after children or other family members that are dependent on it. Therefore, many families have benevolent ghosts living with them. On the other hand, the *chitokwane* is a spirit forced to return immediately after death to carry out the wishes of a shaman or medium. Sometimes *mongo*, or wandering evil spirits, take over the bodies of living individuals. In this case, the tribesmen rely on the spirits of their ancestors to drive out the interloper in a ceremony called the *mandengure*. The possessed person is forced to spend the night in a tree while a *nganga* (witch doctor) oversees the battle between the man's ancestral powers and the offending spirit.

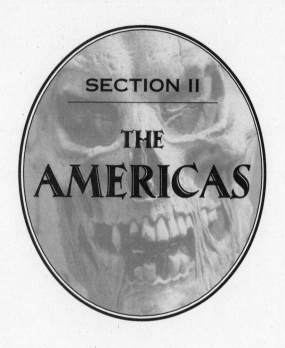

SECTION II

THE
AMERICAS

The Incans and Aztecs were firm believers in ghosts, although most of their spirits tended to be demonic. In Central and South America today, the "cihuateteo" are female demons that hide in the forests and mountains waiting to attach themselves to wanderers and ruin their lives. The same is true of the "ahuizotl," who live in lakes. In Guyana, the local incarnation of the devil is Sakarabru. Perhaps the most feared ghost, however, is "Tezcatlipoca," a fearsome demon who took on four forms, including a hideous golem with pieces of skin hanging from its face and a headless body called the Flayed One.

Members of the Nahuatl tribe of Mexico believe in "tlaciques," shapeshifting entities that can take the form of ghosts, witches, or vampires. The "acheri" is the apparition of a little Indian girl who comes wandering down from the mountains to spread disease among tribal children. Anyone whom her shadow touches will catch the disease, although children can protect themselves by wearing a band of red cloth around their necks.

In Jamaica, ghosts are generally called "goopies," although among the native Obeah tribe, who are the island's specialists in dispatching spirits, they are known as "duppies." The duppy is a ghost that can be called by a secret ritual to do the caller's bidding. According to tradition, if a duppy breathes on you, you will become violently ill, and if it touches you, you will suffer a fit. Duppies are known to hate tobacco seeds, so the seeds are sprinkled around doors and windows of homes to prevent their entry. The duppy can only operate at night and must return to its grave before dawn. If the duppy is prevented from doing this for any reason then, it loses its powers and might as well be returned to the grave permanently.

"Baka" is a Haitian word to describe a ghostly creature that returns after death to eat human flesh. During their natural lives, bakas are said to be members of a secret society that teaches them the ways they must follow after death. "Zombies" are dead bodies and spirits controlled by Voodoo priests to do their bidding. They are similar to duppies but more physical and only last as long as they can be kept from rotting away.

The "wendigo" is a phantom beast, which lives in the forests of Canada and the northern United States. The Algonquin tribe say they are hunters who get lost and are forced to eat human flesh to survive. The Ojibwa say they are spirits of ice monsters who can possess people and cause them to cannibalize their own family members. Shamans who grow too egotistical can also become possessed by a wendigo. In the forest, the wendigo prey on human beings, particularly children. Wendigos are described as brilliantly glowing white phantoms, about 15 feet (4.5 meters) tall, with a star in the middle of their foreheads.

The "spook" is a type of ghost only found in America, and it is said to be a generous rather than a harmful spirit. Casper the friendly ghost is a spook. The first legends of spooks were among the Native Americans, who believed that these spirits could take over control of the body of a living person. Spooks can haunt someone without that person being aware of it, but they are always out to help rather than harm. There are many tales of people whose lives were failures until their spook took them over and enabled them to achieve wealth and position. So if you know you are haunted by a genuine spook, you usually do not want to call in the exorcist.

In the United States, Pueblo tribes believe the spirits of the dead can be captured in "kachina" dolls for use in ceremonies. The ancestral kachina spirits live in the San Francisco Mountains in Arizona and are responsible for bringing rain and other benefits to tribe members. Higher spirits known as "shiwanna" (cloud people) sometimes guide the dead to different regions of the universe and can wait in mountains or below bodies of water until they are needed. The Zuni of New Mexico refer to similar spirits as the "koko," who live in mountains or at the bottom of sacred lakes and sometimes bring water, corn, and general health to tribe members. The Seminole tribe in Florida believes the Everglades swamp is haunted by evil trickster spirits that appear as alluring shapes or balls of light that can lead unwary white men to their death. These vengeful spirits are Indians killed during the Seminole Indian Wars in 1858.

"Gremlins" are modern ghosts that devote themselves to haunting technology. They are small, pesky spirits that were first reported in aircraft. Pilots named the troll-like entities after *Grimm's Fairy Tales*. The creatures have been described as short, furry goblins about six inches tall. The earliest references are from the 1920s, when some pilots began reporting the audacious creatures boring holes in fuselages, biting through cables and wires, and pinching fuel lines. Sometimes, however, gremlins prefer to help pilots and have been credited with helping lost pilots navigate to safety, averting crashes, and alerting pilots to possible dangers.

During his flight across the Atlantic in 1927, Charles Lindbergh observed the apparitions inside his fuselage. He said they discussed navigation with him and reassured him that his flight would be successful, and even shared mystical knowledge. During World War II and the Korean War, gremlins were uniformly annoying presences in airplanes. In recent years, gremlins seem to be expanding their interest to factories, telephone equipment, and computers.

NORTH AMERICA

CANADA

The original inhabitants of Canada were Inuits, and the country was not settled until the fifteenth century by the French and English. The Dominion of Canada, a union of eastern provinces, was established in 1867, and the remaining provinces were either purchased or sought union within the next eighty years. Canada consists of twelve provinces: Nova Scotia, New Brunswick, Prince Edward Isle, Newfoundland, Quebec, Ontario, Manitoba, Saskatchewan, Alberta, British Columbia, and the sparsely populated northern provinces of the Yukon and Northwest Territories.

NOVA SCOTIA

Amherst

TWEED COTTAGE Nova Scotia's most famous and frightening haunting was the so-called Amherst Poltergeist case, which took place at 6 Princess Street in the town of Amherst. The events started in 1878 in the Tweed family cottage and seemed to center around nineteen-year-old Esther Cox. Esther was the younger sister of Daniel Tweed's wife and was living in the tiny cottage with them, their two baby boys, and another of the wife's sisters. Shortly after a man on the street tried to rape Esther at gunpoint, the haunting started. She was in a near-hysterical state for several days, when unexplainable noises started coming from her room and she felt things crawling in bed with her at night. Then, she woke up one morning to find her hair standing on end and her face and arms swelling up, grotesquely deforming her appearance. As the inexplicable swelling continued, she became extremely weak and unable to get out of bed. Four days later, thundering banging sounds rang through the house, objects began flying about in the cottage, and foot-high scribbling appeared on the wall saying "Esther Cox, you are mine to kill." Witnesses came from miles around to see the dinnerware, knickknacks, and other objects flung through the cottage by unseen hands. Then fires ignited by themselves, and Esther said that an entity named "Bob" was communicating to her that he planned to burn the place down.

That was too much for Daniel Tweed, and he ordered Esther out of the house. She got a job and lodging at a local restaurant, but the poltergeist followed her, knocking over chairs and tables and throwing dishes. When Esther was fired from her job, Daniel took her back in. After the activity resumed in the cottage, a traveling showman named Walter Hubbell took Esther on tour, hoping to make a fortune from people who would pay to see the poltergeist in action. However, the effects never worked on stage, and Esther spent the rest of her life wandering from town to town, trying to escape the violent spirit. When a barn of one of her employers burnt down mysteriously, she was accused of arson and sentenced to a short term in prison. The poltergeist followed the poor woman for the rest of her life, although the intensity of the haunting subsided when she married and had a son. She had another son in a second marriage, and died in Brockton, Massachusetts, in 1912.

Halifax

ROBIE STREET PALACE The "Robie Street Palace" is what locals call the haunted house at 1714 Robie Street in Halifax, Nova Scotia. The mansion was built in the 1840s by William Caldwell, the city's first mayor, and now serves as an office. Starting in the 1870s, numerous strange phenomena started manifesting in the house. Poltergeist activity included flying objects, odd noises, and moving cold spots. One elderly man living in the house reported seeing the apparitions of "witches" dancing on the veranda that surrounds the building. Another resident shot a gun through the same upstairs window at a boy stealing apples from a tree in the front yard to scare the lad away. The bullet hit the boy and killed him, and the remorseful man committed suicide by hanging himself. The cursed window was painted over in black paint. The house gained a reputation for being haunted and was turned into offices because no one would stay overnight in the building. In the 1970s, architect Aza Avramovitch bought the house and quickly realized it was haunted, as did many of his employees. Since then, no one has actually lived in the house or spent the night there.

CATHEDRAL CHURCH OF ALL SAINTS The Cathedral Church of All Saints in Halifax, which was built in 1907, is haunted by a former priest named Dean Llwyd. Two weeks after his funeral in the 1950s, clergymen and parishioners started seeing his apparition walk to the pulpit and look out over the congregation, as if he were about to begin a sermon.

FIVE FISHERMEN RESTAURANT A violent, unidentified presence haunts this homey restaurant. Recently, a female employee was trapped in a corner on the second floor of the restaurant by the unseen force. When a male coworker attempted to assist her, the angry ghost started throwing things at him, seriously injuring the young man. In the frenzy, the girl escaped and ran down to the first floor, vowing never to enter the second floor again.

GEORGE STREET ANGLICAN CHURCH A window facing the harbor in this old church is haunted by a former minister who died while he was looking out it. Halifax was nearly destroyed in 1917 when a munitions ship collided with another ship in the harbor. Over two thousand people were killed in the thundering explosions that followed, and whole sections of the city were wiped out. The minister was standing at the window at the moment of the explosion and was killed instantly by flying glass and debris. When the windows in the church were replaced, the man's image was clearly visible in the glass. The windows have been replaced three times since then, and each time his silhouette, noticeably darker than the rest of the glass, can be seen.

McNAB'S ISLAND McNab's Island is a strategically located land mass at the mouth of Halifax Harbor, and the British built two fortifications there in the early eighteenth century. Nearly two centuries later, entrepreneur Bill Lynch built a carnival on the island complete with a Ferris wheel and other rides. By the 1980s, however, the island was completely abandoned, and today there are only a few deserted houses and the two old forts still standing. The only things left behind were the ghosts.

An abandoned white house that sits in an open meadow at the center of the island is haunted by an elderly couple who retired to the island in the 1960s. The man died in the house in 1975, while the woman died there in 1982. Both their ghosts have been reported, and the woman's distinctive perfume seems to foretell their manifestations. Unexplainable footsteps and voices have been heard. Another house nearby is the scene of poltergeist effects such as moving objects, and doors that refuse to open as if someone were holding them shut. Once, all the furniture on the first floor piled itself up into one corner of the living room.

Mahone Bay

OAK ISLAND Oak Island in Nova Scotia's Mahone Bay has been considered haunted for hundreds of years, and the island is known for its ghostly lights that float around at night. Six men have died so far trying to retrieve an alleged treasure concealed in a deep pit on the island, and according to legend, the mystery of Oak Island will not be revealed until seven men have died there. Whoever hid the treasure chose the island for its abundant hardwood and built a complicated, multileveled vertical shaft, thirteen feet in diameter and over two hundred feet deep with log platforms every ten feet to a depth of eighty feet. Their well-concealed treasure pit was discovered in 1795 by three boys exploring the island.

Today, the supposed treasure trove is nicknamed the Money Pit, because so much money has been invested trying to recover the treasure. The only items recovered from the pit so far have been three chain links, a piece of parchment with the letters "V" and "I," and a flat stone encoded with the message "ten feet below ten million pounds are buried." In 1971, a Montreal consortium lowered an underwater camera to a water-filled cavity at the bottom of the pit and sent back images of three chests and a severed hand. But it took so long for a diving team to be organized that the disturbed items were completely eroded by seawater. So far, the mysterious treasure of Oak Island has eluded every attempt at recovery.

Windsor

HALIBURTON HOUSE MUSEUM The Haliburton House Museum in Windsor, Nova Scotia, is a haunted mansion built in 1834. The fifteen-room house is haunted by the original owner, Judge Thomas Chandler Haliburton. The judge had a secret panel in the wall of the reception hall, and it is that passageway from which his apparition emerges. The ghost then wanders around the house and returns back into the secret panel. Another ghost on the property is the spirit of a member of Scotland's Black Regiment, who rode their horses across the property on their way to Annapolis long ago. One of the men dropped his watch and on trying to reach down from his steed to pick it up, fell into a deep pond on the estate and drowned. His ghost, dressed in kilts, was seen emerging on horseback in the middle of the pond. Eventually, the pond was filled in to stop the haunting.

NEW BRUNSWICK

Frederickton

BELMONT HOUSE Not far from Boyce Mansion along the St. John River in Fredericton, Belmont House is another haunted mansion. Built in 1820 by Johnathon Bliss, the first Chief Justice of New Brunswick, the house remained in his politically active family for over a century. During the American Civil War, a secret tunnel that ran from the basement to the river served as an escape route for runaway slaves, who sought freedom in Canada. Later residents reported all kinds of weird noises coming from the cellar, and disembodied footsteps and voices were heard throughout the house. A séance was held that only resulted in increased poltergeist effects, but when the mansion was turned into apartments in 1985, the ghostly activity finally subsided.

BOYCE MANSION If you ask someone in Fredericton if there is a haunted house in town, they will probably direct you to Boyce Mansion. Located on the banks of the St. John River, the three-story

Gothic mansion looks like a Halloween haunted house all through the year. It is now a male dormitory for the University of New Brunswick, and students there will tell you that it is indeed haunted. The apparition is that of a kindly woman who lived here in the early twentieth century, and she is tied to the house because she is waiting for a letter from her dying son. Once she appeared to the dormitory leader to explain herself. To allay his fear, she said she had come in the "name of the Father, Son, and Holy Ghost." Then she explained that her sick son in another city wrote her asking that she come to his bedside, but the letter arrived late, and he died without her coming to his side. Her grief- and guilt-ridden spirit still waits in the house for the letter to arrive on time and set things right. She usually appears to students while they are sleeping, sitting by their bed stroking their hair or holding their hand. If the student awakens during her visit, she calms him by saying, "It's all right, dear."

CHRIST CHURCH CATHEDRAL Christ Church Cathedral in Fredericton is a magnificent Gothic cathedral built in the late 1840s. Reverend John Medley was the first bishop of Fredericton and his marble tomb is in the north part of the church, but it is the ghost of his wife, Margaret Medley, who haunts the place. For over a century, her apparition has been seen praying and kneeling in the church. She has even been spotted floating down Queen Street, and then turning onto Church Street, where she heads for the cathedral and passes through the west door.

PRINCE EDWARD ISLAND

University of Prince Edward Island

The University of Prince Edward Island is made up of St. Dunstan's University and Prince of Wales College, which merged in 1968. The Home Economics Building on campus used to be a male dormitory at St. Dunstan's, and one wintry night, after curfew and all the doors were locked, a student arrived late from town and was locked out. The boy pounded on the door, but as punishment

for being out past curfew, the priests would not let him in. They assumed he would simply return to town to find shelter. Late that night, someone knocked at the door of the boy's roommate, but when he opened the door, all that greeted him was a blast of cold air and an icy puddle on the floor. Thinking it was a prank, he went back to bed. The next morning, the frozen body of the locked-out boy was found on the dormitory doorstep, and his restless, ice-cold spirit has haunted the building ever since.

The woman's dormitory, Benadine Hall, is also haunted. Ghostly activity seems to occur most often in the fourth floor lounge, but the apparitions of two unidentified girls have been seen cowering in fear behind furniture in a third floor room. The Cass Chemistry Building on campus is haunted by its namesake, Father Cass, who died in the early 1900s. Father Cass was a caring and helpful man, who is said to still help students find lost items or put away laboratory supplies after they are finished with their experiments.

NEWFOUNDLAND

Cape Spear

CAPE SPEAR BUNKERS The ghosts of former aviators and soldiers from World War II have been seen in the old bunkers from that era. In 1941, two ten-inch gun emplacements and underground passages connecting the gun sites to men's barracks were constructed at Cape Spear to protect St. John's Harbor. The bunkers, tunnels, and giant gun barrels can still be seen at the restored battery site. In 1942, a German U-boat did approach the harbor and fired two torpedoes, but no serious damage occurred.

St. John's

CARTER'S HILL A private residence on Carter's Hill in St. John's is haunted by an unidentified spirit that likes to lock doors, move around in an icy wind, and stomp on the stairs. In one instance, it made a Christmas tree shake violently by itself. Several tenants have remarked about the paranormal activity. Investigators discovered that a person who lived in the house in the 1950s committed murder, but they have been unable to determine if the ghost is the murdered person or the murderer. The St. John's Haunted Hike departs from the West Entrance to the Anglican Cathedral, Church Hill, in St. John's from June through October. For more information, visit the Web site at www.avint.net/hardticket. The E-mail address is hike@avint.net or phone 709-576-2087.

Placentia Bay

GREEK GALLEY A phantom Greek sailing ship is said to still roam the waters of Placentia Bay, and its flaming presence has on many occasions interfered with the fishing operations of the people in that area. Some fishermen have even reported feeling the heat of the fire that consumes the ship, and have heard the agonizing cries of the figures onboard.

QUEEN'S ROAD APARTMENTS The old Queen's Rows Apartments at 92-A Queen's Road in St. John's is haunted by the sounds of nonexistent babies crying. For many years, tenants complained about the loud crying noises but no source could ever be found. Residents of the house, which has three apartments on three floors, also reported seeing the apparition of a woman walking slowly up the stairs. Investigators discovered that a woman who lived there had murdered her two babies and then put their tiny bodies in a cardboard box. She calmly took the box to the city dump and set it on fire, but was caught before all the evidence of her deed was destroyed.

SUTHERLAND PLACE Sutherland Place on King's Bridge Road in St. John's is haunted by a soldier who died on the property in 1770. The apparition of a tall man in military uniform is seen, although his face is hidden by the high collar of his military coat. He is believed to be a foot soldier who lost his life during the battles between the French and the English. He is seen so often by residents and visitors that he was given the nickname "Peter Paul." King's Bridge Road is a nineteenth-century

roadway built during the reign of King George III to connect Fort William with Portugal Cove and other nearby ports. However, the land was a battleground during the French-English wars.

Sutherland Place is a duplex Renaissance-revival mansion built by William Pitts in 1883 on land purchased from the Church of England just off King's Bridge Road. William died before the house could be completed, however, and the mansion was occupied by his son, the Honorable James S. Pitts.

James rented out the south part the mansion and lived in the north part. His tenants included some of Newfoundland's most distinguished leaders in the years before it became part of Canada. Two lieutenant governors lived there. Sir Leonard Outerbridge lived there from 1884 to 1918, and Gordon A. Winter grew up in the house as a boy. In 1924 the house was purchased and soon was turned into apartments. That was when tenants started seeing the ghost of the soldier wandering around on the property.

After minor renovations in 1998, another unidentified ghost decided to take up residence on the third floor of Sutherland Place. A woman renting a room there started having strange experiences a short time after moving in. She felt uneasy, as if someone were watching or stalking her. One day while she was talking on the telephone, the couch on which she was sitting started to bounce around violently for no apparent reason. Then one of her female roommates woke up to see the form of an old woman with long black hair in a long, flowing black dress standing at the foot of her bed. Residents of a neighboring apartment were experiencing similar phenomena. A woman in that apartment kept seeing the apparition of an elderly lady sitting in the middle of her couch. When the ghost started trying to push people down stairs, both tenants moved out.

TANRAHAN'S TOWN Tanrahan's Town was a nineteenth-century neighborhood that once stood along Willicoff's Lane off Gower Street in St. John's behind the present Masonic Temple. The poor neighborhood of 200 houses and 1,500 residents was burnt to the ground in a devastating fire in 1855. Then when it was rebuilt, it burned down again in 1892. To this day, it is not ghosts but phantom fires that haunt this old neighborhood. Buildings constructed after the Great Fire of 1892 are plagued by ghostly flames that erupt from walls but do no damage. In one home, the ghost fire is confined to a fireplace, making it not as alarming as other homes. But if you place your hand in the fireplace, you feel neither warmth nor fire. Sometimes the floorboards or walls erupt in nonexistent flames, which is much more alarming to tenants.

VICTORIA STATION Victoria Station was used as a doctor's office, surgery, and residence for over thirty years and then became a funeral parlor. In the early 1990s, the building was remodeled into the Victoria Station Inn. The former undertaker is said to still haunt the building and has been seen by employees and guests. One employee working late in an upstairs room saw a Victorian gentleman, dressed in fancy evening clothes, leaning against the mantle of the fireplace, smoking a pipe. The two exchanged glances and the Victorian figure just disappeared into nothingness. The Victoria Station Inn is at 290-288 Duckworth Street in St. John's, Newfoundland.

QUEBEC

Hudson

WILLOW PLACE INN Willow Place Inn overlooks the south shore of Lac des Deux Montagnes in the town of Hudson in Quebec. Built in 1820, the house served as headquarters for Patriotes sympathizers in the Rebellion of 1837. A servant girl in the house overheard conspirators planning the uprising at Saint-Eustache, and she made the mistake of letting them know she disapproved and supported the Militia. The men murdered her and buried her body in the basement.

Her name was Mary Kirbride, and her spirit still haunts the building. Current owners of the inn have nicknamed her "Maude" and report all kinds of paranormal phenomena associated with her. Rocks pile up at the door to Room 8 for

some unknown reason, people report invisible presences in the halls and rooms, chairs and other objects are pushed over by unseen hands, and the voice of a young woman singing can be heard. November is the most active month for the otherworldly manifestations.

Montreal

GRIFFINTOWN A ghost returns every seven years to a vacant lot on the southeast corner of the intersection of William and Murray streets in the Griffintown section of Montreal. So far the apparition has been spotted seventeen times, and it is due to return next in June 2005. The cyclic spirit is a former prostitute named Mary Gallagher, who worked the area with her associate Susan Kennedy. In June 1879, the two women got into an argument over a handsome "john" they had brought to Susan's house on William Street. When the man passed out drunk on the parlor floor, the two women went after each other. Susan got the upper hand and knocked Mary out. Then she took an axe and cut her friend to pieces. Police found the mutilated body in the parlor; Mary's head was in a water bucket in the kitchen. Susan was sentenced to life in prison and died there in 1916. It was rumored that the body and head of the prostitute were not afforded a proper burial by authorities, and that is why the headless phantom of Mary Gallagher started returning to the scene of the crime, roaming the area near Susan's house in search of her severed head.

McGILL UNIVERSITY The McLennan Library at Quebec's prestigious McGill University in Montreal is haunted by an unidentified man in an old-fashioned coat. He only appears on the sixth floor of the library building and looks decidedly out of place or lost. When people talk to him, he looks directly at them and then disappears.

Shawville

DAGG POLTERGEIST Situated on Gatineau Park Road outside Shawville in Pontiac County, Quebec, the Dagg family farmhouse was the center of demonic activity for over two months and became known as the Amityville Horror of Canada. George Dagg lived in the house with his wife, two children, and an adopted eleven-year-old orphan named Dinah Maclean.

The first sign of the evil presence that was to plague this family was some money that disappeared and then turned up unexpectedly. Then on September 15, 1889, the family discovered a mass of filth from the outdoor privy, mixed with sugar, covering both doors to the house and spread on the bed sheets. After that, all hell broke loose. Pails, pots, pans, dishes flew through the kitchen under their own power. Chairs, the sofa, and the kitchen table were turned upside down. Suddenly all the windows in the house broke at the same instant. Unexplainable fires erupted throughout the house. Clumps of hair were yanked and pulled from the children's heads. People came from throughout Quebec to witness the poltergeist activity.

Famous psychic and medium, Elizabeth Barnes, was summoned from nearby Plum Hollow, Ontario. Barnes felt that a witch had put a curse on the family, but her suggestions did little to dispel the uninvited guest. Dinah had grown thin and pale and eventually confessed that she could see the demon and sometimes hear him speak. On one occasion, over twenty witnesses heard the demon speak to Dinah near the woodshed on the property. It began by saying to Dinah, "I'm the Devil! Get out of this, or I'll break your neck." For the next five hours, the "devil" answered questions posed by the people who had gathered. Seventeen witnesses signed affidavits attesting to what has happened.

Finally, an Anglican priest arrived to perform an exorcism, but before he could begin, his Bible disappeared right from his hands. After he had gone, it was found in the kitchen oven. Then, the demon roared that it would return the following Sunday. Word got out and dozens of people showed up to engage the entity in conversation. The voice said it would leave forever at midnight that day, but the crowd was so enthralled by its wit that they kept asking it questions until 3:00 A.M. The following morning, all three of the chil-dren in the house said they could see a white angel floating in the sky, but no one else could see it. After two months of terrorizing the family, the Dagg poltergeist was gone.

ONTARIO

Brockville

FULFORD MANSION Fulford Mansion is now a museum with a ghost of its very own. Many volunteers and visitors have seen the apparition of a man walking the halls. The ghost has never harmed anyone and seems to be friendly enough. The mansion was built by George T. Fulford in the early 1900s, and he is assumed to be the lingering presence.

Etobicoke

ETOBICOKE POLTERGEIST A three-story, white clapboard, former farmhouse at 184 Prince Edward Drive South in Etobicoke, Ontario, became famous in 1968 as the site of a malevolent poltergeist responsible for insane screams, hysterical laughter, strange odors, and loud banging sounds that echoed throughout the house. The house is over a century old and sits near Park Lawn Cemetery in Etobicoke, which is a western suburb of Toronto. The main floor was rented by Roy and Carol Hawkins and their two children, while the basement and second floor were rented out to other individuals. The haunting started with loud thumping sounds that were punctuated with horrifying laughter in a female voice. Then residents were bothered by an evil, invisible presence they felt in their bedrooms at night and loud footsteps that seemed to come from the ceilings and woke them up. One evening, something kicked the family's cat and sent it sailing though the air hissing, while sinister laughter rang out from out of nowhere. A brown, oval light was seen on the attic stairs by several witnesses.

Dozens of investigators descended on the house with all kinds of electronic and infrared measuring devices to document the strange phenomena. An exorcism was performed, but the haunting only intensified. Finally, the Hawkins family and other tenants could no longer stand to be in the house, and everyone moved out. At that point, the haunting lessened. After a thorough study of the evidence, investigators concluded that the Etobicoke Poltergeist was caused by intense emotional energy coming from Carol Hawkins. At the time, her baby boy was undergoing a series of operations to try to save it from a massive head infection that started in the child's ear. The child hovered near death, and it is believed Carol's apprehension and anguish were expressed physically in the house itself.

LAKESHORE PSYCHIATRIC HOSPITAL The haunting here began after three buildings were renovated when the former hospital was purchased by a local college. Not long after the new classrooms opened, two students were in the old tunnels that connect the buildings when they encountered an invisible person who they could hear whistling as it walked in the tunnel and up the stairs. Other students have also felt an invisible presence lurking in the tunnel. A construction worker doing some work in the tunnel encountered the apparition of a nurse in a white uniform. She walked right by him, and then turned a corner without saying a word. The worker followed her cautiously to see what she was up to. When he caught up with her, she turned to face him, and he saw that she only had a "flat, blank area" where her face should have been. Other workers have reported a number of poltergeist effects, such as objects moving and electrical problems, in a room in the basement that used to the hospital's morgue. Students and teachers at the college have also reported sensing the uncontrollable fear and anger of former inmates at the asylum and sense their presence in the former wards.

ROYAL CANADIAN LEGION HALL The Mimico and Humber Bay Branch 217 of the Royal Canadian Legion in Etobicoke is haunted by a young male soldier named Henry. His apparition has been seen since the 1960s roaming around on the third floor of the building. During one investiga-

tion by a journalist from the *Oakville Journal Record*, talcum powder was sprinkled all over the third floor and two witnesses discovered footprints had formed that originated from a wall and disappeared abruptly in the middle of the room. Singer-songwriter Donna Dunlop performed at the legion hall many times and encountered the ghost on several occasions. The hundred-year-old mansion was originally called Eden Court and owned by the Stock family for many years. In the 1930s, it was a glamorous gambling hall owned by gangster Abe Orpen. It was renovated in 1966 and that is when the haunting began. The Royal Canadian Legion Branch 217 is located at 515 Royal York Road in Etobicoke, Toronto.

Hamilton

HAMILTON-BELVIDERE MANSION The Hamilton-Belvidere Mansion is said to be cursed. It is haunted by the ghosts of two murdered families. The first family was killed by their insane, seventeen-year-old son, who afterwards, hanged himself in the attic. The house was sold to another family who inherited the hateful energy. Not long after they moved in, the father murdered his entire family and then hanged himself in the attic.

THE HERMITAGE The Hermitage is the ruins of an old mansion in the Ancaster area near Hamilton. The ruins and the woods surrounding them are haunted by the ghost of a black slave, who hanged himself from a willow tree on the property. He was in love with his white master's daughter and she loved him. But their love was forbidden, and the daughter killed herself. The slave hanged himself after he heard the news.

Hawksville

SIDEROAD 17 Hawksville is a small community in Ontario. In the early 1900s, a Mennonite family died in a house fire and left behind a six-year-old son. The boy was taken into a neighboring family and raised. As the boy grew up, he made it known that if he ever died, he wanted to be buried with his original family members. When he died at the age of forty-seven, however, he was interred in the family plots of the people who took him in. Ever since, witnesses have seen his apparition crossing Sideroad 17, the road that separates the two family's farms, eternally seeking his rightful burial. During heavy fog, his ghostly outline can be most clearly seen.

Lucan

DONNELLY HOMESTEAD The Donnelly family were immigrants from Ireland who came to Canada in the 1840s to set up a new life on land given away by the Canadian government. James and Johannah Donnelly never really got along too well with their neighbors, but in the late 1870s things escalated insanely to the point where the Donnellys were the most hated family in Biddulph Township. Finally, on the night of February 3, 1880, a mob of their neighbors broke into the Donnelly house and brutally bludgeoned and stabbed James, Johannah, two of their sons, and a niece visiting the family. Then they set fire to the place. What they did not know was that a neighbor boy spending the night had witnessed the whole horrible scene.

Despite his testimony, nobody was ever punished for the crimes because local authorities covered it up. But the old homestead has not forgotten that traumatic night. Later residents of the house reported all kinds of paranormal activity. Robert and Noreen Norton, who bought the property in 1974, told reporters horses were especially sensitive to the paranormal energy and ran around as if something was pursuing them. Horses ridden near the old Donnelly property on the old Roman Line road late at night on February 3 will go berserk as if they are possessed or refuse to go any further. If they are forced to proceed the animals soon die mysteriously. That has happened in a least three cases. The ghost of a headless horse has also been spotted on the road at night, and blue balls of lightning have been seen rolling along the road on the anniversary of the massacre. Weird objects have also been seen and photo-graphed near the Donnelly tombstones on the property.

Robert and Linda Salts, the current owners of the Donnelly Homestead, have also witnessed paranormal activity, almost from the moment they walked into their new home and started unpacking in 1988. They constantly feel as if they are being watched, touched, or tested by the unseen presences of the Donnelly family. They hear footsteps going up the stairs late at night, hear their names called by a "soft masculine voice," and see ghostly shadows moving throughout the house at all hours. Their three children have also seen strange things. Several times, the apparitions of four different members of the Donnelly family have appeared in their room. Psychics have also seen the presences. The stern-looking ghosts of James and Johannah are dressed in plain black clothing, while the Donnelly children ghosts are dressed in white.

Tourists visiting the property report the same feelings. The barn is the original Donnelly barn built in 1877 and is haunted by strange footsteps and the sounds of screams. Several visitors to the barn have reported feeling a heavy, oppressive pressure on their chest from some unseen presence. The original Donnelly home burned down on the night of the massacre in the very early morning hours of February 4, 1880. The next year, the remaining members of the family, William, Patrick, and Robert Donnelly, got together and restored the middle part of the original house. The rest of the house was built up new around it. This section of the house from 1877 is the center for a lot of the haunted activity. Psychics investigating the property always pinpoint this area. Other investigators have sensed the presence of a young man in his late twenties lurking in the grove of trees behind the house. It is thought to be William Donnelly, who was known to have loved that area of the property the most.

The Donnelly Homestead is located in Biddulph Township in Lucan, Ontario. For more information, visit the Donnelly Web sites at www.donnellys.com and www.quadro.net/~donnelly. In 1996, J. Robert Salts self-published a book about his experiences called *You Are Never Alone:*

Our Experiences on the Donnelly Homestead, which can be ordered online. The Donnelly Homestead is located at 34937 Roman Line in Lucan, Ontario. For information, phone 519-227-1244 or E-mail rsalts@quadro.net.

London

ELDON HOUSE Eldon House in London, Ontario, is haunted by a British army officer. The man's ghost appeared at a formal ball just minutes after he drowned in the Thames River, which flows through the grounds of the house.

GRAND THEATRE The Grand Theatre in London, Ontario, is haunted by the ghost of Ambrose Small, who owned ninety theaters and opened the opulent London showplace in 1901. On December 2, 1919, Ambrose mysteriously disappeared in downtown Toronto, and his mischievous ghost took up residence in his favorite theater building. He is most often encountered by actors and stagehands in the backstage area, and is blamed for little tricks that bring errors to the attention of performers or protect the theater in some way. The Grand Theatre is on Adelaide Street in London, Ontario.

MIDDLESEX COUNTY JAIL The former jailhouse in London is haunted by the ghost of "Peg Leg" Marion Brown, a notorious criminal who was hanged there. Peg-Leg left an eerie legacy at the county jail where he was hanged in 1899 for murdering a cop. He insisted he was innocent and as he stood on the gallows, proclaimed no grass would ever grow on his grave. None ever did, right up to 1985 when they found the Mexican-Texan desperado's bones while building a parking lot in the former jail area.

Mississauga

CHERRY HILL HOUSE RESTAURANT In Mississauga, Ontario, the oldest building in town never had any ghosts until it was moved to a new location in 1973. The Cherry Hill House restaurant and banquet hall was originally a private residence built by the Silverthorne family in 1822, who lived there until 1932, when it was rented to the Lindsay family until 1972. Then, the building was moved to a new foundation just eight hundred feet from the original. Almost from the day it was opened, the restored building was haunted by poltergeist activity and moving apparitions. The frightening faces of Indians started emerging from the fireplace, and it has been suggested the building was moved on top of an Indian burial ground. Once an apparition arose from a pile of dirt and brandished a sword at a security guard.

Another time, a manager saw the ghost of a "girl in white" running away from something. A medium was brought in, and she contacted the spirit of a sixteen-year-old girl named Miranda, who said she burned to death in the nineteenth century in a fire that started while she was making candles. Cherry Hill House is located a block north of Dundas Street West at Cawthra Avenue in Mississauga, which is a suburb of Toronto. It is located at 680 Silvercreek Boulevard and the phone number is 905-275-9300.

Niagara Falls

FORT GEORGE Fort George at Niagara-on-the-Lake was built over two centuries ago by the British to defend the vital St. Lawrence water communications route from American control. The fort served as the main headquarters of the British Army in Ontario, a meeting place for the Upper Canadian Militia and Six Nations warriors, a depot for the Provincial Marine Naval Department, garrison for the Canadian Army, and the scene of bloody battles during the War of 1812 as Canadians banded together to repulse several American advances.

The United States declared war on Britain on June 18, 1812, and on October 13, the American army invaded the village of Queenston. Canadian commander Isaac Brock rallied an outnumbered band of British regulars, Canadian militia, and Native warriors and counterattacked. In the ensuing twelve-hour confrontation, Brock drove back the Americans but was killed by a sniper's bullet. After their capture of Toronto a year later, the Americans attacked again at Niagara, and took Fort George after a relentless barrage of artillery. The Americans occupied Fort George but were defeated in their attempts to expand further into Canadian territory. In December 1813, the Americans abandoned the fort, and British troops took back control of it and the American Fort Niagara across the river. Fort Niagara is another strategic fort built by the French in 1726. The Americans attacked once again in 1814, but were defeated by the British, who occupied both forts for decades afterwards.

The buildings of Fort George were reconstructed in the 1930s as a historic site. Today, the fully restored fort is garrisoned by a staff wearing the clothing of the War of 1812. Apparitions of former soldiers—American, Canadian, and British—have been seen on the traumatized ground. Ghost Tours of Fort Niagara and Fort George are available from May through September and commence from the parking lot in front of Fort George, just off the Niagara Parkway in Niagara-on-the-Lake. For more information, visit the Web site at www.ghrs.org/ghosttours.

HOUDINI MAGICAL HALL OF FAME Regular séances to contact the spirit of Harry Houdini have been held at the Houdini Magical Hall of Fame in Niagara Falls, Ontario, since 1968. On several occasions it is believed his ghost manifested to mediums there. Houdini died on Halloween 1926 and promised to return from the dead if there was a way. Participants have included Houdini's closest friends like mentalists Joseph Dunninger and Walter B. Gibson, as well as other magicians such as James Randi.

OBAN INN At the Oban Inn in the town of Niagara-on-the-Lake, the ghost of Captain Duncan Mallory, who built the place in 1824, still roams the halls at night. The Buttery restaurant and the Royal George Theatre are just a few of the landmarks inhabited by restless old spirits. The most intriguing mystery, though, is the town's French thorn trees. The story goes they're the progeny of the Golgotha tree that provided the thorns worn by Jesus Christ at his crucifixion. These

creepy trees apparently grow nowhere else in Canada.

OLDE ANGEL INN At the Olde Angel Inn, in Niagara-on-the-Lake, Ontario, the spirit of a British soldier, tortured to death in the basement by American soldiers in the War of 1812, still is felt and seen. To this day, Captain Swayze, whose portrait hangs in a corner of the lobby, harbors ill feelings towards Americans. He has been known to interfere with the operation of beer kegs containing American brew, and even throw beer steins and chairs at them. The bathrooms are said to be haunted by his "cold spot," and his wigged apparition, wearing a blue frock coat and white trousers, is encountered sporadically. Several séances have confirmed the ghost's continuing displeasure with the Americans. The Olde Angel Inn is at 224 Regent Street in Niagara-on-the-Lake, Ontario. For more information, phone 905-468-3411.

Port Perry

GHOST ROAD Port Perry is a suburb of Toronto that has a paved road nicknamed for its most distinguishing feature. Ghost Road is haunted by a man who was riding his motorcycle through an open field at a very high rate of speed. A farmer had put up a barbed wire fence at the intersection of the dirt road in his field and the road. The motorcyclist did not see the fence in the dark and was decapitated. He died instantly and has haunted the spot ever since. The accident took place in 1976, and ever since, witnesses report his motorcycle light coming at them from a distance in the field. The light looks just like the headlamp of a motorcycle, and as the phantom motorcycle passes by through the trees, the red taillight can be seen.

Scarborough

TABER HILL PARK This public park vibrates with otherworldly energy and may have been an ancient sacred site used for spiritual renewal and vision quests. It overlooks Lake Ontario and offers a serene view of the entire area. The large mound at the center of the park is an Iroquois burial site that dates back to A.D. 1250 and contains about 475 bodies. The park is located on Bellamy Road North, one block north of Lawrence Avenue East, in the city of Scarborough.

Toronto

ALBERT'S HALL Albert's Hall, a music house in Toronto, has three ghosts that seem to dangle from ropes in midair. Two of the unidentified apparitions are male, and the other is female. The female is the most frequently sighted. She is seen hanging from her feet from a rope tied to the banister on the stairs that connect the second and third floors. She appears from nowhere with her arms flailing and her mouth opened in a silent scream. There is no record of any such event, although the place has a bawdy history. It was first used as a dancehall, then a vaudeville theater, and finally a blues music hall. A fire in the 1880s gutted the third floor but no one was injured. Musicians performing here report all kinds of strange electrical problems, including an unexplainable high-pitched hum coming from the haunted banister. Ontario is Canada's most haunted province and Toronto its most haunted city. For more information on ghosts in this city, visit the Toronto Ghosts Web site at www.TorontoGhosts.org.

BUDDIES IN BAD TIMES THEATRE This old warehouse building has been home to alternative theater groups since 1968. The Toronto Workshop Productions theater company was the first to be housed here, and after they closed shop, the building was purchased by the city of Toronto, who leased it to a variety of theater groups. In 1994, a gay/lesbian theater company called Buddies in Bad Times took over.

Nobody has ever identified the presence that haunts this building, but most of the activity seems to take place at night. Odd noises ring throughout the building at night, icy cold spots follow people around, and untraceable footsteps are heard. The phenomena are centered in the basement and stage area, and it is generally assumed the unseen poltergeist is associated with former actors or performances. The Buddies in Bad Times Theatre is at 12 Alexander Street in Toronto, Ontario.

C.B.C. BUILDING The old Canadian Broadcasting Company building in Toronto's Cabbagetown area is haunted by a number of ghosts from the thirty years it served the company. It was abandoned in 1993, when the C.B.C. moved to its new broadcasting center on Front Street West, but the ghosts stayed behind. On the fourth floor of the building, the apparition of a tall man in black clothing walks toward the elevator as if he were carrying a heavy box, or perhaps he is injured or disabled in some way. If the elevator stops at that floor, he gets on. Disembodied voices have also been recorded on the haunted fourth floor. The building is currently slated for redevelopment and renovation, which ought to stir up the spirits there even more. The old C.B.C. Building is at 90 Sumach Street in Toronto.

DON JAIL The old Don Jail is an imposing building located at 550 Gerrard Street East in Toronto. Built in 1858 as the original City Jail, the place was expanded into a maximum-security prison where hangings took place until 1962. The building has been shut down since 1993 and is awaiting renovation. The most active ghost of the prison is in the West Wing, where women were housed. The apparition of a blonde-haired woman has been reported floating high in the air in the Main Rotunda. The woman hanged herself in her cell in the 1890s and is still suspended in time, lost between heaven and hell.

COLBORNE LODGE Colborne Lodge is a charming villa on Colborne Lodge Drive in Toronto's west end at High Park. It was built in the early 1830s by the lieutenant-governor of Upper Canada, Sir John Colborne. Sir John's wife, Jemina, suffered from cancer and was confined to her upstairs bedroom for many years before dying there in 1877. Because of devastating pain, she was given morphine and opium, which kept her in a dreamy, disconnected state. She spent most of her time staring out her window at her burial plot on the property. To this day, her apparition is seen staring out that same upstairs master bedroom window, looking down at her iron-fenced gravesite and massive monument. Her silhouetted apparition was first reported by a motorcycle policeman in 1969. Sir John died in the house in 1890 and willed his house and property to the city. Colborne Lodge is now a public museum run by the Toronto Historical Board.

ELGIN THEATRE This old Toronto theater is haunted by some powerful presence. The entity is strongest in the ladies restroom, where two separate murders have allegedly taken place. Many employees have noticed odd things, such as footsteps, voices, screams, vibrating objects, and the smell of a distinctive perfume when no one is wearing it. In the 1980s, two night watchmen encountered an invisible presence that locked them out of the bathroom. In another incident, a woman janitor was accosted in the restroom by an invisible entity and had to go to the hospital for treatment of her wounds. To date, no investigation of the premises has been undertaken.

FORT YORK Fort York is located on Garrison Street, off Fleet Street between Strachon Avenue and Bathurst Street in Toronto. Built in 1793, the old British fort was occupied by American forces twice during the War of 1812 and witnessed a lot of heavy fighting. Apparently, the ghostly soldiers are still on alert at the fort, for they seem to be caught in the middle of a battle. People walking on the parapets and near defensive positions are pulled out of the line of fire by invisible hands, the apparition of a red-coated guard is seen in the barracks and near the front entrance to the fort, and sometimes, full regiments materialize to drill in the yard. The sounds of disembodied footsteps running for cover are still heard inside the fort. Recently, a militiaman of the Royal Regiment of Canada was jogging along the old earthworks in front of the fort, when "something" yanked him down into the fort, as if forcing him to take cover. The apparition of a woman also was spotted at the fort, walking around the officers' quarters. In 1996, modern cadets sleeping overnight at the fort reported the lady's ghost trying to hold their hands while they were in bed sleeping. For information on tours of Fort York, call 416-392-6907.

GIBRALTAR POINT LIGHTHOUSE The Gibraltar Point Lighthouse is located on Ward's Island in Toronto Harbor. A bronze plaque near the lighthouse commemorates its ghost, a former lighthouse keeper who disappeared mysteriously and returned to haunt the site. John Paul Rademuller was appointed the first lighthouse keeper in 1809 and was soon using his spare time brewing bootleg beer. When Rademuller refused some of his brew to two drunken soldiers, they bludgeoned him to death and helped themselves to his beer. To cover up the murder, they cut up the body in small pieces and buried it in the ground surrounding the lighthouse. The two men were arrested for the crime in 1815, but with no evidence of a body, they had to be released. Today, the apparition of John Paul Rademuller is seen walking up the stairway to light the beacon or roaming the grounds looking for his scattered body parts. Some human bones were discovered buried near the lighthouse in 1893, but it is still not certain if they were Rademuller's.

GRANGE The Grange is the name of a Georgian mansion built in 1817. Canada's famous essayist Goldwin Smith lived in the house from 1871 till his death at home in 1910. Some have suggested it could be Smith's shadowy apparition that is still seen in the library. Others believe the revenant is his assistant, the aspiring horror writer Algernon Blackwood. Another candidate might be William Chin, who served as the butler at the Grange for over fifty years. In 1973, the Grange was renovated and became the Art Gallery of Ontario. The restorers have been very careful to preserve the mansion exactly as it was in its heyday. The Art Gallery of Ontario is at 317 Dundas Street West in Toronto. The phone number is 416-979-6648.

HOCKEY HALL OF FAME This ornate beaux-arts building was the home of a branch of the Bank of Montreal from 1847 to 1983. When it became home to the Hockey Hall of Fame in 1993, the group hardly expected to take possession of the bank's ghost as well. In the early 1900s, a teller by the name of Dorothy had a love affair with a married teller at the bank that went bad. One day the distraught woman took the bank's pistol, went upstairs to the restroom, and shot herself in the head. Not long afterwards, her apparition started appearing near the offices and vault. That was followed by a variety of poltergeist activity, and the bank got such a reputation for being haunted that tellers refused to be transferred there and staff refused to use the upstairs restroom.

There have been a few encounters with Dorothy by the new owners. According to the Hall of Fame's publicist, employees have formed a positive relationship with the ghost, although they tend to blame her for taking misplaced items. When asked if he had any run-ins with the ghost, Ron Ellis, former Toronto Maple Leaf player and Hockey Hall of Fame member, said that he has heard Dorothy moving around but that after working with Punch Imlach, nothing scares him anymore. The Hockey Hall of Fame is located on the corner of Yonge and Front Streets in Toronto. For information, call 416-360-7765.

Hsin Kuang Centre The Hsin Kuang building at 346 Spadina Avenue in Toronto was constructed in 1929 as the headquarters for unionists known as the Labour Lyceum. The building was remodeled into a beautiful Chinese Mandarin restaurant in the 1970s, but the place was cursed with bad luck from the beginning and soon closed down. Rumors spread that the building was haunted by spirits from a Chinese funeral parlor and morgue that stood on the property long ago. Some witnesses reported seeing a male apparition in the washroom of the restaurant.

Finally, the owners called in a traditional Chinese exorcist, who thought the problem could be solved with Feng Shui. He pointed to two billboards on top of the building across the street that directed negative spiritual energy into the front entrance of the restaurant. At his urging, two huge protective gargoyles were placed at the front entrance, special mirrors were installed inside to redirect the energy, and the main entrance was moved around the corner. That seemed to work and a new sense of wholesomeness pervaded the building. The owners decided to open up the building to several different merchants, and so far, they have been very successful—and ghostfree.

Keg Mansion Restaurant This exclusive Toronto eatery is in a real Gothic mansion, built in 1853 by the founder of McMaster University, Lord William McMaster. It was purchased in 1860 by Hart Massey, founder of the giant farm implements company, Massey Ferguson. Actor Raymond Massey grew up here, and the house remained in the Massey family until the 1920s. After that it served as an art gallery, convalescent home, and bar. It became part of the Keg Mansion Restaurant chain in 1976.

Stories that the mansion was haunted began circulating in the 1950s. The sound of ghostly children running and playing are heard in the upper floors and in the kitchen, and an especially hyperactive boy ghost is encountered in the bar area. After the death of matriarch Lilian Massey in 1908, a faithful maid was so stricken by grief that she hanged herself in the house. Her grisly apparition is seen dangling from a rope in the oval vestibule over the main foyer. The Keg Mansion Restaurant is at 515 Jarvis Street in Toronto. For reservations, call 416-964-6609.

Mackenzie House The most haunted house in Toronto is said to be the Georgian home of its first mayor, William Lyon Mackenzie. Mackenzie moved into the house in 1859 and died in the second-floor bedroom in 1861. His distinctive apparition, a short, bald man in a red wig and frock coat, is often seen in the house, most often in his second-floor bedroom. Today, the ex-mayor seems fascinated with modern indoor plumbing and is blamed with flushing toilets and turning on water taps. His presence is also felt in the basement near the printing press. Mackenzie was a firebrand political rebel and led the Rebellion of 1837. The apparition of his wife, a lady with long, flowing hair, has also been seen on both the second and third floors. She liked to appear at the foot of the beds of sleeping residents.

Scores of reports of poltergeist activity and ghostly sightings have been made by residents, workmen, and visitors to Mackenzie House over the years. A séance and exorcism under the auspices of Anglican Archdeacon John Frank was held in 1960, and when ownership of the house was transferred to the Toronto Historical Board, among the contents listed on the official inventory list was "One Ghost (exorcized)." That is still the view of the Historical Board, which downplays any reports of recent activity. Mackenzie was the grandfather of Canada's spiritualist prime minister, William Lyon Mackenzie King. Mackenzie House is at 82 Bond Street in Toronto. For information on tours, call 416-392-6915.

MASSEY HALL Toronto's Massey Hall, a former symphony auditorium, is now a concert hall for rock bands and choral groups. Built by industrialist Hart Massey and opened in 1894, it was the city's only major concert hall until Roy Thompson Hall opened in 1983. The Massey is haunted by two ghosts. One is a male apparition in old-fashioned clothing who wanders the backstage area and seems interested in getting sets up on stage. The other ghost is "Diva," an apparition who walks through the auditorium seats and sings out in a high-pitched wail that disrupts performances. She is thought to be a former opera singer who does not like the change in musical venue at her old symphony hall, while others argue she is a more diffuse poltergeist spirit created from the emotional energies of the performers themselves. Massey Hall is at 15 Shuter Street in Toronto, Ontario. For information, phone 416-593-4828.

Perhaps old Massey Hall is where Toronto's Sci-Fi Band picked up their ghost. The popular rock group, led by Patrick Cross, is haunted by a nasty poltergeist spirit. The ghost has manifested at places the band performs, caused fires, messed with equipment, and thrown objects about on stage. Psychic Eugenia Macer-Story contacted the spirit and discovered it is a female entity that has attached itself to an electric guitar used by the group. To protect themselves, band members have taken to treating the ghost as a member of the group. "Since we tried talking to the ghost," says

Sci-Fi Band Ghost, Toronto, Canada (Patrick Cross)

Patrick, "things have calmed down a bit, but there are still things being moved around and the ghost-energy doesn't want to leave or pass on to the Other Side. She still wants to be noticed!" The group now bills itself as "Canada's Most Haunted Rock Band." For updates, visit the band's Web site at www.globalserve.net/~scifi/enter.htm.

MYNAH BIRD COFFEE HOUSE The Mynah Bird was an unusual establishment located at 144 Yorkville Avenue in Toronto. True, it was a coffeehouse with topless dancing and nudie films, but what made it really unusual was the angry and sometimes violent ghost that haunted the place. The coffeehouse always had a dance floor, but when owner Colin Kerr added seminude dancing girls to boost business, he found that some invisible presence objected. Something started interfering with the striptease shows, and all kinds of unexplainable electrical and mechanical problems started popping up. Musical instruments would disappear, and strange noises interrupted performances. Then, the girls began encountering a decidedly unfriendly presence on the upper floor that even took to throwing chairs around. Once, the apparition of a man with gray hair and a beard was seen. The upstairs area used to be an artist's studio, and it is thought that the activities ran counter to the spirit's artistic sensibilities. The ghost finally had its way, and the Mynah Bird closed down, to be replaced by a nice quiet commercial building.

OLD CITY HALL Built in the late 1890s, the Old City Hall is a Gothic building with a 260-foot clock tower that was the headquarters of the city of Toronto and county of York until 1966. Today it is the seat of the Toronto municipal court system. Judges, staff, and visitors have reported all kinds of strange poltergeist effects, such as untraceable footsteps and voices echoing through the corridors, judges' robes being tugged by unseen hands, groans and moans from the building itself, and roaming cold spots. Scenes of increased activity include the rear staircase, the northwest attic, and the cellar, which served as a holding area for prisoners. Courtroom 33 is the most haunted area and the presences responsible are thought to be the spirits of the last men sentenced to hang in Canada. In the late 1980s, a *Toronto Star* reporter attempted to spend Halloween night in Courtroom 33 but was forced to flee at 4:00 A.M., after experiencing spooky effects that included her feet being "glued to the floor" so she could not move. Toronto's former City Hall is at 60 Queen Street. The telephone number is 416-327-6092.

ONTARIO SCIENCE CENTRE This popular interactive science museum was opened in 1969 in the Don Mills section of Toronto. The planetarium at the center is called the Star Lab and is located in the Hall of Space. However, starting in 1980, the stellar show was augmented by an astral visitor that employees have dubbed the Star Lab Ghost. According to the facility's astronomy researcher, Ivan Semeniuk, the poltergeist presence was responsible for numerous unexplainable glitches in equipment and other ghostly phenomena, including strange balls of light that would interrupt the planetarium performance. The haunting lessened noticeably when the exhibit was computerized in 1985, although employees go to extra precautions to make sure the ghost does not "slip back in among the stars" in the darkened room. The Ontario Science Centre is located at 770 Don Mills Road in Toronto. For information, call 416-696-3127.

OSGOODE HALL This classical columned building is home to Ontario's Supreme Court and headquarters for the Law Society of Upper Canada. Built in 1829, the place is haunted by a wide variety of presences. The apparitions of several unidentified women have been reported floating through the hallways, and the ghosts of former lawyers and judges have also been seen. The voices of a group of invisible people chattering away can be heard in one chamber in the early morning hours. The ghosts even go so far as to close the doors to the room before their meeting begins, but if someone opens the door, all the talking suddenly halts. Osgoode Hall is at 130 Queen Street West in Toronto, Ontario. For tour information, call 416-947-4041.

PADDOCK NIGHTCLUB The Paddock is one of several alternative culture nightclubs in "Goth Alley," an area near Queen and Bathurst streets in Toronto. Its major distinction is that it is haunted by a former customer. Both employees and patrons have seen the apparition of a man or felt his presence. Most of the encounters have taken place in the basement storage area, where it is said there was a gangland slaying back in the 1930s. The ghost is supposedly of this unidentified gangster, who was shot to death there. Another version of the story is that he hanged himself in the basement rather than face the wrath of the mob boss who was after him.

QUEENS PARK Queens Park is the site of the Ontario Legislative Building located on Queen's Park Crescent in Toronto. The pink sandstone building, constructed in an eerie Gothic-Romanesque style, looks haunted before you even get inside. The legislature was built in 1893 on top of an old insane asylum that dated back to 1842. While some politicians might jest that is all too appropriate, the former asylum appears to actually have contributed a few spirits to the government building. At least three female inmates haunt the basement area and the tunnels that connect the legislature to the Whitney Block buildings.

The most often seen of these former inmates is the grief-stricken White Lady, who wears a long white gown and has long flowing hair. One of the other apparitions is the Modest Maiden, a shy ghost in a checkered dress. The most frightening of the three is the Hanging Woman. She is seen hanging from a hook on the wall of the basement tunnel. Another apparition of Queens Park is the Old Soldier, who appears sporadically in full regimental dress. He is most often seen at official state ceremonies descending the Grand Staircase in the building. Tours of Queens Park take place seven days a week during the summer season. Phone 416-325-7500 for information.

ROYAL ALEXANDRA THEATRE Three ghosts haunted the Royal Alexandra. The apparition of a prop man known as the "Phantom Flyman" lurks up in the rafters or the backstage area of his former workplace. He died in an accident at the theater in 1982. The ghost of an audience member can sometimes be seen in the upper balcony. The woman died in her seat at the Royal Alex many years ago, and most employees of the theater admit to sensing her continuing presence there. And an unidentified man in a beige shirt and brown pants haunts the backstage, and may in fact be the notorious Phantom Flyman in a different guise. Built in 1907, the ornate theater has seen many spectacular and "specter-acular" events. The Royal Alexandra Theatre is at 260 King Street in Toronto. For information, phone 416-872-3333.

ROYAL ONTARIO MUSEUM The Royal Ontario Museum at the corner of University Avenue and Bloor Street West in Toronto is haunted by the ghost of its first curator. The apparition of curator Charles Trick Currelly has been reported several times by night watchmen in the Bishop White Gallery. Currelly was known to work long hours and often slept in his office at the museum, and that is thought to explain the fact that his apparition is sometimes seen wearing only a nightshirt. Currelly was responsible for obtaining the priceless Buddhist sculptures and Chinese wall paintings, which are on display in the Bishop White Gallery at the museum. Perhaps his proud spirit is still admiring the beautiful works. The Royal Ontario Museum is located at 100 Queen's Park in Toronto. For information, phone 416-586-8000.

ROYAL YORK HOTEL The Royal York Hotel is one of Toronto's most enduring landmarks and also has one of the city's most enduring ghosts. For many years, the apparition of an elegant, gray-haired gentleman in a maroon smoking jacket has been seen moving quietly through the corridor of the eighth floor of the tower. There is also another ghost of a former employee who hanged himself in 1994 from a stairwell railing above the nineteenth floor. While the hotel has only nineteen floors, there are stairways that lead to the upper-roof areas on the twentieth to twenty-third floors. The reason for the suicide is unknown, but many employees have reported untraceable sounds of footsteps and screams in that area. Maintenance personnel, who have to access the "Royal York" sign from that floor, also have reported paranormal disturbances. The area is under security surveillance and no explanation for the mysterious sounds has ever been found.

RYERSON UNIVERSITY THEATRE SCHOOL Ryerson University Theatre School at the Ryerson University campus on Gerrard Street in Toronto is haunted by an unidentified apparition that has recently started manifesting there. Visitors and employees are suddenly reporting "creepy feelings" in certain parts of the auditorium, and a female student rehearsing on the stage saw something so terrifying in the audience seats that she has refused ever to go into the building again. Two cursory investigations have turned up no evidence of the source for the haunting.

ST. MARY MAGDALENE CHURCH A ghostly Gray Lady has been seen both inside and outside St. Mary Magdalene's since the 1920s. Construction on the church began in 1888 and ended in 1908. The haunting began when the church organist-choirmaster, the well-known and respected musician Dr. Healey Willan, was practicing alone in the locked church and noticed an elderly woman dressed in gray standing to the side of the pews below him. She disappeared as soon as he got up to look for her. He later discovered that other members of the congregation had also seen the apparition both inside the church and outside in the garden area. In 1991, the new choirmaster, Dr. Elmer Iseler, saw the Gray Lady outside in the northeast corner of the church property. Most church members believe the ghost is a former charlady, who loved the church so much she does not want to leave. St. Mary Magdalene Church is at 477 Manning Avenue in Toronto.

ST. MICHAEL'S HOSPITAL Ward 7B at St. Michael's Hospital is haunted by a nun who used to work in the hospital. The hospital was opened in 1892 and is operated by the Sisters of St. Joseph. The ghost of Ward 7B is Sister Vincenza, or "Vinnie" as the staff calls her, whose apparition is seen still making her rounds in the ward. Vinnie died in the 1950s, but the devoted woman kept up her duties. Witnesses who have encountered the hooded apparition head-on say there is only a black emptiness where her face should be. St. Michael's Hospital is located at 30 Bond Street in Toronto.

TODMORDEN MILLS Todmorden Mills in the Toronto borough of East York has served as a mill, riding stable, theater, and now historical site. Volunteers and employees say the building is haunted. The apparition of an elderly lady, who seems harmless enough, has been glimpsed walking through the theater at night by several witnesses. Another, perhaps less pleasant, apparition is a gray form that is seen floating about twenty feet above the stage in front of the sound booth window. The loud and unexplainable sounds of moving furniture or props can be heard from the loft spaces late at night.

UNIVERSITY OF TORONTO The University of Toronto is composed of four separate colleges, three of which are haunted. Trinity College, which is affiliated with the Anglican Church of Canada, was founded in 1851 by the first bishop of Toronto, John Strachan. The original building was constructed in 1851 at 999 Queen Street West, where the original gates are still standing.

The college moved to its current Gothic building at 6 Hoskin Avenue in 1925. However, a long tradition connects the two sites, for at the beginning of every new term, Trinity students make a ceremonial march from the new school to the gate of the old. That same tradition brings the ghost of Bishop Strachan to the new school building. He died on November 1, 1867, and never saw the new building, but every November 1, his apparition is said to walk the corridors of the new school. The rest of the year, he spends his time in the Provost's Office, where his stern portrait hangs. There is a distinct feeling in that room that the school's founder is still overseeing things.

The second college at the university that is haunted is University College, the main campus of the University of Toronto located just west of Queen's Park Crescent. The Gothic building was built in 1857 and is haunted by a Russian stonemason who worked on it. His name was Ivan Reznikoff, and he seems to still be seeking out Paul Diabolos, the Greek man who stole his beloved Susie. Reznikoff caught Diabolos in a tryst with Susie in the dark passageway that connects Croft Chapter Hall and University College. The enraged Russian went at the Greek with his cutter's axe. He missed his target, although the mark of his axe can still be seen on the oak door at the hall's portico. Later that night, the wily Greek cornered Reznikoff and knifed him to death and dumped his body in a hole being dug for a stairwell. In 1890, workers discovered Reznikoff's remains beneath the stairwell landing and his skull became part of the university archives. (Tours of the campus take place every weekday. Phone 416-978-5000 for more information.)

Massey College at 4 Devonshire Place in Toronto is the university's most recent addition and third haunted college. Founded in 1963, the modern building is haunted by its first Master, Robertson Davies. Davies was a charismatic author and essayist, who earned the nickname "Merlin of Massey." Shortly before his death in December 1995, Davies promised to return to haunt the college or at least "give some signs." He also urged his successor "never to doubt that the college was haunted."

WINTER GARDEN THEATRE The Winter Garden opened in 1913 as a vaudeville theater and was originally called Loew's Yonge Street Theatre. Due to poor attendance during the Depression years, the upper balcony in the huge theater was closed off and remained sealed for nearly fifty years. The lower section eventually was turned into a movie house. In 1981, the Ontario Heritage Foundation bought the landmark in hopes of restoring it. When they opened up the upper balcony, they found priceless memorabilia from the 1920s stored there, as well as a few ghosts. Workers reported spring-loaded seats that would fold down as if someone were sitting down to watch a performance, and would then watch them close hours later as the ghostly audience departed. After the balcony was reopened the elevators seemed to take on a mind of their own, and the apparition of a woman in Edwardian dress started appearing in the lobby. She appears briefly to employees or patrons, and then as soon as she is spotted, disappears.

WONDERLAND Canada's Wonderland Amusement Park is located just north of metropolitan Toronto. The popular attraction is owned and operated by Paramount Studios. Not long after the park opened, a maintenance man working on a ride called Thunder Run was decapitated when a train's brakes failed and it came roaring down the incline toward him. Today, the ride is called the Alpenfest, and it is haunted by his ghost. The Alpenfest Ghost is said to wander throughout the entire park at night after closing. Games and rides start up by themselves and lights mysteriously turn on and off.

YORK UNIVERSITY Glendon College, part of York University in Toronto, is located away from the main campus in the central part of the city on a beautifully wooded campus. York Hall, one of the main buildings at Glendon, is haunted by the ghost of a despondent student who committed suicide there. Doors open slowly then slam shut with no one there, and odd noises such as footsteps and gasping sounds are heard. No apparitions have yet been reported.

Schomberg

COUNTRY BOOKSHOP The Country Bookshop is haunted by the apparition of a hooded lady wearing a cloak, and she never shows her face to anyone. Located north of Toronto and just south of Schomberg in the community of Lloydtown, the haunted bookstore was opened in 1967 in a converted barn. According to locals, in the nineteenth century, a woman's baby died in the barn. One version of the tale says the child died at birth; another says the woman killed it in the barn. Whatever the circumstances, the woman's ghost returns to search for her lost child. She most often appears at twilight in front of the store. She walks slowly from a walnut tree at the beginning of the driveway towards the bookstore and then back again.

Uptergrove

ST. COLUMBKILLE'S CHURCH St. Columbkille's Church in this Ontario city is haunted by an apparition that once sat down at the organ and played hymns. The one hundred-year-old Roman Catholic church has been haunted by the unidentified presence for over fifty years. It is usually seen wearing a black hat and choir gown with a white face and no mouth or nose. When the ghost appeared in the gallery and started playing the organ, parishioners started screaming and the burly custodian darted up the stairs to catch the "prankster," but when he put his arms around the phantom he grasped at thin air. The apparition then shot up the stairs to the belfry, yet when the custodian and others followed it, the area was empty. Another time, the ghost appeared on the church balcony, and when people started yelling at it, it simply faded out of existence.

Wainfleet

HOPKINS TOMB Hopkins Tomb is a public memorial on Lakeshore Road. John Hopkins was a pirate on Lake Erie. As punishment for his deeds, he was sealed into a tomb alive with his dog and left to die. According to legend, the crazed man put a curse on the tomb in which he died. It is said that anyone who tries to get into it or run around it during a full moon, will suffer a nasty accident or die. Witnesses brave enough to visit the tomb at night have reported hearing the howling of a dog coming from the tomb, along with someone pounding on the door demanding to be released.

Windsor

YE OLD BOWIE HOUSE This historic Ontario pub is haunted by a ghostly figure that floats in and out of the rooms. The apparition resembles Sir James Bowie III, who vanished on Lake St. Clair after a boating accident. His snide and childish spirit seems to be taunting or teasing people, and most witnesses describe their encounter not as frightening but rather as "disappointing."

MANITOBA

Winnipeg

FORT GARRY HOTEL The Fort Garry Hotel is a Gothic-style building in Winnipeg that looks haunted before you even get inside. The eighty-five-year-old castlelike structure has plenty of dark corners where ghosts lurk. The hotel even has its own spooky "catacomb," a dark and deserted sub-subbasement that has a haunted tunnel connecting the hotel and the steam plant at the Forks. But the most active spirit is the ghost of a lady in a white ball gown, who is seen hovering at the foot of the beds in some guest rooms. Descriptions of the apparition match Lady McMillan, who wore a white, laced, brocaded gown to a high society ball held by the Victorian Society of Nurses at the hotel in December 1913.

Newspaper reports from the time perfectly describe the ghost currently seen in the hotel. Sometimes she appears as a soft ball of light that moves slowly up and down the hallways, while at other times, her invisible presence is felt pushing down on the bed next to sleeping guests. Apparently, the lonely spirit has yet to hook up with the hotel's other ghost. Hotel employees have seen the apparition of a handsome gentleman eating alone at a table in the dining room in the middle of the night. The Fort Garry Hotel is at 222 Broadway in Winnipeg, Manitoba. For reservations, phone 204-942-8251 or fax 204-956-2351.

LAKE MANITOBA The University of Manitoba's Delta Marsh Field Station administration building is haunted by a caretaker, who dates back to the 1930s when the log-sided building was used as an aristocratic hunting lodge. Murray was the faithful caretaker who catered to the whims of rich men and such celebrities as Cary Grant and Clark Gable. Today, Murray's apparition is seen looking out windows and wandering the halls. He has even been seen sleeping in one of the bunk beds. Murray is also blamed for doors that open and close by themselves, ringing the station bell, and unexplainable sounds at night.

MANITOBA PROVINCIAL ARCHIVES The Manitoba Provincial Archives are housed in the former Winnipeg Civic Auditorium. Over the forty years it served as the city's auditorium, the building saw many illustrious performers who were always enthusiastically received by Winnipeg's citizens. The powerful energy left over from those magical performances is thought to be responsible for the variety of poltergeist effects that manifest in the building to this day. Motion sensors go off for no reason, items are mysteriously taped or glued to workers' desk, strange sounds and footsteps are heard when no one is there, and many unexplainable electrical problems occur.

MANITOBA THEATRE CENTRE The Manitoba Theatre Centre has a ghost that came with the building when it was moved to the present location. Shortly after World War II, the Dominion Theatre building was moved and reopened as the Manitoba Theatre Centre, and the ghost of an adolescent boy named George followed it. George lived at the Dominion with his caretaker father in an upstairs apartment. Though he was confined to a wheelchair, George always wanted to be an actor. Unfortunately, the boy was trapped upstairs when a fire erupted in the building and he was burned to death. Like many other adolescent ghosts, George rarely manifests visibly and prefers to remain an unseen presence. His friendly though mischievous ghost is blamed for stealing files and other objects, turning on appliances to interrupt conversations, throwing books around, and other harmless pranks. Once, witnesses watched in amazement as George's invisible spirit moved through the auditorium and lifted up every folding seat in order, like someone was running up and down the rows flipping seats up.

MOTHER TUCKER'S FAMILY RESTAURANT Mother Tucker's Family Restaurant in Winnipeg is haunted by the ghost of a Freemason. The building was constructed as a Masonic Temple in 1895, and thousands of secret initiation ceremonies were performed here. That energy trapped in the walls is thought to be what keeps the former Mason attached to the property. Efforts to identify the spirit have proved unsuccessful, although it is thought the entity dates from the 1920s. In fact, the ghost allegedly made a telephone call to the restaurant one day to inform the owners that the year was 1919 not 1979. The ghost's activity seems tied to electrical disturbances, as if it is tapping into that energy to manifest. The third floor bar area seems to be the most active. Custodians, waitresses, managers, and client have all had encounters with the misplaced spirit. Mother Tucker's Family Restaurant is at 335 Donald Street in Winnipeg, Manitoba.

ST. NORTBERT MONASTERY RUINS This monastery on the outskirts of Winnipeg burnt down in the 1980s. The brick building survived the flames and the walls are still standing. Visitors to the ruins have reported seeing the apparitions of monks jumping off the walls and through former windows, but it is not known if they are reenacting the night of the fire or just having fun. The inquisitive spirits have been known to stop their activities long enough to watch people talking at the site.

SASKATCHEWAN

Pelican Narrows

PELICAN NARROWS RESERVATION Pelican Narrows is a Native Candian reserve in northern Saskatchewan. The cemetery for the reserve, which is located on an island, is haunted. Glowing spheres of light are seen floating in and out of the trees of the island as if they were performing a ceremony or dance ritual. Sometimes the balls, which vary in brightness and size, move at rapid speeds through the woods. At other times the globes of light follow people. The Native Canadians believe the balls of light are the spirits of their dead ancestors.

Regina

GOVERNMENT HOUSE Government House in Regina is haunted by an unidentified ghost nicknamed "Howie." His footsteps can be heard stomping down the back stairways, and he is blamed for playing little tricks on employees, like moving small, personal objects and placing them in odd locations.

HOTEL SASKATCHEWAN The Hotel Saskatchewan in Regina was built in the late nineteenth century during the heyday of the Canadian Pacific Railway, but where the ghost of the fourth floor came from no one knows. Some say it is a man who hanged himself in one of the rooms in the 1930s; others say there was a gruesome murder on that floor. But guests and employees who have encountered the presence have no doubt something traumatic happened on that floor. Many who have felt the unpleasant energy do not like to talk about it, but two guests who stayed in Room 420 in 1992 insist something is attached to a comfortable old chair in the room. Before they went to bed, the man left his tennis shoes in front of the chair where he had taken them off. In the morning they were filled with water. The room was locked and the guests never left their bed during the night.

REGINA GENERAL HOSPITAL The Regina General Hospital is haunted by a former nurse. Witnesses see what looks like a woman in a nursing uniform dart about the halls faster than any human being could possibly move. The only place the super ghost slows down is in the restroom, where people get a glimpse in the mirrors of an elderly nurse behind them. As soon as they turn around, she is gone. The apparition is thought to be of a dedicated nurse who never caught up with her work even after death.

Runnymede

FAMOUS PLAYERS MOVIE THEATRE The Famous Players theater at Runnymede closed down a few years ago, but before that is served as a vaudeville theater. The building has been haunted for decades by the ghost of a little girl who was killed while performing on stage, when a sandbag fell from the catwalk in the early 1900s. Former employees and managers at the movie theater told of several encounters with the pathetic spirit. She could be heard sobbing quietly and was felt most often in the storage area behind the main screen.

Saint Louis

GHOST LIGHT Saint Louis is a tiny Saskatchewan village about 30 kilometers (19 miles) from Prince Albert. Near the town is a ghostly light that has been witnessed by dozens of people. The Saint Louis Ghost Light travels down a bumpy gravel road that once was a railroad bed. At first the light appears as if someone is carrying a lantern towards you. It seems to be swinging slightly from a person walking. According to local legend, a railway worker was walking on the tracks with his lamp and was killed when the train backed into him.

Saskatoon

HOUSE ON SASKATCHEWAN CRESCENT The house at 844 Saskatchewan Crescent in the city of Saskatoon, Saskatchewan, has been haunted by the wife of a former owner who lived there in 1930s. People experienced unexplainable cold spots, foot-

steps, and other paranormal clues. The woman has been sensed staring out the top floor front window "waiting patiently for her husband to return from work" and looking pensively out the back window toward the stables, "as if she were watching a hired hand working." The three-story house was one of the finest in town, with oak trim and railings and a ballroom on the third floor. But nobody wanted to live there, although many people wanted to turn it into a museum. Finally in August 1995, the house was torn down and two new houses constructed on the former estate. Now there are rumors that the new homes are haunted by the woman's presence.

ALBERTA

Banff

BANFF SPRINGS HOTEL A ghostly bagpiper walks around the halls of the Banff Springs Hotel at night playing his bagpipes, and the apparition of a bellman sometimes appears at the doors of guests. Located in the city of Banff in the heart of the Canadian Rockies, about 129 kilometers (eighty miles) from the Calgary Airport, the resort hotel has 849 rooms and looks like a Scottish Castle. The hotel was opened in 1888 by rail baron Cornelius Van Horne, and one of the resident ghosts is Sam McAuley, a former bellman. However, who exactly is playing the bagpipes remains a mystery. To contact the Banff Springs Hotel, call 403-762-2211 or fax 403-762-5755.

Calgary

CANMORE OPERA HOUSE The Canmore Opera House, which was built at the turn of the century, was moved to Heritage Park in 1966. It is still used as a theatre, but at times seems to house more than one group of players. Costumes are thrown around the dressing rooms when the theater is supposedly empty, actors report hearing heavy footsteps and the sounds of a party going on in the distance. The grand piano that sits on the stage plays occasionally, even when no one is nearby. The Canmore Opera House used to be a miner's hospital and some of the spirits date from that era, though the most frequently sighted apparition is that of civic pioneer Sam Livingstone, whose long, blond-haired apparition is seen sitting in the front row, still enjoying the performances, or just sitting on the stairs backstage.

The old opera house was moved to Heritage Park in 1965, and the haunting started ten years later. The history park in Calgary is haunted by many ghosts associated with the historical buildings there. It was established in south Calgary in 1964 as a western theme park and history center, and many old buildings from throughout the city have been moved to the site.

COSTE HOUSE The Coste House on Amherst Street in Calgary is a twenty-eight-room mansion said to be haunted by the spirit of Dr. Carmichael, who once lived in there. His ghost flits nervously from room to room, slamming doors, and making floors creak as he dashes about. The house was built in 1913, but was abandoned during the Depression and fell into disrepair. It was renovated and served as the headquarters of the Allied Arts Council from 1946 to 1958.

DEANE HOUSE Deane House is a three-story home built in 1906 on what is now the Fort Calgary Historical Site. The first resident of the house was Richard Deane, Northwest Superintendent of the Royal Mounted Police. In 1914, the house became a train station on the Grand Trunk Pacific Railway. In 1929, the house was moved across the Bow River to its present location and reopened as the Gaspe Lodge, a room and board. In 1973, it was bought by the Dandelion Artists' Coop and contained studios rented by painters, sculptors, and writers. In 1986, the house became a historical museum, part of the Alberta Culture Center.

Starting in 1979, an apparition of a woman started appearing on the front porch of the house, and the ghost of a man resembling Richard Deane was seen several times sitting in a chair in the study, smoking a pipe. Numerous poltergeist effects have been reported that include mysterious fires, loud unexplainable laughter, a mock telephone in the study that rings without being connected to anything, and a cabinet in the parlor that had to be locked away in storage because the glass door kept bursting, sending shards of glass all over the room.

During the time the house was used as a rooming house, there was a murder-suicide in which a man took an axe to his wife and then committed suicide in front of his two children. Then, it was discovered the house had been relocated over a Native-Canadian burial ground. At a meeting at Deane House, an elderly Native man with braids once told a guest who ventured into the basement to get out because it was "sacred." When she complained to the staff about his rudeness, the mysterious man was nowhere to be found. His description, however, matched that of a legendary chief named Deerfoot, who vowed to come back from the dead to avenge any evil perpetrated against his people. Deane House was exorcised in the spring of 1990, and the intensity of the haunting decreased noticeably.

FIRE STATIONS Two of the former fire stations in Calgary are haunted by phantom horses that used to pull fire wagons. The horse-drawn rigs were replaced by trucks around 1925, but the sounds of horses' naying and stomping feet still are heard in the areas where the horses were quartered. Maintenance staff and tenants of the buildings, as well as people walking past on the front sidewalks, have also reported hearing the distant clanging of the old fire alarm bells and the sounds of wooden wagons leaving the station. Firehall No. 3 in East Calgary is now a restaurant, and Firehall No. 6 in Hillhurst is now a warehouse.

GHOST HILLS There are reports of ghosts from the Native tribe area near Morley, which is west of Calgary. Chief White Eagle of the Stony Tribe led his people to this area after a vicious attack by a rival tribe. He died as a result of battle wounds, but as he lay dying his braves created a rockslide that obliterated the enemies following them below. His indomitable spirit can sometimes be seen riding his white horse, parting the fog that gathers around the Ghost Hills.

HILLHURST SCHOOL Hillhurst School in northwest Calgary is haunted by the ghost of its former custodian Ernest Stevenson, although most of the children call him "Stevie." The apparition of the good-natured man has been witnessed by children, employees, teachers, and parents, and the school even enters ghostly activity into its logbooks. The only time the ghost gets upset is if someone takes his picture down in the hallway. Then, doors start swinging wildly by themselves, and other odd poltergeist effects are likely to occur. Stevenson worked at the school for many years and lived on the third floor of the building.

LOUGHEED HOUSE Calgary's Lougheed House on 13th Avenue was built in 1900 by James Lougheed, and it is his wife's ghost who still haunts it. She is observed only on the third floor, which is also the scene of other ghostly phenomena, such as doors opening and closing slowly by themselves, and untraceable footsteps and other sounds. Encounters reached a peak in the 1940s and 1950s, when the Red Cross used the building as a training facility and dozens of young ladies encountered the ghost. The dignified overseers of the Red Cross were caught up in a controversy as to whether to admit their building was indeed haunted. It ended up an unresolved issue "best left alone."

PETER PRINCE HOME The Peter Prince Home, which is also at Heritage Park, is another supposedly haunted house. This grand old home was built by early Calgary lumber baron Peter Prince, and was also moved to its present site at Heritage Park in 1966. Numerous visitors have reported on the nice touch of the costumed "beautiful woman in white holding a baby" in one of the upstairs bedrooms. Park staff have come to expect reports of this apparition, who seems content to cuddle her infant and smile at visitors. In addition the third floor of the home is closed off, and is not wired for electricity, yet at times is seen to be illuminated as if there were lights on inside.

WAINWRIGHT HOTEL The Wainwright Hotel, another historical attraction in Heritage Park, seems to have attracted some former guests who died long ago, even though it is only a reproduction of the original. At an old family mansion in the park, there have been sightings of a pleasant, young lady holding her baby on the third floor of the building. Sometimes she smiles at onlookers, while at other times, only a ghostly light moves around on the third floor, even though that floor has no electrical supply. Other ghosts at Heritage Park include an unidentified male apparition seen in the Sam Livingston House and a mother and child ghost who are observed in the old Sandstone House. There is also a wandering ghost, and a mysterious crying woman who disappears when approached by the park's employees.

Dunvegan

CATHOLIC MISSION Dunvegan is a small missionary settlement that is haunted by a nun who died under suspicious circumstances. Her apparition, known as the Gray Lady, still is seen descending the hillside and crossing the bridge over the Peace River toward the settlement. Her body was found in the woods and no cause of death was ever given.

Fort Edmonton

FIRKINS HOUSE In 1992, a family donated their haunted house to the city of Fort Edmonton, Alberta, and the city gladly accepted. For many years, residents of the house had been reporting the apparition of a young man, who is believed to be a former owner's son who died in the house. The ghost was very content, and was even known to sing lullabies to infants in the house. Although everyone knew the house was haunted, the city wanted to move it to Fort Edmonton Historical Park, which contains replicas and actual buildings from the city's past. The Firkins' House, named for its first family, was unique in that it had never been remodeled or altered in its eighty-year history. What the city did not count on was that moving the house to the new location would upset the ghost so much. From the moment the house was placed at the new location, the ghost started showing his displeasure. Doors refused to open, but windows flew open for no apparent reason. Many of the workers in the house felt an uneasy presence that interfered with their work. Today, the ghost is blamed for making unexplainable noises, creating icy cold spots, and shoving visitors from behind.

Fort Macleod

EMPRESS THEATRE Renovations at the Empress Theatre in Fort Macleod in Alberta stirred up a lot more than just some dust. In 1992, shortly after remodeling, strange sounds started coming from the main stage area. The sounds were described as "a whirlwind walking around on the wooden floor." The otherworldly footsteps have been heard by custodians and managers, who have never been able to explain them. Employees, performers, and audience members have all reported an unseen presence that touches them or breathes on their necks. While the spirit remains unidentified, many at the theater believe it is former owner Dan Boyle, who operated the building from 1937 until his death in 1963.

Galt

GALT MUSEUM The ghost of the Galt Museum in the town of Galt, near Lethbridge in Alberta, dates from a time when the building was used as a hospital. In 1933, sixty-year-old George Benjamin Bailey, a farmer from Magrath, was being wheeled to surgery when his gurney got caught in the door of the elevator. As it continued to rise, Bailey fell off the cart and swung into the shaft, falling to his death. When the old hospital was remodeled into a museum, workers and visitors started reporting the sounds of shuffling footsteps when no one was around and felt like someone was watching over their shoulders. The phenomena happen most frequently in a workroom near the former elevator shaft where displays are prepared. Odd noises and other strange events continue to haunt the room, although no one as yet has actually seen old George's apparition.

Ghost River

GHOST DAM Ghost River in Alberta got its name from all the ghostly sightings there over the last two centuries. French explorers called it the "River of Death," because the area around the river was a burial ground for the Stoney Indians. According to the Indians however, that is not how the river got its name. In 1870, there was a great gathering of hundreds of tribesmen at the plateau where the Ghost Dam now sits, but their group was decimated by a strange sickness that took most of the tribe's leaders. According to records, an epidemic of smallpox hit Alberta that year and killed over one-third of the Indian population. Not long afterwards, settlers, Indians, and others started reporting the ghosts of Indians along the river. Sometimes, the Indian apparitions tried to hunt buffalo in open areas along the river, and the herds would run back and forth as if being chased, while onlookers observed bands of phantom Indians on horses chasing them.

Jasper

TONQUIN INN The ghost of a railroad worker haunts the 135-room Tonquin Inn in Jasper, Alberta. He made the inn his home for two years, but one night went to work after a few too many beers and fell out the back of the caboose. At least that is what people assume happened, for the man's body was never found. But his ghost found its way home to Tonquin, and his presence is still felt at the inn. To contact the Tonquin Inn, phone 403-852-4987 or fax 403-852-4413.

New Sarepta

HIGH SCHOOL OF NEW SAREPTA The High School of New Sarepta is haunted by an eleventh-grade student killed in the parking lot when he crashed his Corsica after a school dance in 1963. His mutilated apparition is seen in the gymnasium, where the dance was held. Students report seeing his bleeding, one-legged body crawling on the gym floor.

Okotok

OKOTOK CULTURAL CENTRE The Cultural Centre in Okotok, Alberta, was built as a train station in the 1920s and the ghost is an impatient woman who seems to be still waiting for a train. The unidentified apparition wears a flowered hat and long black dress with a bustle, and a high-pitched whine sometimes accompanies her manifestation. She is most often seen in the Cultural Centre's art gallery, which used to be the waiting room. She also emerges from the shadows in the theater and startles visitors. "On a couple of occasions she walked right through me," says Cultural Coordinator Brenda Cupelli. "I felt like she was bitter and waiting for someone who had never come."

Waterton Park

KILMOREY LODGE Kilmorey Lodge in Waterton Park, Alberta, is haunted by the apparition of an elderly, small-framed woman wearing a blue and white dress. She spends most of her time sitting in a large red velvet chair in the lobby, although she has been known to wander through guest's rooms at night. Some believe she is Isabella Brown, a Cree Indian whose Indian name meant "Blue Flash of Lightning." She married a mountain man, and they often stayed at the lodge. She died in 1935 and was buried next to her husband along the western shore of Lower Waterton Lake.

BRITISH COLUMBIA

Burnaby

BURNABY ART GALLERY The Burnaby Art Gallery is housed in a former mansion known as Fairacres. It was built in 1909 by real estate tycoon Henry Ceberley. The estate is composed of the house itself, the remains of an old barn, and the carriage house. Fairacres remained in the Ceberley family only ten years and has been used as a tuberculosis clinic, a Benedictine abbey, a cult temple, and a university dormitory. However, it was not until 1967, when the house was purchased by the city and remodeled into an art gallery, that the haunting began. The apparition of Mrs. Grace Ceperley started being reported by security guards and custodians on the third floor. She is described as wearing a long, flowing white dress. During working hours, the apparition changed into a blue gown and appeared in the downstairs gallery. Mrs. Ceperley left instructions in her will that the mansion be turned into a children's home, but her instructions were never carried out. Now her spirit seems a little upset, and it appears she has invited some ghostly children to join her in trying to take back the house. In the present art gallery, paintings float off the walls, the eyes of people in portraits "follow" visitors as they walk by, and the faces of ghostly children peer out from the upper windows.

Chilliwack

OLD CITY HALL Chilliwack is a quiet farming town in the Fraser Valley of British Columbia, but the staid community's former City Hall is haunted the ghost of a Chinese opium smoker. The man was arrested in 1928 for possession of opium and placed in the small cell at the Chilliwack City Hall. Faced with the humiliating prospect of years in jail, the man took the belt of his cellmate and strangled himself. Now the Chilliwack Museum, the building remains haunted by his presence on the upper floor. Most often, it is only his slow, shuffling footsteps that are heard, sometimes opening and closing a door behind him.

FREDERICKSON HOUSE The old Frederickson House on William Street North in Chilliwack is a twelve-room house that the resident spirits would rather keep to themselves. Douglas and Hetty Frederickson moved into the place in December 1965 and were forced to move out three years later because of the frightening haunting. A family who moved in later went through the same experiences as the Fredericksons and also had to leave the house because of the haunting. It started the same way in both cases. The women and children of the household started having graphic, recurring nightmares about a woman covered in blood lying on the floor of attic. Next, poltergeist activity broke out in the house. Doors banged open and closed, bedstands moved, and dresser drawers opened and shut by themselves. A scary, icy-cold presence wandered the hallways, and when it touched people, they froze in their tracks. Once, the apparition of a woman was seen standing by a window. Unfortunately, no historical evidence of the identity of the spirit (or spirits) was ever found, although there were rumors that a man committed suicide in the house and that the body of a woman was bricked up in the chimney. Current residents have reported nothing unusual.

Coquitland

BURQUITLAM FUNERAL CHAPEL The ghost at the Burquitlam Funeral Chapel in Coquitland has nothing to do with the funeral parlor. The original building was a private residence built in 1924, and it did not become a funeral chapel until 1964. But the apparition of a fifty-year-old man, dressed in a sloppy brown sports coat and dark fedora hat, has been seen in the basement suite in the building since the 1950s. He usually appears at the bottom of the basement stairs, and then wanders through the basement bedroom and disappears into the kitchenette, an area of the basement suite that used to be open to the outside. In 1996, the apparition started appearing outside the basement area. Once he was seen near the altar in the chapel. Another time he was seen walking on the road in front of the house. One thing people notice about this unidentified ghost is that his apparition is not completely transparent, and if he passes in front of a window or lamp, he blocks the light momentarily. The Burquitlam Funeral Chapel is at 625 North Road in Coquitland, British Columbia.

RIVERVIEW HOSPITAL Another Coquitland haunt is the old Riverview Hospital on the Lougheed Highway. The psychiatric hospital's three buildings have held as many as eight thousand patients, and many parts of the remaining structures are considered haunted. Ward E2 in the Centrelawn building is haunted by a Casper-like apparition that looks like a "sheet floating in midair." The elevator in the Eastlawn building has long been considered haunted. Cold spots "ride" the elevator and exit at certain floors and unexplainable electrical problems cause it to operate erratically, even after the elevator was modernized and then replaced. The ghost of a staff member who lived in the attic of the Westlawn building has been encountered many times over the years. The man committed suicide there and the fourth floor has been haunted ever since. Westlawn is so spooky-looking that it is often used to represent various buildings in the filming of *The X-Files* television series.

Courtenay

SIWASH HILL CEMETERY The Native cemetery on Siwash Hill just outside the town of Courtenay in British Columbia has been considered haunted since 1940, when several witnesses reported seeing a strange apparition that was seen again a week later by amateur investigators. The ghost first manifested as a misty ball that started glowing with a diffuse green light and then took the form of a human figure. Finally, it dissolved back into nothingness.

Creston

CRESTON VALLEY MUSEUM The Creston Valley Museum on the outskirts of Creston, British Columbia, is a unique stone building built by a Russian immigrant as his final resting place. Rudolph Schultz built the house in the 1950s and included a crypt in the floor where he wanted to spend eternity. However, it is against the law in Canada to be buried in dwellings, and when he died in 1967, he was interred in a cemetery like all respectable folk. Schultz's very odd stone house never made a suitable home for anyone else, even after the stone floor was concreted over and a carpet laid. Eventually, the house was purchased by the Creston and District Museum and Historical Society.

The haunting began during restoration work, when workers removed the concrete floor to reveal the original stone floor—and Schultz's underground crypt. Workers heard Schultz's low voice speaking to them, and when the museum opened in 1982, visitors and guides felt his presence following them around and numerous minor poltergeist effects were observed. Schultz's body may be buried in the public cemetery, but his spirit has returned to the spot where he wanted to spend eternity. To this day, mysterious white fuzz appears overnight on the floor to mark the outline of his hidden crypt.

Greenwood

GREENWOOD MUSEUM The Greenwood Museum used to be the courthouse and jail for the tiny hamlet of Greenwood in British Columbia. Built in 1902, the building has had a number of interesting occupants over the years, but the one who stayed the longest is the ghost of a man who hanged himself in the basement jail in July 1915. Nicknamed "Charlie," the man's ghost still haunts the place, and he has been blamed for a variety of macabre and unexplainable incidents. His ghost took a particular disliking to a manikin. Inexplicably, museum workers found the manikin facedown in a tub of water, as if someone were trying to drown it, and finally discovered the head smashed to pieces one morning.

Kamloop

BLACK NUGGET MUSEUM The Black Nugget Museum is a privately run museum on Gatacre Street in the island town of Ladysmith that is haunted by its exhibits. The remains of an elderly Native woman on display in her original coffin box is part of the problem. Psychics have detected her spirit and even had conversations with it. A group of elephant figurines on the fireplace mantle seem to keep changing the direction in which they are lined up. For some reason, they like to face the west. The museum is also haunted by at least one ghost of its own. The century-old building used to be a hotel and gambling den, and at least one man, caught cheating at cards, was murdered here. His presence is sensed in the former barroom area.

HATTE CREEK RANCH Just outside Kamloop, at the Hatte Creek Ranch, is an old roadhouse and ranch that was turned into a historic museum. The sounds of the horseshoeing anvil being struck by a hammer are heard in the early morning hours, and phantom horses can be heard traveling along the trail near the ranch. Inside the roadhouse, curtains rearrange themselves and loud banging and scratching sounds emanate from the wallboards. A glowing orb moves through the house and a transparent apparition has been seen near the front door. The identity of the haunting presences has never been determined.

Ladysmith

PLEASANT STREET CEMETERY Some people believe the presence haunting the theater is a lost soul who wandered over from the Pleasant Street Cemetery nearby. In 1939, city fathers disinterred early residents from their resting places at the Lorne Street Cemetery and moved them all closer to the city center at Pleasant Street. Many spirits were apparently disturbed, because residents living near both graveyards reported strange activity. One couple living near the Pleasant Street Cemetery started being visited by a presence they named "Herbie," a harmless ghost who was fascinated with lighting and electrical appliances.

SAGEBRUSH THEATRE The Sagebrush Theatre in Kamloop, which is home to the Western Canada Theatre Company, is haunted by an unidentified man in nineteenth-century clothes. Sometimes he is seen standing on the catwalks above stage or sitting in the same seat in the audience, but when anyone tries to approach him, he disappears into thin air. The ghost has grown so familiar that employees have named him "Albert" and talk to him when no one else is around. Likewise, Albert has helped out with a few projects and even saved the life of one employee. When a technician was alone in the building working on a spotlight in the catwalk, she heard some say in her ear, "Put your safety harness on!" Moments later the spotlight broke from its bracket and dropped to the stage below. Only her safety belt prevented her from plummeting to the floor with the heavy spotlight.

New Westminster

IRVING HOUSE Irving House was built in the early 1860s by Captain Irving, who died in his bed at home but never left the place. The house has been considered haunted for decades but renovating it into a museum seems to have accentuated the ghostly activity. Strange noises are heard throughout the building, and the walls seem to shiver in the dining room. People touring the upstairs den say the trophy heads of a moose and a caribou seem to watch you, and some people insist these stuffed animals slightly turn their heads to follow you around. In the master bedroom, where Captain Irving died, sometimes an indentation forms in the bed, as if someone were lying in it. Just to be sure tourists know who is haunting the place, a disembodied voice asking, "Say my name!" is sometimes heard.

Penticton

PENTICTON MUSEUM The Penticton Museum in Penticton, British Columbia, is a modern building that was haunted by the Blue Lady apparition for many years. Built in the late 1960s, the ghost of an unidentified woman in a blue dress is associated with the bones and skull of a woman found in the 1920s on the east side of the river near the town. The bones were stored in the museum archives for many years, and when they were removed from the premises in 1992, the haunting stopped. Before that, eight janitors had quit work during the previous eighteen months because of late-night encounters with the ghost.

Port Moody

JAKE'S CROSSING PUB Jake's Crossing Pub on St. John's Street in Port Moody, British Columbia, is haunted by the phantoms of a man and his dog. Formerly called the Port Moody Arms Pub, the hotel bar's employees and clients all report seeing the apparition of a former caretaker named Slim

Kirkpatrick and his dog, Jimmy Joe. Slim and his dog lived in the basement of the building from 1973 to 1978, the year the seventy-year-old Slim died in Surrey Memorial Hospital. Not long afterwards, the gray-haired apparition of Slim, wearing his familiar plaid flannel shirt, started being encountered in the basement of the pub. Then, the ghost started showing up in the bar area, as well as in the lounge and hallways of the hotel. Most of the time, Slim's apparition is accompanied by the phantom of a black cocker spaniel, his eternally faithful dog, Jimmy Joe.

But in recent years, Slim seems to be seeking human company and has even tried to start up some conversations with employees. In 1997, a relief cook was in the basement using the laundry washing machine and felt the presence of someone else in the room. Suddenly, an empty chair six feet away from him started moving slowly towards him. When it touched his knees, a disembodied voice invited him to sit down. Instead of sitting down, however, the frightened man ran upstairs to tell the others what happened. Today, most employees take time out to talk with the unseen presence when they are in the basement. It seems to "calm things down," and "things seem to go better" for them. They insist that if they keep talking to Slim, he is more likely to "help them out" in times of need.

Princeton

PRINCETON HOTEL The entity haunting the basement of the Princeton Hotel is nicknamed "Friday." Princeton is a small mining town located at the confluence of the Similkameen and Tulameen rivers in British Columbia. The hotel was built in 1910, and Friday was a Chinese handyman hired by the original owners. He earned his nickname because every Friday, like clockwork, he drove to the train station to pick up guests arriving in town. The only time he ever missed his appointment was the day he fell down the cellar stairs and cracked his skull open. He died instantly. The large wooden support pillar where he hit his head still carries a bloodstain and a few strands of hair from the accident. Friday is a polite and good-natured ghost who only mani-fests in the cellar and has never been encountered anywhere else in the hotel. To this day, the own-ers treat their faithful and kind handyman with the respect due him.

Quadra Island

HERIOT BAY INN The Heriot Bay Inn on Quadra Island was built in 1894 and has been remodeled several times, but the one constant in its history seems to be the ghost of a lumberjack. The logger was killed in a fight at the inn and buried in a triangular plot of land across from it, but his spirit took refuge at the inn. The apparition of a tall, thin man wearing heavy logger's clothing has been reported by staff and guests for many decades. Ac-cording to the accounts, the apparition is most active in the bar area, which most assume is where the brawl that killed him began.

QUESNEL A haunted doll at the Quesnel and Dis-trict Museum in the central British Columbia town of Quesnel is possessed by a spirit that does not like it photographed or moved around. The grotesque doll is named Mereanda (or Mandy for short) and has a large crack in the face that makes her right eye look leeringly out at people. "Mandy reminds me of Chucky," says the museum's direc-tor Ruth Stubbs, referring to the horror film doll that is possessed by the sprit of a dead murderer. Dozens of people would agree with her. Photogra-phers who attempt to take pictures of the doll say the film never turns up. Negatives are ruined or eaten up by processing equipment, print paper just disappears or comes out blank, VCR cassettes get stuck or explode, and camera equipment sud-denly malfunctions.

The twenty-four-inch, antique doll was made in Germany in the 1920s and has a history of being haunted. The doll was given to the museum by a young woman who found it in the trunk of her dead grandmother's car. When she took it home, she was awakened in the middle of the night by the doll's crying, even though there is no sound box in the doll. The doll also seemed to have supernatural powers such as opening win-

dows, even if they were nailed shut, and moving about on its own. Sometimes the doll threw tem-per tantrums, and everything in the room was dis-turbed or tossed around. Museum workers also became suspicious of the doll and enclosed it in a clear Plexiglas case to be sure it was not infested with insects or some other animal. But they soon realized something much more sinister must be behind the doll's unexplainable behavior.

Salt Spring Island

HARBOUR HOUSE HOTEL The Harbour House Hotel in the town of Ganges on Salt Spring Island is haunted by the stubborn ghost of Walter Her-zog, the original owner. Herzog was murdered in the early morning hours on September 15, 1973, by a burglar he encountered in his hotel suite. The desperate thief fired five bullets into Herzog's chest, and ever since that day, the hotel has been haunted by his ghost. Manifestations usually occur in the hotel pub, which is the location of his for-mer suite, and also in Room 206, which is directly above the former suite. Beer taps fly open by themselves, the juke box operates even if it is un-plugged, the pinball machine plays games by itself, telephones constantly ring in Room 206 for no apparent reason, and most of the appliances in the bar area come on and off with no human hand touching them. A psychic who contacted Herzog's spirit recently described him as a confused spirit suffering from turmoil and unbalance. She also predicted his disturbed presence will grow stronger and more dangerous.

South Pender Island

BEDWELL HARBOUR ISLAND RESORT The Bed-well Harbour Island Resort on South Pender Is-land near Vancouver is haunted by the ghost of a young Native woman who was murdered. The is-land was settled in 1791, when a Spanish schooner visited it and discovered fresh water springs that later served to replenish the supplies of other sail-ing ships. The most active ghost on the island stems from an incident in the nineteenth century, when two European men raped a young Indian girl who was digging for clams along the beach. They chased her into the forest, raped her, and then beat her to death with a pair of heavy oarlocks. The oarlocks became wedged in a small yew tree at the scene and can still be seen today, almost completely overgrown by the tree.

Today, the ghost of the poor girl still lingers near the yew tree where she was murdered, and her apparition has been seen on the hill above the resort and even wandering in the nearby employee apartments and Bedwell Harbor Island Pub. Her rather indistinct apparition manifests as a glowing mist or thick fog that forms near the tree or from the ceiling in buildings. Once, when the owners of the pub put up a landscape painting resembling the murder scene in the forest behind the place, the ghost was displeased and kept knocking it off the wall. When the painting was replaced, the odd phenomena ceased. Another Indian spirit haunts the island area opposite the resort. The sixteen-acre Indian Reserve on the east side of Bedwell Harbor is sacred to Natives as the site of a great tribal battle and is said to be haunted by the tall apparition of a warrior from that time.

Vancouver

AMBASSADOR HOTEL A ghostly guest at the Ambassador Hotel behaves very differently from the typical client. The original Senator Hotel that occupied the building was an upper middle class establishment at the heart of the city, but after World War II, the clientele changed to the down-and-out and transients. Then, in the 1960s, the theater district between Smithe and Hastings streets in Vancouver became a Mecca for hippies and youth seeking a new life. So many homeless children came to Vancouver that in 1980, the old Senator Hotel was taken over by the city and run as a youth shelter. Hundreds of desperate, penniless teenagers lived at the group residence and took advantage of the social services being offered. It was not long before those pent-up adolescent frustrations took the form of frightening poltergeist phenomena.

Residents and employees started noticing that objects were missing or placed in odd spots, doors mysteriously opened and closed or locked and unlocked themselves, and strange sounds and voices echoed throughout the halls at night. Once, a kitchen worker received serious burns to her legs when she brushed against an oven that was not even hot. Apparitions started appearing too. Most were the faces of old people, ghosts of parents and other authorities who haunted the children, but others were more bizarre, like the pair of olive-skinned legs that walked about in the ladies lounge. In the 1990s, the building was once again turned into a hotel and opened its doors as the renovated Ambassador, which now caters to businessmen and tourists. But every once in a while, the mysterious energies from the youth shelter still manifest. The Ambassador Hotel is at 1212 Granville Street in Vancouver, British Columbia.

ANMORE VILLAGE HALL The Village Hall in Anmore, a small community twelve miles from Vancouver on the opposite side of the Upper Burrard Inlet, is haunted by the presence of a man who committed suicide there. The incident took place in the 1930s, when the house was owned by the Murray family. Their hired hand hanged himself in their kitchen, and ever since the 1940s, residents of the house have reported disturbing creaking and groaning sounds, strange footsteps, cold spots, and a mysterious unseen presence. The old Murray house became the Anmore Village Hall when the town was incorporated in 1987. Staff members and visitors still report paranormal activity.

CRAIGFLOWER SCHOOLHOUSE The Craigflower Schoolhouse is the oldest surviving school building in western Canada, and today, it is a heritage museum operated by the government of British Columbia. It is located in the town of Saanich on Vancouver Island. Built in 1855 for the children of employees of the Hudson Bay Company, the school was rebuilt several times over the years. It was during one of those construction phases in 1911 that five human skulls were found along with some ancient arrowheads. Then in 1918, during more construction, a complete human skeleton was unearthed. Almost from that day, an outbreak of frightening ghostly phenomena took place on the property that did not stop until the bones were reburied in a secret location on the property. For no known reason, the haunting started up again sixty years later and continues to this day. The old school bell rings violently for no reason, the sounds of chains are heard being dragged through the hallways, and the upper floor is plagued by raucous banging sounds.

HOTEL VANCOUVER A former resident of the Hotel Vancouver liked the place so much, she never left. The woman stayed at the hotel from 1939 to 1940, and her thin apparition, wearing an elegant evening gown, is most often glimpsed riding up and down in the elevator. According to those who remember her, she loved to take the shiny brass elevators to the top floor and look out over the city lights at night. Both employees and guests have glimpsed her apparition in the elevators. The magnificent hotel was built in the late

Hotel Vancouver, British Columbia, Canada (Hotel Vancouver)

1800s by Cornelius Van Horne to encourage people to use his Canadian Pacific Railway to see the country. The Hotel Vancouver is at 900 West Georgia Street in Vancouver, British Columbia. For information, call 604-684-3131 or fax 604-662-1929.

MANDARIN GARDENS The Mandarin Gardens is a popular Vancouver nightclub haunted by the ghost of its former owner. The place was opened in the 1930s by Chan See Wong, who died in the building in 1938. Now his voice is heard giving orders during daylight hours, and at night, he plays tricks on employees and then bursts out in mocking laughter. He is blamed for unplugging appliances, jiggling dishes and utensils in the kitchen, and scaring people with his disembodied hand. The nightclub, located at 98 East Pender Street, was finally closed by the city.

MUSHROOM STUDIOS Other entertainers, performing for recording sessions at Mushroom Studios in Vancouver, seem to be responsible for their own ghostly activity. Investigators believe the poltergeist activity is caused by the young, frenzied musicians doing their creative best to make hit records. Effects include discarnate voices, singing, and humming sounds in tune to the music. So far, the haunting is under control, as technicians have been able to block the sounds from being recorded on album tapes. The Mushroom Studios are located at 1234 West 6th Avenue in Vancouver, British Columbia.

OAKHURST NURSING HOME Chairs rock by themselves, curtains part as if someone were looking out the window, and strange dragging sounds emanate from the basement at the former Oakhurst Nursing Home in Vancouver. The mansion was built in 1913 and used for many years after World War II as a nursing home. The estate was also the location for the 1995 movie *One Foot in Heaven*, during the filming of which many crew members reported experiencing paranormal phenomena. The old Oakhurst Nursing Home is at 7430 Oak Street in Vancouver, British Columbia.

VOGUE THEATRE The Vogue Theatre on the west end of Vancouver in British Columbia is haunted by an unidentified male apparition that appears only fleetingly. Other evidence for a haunting includes poltergeist activity such as drums that play themselves, equipment unplugged by an unseen hand, doors slamming, objects being strewn about, and people being touched from behind when no one is there. The theater opened in 1941 as a movie theater but was shut down in 1985, until it reopened again in 1992 as a combination film and live performance theater. It was then the employees first began reporting the ghostly figure. Technical Director Ken St. Pierre and Operations Manager Bill Allman saw the apparition in separate incidents in the basement of the building. In November 1995, during his performance on stage, popular singer/dancer Shane McPherson saw the apparition of a man standing under the Exit sign, stage left near the front row. He described the ghost as a tall man in his mid-thirties with close-cropped dark hair, a narrow face, and wearing a cream-colored dinner jacket. "The only way I can describe it," said McPherson, "is as television would do a fade-out, this individual dissolved. He simply dissolved in front of my eyes."

In the summer of 1996, a box-office attendant saw the same ghostly figure climbing the balcony stairs before it disappeared into thin air. In June 1997, during the taping of a CBC radio broadcast of "Gabereau," the announcer made a sarcastic reference to the theater's ghost, at which time a deafening squeal issued from the house speakers, forcing technicians to halt production. The ghost of the Vogue remains unidentified. There is no record of a fatality in the building, and most witnesses seem to think it is the restless spirit of a member of the stage or maintenance crew. The Vogue Theatre is at 918 Granville Street in Vancouver, British Columbia.

ZEBALLOS HOTEL The Zeballos Hotel on the west coast of Vancouver Island was built in 1939, in the middle of a gold rush. Today, the place is haunted by the ghost of one of its first residents, a Chinese immigrant named Susie Woo. She died after a short illness in 1940 in Room 1 of the hotel, and apparently, still thinks the room belongs to her. She has chased away guests she does not like from her room, including three loud and burly fishermen. The men ran down the stairs into the lobby and were so afraid they refused to return to their room to get their belongings. Other guests reported disturbances such as footsteps, knocking sounds, and an eerie feeling of being alone in the room. Finally, in 1997, the hotel turned the inhospitable room into an office.

Vernon

TOWNE THEATRE Vernon's discount movie house, the Towne Theatre, is haunted by a former projectionist, who is likely to knock down the film posters overnight if he does not like what is playing. Basically, the presence likes to help out, such as locking the doors at night if the manager forgets or moving things around for cleaners. Phantom footsteps are often heard in the empty projection booth, which is where the ghost likes to spend most of his time. The building was completely renovated in 1939 and again in 1992, and no one has been able to determine an identity for the determined presence.

Victoria

FAIRFIELD HEALTH CENTRE The Fairfield Health Centre in Victoria is haunted by the apparitions of nuns and patients, who are seen and heard wandering the old halls. One female ghost calls out the name "Peter" over and over again. One of the spirits is obsessed with water and is blamed for flushing toilets and turning faucets on and off. The George Road Hospital is another Victoria hospital with a reputation for being haunted. The former mansion was moved from Ashnola to Victoria and used as a clinic. The structure was haunted for many years by the apparition of a nurse or "woman in white." Sometimes she appeared as a moving globe of white light that gradually diminished in size and then disappeared.

FOUR MILE HOUSE The haunting at Four Mile Hill House, a nineteenth-century roadhouse north of Victoria on Metchosin Road, did not begin until it was being renovated in 1979. The new owners planned to turn it into a store selling reproductions of antique furniture, but what they really achieved was to free an antique spirit sleeping in the woodwork. During the work, the apparition of a man wearing pre-World War II clothing started showing up. His footsteps were also heard late at night, along with the sounds of construction work, as if the ghost were trying to help finish the work. Once, the apparition came up behind a young woman, touched her, and then chased her into the kitchen. At other times, he was seen sitting in a tearoom in another part of the store.

The furniture store closed in 1988, and once again the place was remodeled. This time it opened as a pub and restaurant, and before long the ghostly apparition was seen sitting at empty tables in the dining room. Sometimes, the ghost would sit at its table and hit the side of a coffee cup with a spoon to ask for service. All the remodeling also released a few more trapped souls from the building. The oldest ghost is thought to be Jake Matteson, who owned the property in the 1850s and died there waiting for his young bride to join him from Scotland. Another ghost is Margaret Gouge, who lived in the roadhouse in the later half of the nineteenth century. She loved flowers and is most often seen looking out from the laundry room into the garden. Still another ghost is the Lady in White, who is seen waiting outside the old inn and on Thetis Point. She is the spirit of a sea captain's wife who died before she could be reunited with her husband. In the pub, there is a lovely stained-glass portrait of the Lady in White.

MCPHERSON PLAYHOUSE Two ghosts haunt the McPherson Playhouse in Victoria, British Columbia. Despite the ultra-modern façade of the theater, it opened before World War I as a vaudeville stage and has had a lot of time to produce some ghosts. The theater always ran at the edge of economic collapse for years, until it was willed to the city and renovated in the 1960s, and afterwards became home to the Bastion Theatre Company. Over the years, many performers and patrons have seen the ghosts here. The dark phantom of a man in formal attire is seen in the second-floor balcony or his brooding presence is sensed walking across the stage.

The ghost of a woman, the Gray Lady, is seen walking back and forth across the upper balcony in front of the projection booth. Both ghosts remain unidentified, although according to local legend, a theater manager committed suicide by hanging himself from a rope tied to the dress-circle rail on the second-floor balcony. As for the Gray Lady, she wears clothing from the nineteenth century, which may be an indication she was an actress or vaudeville performer, or, as some have suggested, she might be a wandering spirit from Victoria's original cemetery. The cemetery was located not far from the playhouse at Douglas and Johnson streets, but *most* of the bodies were moved to the Quadra Street Cemetery in 1869.

A few blocks from the McPherson Playhouse stands another of Victoria's haunted theaters, the Royal. Despite its prestigious name, the Royal Theatre began as a vaudeville house in 1913 and ended up as a discount movie house by the 1960s. In 1973, it was saved from the wrecking ball by a consortium of local cities that banded together to refurbish and restore the theater. In 1982, it became part of the same theater company that runs the McPherson. The ghost at the Royal is shyer than the one at its sister theater, and its presence is usually sensed rather than seen. When the apparition is observed, usually late at night by custodians, it is a fleeting male figure.

OCEAN POINTE RESORT The spirits that haunt the Ocean Pointe Resort in Victoria, British Columbia, are not from the brand-new, 250-room hotel. Instead, they came with the property, for the luxurious hotel on Vancouver Island was built on top of an Indian burial ground. During construction of the hotel in 1992, workers unearthed bones and Native artifacts that indicated the ground was sacred. Some of the workers reported feeling strange and having odd dreams as a result of the discovery. The owners wisely halted construction and called a Native shaman as well as a Catholic priest to conduct purifying ceremonies and an exorcism. That seemed to transmute the negative feelings into a positive, peaceful presence that permeates the place to this day. The Ocean Pointe Resort is located at 45 Songhees Road in Victoria, British Columbia. For information, telephone 604-360-2999.

ROYAL ROADS MILITARY COLLEGE The Royal Roads Military College, just outside Victoria, has a ghost that dates back to the family of James Dunsmuir, who served as premier of Canada at the turn of the nineteenth century. The Norman-style mansion built by James cost over four million dollars and required a staff of over a hundred to keep running. He called it Hatley Park, and it remained in his family until 1937. Since the military college was established there in 1940, dozens of cadets and instructors have encountered the apparition of a short, elderly woman. She is thought to be James's wife, Laura Dunsmuir, who died in the house in 1937. Sometimes she materializes next to the cadets' beds at night, and has even been known to grab a hold of a cadet's legs and try to yank him out of bed. For some reason, the former mistress of the house does not like so many uninvited young men staying at her beloved Hatley Park.

ROYAL VICTORIA GOLF COURSE Royal Victoria Golf Course in Victoria is haunted by a "Woman in White," seen screaming for help. Sometimes she rings the bell trying to get help. She is Doris Gravlin, who was murdered on September 22, 1936, by her estranged husband. He had followed her to the golf course and arranged to meet her in private at the seventh hole around 9:00 P.M. The man had a serious drinking problem but still loved his wife, and the only solution he could think of was murder-suicide. When they met on the golf course, he attacked and strangled her, then dragged her lifeless body by a cord still wrapped around her throat down to the beach at Golf Course Point. Next, he walked slowly into the water and drowned himself.

His wife's screams were heard by witnesses that day and are still heard up to the present time. At first her apparition was nothing more than a diffuse ball of light, but over the years she has grown more distinct. Her five-foot-tall, easily recognizable apparition is usually encountered walking along the edge of the water on the lee side of Golf Course Point. Others have seen her apparition floating gracefully over the beach or amongst the tall grass. In recent years, the ghost has even taken to following people around.

Whistler

WHISTLER CREEK LODGE The apparitions of a mother and her twelve-year-old son haunt the Whistler Creek Lodge and Serrebello Restaurant in the British Columbia town of Whistler. The distinctive apparitions are seen by employees and patrons in the restaurant area. The ghosts sit up in the rafters of the building and can be seen laughing uproariously at the people below. A more sinister presence has been detected roaming the halls of the adjoining hotel. Where the ghosts come from or what they want is anyone's guess.

UNITED STATES

The original inhabitants of the United States were probably of Asian descent. The land was not colonized by Europeans until the sixteenth century. After the Revolutionary War with Britain, the United States became independent and was organized as a federal republic in 1781. Presented here are a few representative cases from the United States. For more information, visit the Haunted Places Web site (www.haunted-places.com). For a complete listing of over two thousand cases from all fifty states, see the author's *Haunted Places: The National Directory* (Penguin 1996).

DISTRICT OF COLUMBIA

THE WHITE HOUSE The residence of the president of the United States has long been considered haunted. In the attic, the ghost of

William Henry Harrison can sometimes be heard rummaging about, although exactly what he is looking for has never been determined. During the Truman administration, a guard heard the voice of David Burns, who owned the White House property in 1790, coming from the attic area above the Oval Room. On the front porch of the White House, the ghost of Anne Surratt has been seen pounding on the doors, pleading for the release of her mother. Mary Surratt was executed in 1865 for her part in the conspiracy to assassinate President Lincoln. Her daughter is said to appear on the steps of the White House on July 7, the anniversary of her mother's trip to the scaffolds.

The Lincoln Bedroom is the most haunted part of the White House. President Lincoln was the nation's most mystical leader, and he generated tremendous psychic energy. While living in the White House, he and his wife held several séances in an attempt to contact the spirit of their son, Willie, who died there. One medium who visited the White House regularly gave Lincoln advice from great leaders of history. At one of those séances, the spirit of Daniel Webster pleaded with Lincoln to follow through with his efforts to free the slaves. Medium J.B. Conklin conveyed a message to Lincoln from his close friend, Edward Baker, who had been killed at the battle of Ball's Bluff. The cryptic message said: "Gone elsewhere. Elsewhere is everywhere." In 1863, medium Charles Shockle visited the White House and performed a levitation. At another levitation, Lincoln allegedly ordered a Maine congressman to sit on top of a piano that was floating in midair. In November 1860, Lincoln told his wife he knew he would be elected for a second term but would die in office, and he saw his own assassination in a series of dreams ten days before that fateful day of April 14, 1865.

Afterwards, many people reported seeing the ghost of this great man in the White House. The first person to see him was the wife of Calvin Coolidge, Grace, who said she glimpsed him in a window in the Oval Room. When Lincoln was alive, he used the room as a library and spent a lot of time meditating, while gazing out the windows.

White House employees still see his figure standing in front of those same windows. Army Chaplain E.C. Bowles remembers Lincoln's sad look as his ghost stared out a window here. The sixteenth president's biographer, Carl Sandburg, said he felt Lincoln come stand beside him at that window. Above this office, in the Yellow Oval Room, Lincoln's wife encountered the ghosts of Thomas Jefferson and John Tyler.

Franklin D. Roosevelt's personal valet ran screaming from the White House one day, after seeing Lincoln's ghost. Eleanor Roosevelt's maid, Mary Eben, saw the ghost sitting on his bed pulling off his boots. Even the Roosevelts' dog, Fala, was said to have sensed Lincoln's presence. Grace Coolidge, Theodore Roosevelt, Eleanor Roosevelt, Winston Churchill, Harry Truman, Margaret Truman, Dwight Eisenhower, James Haggerty, Jacqueline Kennedy, Ladybird Johnson, Susan Ford, and Maureen Reagan have all admitted sensing the presence of the Civil War president in the White House. The wife of Lyndon Johnson witnessed Lincoln's mysterious presence, while she watched a television program about his assassination. She felt compelled to read a plaque above the fireplace, which explained the dead president's connection to the room. Gerald Ford's daughter, Susan, saw Lincoln's ghost in the room in the 1980s. In 1987, Ronald Reagan's daughter, Maureen, and her husband, Dennis Revell, both saw Lincoln's transparent form next to the bedroom's fireplace. President Clinton's press secretary, Mike McCurry, told reporters he had no doubt that Lincoln's ghost still walks in the White House.

Household members of the family of Ulysses S. Grant are said to have conversed with the ghost of young Willie Lincoln. President Johnson's daughter, Lynda Johnson Robb, sensed the child's spirit in his former bedroom. The cries of Mrs. Grover Cleveland have also been reported coming from this area of the White House. She was the first president's wife to have a baby in the building. In another bedroom, in 1953, the ghost of a British soldier appeared carrying a torch. The husband and wife who stayed there said the ghost tried to burn their bed. The same ghost has been seen on other occasions in the White House and is thought to be the spirit of a soldier involved in setting fire to the structure on August 24, 1814.

The ghost of Andrew Jackson is said to haunt his canopy bed in the Rose Bedroom on the second floor. White House personnel have reported an inexplicable cold spot and the sound of hearty laughter coming from the empty bed. In 1865, Lincoln's wife reported encountering Jackson's ghost, and in the 1950s, White House seamstress Lillian Parks felt Jackson's presence lean over her, while she sat hemming a bedspread in a chair next to his bed. An aide to Lyndon Johnson heard the cussing, hollering ghost of Jackson in this room in 1964. The Rose Bedroom is also known as the Queen's Suite, because visiting queens have often stayed there. Queen Wilhelmina of the Netherlands was sleeping in this room, when she answered a knock at the door. Standing in the hallway was the ghost of Abraham Lincoln, whose bedroom was right across the hall.

The ghost of former First Lady Dolley Madison appeared in the Rose Garden during the administration of Woodrow Wilson. Dolley had planted the garden a hundred years earlier, but Mrs. Wilson gave orders to have it dug up. Workmen reported Dolley's ghost appeared in the garden and kept them from carrying out their job. After that, no one dared harm the famous White House Rose Garden. In the East Room, staffers have reported the ghost of President John Adams's wife, Abigail, hanging laundry in this airy room. Her apparition passes through closed doors with her arms outstretched, as if she were carrying a laundry basket. Sometimes the faint smell of damp clothes and soap can be detected in this area. During William Taft's presidency, Abigail was reported passing through doors on the second floor of the White House. More recently, she has been reported roaming through the second floor hallways. The second floor hallways at the White House are trafficked by numerous ghosts. The footsteps of Abraham Lincoln have also been reported in this corridor by several residents, including Eleanor Roosevelt. No wonder Harry Truman wrote to his wife: "I sit here in this old house, all the while listening to the ghosts walk up and down the hallway. At four o'clock I was awakened by three distinct knocks on my bedroom door. No one there. Damned place is haunted, sure as shooting!"

ILLINOIS

Chicago

BACHELOR'S GROVE CEMETERY Chicago is known for its haunted cemeteries. One of the most active spots for sightings is Bachelor's Grove Cemetery, even though no one has been buried in this small graveyard since 1965. Over a hundred reports of paranormal activity have taken place on this acre of land. The property was set aside as a cemetery in 1864, though some of the plots date back to the 1830s. Bachelor's Grove is named for the large number of single men resting in its graves, yet one of the most prominent ghosts is a woman known as the White Lady, the Madonna of Bachelor's Grove, or affectionately, as "Mrs. Rogers." She appears only during the full moon and is thought to be a woman who was buried in a grave next to her young son. Other ghosts congregate at the lagoon, still a favorite spot for animal sacrifices and voodoo rituals. Apparitions seen near the lagoon include a two-headed man and a farmer with a horse and plow. The farmer died in the 1870s, when his horse suddenly bolted into the water, taking the man and the plow with it. Nobody has yet suggested an identity for the two-headed ghost, although, during the late 1920s, the site was a favorite dumping ground for victims of Chicago mobsters. Perhaps the unique phantom is a remnant of those violent times.

In the 1950s, a ghostly farmhouse, complete with a white picket fence, appeared on several occasions. Strange blue lights are sometimes seen dancing from tombstone to tombstone here, and in December 1971, a woman said she put her hand right through the ghost of a figure walking down a path in the cemetery. In 1984, a skeptical investigator encountered the yellow, glowing apparition of a man. The image only lasted for a few seconds but was followed by a display of darting red lights. Phantom cars have materialized on the roads surrounding the cemetery. The Ghost Research Society undertook an extensive investigation of Bachelor's Grove in 1982. Using infrared film, they were able to capture the image of a ghost in an old-style dress sitting on a tombstone. Bachelor's Grove is located west of Midlothian, a suburb south of Chicago.

EVERGREEN CEMETERY The ghost of a brunette girl buried in this cemetery likes to see the sights of Chicago. In the 1980s, the child's phantom was reported hitchhiking rides in the west Chicago area. Once, she even got on a CTA bus. When the driver walked back to tell her she had not paid, the girl vanished in front of him. Now she is seen walking down Kedzie Avenue. Evergreen Cemetery is located at 87th Street and Kedzie Avenue in Chicago. The phone number is 708-422-9051.

GRACELAND CEMETERY Graceland Cemetery, opened in 1860, is haunted by a variety of spirits. The lifelike statue over the grave of a seven-year-old girl reportedly sheds tears and moves around the grounds. The statue marking the grave of Inez Clarke is covered by a glass case, but that does not stop it from disappearing, especially during violent thunderstorms. Guards have reported it gone on several occasions, only to find the statue in place the next morning. Inez died in 1880, but her ghostly figure is still seen walking among the tombstones. Another eerie statue marks the grave of Dexter Graves, who died in 1844 at the age of fifty-five. The menacing, hooded figure of Death is said to give those who look into its face a taste of what is to come. But Graceland's most lavish monument is the thirty-foot-long, twelve-foot-high tomb of Ludwig Wolff. The area around the stone building is the stomping ground of a green-eyed ghoul, who likes to howl at the full moon. Graceland Cemetery is at 4001 North Clark Street in Chicago. The telephone is 312-525-1105.

HOLY SEPULCHRE CEMETERY The grave of a girl believed to have healing powers gives off the odor of fresh roses, although none are in sight. Hun-

Inez Clarke Gravesite, Graceland Cemetery, Chicago, United States (Bruce Schaffenberger)

dreds have made the pilgrimage to the grave in hopes of finding relief to their ills. She is Mary Alice Quinn, who died in 1935 at the age of fourteen. A gentle, pious child, she reportedly healed several people before she died. Mary is buried in the Reilly plot. Holy Sepulchre Cemetery is at 6001 West 111th Street in the town of Worth, which is a southwest suburb of Chicago. The phone number is 312-445-2022.

JEWISH WALDHEIM CEMETERY The ghost of a 1920s flapper girl has been reported near the Jewish Waldheim Cemetery. Sightings peaked in 1933 and 1973, and the apparition is still seen at the cemetery gates and on Des Plaines Avenue, between the Melody Mill Ballroom and the cemetery. Jewish Waldheim Cemetery is in North Riverside, a northwest suburb of Chicago. The phone number is 708-366-4100.

MOUNT CARMEL CEMETERY The gravesite of Al Capone is haunted by the mobster's ghost, which is said to appear to disrespectful people visiting his family plot. Capone himself was haunted by the ghost of James Clark, brother-in-law of Bugs Moran and one of the victims of the St. Valentine's Day Massacre. In another part of the cemetery, the life-sized statue of Julia Buccola Petta, who died in childbirth in 1921, is haunted by her ghost, which is seen wearing a white dress near the grave. Her casket was opened in 1927, and her body was still in perfect condition. So astonished were the family members that a photograph of the corpse was taken and is displayed on her tombstone. The cemetery is located on Harrison Street in the town of Hillside, a western suburb of Chicago. The phone number is 708-449-8300.

RESURRECTION CEMETERY The ghost of a blonde, blue-eyed girl has haunted the district around this graveyard since 1939, five years after a young Polish girl was buried here. Mary Bregavy, or Resurrection Mary as she has come to be called, died in a car accident after an evening of dancing at the old O'Henry Ballroom (now the Willowbrook Ballroom). Sometimes, her glowing, faceless ghost is seen walking along the shoulder of the road, but most often, her white apparition is seen hitchhiking. Sometimes her aloof ghost even dances with a few young men at the ballroom and asks for a ride home. During renovations at the cemetery in the 1970s, sightings of her ghost reached a peak.

In December 1977, a passing motorist saw Mary holding onto the bars of the cemetery gate. He called police, thinking a girl was trapped in the cemetery. Investigators found no one in the cemetery, but two bars in the gate were bent apart. Etched into the iron were two small handprints. Supervisors had the sections cut out to keep curiosity-seekers away, but embarrassed officials welded the pieces back in place a year later. Dozens of witnesses, including many taxi drivers,

have seen Mary's ghost along the road. In 1989, a cab driver picked up a girl fitting Mary's description in front of the Old Willow Shopping Center. As they passed Resurrection Cemetery, the girl vanished from the front seat. Today, her ghost is seen most often along Archer Avenue in south Chicago. Resurrection Cemetery is located at 7600 South Archer Avenue in the south Chicago suburb of Justice. The telephone number is 312-767-4644.

WHITE CEMETERY Eerie, glowing globes have been seen hovering in this 1820s cemetery. The lights float near the fence and sometimes over the road surface. A phantom black car has also been reported in the cemetery and near an old house that stood a block away. Although the house burnt down years ago, it sometimes reappears, only to vanish from view within a few seconds. The cemetery is located on Cuba Road in Barrington, a northwest suburb of Chicago.

CALIFORNIA

San Francisco

ALCATRAZ The Miwok Indians thought evil spirits inhabited this island and never set foot here until 1859, when they arrived in shackles as the island's first prisoners. By 1912, the U.S. Army had built the largest reinforced concrete structure in the world, a huge fortress that would later house the nation's most dangerous criminals. In 1963, the island was taken over by the National Park Service and only the ghosts of its tormented inmates remain. Clanging sounds, screams, and crying can sometimes be heard in Cell Block B and the dungeon area near Cell Block A.

Disturbances in Cell Block C became so frequent that the Park Service called in psychic Sylvia Brown to try to figure out what was happening. She made contact with the spirit of a man called "Butcher," who resisted all her efforts to calm his violent soul. Prison records confirmed that Abie Maldowitz, a mob hit man with the nickname of Butcher, was killed by another prisoner in the laundry room of the cell block. In Cell Block D, four cells are thought to be haunted. Strange voices have emanated from cells 11, 12, and 13 there.

Even in the summer months, cell 14-D feels ice cold, and some visitors have been overcome by emotion in one corner of the cell. This was the tiny cell where killer Rufe McCain was kept in solitary confinement for over three years. Sometimes the sounds of banjo playing are reported coming from the deserted Shower Room, where Al Capone frequently played the instrument. Boats to Alcatraz Island leave every few hours from Pier 41 in San Francisco. Call 415-546-2700 for tour information.

HASKELL HOUSE The two-story, white frame house known as Haskell House in the former Fort Mason military compound is haunted. It was in this house that U.S. Senator David Broderick died from a gunshot wound in a duel with State Supreme Court Justice David Terry. The year was 1857. Terry was a powerful Southerner who wanted California to become a slave state. Broderick was a vociferous critic of a new California law that allowed any white person to bring a freed slave to authorities and claim him as his own property. When the smoke cleared, Broderick lay on the ground bleeding from a chest wound, and Terry stood over him. Broderick was taken to the home of his close friend, Leonides Haskell, and died there three days later.

The Senator had spent the evening before the duel at his friend's house, where he paced about anxiously all night long. Haskell's home was confiscated by the Union Army in 1863 and remains a military quarters to this day. Many of the officers and family members who lived there have reported seeing the ghost of Senator Broderick pacing back and forth, reliving his anguish the night before the duel. Recently, Captain James Lunn's family reported disembodied shadows moving back and forth in the parlor. Colonel Cecil Puckett felt someone following him around the house, even watching him in the shower. Captain Everett Jones and his family experienced a variety of frightening poltergeist activity—until they stopped joking about the ghost. According to

Mansions Hotel, San Francisco, California, United States (Bruce Schaffenberger)

Captain James Knight: "There's no doubt the house was haunted." Haskell House is the old Quarters Three at Fort Mason in San Francisco. For information, call 415-776-0693.

MANSIONS HOTEL When you check into the Mansions Hotel, be sure to tell the desk clerk if you want a Non-Haunting Room. The unique hotel consists of two magnificent mansions. The newer one is free of ghosts. The older one is haunted. The hotel documents its uncanny history in a display that includes affidavits of witnesses, transcripts of séances, and photographs of ghosts. For years, guests have complained about strange noises, cold shadows moving about, and even toilet seats flying across the room. Actor Vincent Schiavelli, who portrayed the disturbed subway spirit in the movie *Ghost* (1990), encountered a female ghost as he entered his room at the hotel late one night. In 1991, an apparition materialized in front of several witnesses during a séance in a third-floor suite. That ghost's photograph is now part of the hotel's haunted gallery. In July 1992, a scientific study conducted by the Office of Paranormal Investigation discovered powerful electromagnetic forces in the old section of the hotel. The results confirmed the impressions of psychic Sylvia Brown, who sensed numerous spirits in the hotel.

In August 1992, a man and his wife checked into a room in the old mansion. Ten minutes later, the man returned to the front desk in a state of shock. His face was ashen. His whole body was shaking. Something had frightened him badly, but he refused to talk about it. Since he had already checked in, the clerk was forced to charge him. "I don't care," the man said, "I just can't be here anymore!" Owner Bob Pritikin commented: "The man just didn't know there were ghosts in the hotel. We get all kinds of weird things happening in this place." The Mansions Hotel is at 2220 Sacramento Street in San Francisco. For information, call 415-929-9444.

SAN FRANCISCO ART INSTITUTE The San Francisco Art Institute is located in the Russian Hill area of San Francisco, where more hauntings are reported than any other area of the city. An old cemetery, now buried under tons of concrete construction, might be the source of the manifestations, and at least a few of those lost souls seems to have found a home in the tower of the San Francisco Art Institute. The monastic tower, which is adjacent to the cemetery site, has been considered haunted for fifty years. Unexplainable footsteps are heard climbing the stairway to the observation platform, lights turn off and on again for no reason, and doors open and shut by themselves. One former student was taking a break on the tower's third level when he heard footsteps coming up the stairs. He watched in disbelief as the door opened and closed, and the invisible footsteps went past him to the observation deck. Other students, a watchman, and a janitor have also witnessed apparitions climbing the stairs of the tower. During remodeling of the tower, workers reported an evil presence that caused "breaking sounds," and three near-fatal accidents

occurred. A group of psychics attempted to contact the ghost during a séance, but they only succeeded in verifying the presence of many "frustrated" spirits. The San Francisco Art Institute is at 800 Chestnut Street in San Francisco. For information, phone 415-771-7020.

MOSS BEACH DISTILLERY The gruesome ghost of a lady in a blue dress, soaked in blood, haunts this old speakeasy on Half Moon Bay, just south of San Francisco on the coast. Waitresses, chefs, managers, and customers have seen the young woman's phantom standing near the piano, outside the ladies room, or dancing alone in deserted rooms. Once, a boy ran screaming from the restroom, insisting that a lady covered in blood touched him. In February 1992, two waitresses saw a stool tip over and do a somersault. The woman's bloody phantom was even spotted standing in the middle of Highway 1, which runs in front of the restaurant. On average, her ghost has been sighted once or twice every year for the last fifty years. In August 1992, all the settings in the restaurant's automatic thermostat system were mysteriously changed. The complicated reprogramming would have taken most people three or four hours to perform. "The company told me that there was no way it could have been done except manually," owner John Barber related, "but I had the only access key!" Previous owners say the ghost of the Moss Beach Distillery is the spirit of a young woman stabbed to death by a jealous lover on the beach in front of this cliffside restaurant, over seventy years ago. Moss Beach Distillery is located on Highway 1 on the corner of Ocean and Beach Streets in the town of Moss Beach. For more information, phone 415-728-5595.

WINCHESTER HOUSE Sarah Winchester started building this house in 1884 and never stopped. She was living in New Haven, Connecticut, when her husband and only child died within months of each other. In an attempt to contact her lost loved ones, she went to Boston medium Adam Coons. He contacted her husband, who asked Sarah to build a house for all the spirits of people killed by the rifle that bears the Winchester name. She traveled west and came upon an eight-room farmhouse being built in the Santa Clara Valley in California. Immediately she knew it was the right place and bought the entire forty-acre farm. Work continued on the house around the clock for the next thirty-eight years. She eventually spent six million dollars and ended up with a house of 700 rooms, 950 doors, and 10,000 windows. She had a special room for séances, called the Blue Room, where she received building plans direct from the spirit world. Every night at midnight, 1:00 A.M., and 2:00 A.M., a large bell in the bell tower rang out to summon spirits. To discourage evil spirits from entering her home, she built many blind passageways and based much of the construction on the number thirteen. She even slept in a different bedroom every night to keep one step ahead of them.

Sarah was convinced that evil spirits had found her when the 1906 earthquake leveled the upper stories of her mansion. Only 160 rooms remained, and she had the bedroom where she slept that night boarded up. On the other hand, Sarah treated good spirits royally. She held regular banquets in her lavish Dining Room, where servants set out five-course meals on thirteen solid gold plates and cutlery. The only guests were herself and twelve invisible ghosts. Real people rarely set foot in her home, and she even turned away such notables as Theodore Roosevelt and Mary Baker Eddy. One of her few guests was Harry Houdini, who never spoke of his single visit to Winchester House. Sarah died in September 1922 and bequeathed her estate to a niece with the instructions that "the ghosts continue to be welcomed and provided for." Guided tours of the house have been offered since 1923.

Several famous psychics have contacted ghosts here, and staff members have seen moving balls of light and a gray-haired female apparition floating through the halls. Visitors have heard organ music, whispering voices, and slamming noises. The management of Winchester House maintains a file of affidavits by witnesses of unusual events. Winchester House is located about fifty miles south of San Francisco in San Jose. Winchester House is at 525 South Winchester Boulevard in San Jose, California. For tour information, call 408-247-2101.

CENTRAL AMERICA

BARBADOS

Barbados is an island of the Lesser Antilles chain in the West Indies. It is an independent nation within the British Commonwealth that was first settled by the Arawak people.

Bridgetown

CHRIST CHURCH GRAVEYARD Barbados is an island in the West Indies that was the scene of one of the world's first scientifically investigated hauntings. The phenomena centered on the Chase Family Vault, a massive crypt that sits half below ground. The crypt is open and all the coffins have been removed, and the reason they were taken out was that they kept repositioning themselves, even when the empty tomb was sealed. The phenomena started with the burial of Thomas Chase in August 1812. Thomas was a powerful judge and one of the most hated men on the island. He was known as a ruthless and stubborn man, traits that he is said to have taken to the grave. Unfortunately, there was the spirit of an equally stubborn woman waiting for him in the crypt.

The vault was purchased by the Chase family from relatives in the Goddard family in 1808, even though it already contained the wooden coffin of Thomasina Goddard, who had died on July 31, 1807. Thomas Chase needed a final resting spot for his daughter, two-year-old Mary Ann Chase, and her small lead coffin was added in 1808. Four years later, in July 1812, her sister Dorcas was laid to rest in the family tomb. The teenager had starved herself to death, driven to depression and despair by her tyrannical father. Just one month later, the body of Thomas Chase joined his daughters in the tomb. But when the vault was opened to bury him, her heavy lead coffin had been pushed against the opposite wall from where her father would lay and her baby sister's coffin had been moved too. There was no way anyone could have gotten into the crypt. After each interment, a heavy marble slab was cemented in place over the only opening.

The next burial took place in September 1816, when an eleven-year-old-boy from the Chase family was interred in the vault. But when it was opened, all the coffins except Goddard's were in complete disarray. Even the lead coffin of Thomas Chase, which had taken eight burly men to move, was flung on top of the others. In November 1816, the father of the boy previously interred joined his son in the vault. Again, when it was opened, the coffins had obviously been thrown about. This time Thomasina Goddard's wooden coffin was so badly damaged that it had to be wrapped in wire just to hold it together. The next interment was in 1819, and once again the coffins were strewn about in the vault, and the only one not moved was that of Thomasina Goddard.

At this point the British governor of Barbados, Lord Combermere, stepped in and organized a thorough investigation. The vault and coffins were meticulously examined and no hidden cavities or anything out of the ordinary was found. No evidence was found of earth movement or flooding. Sand was sprinkled on the vault floor to detect any footprints of intruders, and the marble slab cemented in place. Then, the personal seals of the governor and two other dignitaries were pressed into the wet mortar.

On April 18, 1820, Lord Combermere ordered the vault opened for inspection. All the seals were still intact, but the coffins were in the worse disarray yet. Some were turned over and broken, yet there were no footprints or other marks in the sand. Only the wooden Goddard coffin had not moved. Panicked islanders were now convinced the Christ Church graveyard was haunted, and the governor had to find a way to put an end to the mystery. He ordered the quarreling coffins reburied in separate plots and the Chase vault left open, never to be used again. Christ Church is located seven miles from the capital city of Bridgetown, overlooking Oisin's Bay in Christ Church graveyard. If you visit the site, you will find the Chase vault lying open and still unused.

EL SALVADOR

El Salvador was once controlled by Guatemala and then by Spain, from which it became independent in 1821. After a lengthy civil war, a new constitution was adopted in 1983.

San Salvador

LA SEGUANAVA The foothills north of the city of San Salvador area are haunted by the sadistic spirit of a witch called "La Seguanava." She enjoys causing pain and fear in witnesses, and the more frightened they become the more powerfully she manifests. She has been known to follow hikers home and haunt their homes with poltergeist effects for weeks at the initial encounter. Some say she was an old lady who lived in the mountains and sometimes came into the city. One night over fifty years ago, she was waiting at a bus stop, and several youths started tormenting her because of her odd appearance. Before the night was over they had beaten the poor woman to death, but she apparently has not forgotten.

GUATEMALA

Mayan settlements here go back to 2500 B.C. After being under Spanish and Mexican control, it became an independent republic in 1839.

Guatemala City

SANTA ROSA DE LIMA CHURCH The apparition of a beautiful woman in a white dress haunts the front of the Santa Rosa de Lima Church in Guatemala City. She is said to appear about once in a decade but always on November 1, the Day of the Dead. She materializes with open arms at the main entrance to the church. Sometimes she can be heard whispering, "Come here!" The unidentified apparition most often appears around 3:00 A.M. and sometimes approaches people on the street at that late hour. It is said anyone who follows her will meet their death, and the deaths of at least three men have been blamed on her. One young man described his experience when returning from a funeral late one night with some friends: "We all saw a beautiful lady. She had a white dress on and her arms were spread out like she wanted a hug. We started to walk to her because in our minds we heard her say, 'Come to me!' When we went closer, we could see she had no feet and looked like she was flying."

HAITI

A slave revolt in 1804 took back the entire island from Spanish control. In 1844, the east part of the island revolted and formed the Dominican Republic. Francois Duvalier ruled the island from 1957 to 1971. Today, it is a presidential republic.

Port-au-Prince

BEL AIR DISTRICT Voodoo priests ("hougans") are said to have the ability to control a person's dead body ("Zombie") as well as their spirit ("Iwa"). In one well-documented case, Hougan Luc Gedeon restored the spirit of an outspoken black man named Arapice La Croix, who was murdered in the Bel Air district of Port-au-Prince at the age of twenty-one. The black man's ghost approached Luc Gedeon and asked to become part of the hougan's spiritual family. In a ceremony witnessed by many of his relatives and others, Arapice's apparition appeared out of thin air and lay down in the middle of a huge bonfire to be cleansed. Afterwards, the hougan placed Arapice's spirit in a virgin clay pot called a "Govi." The Govi and its spirit became part of the hougan's family and continues to manifest under the control of his descendents.

Voodoo is a mixture of native and Catholic beliefs that is directed to controlling the spirits of the dead. When a Vodouisant (member of the Voodoo cult) dies, he or she is buried in a Roman Catholic ceremony that lasts nine days. Then, the Voodoo ceremony of "Desounin" starts, during which the parts of the person's soul and life force and the primary spiritual identity in the head (the Iwa) are separated and go to their different destinations. Sometimes, if the Iwa or spirit of the dead person is to be revived on the earthly plane, a ceremony known as "Retire mo non dio" ("Take the dead out of water") is held. One year and one day after the person has died, his or her spiritual identity is summoned through a vessel of water and put into a Govi. The deceased person's spirit may speak from the Govi or through one of the priests present to show it has been successfully contained. Govis are stored in the Djevo, or the sacred inner room of a Voodoo temple. If a spirit is especially strong, as was the case with Arapice La Croix, he or she may appear to a Voodoo priest and ask to be "stored" in a Govi for summoning later. The spirit of such a person is called an "Iwa Ghede." Also roaming the night in Haiti are the "Bakas," former members of a secret society who agreed to return from the grave to serve their group's needs.

CEMETERY OF PORT-AU-PRINCE This city's main cemetery is haunted by the ghastly apparitions of decomposing bodies that have been witnessed walking the grounds. Most of the sightings in this 233-year-old graveyard are during the early evening twilight hours. Sightings have increased in recent years because of rampant grave robbing that is disturbing the final resting place of thousands of dead people. Haiti is the poorest country in the Western Hemisphere, and people will dig up a coffin just to salvage the brass handles and hinges. They also rip open the coffins looking for jewelry and even take belts and shoes. Often they leave the coffins sticking up out of the graves with skeletons lying half out of the busted boxes. Elaborate mausoleums are ransacked and destroyed; skulls and bones litter the grounds. The situation grew out of control in the early 1990s, when a trade embargo was put in place to try to oust the island nation's military leaders. The Haitian economy suffered and black markets became the only place to secure many items. Most of the pilfered brass and iron coffin fittings are bought back by funeral directors to adorn new coffins.

HONDURAS

The indigenous culture here included remnants of the Mayan civilization. Honduras declared independence from Spain in 1821. A civilian government was elected in 1982.

Roatan Island

FLOWERS BAY The hills around Flowers Bay on Roatan Island in the Islas de La Bahís chain are the most haunted in all of Honduras. At Coxen Hole, the ghost of English pirate John Coxen lies in wait for anyone that gets too interested in "his" mysterious hole. At the sign for the old Arnold Auld School, now rebuilt at another location, pirate ghosts protecting buried treasure are also seen. Between Coxen Hole and a village called Watering Place (where pirate ships once loaded on fresh water), the local cemetery has apparitions dressed in naval uniforms.

Santa Fe

GUADALUPE Guadalupe is a fishing village close to the Honduran city of Santa Fe. Not far from the village is a haunted section of beach called Punta Betulia. The area has long been considered haunted and, according to native tradition, was once a site where people were sacrificed to the Jaguar God. Witnesses report apparitions walking aimlessly about and the sounds of chains and people screaming. The focal point for the activity is a structure about fifty meters from the water. There are many sculptures there, some weighing as much as five tons, and a small chapel with an empty altar. There is also an elongated table with the sculpture of a skull at one end that may have been used as a sacrificial altar.

PUNTIACO The ghosts of natives who were forced to vacate their homes to make way for the modern city of Santa Fe are still seen on the streets. The apparitions seem upset that their ancestral grounds have been concreted over with streets and buildings. The natives lived here for centuries before being pushed out of the area by heavy construction equipment. They long to return to their native land and town, which they called "Puntiaco."

Tegucigalpa

TALGUA CAVES The caves of Talgua, about two hundred kilometers east of the city of Tegucigalpa in the Honduras, are haunted by the luminous ghost of a giant being. A possible source for the hauntings was discovered in 1994, when explorers discovered a ritual chamber in the cave that contained the crystallized copses of several giant beings. In 1940, gigantic human bones and skulls were found near a tomb on the Humuya River, and other giant remains have been discovered in La Union in Olancho. The skeletons are around three meters (8–10 feet) tall with extremely large and thick skulls. According to Sabanagrande natives, the giant race lived in the forest long ago. The giant ghost seen in the area, however, is from a single man, who murdered his brother and other family members. The man's soul still wanders through the forest, lost in eternity.

JAMAICA

Jamaica was settled by Arawak people. It was a Spanish colony from 1509 to 1655 and a British colony from 1655 to 1958. It became an independent nation within the British Commonwealth in 1962.

Montego Bay

GREENWOOD GREAT HOUSE Fifteen miles east of Montego Bay lies Greenwood Great House, a manor house built in 1800 that once belonged to the family of British poet Elizabeth Barrett. The place is haunted by the Lady in Gray, who has been identified as the wife of the original owner. In fact, there is still a photograph on display that shows her apparition floating behind her husband, who is seated in a rocking chair on the veranda. The current owners say they live with the ghost "on a daily basis," and many tourists visiting the property have felt her presence. Oddly, though, no one has been able to capture her apparition on film. Ever since the ghost photo was taken, people's cameras break down or fail mysteriously. As soon as they leave the house, their cameras work fine.

ROSE HALL PLANTATION Built between 1770 and 1780, Rose Hall was one of the largest estates on the island of Jamaica during British colonial times, but by the nineteenth century, the magnificent three-story mansion was abandoned and fell into disrepair. Nobody would live there because it was considered haunted. At one time, it was known as the most haunted house in the Western Hemisphere. Even today, some natives refuse to go near the place for that reason, and people touring the basement dungeon often hear tortured screams or are overcome by feelings of sadness.

Actually, the ghost of Rose Hall is not someone with whom you would want to mess around. The former mistress of the estate, Annie Palmer, was a sadistic woman, who dressed like a man and rode around on her horse with a whip she took to slaves or anyone else who got in her way. It is her mean spirit that haunts her former home. Annie studied Voodoo with a Haitian princess, and locals still refer to her as the "White Witch of Rose Hall." Annie came to the prosperous Rose Hall sugar plantation in 1790 as the second wife of owner John Palmer. What he did not know was that the comely young lady had already poisoned her previous two husbands. When John discovered that she was having an affair with a slave, she also poisoned him, and, as he lay dying, she made love to the slave in front of him. Annie seduced many handsome slaves and promised them their freedom if they would perform well. Then, when she got tired of them, she watched her overseers torture them to death. Finally, in 1833, a young slave survived long enough to kill her before she killed him. He raised her lifeless body above his head and threw it from the balcony for all the other slaves to see. Her gravestone on the property carries deep gouges and other signs of abuse from her former slaves.

After her death, it was believed her spirit still controlled the house, and no one would live there until 1905, when the estate was purchased by the Henderson family. However, a maid preparing for the Henderson's arrival was "pushed" to her death from an upstairs window, and the Hendersons never even stayed a night in the house. The deserted estate defaulted to the British government.

In 1952, famed medium Eileen Garrett attempted to exorcise Annie's tortured spirit from her estate but was unsuccessful. Despite being terror-stricken at her predicament, the stubborn ghost of Annie Palmer refuses to leave the property she ruled with an iron hand. "Let no one think this is the end of me," she said through the medium.

Rose Hall sat empty until 1965, when it was purchased by John Rollins, former governor of Delaware. He spent over $2.5 million restoring the house and opened it in 1971 as a hotel. In 1978, over eight thousand people arrived at the estate to watch famous mediums and psychics from around the world contact Annie Palmer's spirit. One of them, a Greek channeler named Bambos, received a communication to look in a giant termite mound on the property. Concealed within the insect mound was a brass urn containing a Voodoo doll that allegedly belonged to Annie Palmer. Apparently, Annie is pleased with all the attention. Her once-ruined mansion has been fully restored and is now an upscale resort hotel within easy reach of the Montego Bay Airport. Of course, she has not given up the place. Photographs of her ghost and letters from guests who have seen her apparition are on display in the former dungeon.

MEXICO

The Olmec, Maya, Toltec, and Aztec civilizations flourished in Mexico before the country was conquered by Spain. After a revolt in 1821, it declared its independence as a constitutional republic.

Acambaro

ACAMBARO TOMBS Ancient tombs located on the cliffs of the Hill of the Bull near the town of Acambaro in the state of Guanajuato is said to be the source of strange apparitions reported by residents and visitors. Villagers believe the hill is haunted and will not walk its slopes. The site was discovered in 1944 by German merchant Waldemar Julsrud and has produced over 33,500 clay and stone artifacts that include numerous statues resembling ancient Egyptian deities. The discoveries have so upset traditional archeologists that they have labeled them frauds and refuse to acknowledge their existence. However, recent studies at Ohio State University have concluded that the artifacts are genuine and could date back as far as 4,500 B.C.

Famous medium and psychic Arthur Ford was asked to try to contact spirits using the artifacts from the site. To everyone's surprise, the apparition of Egyptologist Arthur Weigall manifested. He was a victim of an Egyptian curse for opening Pharaoh Tutankamen's tomb. His message was that early Egyptians had visited Mexico and made the tombs. Dutch psychic Peter Hurkos, who visited the site in Mexico and examined some of the artifacts, declared that he was unable to handle the artifacts for more than a few minutes because of their powerful spiritual vibrations. He also said that there were more tombs waiting to be discovered on the hill.

Chichen Itza

ASTRONOMICAL OBSERVATORY Located about thirty-two kilometers (twenty miles) west of Valladolid in the Yucatan state, Chichen Itza is an ancient Maya site with extensive ruins, including well-preserved temples, pyramids, and sculptures. The place where ghosts are seen, however, is just one building, the so-called Astronomical Observatory. Sacrifices were made inside the observatory in hopes of reading propitious signs in the heavens, and apparently, people were butchered and their body parts strewn around the core of the observatory by the priests.

There have been several reports of sightings of priests and victims inside the building. One of the most vivid occurred in 1986. American tourist Lorraine Butler Glessner encountered a frightening apparition in a corridor near the inner core of the observatory: "As I strolled down the corridor, I saw a man eying me. He was angry about my being there. His eyes were piercing and he looked at me angrily with his head slightly lowered. I felt strange, like there was a 'fold' or crease in time surrounding him. Then I realized he was a Mayan,

Chichen Itza, Mexico (Lorraine Butler Glessner)

rather short and dressed in drab clothing. I sensed that he was not a priest or astronomer but rather some kind of assistant. Something told me to get out of there fast, and I did. I took off and exited at a side door, where my husband looked at me and immediately asked if I were okay. I guess I looked pretty shaken. Once I had a few minutes to mull over the encounter, I thought it was really a cool thing to happen to me. But I will never forget his eyes."

Durango

DURANGO DEAD ZONE The desert forty kilometers (twenty-five miles) from the town of Ceballos in the Mexican state of Durango is a mysterious region where all kinds of strange apparitions are seen. Balls of light that constantly change color are seen floating over the desert, and encounters occur with tall blond-haired men and women, and short people in silvery outfits. Whether these sightings are the work of ghosts, interdimensional beings, or UFO aliens is still a matter of debate. The Mexican government has established a research lab in the area. The Dead Zone got its name in 1968, after Pemex Oil company engineers looking for oil deposits discovered that no radio, microwave, or television communication was possible in the area. Some sort of powerful magnetic source in the rocks or buried deep underground was dampening electromagnetic energy. The geographical title for the region is "Mar de Tetys," the name of an ancient sea that once covered the now arid desert.

El Pedregal

CUICULICO PYRAMID The ghosts of Toltec shamans have been reported in a few of the apartment buildings of this affluent Mexico City suburb, and it is generally believed the source of the wandering spirits lies beneath the city streets. El Pedregal and the neighboring suburb of San Angel sit on top of the largest pyramid in the world, now buried under ancient lava flows. Discovered in 1922, the pyramid is really several structures in one, layers of pyramids within pyramids, which were built on top of each other every fifty-two years for many centuries. The construction cycle corresponds with a sacred ritual called *Fuego Nuevo* (New Fire) that was celebrated by Toltec priests every fifty-two years. Archeologists estimate the structure is around eight thousand years old, but the hard lava rock that encases it makes excavation nearly impossible.

Guanajuato

MUSEUM OF THE MUMMIES The Museo de las Momias (Museum of the Mummies) is a macabre place where the spirits of the dead have definitely been disturbed. The Pateon Cemetery located in the town of Gaunajuato on the summit of the Cerro del Trozado Mountain is a cramped graveyard with many beautiful stones and tombs, but it relies on its income from burial fees that must continue to be paid by the descendents of the deceased. If payment is not made, the bodies are "repossessed" and earn their keep by being put

Museum of the Mummies, Guanjuato, Mexico (Museum of the Mummies)

on public display. Owners have so far exhumed one hundred eight delinquent corpses, put them on public display, and charge people about $2.00 to see them. The bodies are remarkably well preserved from being in the dry earth so long, and most have hair, skin, nails, teeth, genitalia, and even clothing intact.

Several shelves are devoted to babies, and psychically sensitive people visiting the museum of death report hearing the sounds of babies whining and crying for attention. In 1969, the apparition of a tall woman was seen facing these shelves, as if she were looking for her lost child. The sounds of adult corpses talking amongst themselves in hurried whispers is also reported.

In the middle of the sixteenth century, the town became one of the richest in Mexico because of its huge silver deposits. Many mansions were built and the town attracted artistic and cultured people. The famous muralist Diego Rivera was born there. Most of the bodies at the infamous museum date from the twentieth century, and because of the hot, dry climate, they are remarkably well preserved. Despite the T-shirts with pictures of skulls and coffins sold in the gift shop, Mexican

Museum of the Mummies, Guanjuato, Mexico
(Museum of the Mummies)

visitors to the museum treat the dead with a great deal of respect. For more information, visit the Web site www.sirius.com/~dbh/mummies/index.html.

Mexico City

METRO SUBWAY SYSTEM Mexico City grew from the Aztec city of Tenochtitlan, which was founded in the middle of a swamp in the mid-1300s. Today, it is a teeming city full of smog and dirt, but there is one part of the city that is always immaculate. Mexicans are very proud of their subway system, and tourists often comment how clean and beautiful are its floors and glistening ceramic walls and murals. Some Mexicans have a reverent attitude toward their "metro" not out of pride, but rather because they believe it is haunted. Many apparitions have been reported in the underground stations. Some of the ghosts appear to be glorious Aztec warriors, while others are just wandering children in rags. During construction of the subway system, several skeletons and over one hundred tons of clay artifacts—mostly bowls, masks, and idols—were unearthed. There were

also rumors that two thousand children were sacrificed in the construction of the subway to appease malignant spirits offended by the huge scar in the earth's skin.

Human sacrifice is an old tradition in Mexico. The Aztecs rose to power in the twelfth century, settled down and formed cities in the fourteenth century, and were conquered by the Spanish in the sixteenth century. During the Aztec empire, however, human sacrifice was an everyday fact of life. Bloody sacrifices were regularly made to entice the sun to reappear each morning, and specific sacrifices were made to appease the gods or ask them for something. For instance, in 1487, twenty thousand people were ritually murdered to gain the support of the war god Huitzilopochtli. According to Aztec lore, the best sacrifice is young children, and they must be offered any time some human undertaking will alter the earth or balance of nature. It is a long tradition that allegedly resurfaced during the building of the subway.

Rumors of human sacrifices were so widespread that the governor of the state of Morales and the head of the Department of Public Works had to issue official denials. The situation came to a head when an eight-year-old boy was abducted from the town of Cuernavaca by kidnappers. When police stopped the kidnappers' vehicle for speeding, the boy told them he was being taken to Mexico City so his kidnappers could collect a thousand peso bounty. The boy told authorities he was going to be "buried alive in the metro." His adult abductors were indeed rushing to Mexico City with a kidnapped child, but they never admitted to being part of plot to provide human sacrifices. Nonetheless, to this day, many users of Mexico City's subway are convinced it was built on the bodies of sacrifice victims and treat it with as much respect as they would show the inside of a church.

Monterrey

YERBA BUENA Yerba Buena is a small farming community thirty miles south of Monterrey in the Tamaulipas state of Mexico. Near the town's school is a large cave in the Sierra Madre foothills that is haunted by a gruesome apparition. The ghost is of a woman who staggers around in the cave looking for her heart, and there is a hole in her chest where it should be. The apparition is of Celina Salvana, a member of a religious cult that met in the cave in the 1960s.

The cult was established by a sister and brother, Magdalena and Eleazar Solis, and was based on ancient Aztec beliefs. They attracted recruits by showing them the "divine presence" after they drank a concoction that contained human blood and marijuana leaves. Before long they had assembled a group of forty members from the area, and their ceremonies became more and more violent. On May 31, 1963, they performed their most terrifying ritual. May 31 corresponds to the Aztec festival of Huixtocihuatl, in which a woman must be sacrificed to the gods. Under the influence of the drink, Celina, a thirty-year-old mother of two, stepped forward to volunteer for "eternal bliss." The others stoned her to death, and then they quickly opened her chest with a serrated knife, cut out her heart, and held it up, still beating, as an offering to the gods. When authorities finally learned of the cult's activities, they raided the cave and discovered human bones from several victims piled in a corner. All forty members of the cult were arrested.

Teotihuacan, Mexico (Mexican National Tourist Council)

Teotihuacan

AVENUE OF THE DEAD The apparitions of Olmec tribesmen are seen walking somberly down this wide roadway that stretches through the ancient ruins of Teotihuacan. They wear elaborate costumes and colorful woven hats. The Olmecs were a people of unknown origin who settled in the area now bounded by the Mexican states of Veracruz and Tabasco. They were exquisite sculptors and left behind intricate black basalt carvings of feline faces on human bodies, as well as dozens of stone temple sites. Lining the Avenue of the Dead are pyramid temples where sacred ceremonies were performed. Among the most important were the temples of the Sun and Moon, and the Temple of Quetzalcoatl. Photographs taken at the site sometimes show unexplainable red-colored human shapes among the temple ruins.

Tijuana

AGUA CALIENTE HIGH SCHOOL This high school is housed in the old Agua Caliente Casino building and is haunted by a ghost from the 1940s. The apparition of a former singer at the casino seems to want people to follow her outside the building. She appears most often when it is raining outside, and her form is outlined by the falling raindrops. She is said to have poisoned her lover to run away with two suitcases of money he had hidden in the desert, but the man realized he had been poisoned and followed her outside, pleading for the antidote. She refused, and he drew a pistol and shot her. Both died outside the casino, and the suitcases have never been found.

TLATELOLCO APARTMENTS Several residents of this modern, high-rise apartment building were haunted by the apparition of a beautiful, young woman in an old-fashioned black dress with a ruffled collar. The ghost was first reported in the building in 1968 in the Pantoja residence. The apparition was always in tears and sometimes held a handkerchief to her eyes. After she disappeared, witnesses could still hear her mournful sobbing.

The apartments are located in a section of Mexico City that witnessed a final, bloody battle in 1523 between the Aztecs and the Spanish warlord Hernando Cortez. The Crying Phantom of Tlatelolco has appeared many times there since, and she always seems to presage some kind of disaster or loss of human life. She was witnessed in the area in the seventeenth century before flooding and earthquakes claimed the lives of tens of thousands in Mexico City. She appeared in the nineteenth century, just before France invaded Mexico and conquered the people. More recently, she appeared in the Tlatelolco area in 1958 a few days before a devastating earthquake hit the area.

And in 1968, when she materialized to residents of the apartment building, there was a massacre of students by the armed forces at the Plaza of the Three Cultures, right in the heart of Tlatelolco. Hundreds died or were seriously injured and 10,000 residents of the area lived under military siege for a day. The Chihuahua apartment building was nearly destroyed by tank cannons, and hundreds were left homeless.

Uxmal

PYRAMID OF THE MAGICIAN Visitors have reported seeing the apparition of a Mayan priest in full-feathered regalia on the top front platform of the Pyramid of the Magician at Uxmal. Uxmal is a ceremonial city set out from the lush jungle by a natural plateau. A carving on its walls shows a

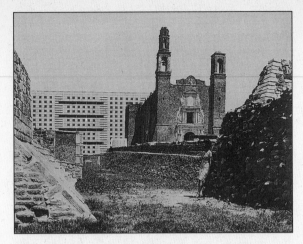

Plaza of the Three Cultures, Mexico City, Mexico (Mexican National Tourist Council)

serpent disgorging a large egg from its jaws, a symbolic rendering of the magical act of manifestation. It is an art the priest learned well, for he still performs his magical evocations.

Behind the pyramid is a ball court in which a ritual game was played that mimicked the archetypal struggle the spirit of the sun makes to cross the empty sky. In front of the Governor's Palace

Uxmal, Pyramid of the Magician, Uxmal, Mexico (Mexican National Tourist Council)

is an intricately carved stone throne, and people who sit on it have reported feelings of great power and spiritual conductivity.

Veracruz

CHENEQUE Supernatural beings known as the *Cheneque* haunt the Mexican state of Veracruz and have been sighted for many centuries. The short entities "emerge from out of nowhere and disappear into nothingness." According to the local Totonac tribe, the *Cheneque* have always inhabited this part of Mexico and are depicted in the ancient statues at the temple of Tajin. Most sightings have been in the forests near Mt. Orizaba. The ghostly entities have been known to play with little children, who sometimes follow them into the woods. To discourage the spirits from approaching their children, Native parents fashion little, smiling clay dolls and put them around their homes to fool the *Cheneque* into playing with the dolls and not their children. Even so, children still disappear for days, saying they have gone off to play with the gnomish beings. In 1970, a six-year-old boy was taken for thirty-three days, and the last person to see him, his uncle, was indicted for murder. Yet the boy turned up at the family doorstep, saying the *Cheneque* had fed and sheltered him and "played lots of games."

Many truck drivers on the road between La Tinaja and Tierra Blanca in the Veracruz province see the fleeting apparitions of the little people in their headlights at night. On several occasions the drivers have chased the ghosts into the forest, where they confront the beings, only to see them dissolve into thin air, as if they "had come from another dimension." In the 1970s and 1980s, it became a challenge among the drivers to see who could capture one of the beings or bring back some evidence that they were real. One trucker from the Lopez Transportation Company in Catemac, Veracruz, stopped his truck and cornered a group of the *Cheneque* on the road one evening. As he approached them, one turned and shot a beam of intense light at his truck and it burst into flames. In less than thirty minutes, his truck and

entire load of nonflammable contents were reduced to a pile of dust by mysterious blue flames. Amazingly the fuel and fuel tank were selectively omitted from the fire and survived intact.

The case was so bizarre that local authorities sent samples of the ash to the Department of Thermodynamics at the National University of Mexico for analysis. The physicists concluded the carbonization of the metal and asbestos components of the truck could only be achieved with "an unknown type of light-heat beam with a very selective wavelength corresponding to a laser ray but many times more powerful and not known to modern science." The same "intense blue flame" directed by the interdimensional beings burnt two more trucks before the truckers gave up the idea of capturing a *Cheneque*. One incident took place on the Cordoba Highway and the other on the Costera del Golfo Highway. To this day, it is not known what the *Cheneque* represent, but the list of possible explanations ranges from ghosts to extraterrestrials.

PANAMA

Panama was a Spanish colony and then part of Colombia. After a revolt in 1903, it was declared an independent country. Construction on the Panama Canal began in 1904 and lasted ten years.

Panama City

FORT CLAYTON The ghost of a soldier haunts the Fort Clayton Army Base clinic and has even been seen on buses that stop at the clinic. The clinic serves as a halfway medical facility for soldiers who have checked out of the base hospital but still need treatment for chronic conditions. The apparition appears to be a real person until he dematerializes into thin air or disappears from his seat in the back of a bus. The apparition has been seen by many witnesses in the military and by several different bus drivers. He is a tall man dressed in World War II fatigues. He coughs a lot and has a pale face with sunken eyes. He walks very slowly and when seated just stares out into blank space. No one has identified the man, but many have encountered his ghost.

PANAMA LA VIEJA Two miles from the center of modern Panama City are ruins of the first capital, known as Panama La Vieja (Old Panama). Founded in 1519, it was Spain's first settlement on the Pacific Ocean. As the center for Spanish exploration and trade throughout the New World, the city grew fantastically wealthy and attracted pirates from all over the world. When notorious pirate Henry Morgan attempted to loot the city in 1671, the governor ordered the powder magazines ignited and the whole city went up in flames. In the ruins of the remaining buildings many phantoms have been seen. The old cathedral is haunted by a Catholic priest, who is sometimes also seen in the bell tower and the Bishop's House. In front of the ruins, alongside the ocean, near the present artisan's market, the ghosts of pirates and Spanish sailors are seen.

PUERTO RICO

The island of Puerto Rico was settled by Arawak people and colonized by Spain. It was ceded to the United States after the Spanish-American War of 1898. It became an independent country in a United States commonwealth in 1952.

Canvanas

CHUPACABRA The glowing phantom of a terrifying entity called "Chupacabra" is seen in the area around this quiet Puerto Rican town. The short, gray creature has large red eyes, three-fingered claws, and long spines on its back that change in blinding colors following the spectrum from red to violet. Sometimes it appears to float in midair or fly with wings. Hundreds of witnesses, ranging from policemen to simple farmers, have encoun-

tered the creature, and there is some difference of opinion among investigators as to whether it represents an apparition, a demon, an extraterrestrial, or some kind of mutated animal. Many locals believe that Chupacabra is the spirit of the El Yunque rainforest that is seeking revenge against humans for destroying the lush forests. However, there is some evidence that it could be an ancient entity. Drawings by the Tainos, Puerto Rico's first inhabitants, show creatures remarkably similar to some modern descriptions of Chupacabra.

One thing that everyone agrees on is that Chupacabra is mean and violent and has the power to make witnesses feel ill or cause them to enter altered states of consciousness. The creature has been blamed for mutilating sheep, dogs, and other animals. While Canvanas seems to be the center of its activity, Chupacabra has also been encountered in Orocovis, Humacao, Naranjito, Gurabo, and even in the San Juan suburb of Rexville.

VIRGIN ISLANDS

The Virgin Islands were settled by the Carib natives and taken over at one time or another by the Dutch, British, French, Spanish, and even the Knights of Malta. Today they are administered by the United States Navy with their own elected governor.

St. Thomas

BLUEBEARD'S CASTLE HOTEL This old fortress in St. Thomas was home to the famous pirate Bluebeard, and today it is an upscale hotel. Bluebeard converted the tower into a classy home for his bride, Mercedia Cordovan. The suave buccaneer later saved the beautiful woman from her executioners. The ghosts of both Bluebeard and Mercedia haunt the place. Bluebeard's Castle Hotel is located on the Charlotte Amalie in St. Thomas, U.S. Virgin Islands. For information, phone 809-774-1600.

SOUTH AMERICA

BOLIVIA

Bolivia is home to two pre-Incan cultures, the Tiahuanaco and the Aymaras. It was conquered by Spain and achieved its independence in 1825. The civilian government was overthrown in a military coup in 1964.

Lake Titicaca

TIAHUANACO The mysterious haunted city of Tiahuanaco near Lake Titicaca on the Bolivian high desert was an ancient ruin when the Incas discovered it and gave it its present name, which means "City of the Dead." The area was first settled around 1600 B.C. by an unknown civilization that predated the Aztecs, Incans, and Mayans—a civilization that archeologists say flourished in South America as long as twelve thousand years ago. No one has been able to identify the people who lived here, but scholars do believe that whoever they were, they abandoned the site voluntarily and disappeared from the continent within a short time. The only clue to who these people were comes from the ghosts they left behind. Amateur explorers and tourists off the beaten path have reported seeing the apparitions of ancient Egyptians here.

Most of the sightings of Egyptian ghosts take place in the Kalasasaya, a polished-stone temple put together in a fashion that archeologists admit was used only by the Egyptians. In fact, recently it was discovered that the temple is almost an exact one-fifth-scale model of the Egyptian temple of Karnak. The builders of Tiahuanaco, like the builders of the pyramids, used some unknown technology to transport giant stone blocks weighing over one hundred tons to the site and assemble them. The Gateway of the Sun is composed of massive blocks of brown stone that contain large rectangular holes that once held giant slabs of gold. Arkpana and Pumapunku are former pyramids at the site that have been reduced to rounded mounds because looters have carried off their magnificent polished cover stones. The original residents also maneuvered about on Lake Titicaca in reed boats of exactly the same method of construction as used by the Egyptians. Copper surgical instruments found at the site are exact duplicates of similar instruments that date from ancient Egypt, and both cultures practiced the art of trepanning, in which a large round hole was made in the top of a person's skull for some sort of spiritual or therapeutic purpose. The technique was picked up by the Incas but did not originate with them.

Nonetheless, the idea that ancient Egyptians settled in South America is too much of a leap for most scholars. Only one archeologist has ever come close to accepting the evidence at face value. Austrian engineer Arthur Posnansky was so convinced that the site was from a pre-Columbian culture that he became a Bolivian citizen and spent fifty years living here. He was convinced that such an advanced and deliberate civilization would have left a message about their identity. Many believe he was about to reveal proof of the Egyptian connection, but he died in 1946 before he could reveal his findings. Perhaps it is the time for a new science to emerge, something merging the skills of scientists with those of psychics and mediums. For if any site on earth begs for such a science as "para-archeology," Tiahuanaco is it. The site is an hour's drive from La Paz and is located in a small valley at thirteen thousand-feet elevation.

BRAZIL

Little is known about the people who first settled Brazil. Portuguese, Dutch, and Spanish colonists settled here in the sixteenth century, and it was claimed by the Portuguese. An independent empire of Brazil was set up in 1822. It has had a tumultuous government, alternating between dictatorship and civilian rule ever since.

Minas Gerais

VARGINHA Dozens of witnesses in the city of Varginha, in the state of Minas Gerais in southern Brazil, have reported seeing a terrifying brown-skinned apparition with blood-red eyes, three small horns on its head, and a tiny mouth. A buzzing sound seems to follow the entity around. The first sighting was in 1996, in a public park in the Varginha suburb of Jardim Andere. That was followed by dozens of other encounters, including a well-documented sighting at 76 Benevenuto Bras Vieira Street in Jardin Andere. What the apparition represents is a matter of some controversy. Some believe it is the ghost of a deformed human,

others believe it is an incarnation of the devil. Many believe it is some kind of interdimensional or extraterrestrial creature. According to some reports, the creature was captured by the Varginha City Fire Department and taken to the military base at Tres Coracoes, 25 kilometers (15.5 miles) from the city.

SAN PAULO

City of San Paulo

CITY COUNCIL BUILDING The twenty-eight-year-old City Council Building in the city of San Paulo, Brazil, is haunted. At least that is what council members and employees in the twelve-story building insist. The ghosts seem like normal people, then disappear into thin air, and the place is plagued by a variety of poltergeist phenomena, including ghostly footsteps, phones that ring constantly with no one there, and disembodied voices. Council member Paulo Roberto Faria Lima and his staff were at a late-night meeting that broke up around 12:30 A.M. "We wanted to leave," he told reporters, "but couldn't open the door—weird because it can only be locked from the inside. Then, we started hearing voices speaking in an unidentifiable tongue and heard furniture moving around on the other side. I phoned security, and a guard came and opened the door easily. He told us we were the only ones in the building."

The phenomena continued to escalate, and in the spring of 1999, the council decided to call in two paranormal investigators. After using sophisticated electronic equipment to monitor the strange energy, the pair concluded that the building was inhabited by "playful spirits" or poltergeists that are caused by mental energy projected by disturbed employees. Others are not so easily convinced. They are certain the energy in the nearly new building comes from ancient spirits and not disgruntled employees. The area has a long tradition of hauntings and is situated in the Vale do Anhangabau—the Valley of Spirits.

SAN PAULO POLTERGEIST The Ulhoa Hacienda in the city of San Paulo became the center of worldwide attention in April 1959, when some un-seen force started hurling rocks inside and outside the home. Soon the poltergeist was throwing dishes, pots and pans, and food in the kitchen. The events started when Don Cid de Ulhoa was reading a paper in the living room, while his wife and young maid worked in the kitchen, and their three children were playing in the hallway. All of a sudden, two stones thumped down the hallway toward the children. Within minutes a flurry of stones started dropping out of midair and flying off walls and furniture and bouncing like rubber balls off the floor. The stones were falling in every room in the house except the room in which the children took cover.

The rain of stones continued for forty-eight hours. Other objects in the house also took flight. Don Cid was convinced someone was try-ing to drive the family from their home but never was able to find any human responsible. Finally, he called a priest to perform an exor-cism. Father Henrique de Morais Matos arrived and soon became fascinated by the phenomenon. He grabbed an egg floating in the air, put it in the refrigerator and shut the door. Moments later he saw an egg hit the pantry door without breaking. He picked it up and noticed it was cool. When he opened the refrigerator, the egg he had placed there was gone. Convinced the effects were genuine, he performed an exorcism. The poltergeist activity lessoned but then started up again, and two more exorcisms had the same effect. Finally after forty days and nights, the haunting stopped.

Investigators concluded that the source of the poltergeist energy was the teenaged maid, Fran-cesca. She remained remarkably calm during the phenomena, saying she was convinced the stones would not hurt her. Local psychics said the girl possessed great mediumistic powers and was channeling spirits. The more scientific research-ers said the girl was psychokinetically expressing tensions that had built up in the household. Francesca left her employment with the Ulhoa family a few days later, and the poltergeist never returned.

Limeira

LIMEIRA LIGHTS Strange apparitions and lights have been seen above the Roman Catholic church in the Pires district of the city of Limeira for many years. In February 1997, a wedding at the church was completely disrupted by a luminous ball of light floating above the church, and photographer Carlos Pancieri was able to videotape five minutes of the light's presence. "Within all my experi-ence," he told reporters, "I have never seen a phe-nomenon like this." The ball of light moves low over rooftops in the area of the church. No identi-fication of the luminous form has ever been made. Limeira is a city of one hundred thousand popula-tion located 112 kilometers (70 miles) northwest of Campinas in the Sao Paulo state in Brazil. It is an area known for paranormal phenomena of all types.

CHILE

Chile was originally part of the Incan Empire. It was under Spanish rule from 1536 to 1818, when it became an independent republic. After twenty years of military rule, Chile developed a civilian government in 1989.

Easter Island

RAPA NUI This famous island is known as Rapa Nui to Polynesians and has long been considered haunted and inhabited by spiritual powers. It was named Easter Island because it was discovered on Easter Sunday by a Dutch explorer. Although it lies 2,200 miles (3,600 kilometers) off the coast of Chile, the 63-square-mile island was annexed by Chile in 1888. Today, the island is barren and desolate, and the only distinctive features are over a hundred fifteen-foot-tall monolithic statues called *moai*. Around 400 A.D., however, Rapa Nui was covered in lush forests and teeming with life. It has been deduced that about one hundred Poly-nesian colonists arrived about that time, and within a thousand years, their progeny had completely exhausted the island of its resources. By 1700, the people were starving and resorted to cannibalism, as bloody battles between rival clans erupted all over the island.

Easter Island, Chile (Martin Gray)

All that is left today is a ghost island inhabited by the enigmatic statues. Weighing between 80 and 270 tons, the giant faces once held great significance for the islanders, but today, no one is really sure exactly what they meant. Some of the statues carried crowns of red volcanic stone, and it is known from similar practices among Polynesians that the statues were considered storage vessels of sacred spiritual powers. This power (*manna*) is a magical, intelligent energy that can be accessed by the human mind. When explorer Martin Gray visited the summit of Rano Raraku on the island, he received a clear and powerful message that told him to "follow the pilgrimage routes of the ancient religions." That is exactly how he spends his life, and he had become one of the world's leading authorities on sacred sites and world spiritual traditions. Immediately after his experience, he began writing his book *Places of Peace and Power*.

COLOMBIA

Símon Bolívar led this country (and most of South America) to independence from Spain in 1819. It formed a united Gran Columbia that consisted of Panama, Venezuela, Ecuador, and Columbia in 1819, but by the early 1900s the confederation had broken up. Since then the country has suffered at the hands of political violence and opportunism.

Cordillera Occidental Mountains

CALI BUENA VENTURA HIGHWAY The Cali Buena Ventura Highway runs through the Cordillera Occidental Mountains in the giant Los Farallones National Park in Colombia. The road is haunted by the apparition of a short black man, who is seen walking along the shoulder. There have even been reports of drivers offering him a ride, only to see his silent apparition disappear from the seat next to them. The ghostly figure is thought to be a native man who fell to his death during the construction of the Alto Anchicaya Dam. He is among the names of the sixty workers listed on a plaque at the dam honoring those who died during its construction.

El Danubio

YATACUE BRIDGE Yatacue is a tiny village eight kilometers (five miles) southwest of the town of El Danubio on the Anchicaya River near where it comes together with the Digua River. The roads in the area are haunted by the phantom of an empty, silent pickup truck that appears from nowhere and disappears just as mysteriously. Sometimes only the dim yellow headlights of the truck are seen. According to local legend, the truck was involved in an accident at the Yatacue Bridge in the early 1970s. The truck went sailing over the edge of the bridge, crushing a passenger to death and paralyzing the driver. It is believed the same accident is responsible for the luminous green apparition of a human figure that is seen floating slightly above the ground in the area. The ghost has been encountered many times over the years.

The Ghost of Anchicaya, as it has come to be called, was witnessed by Peace Corps volunteer Craig Downer and a friend in 1978. "What I saw," he reported, "was a bright, quavering, luminous cloud in the shape of a man. It was approaching from one hundred fifty feet away, between the waterfall and the bridge. As it approached me, I had communicated to me a horrible, hellish despair, a malignancy that gave me the shudders. When the ghost was within about sixty feet of us, I drew my machete, and then we beat a quick retreat up the road along the mountain slope."

PERU

Peru was the seat of the Incan empire, which was established around A.D. 1230. The Spanish conquered the country in 1533. Peru declared its independence in 1821. Since then the country has alternated between military and civilian rule.

Cuzco

MACHU PICCHU This ancient Incan city is located in the Andes Mountains, northwest of the city of Cuzco in Peru. Discovered by the American explorer Hiram Bingham in 1911, the beautiful ruins on a lush mountain peak are often surrounded by clouds. Tourism to the ancient city has peaked in recent years, largely because of its mystical aura and tales of strange experiences by visitors. Apparitions of Incan priests are often seen, especially in the temple and on the pathways through the terraced gardens. While archeologists insist it was used as a citadel and fortress, most

Machu Picchu, Andes Mountains, Peru (Andrew Hayden)

people visiting the site are impressed by its peaceful and wholesome atmosphere, which is unlike other Incan sites.

Nazca Desert

NAZCA LINES The Nazca Plain is a portal to the Other Side. The desert is located about 400 kilometers (250 miles) from Lima, Peru, between the Nazca and Ica valleys, and the Pan American Highway parallels the site. The desert is covered by strange markings of animals and geometric figures that can only be fully appreciated and deciphered from high in the air. Among the hundreds of figures are whales, spiders, eagles, pelicans, spirals, squares, triangles, and trapezoids. It is believed the drawings were intended to guide shamans on drug-induced flights out of their bodies to multidimensional universes.

The San Pedro cactus is native to the area and a source of psylocybin, the powerful "ally" drug used to induce the shamanic flight. Many of the ancient drawings depict the sacred ceremonies during which the potion was taken, as well as shamans showing the runny nostrils and vomiting characteristic of entheogenic drug usage. The shamans believed the altered state of consciousness took them to worlds more real than the everyday world, and the Nazca markings testify to the truth of their out-of-body incarnations. Many of the drawings depict the animal powers, or archetypal essences, that became part of the shaman's psychic toolkit.

Scores of strange elongated skulls have also been found in the area around the Nazca Desert. It is only since President Fujimori took power in Peru that the controversial skulls have been allowed to be photographed and knowledge of them spread outside the country. The skulls are so numerous that many makeshift museums exist in the homes of locals. People living near the desert have been afraid of the skulls in the past and believed those who take them home invite ghosts. Some shamans have tried to deliberately deform their heads to resemble the ancient skulls, which they believe belonged to a race of magical and wise people.

Catholic priests have told villagers the deformed skulls are evil and represent the offspring of fallen angels. Others believe the skulls represent a race of extraterrestrial beings who settled here. The coned skulls look remarkably like portraits of Akhenaten, the "Heretic Pharaoh," who ruled Egypt 3,500 years ago. North of Nazca, in the Paracas Desert, hundreds of mummies prepared in the Egyptian fashion have been discovered. The remarkably well-preserved mummies of chiefs and other noblemen have been found wrapped in many yards of woven fabric ribbon, with pieces of gold, food, and other offerings for use in the next world tucked between the wrappings.

Archeologists agree that whoever made the gigantic markings predated both the Incas and the Aztecs. Perhaps the next phase of research should include psychics and shamans who can still make a connection with those ancient souls, for the ghosts of the mysterious creators of the Nazca Lines have been seen by both dedicated archeologists and everyday tourists in the deserted desert region.

San Pedro de Costa

MARCA HUASI The road from Lima into the Andes Mountains ends at a town called San Pedro de Costa. Another 915 meters (three thousand feet) above the town lies a mysterious plateau called Marca Huasi that is covered with scores of twenty-five-foot-tall carvings of human faces and animals never seen in this area such as polar bears, camels, and even dinosaurs. But even more mysterious are the strange apparitions seen by people visiting the carvings. The apparitions of men and women are frequently reported. The levitating figures, sometimes showing only half their torso, usually look like normal people at a distance. But as they approach, witnesses realize that the figures are really ghosts. During a 1997 expedition to the plateau led by guide Jerry Wills, a man saw a woman on the rocks above him and climbed up to join her. As he got closer, he realized she had no legs and was floating in midair. She had long black hair and the face of a cat. The entity snarled

at the man and scared him so badly, he had to be immediately evacuated from the area.

SURINAM

Surinam is the former Dutch Guiana. It received its independence in 1975, but its government has been plagued by bitter fighting between military and civilian factions.

Backhuis Mountains

AZEMAN The villages that stretch between the Backhuis Mountains and Kayser Mountains in western Surinam are haunted by the spirit of the "Azeman," a ghostly woman who haunts people living in native huts. In the middle of the night, the unwelcome phantom bites a piece of flesh from the big toe of sleeping persons and saps their blood. Where the Dracula-like phantom originated is not known.

VENEZUELA

Venezuela was inhabited by indigenous people as far back as 2000 B.C. It was conquered by Spain and declared its independence in 1811. Its people overthrew a dictatorship in 1958 to become a constitutional republic.

Miranda State

TUY RIVER VALLEY The Tuy River Valley, which stretched between the towns of Ocumare del Tuy and San Francisco de Yare in the Miranda state of northern Venezuela, is haunted by the "Ghost of Infiernito," the white-clothed apparition of a man who jumps out into the headlights of approaching vehicles. The apparition is named for the El Infiernito, a stretch of the Ocumare-Yare Highway. According to local tradition, the apparition is of a man who died in a bloody machete duel, in which two men fought over the love of a woman. The distinct apparition is described as a middle-aged man in black boots wearing the traditional white attire of the area called a *liquiliqui*. His face is so pale that it appears as if he has no eyebrows or eyelashes.

The ghost has been blamed for several accidents and has even taken to showing up in the back seats of cars and taxis passing through the area. Sometimes people offer him a ride, other times he just materializes in their back seats. Then, in a few minutes, he disappears into thin air. Once he appeared on the back of a horse holding onto its rider. Locals have no doubt the ghost is real and have even requested assistance in getting rid of the troublesome spirit. As if to confirm the ghost's identity, a state tractor involved in construction along the Ocumare-Yare Highway at El Infiernito uncovered scattered human remains that suggested someone had been hacked to death and the pieces scattered in the underbrush.

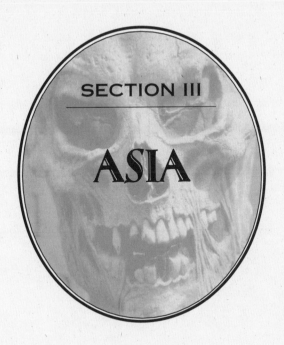

SECTION III

ASIA

In China, ghosts are divided into sixty different kinds of "shin" or spirits. To keep these ghosts outside their homes, the Chinese traditionally leave gifts of cakes that bear prayer tags that beseech spirits to take the food and go on to someone else's house. Shin first manifest as misty forms that morph into humanoid shapes with the heads materializing first and then the feet. The body fills in last, though oddly enough, Chinese ghosts never have chins. Tibetan exorcists believe there are eighty-four thousand possible ghosts, and they have to identify which one it is before they know what ritual to perform.

"Po" is Chinese for the soul or the spiritual essence that survives bodily death. If the po does not leave the physical realm at death and go towards the light of the spiritual realm, it becomes an evil spirit or ghost. The Chinese Hopping Ghost is a person's po that has not left the body at death and continues to animate a person's corpse. The Hopping Ghost does not have full control of the body's functions. The joints of the body have stiffened in death, the hands and arms are straight and thrust forward, and the body moves in a rigid jumping fashion. Hence the name "Hopping Ghost." The fingernails continue to grow after death and become sharp and lethal weapons, and hopping ghosts lunge forward at their victims and try to cut arteries in the neck. The Hopping Ghost lives off of dark or lunar (yin) energy and stays in caves or cellars. It is said that the first rays of the sun at dawn can kill them. The only other way to stop a Hopping Ghost is to paste a traditional Chinese blessing in the center of its forehead or just burn it up in a bonfire.

Japanese ideas about ghosts are tightly bound to Buddhist philosophy, and the most general Buddhist term for ghost or spirit is "gaki." The gaki is generally seen as a lower energy form from the underworld. All gaki suffer eternal hunger and thirst, although there are degrees of suffering. The muzai-gaki hunger without ever getting any food. The shozai-gaki feed on unclean substances and fecal matter. The usai-gaki eat any remains of food that are discarded by mankind, as well as offerings of food humans give to the gods or ancestors. Gakis are considered to be the cause of disease and fever because they sometimes enter the human body and sap the life force from a person. Very specific kinds of gaki manifest on the lower plane of existence as insects. For instance, jiki-ketsu-gaki are bloodsuckers, ju-chu-gaki are born in the wood of trees, and jiki-fun-gaki are feces eaters. There are literally hundreds of possible varieties of gakis.

The Japanese also have a wide variety of traditional ghosts. "Obake" is the general name for a bad ghost or demon. The ghost of a mother returning to protect her children is called an "ubumi." "Koki-teno" is the ghost of a beautiful woman in a white, flowing gown, who usually appears first as a fox to trick men. Sea phantoms called "shojo" have red hair and are attracted to sake. Also attracted to sake are the "tengu" or mischievous spirits who live in trees. The "umi bozu" ("sea priest") is a giant black sea phantom with a shaved head and huge glaring eyes who likes to frighten Japanese sailors. "Kappa" are little green phantoms that haunt lakes and rivers. They survive out of water by keeping a reservoir of water in a bowl-like depression in the top of their heads. "Hengeyokai" are phantoms of the animal kingdom that are capable of shapeshifting into human form. The "Zashiki Warshi" is the Japanese poltergeist, depicted as the spirit of a little boy.

India also has a seemingly endless categorization of ghosts. "Rudra" is the Indian god who rules over ghosts, and Hindus often leave offerings to Rudra at crossroads where ghosts are said to gather. Offerings are also left for spirits known as "virikas," small, red-colored phantoms with sharp teeth who make jabbering noises. The offerings are so the virikas will be satisfied and not go searching for human victims. "Vetala" is the Indian vampire spirit that has taken over a corpse. "Rakshashas" are a whole family of demons led by the ten-headed devil Ravana. "Bugaboos" are friendly towards humans and very useful to mothers who want to make their children behave.

The "brahmadaitya" is the spirit of an unmarried Brahman or priest. He lives in a tree and does not bother humans unless they climb his tree, in which case they will end up with their necks broken. The "mumiai" are Indian poltergeist spirits that never show themselves and like to throw things or physically attack people. "Pretas" are the ghosts of violent men who have not been given a proper burial. The Indians also have two unique ghosts whose job it is to protect them from other ghosts. The two spirits are male and female entities called the "jak" and the "jakni."

In Eurasia and Arabia, "zinn" is the general term for a spirit or ghost. The "jinne" is a member of a race of spirits called the "children of fire," who will perform tasks and grant wishes if enclosed in a vessel. On the other hand, the "ghoul" is a horrendous phantom that steals dead bodies and haunts any area used for the preparation and burial of the dead. The "afrit" is the apparition of a murdered person who wants to revenge his or her death. The afrit rises out of the murdered person's spilled blood, wherever it falls on the ground. The only way to prevent their materialization is to drive a new nail into the bloody ground at the murder scene.

"Mura-muras" are the ancestral spirits of Australian Aborigines who control the weather. During a drought, the Aborigines place small stones covered with blood as high as possible in trees to symbolically get the attention of the mura-muras and hope they will respond with a rain shower. The "yowie" is an Australian dog-sized phantom of the night that looks like a cross between an insect and a reptile. The New Zealand Maoris believe that places, persons, and things can be "tapu" (taboo) or charged with negative spiritual energy. Many Maoris believe that ignoring tapu or inadequately following rituals can lead to sickness or even death.

AUSTRALASIA

AUSTRALIA

Australia was populated forty thousand years ago by the Aborigines. It was claimed for Great Britain in 1770 by explorer Captain James Cook, and the first colonies were established in 1788. There were about a million aborigines when the white settlers arrived. Because they "hunted" cattle for food, aborigines were considered predators and settlers slaughtered tens of thousands of them. By 1900, there were only about sixty-six thousand left, although their population has grown considerably since. Australia gained complete independence from Britain in 1986, although it is still one of the original members of the British Commonwealth. Australia consists of the states of New South Wales, Victoria, Queensland, Tasmania, South Australia, Northern Territories, and Western Australia.

NEW SOUTH WALES

Campbelltown

FISHER'S GHOST CREEK The first sightings of a ghost near this creek on the outskirts of Sydney in Campbelltown date from the late 1800s. The apparition is of a man sitting on a fence near a creek that ran along the main road in town. Numerous sightings occurred until someone got up the gumption to ask the ghost what it wanted. Amazingly, the spirit spoke and said his name was Fisher and he had been murdered. Local police brought in Aboriginal trackers, who found the body further downstream in the creek. To this day, the creek is called Fisher's Ghost Creek.

Junee

MONTE CRISTO Monte Cristo is a haunted mansion in Junee, a small town near the cities of Albury and Woodonga in New South Wales. The mansion is located high on a bluff overlooking town, and it is said to be so haunted that the entire house emits an eerie glow at night. For over a century, residents and visitors have told of their encounters with apparitions, cold spots, disembodied voices and footsteps, and numerous other paranormal manifestations. The ghosts turn up most frequently in the Drawing Room. The feeling of wicked energy is so strong here that some tourists never leave their cars; they just turn around in the car park and drive away without ever getting out.

The mansion was built in 1884 by the Christopher William Crawley family. Christopher died in

1910 in the house from gangrene of the neck. His wife ruled the house with a stern hand until her death of heart failure in 1933 at the age of ninety-two. She also died at home, and both Crawleys are buried in the local cemetery. The property sat abandoned for many years, until 1963 when Reg and Olive Ryan purchased and restored the mansion and opened it for tours. They admit to feeling the ghostly presences of the Crawley family in the house but say they have learned to live with them. In April 1999, the Australian Ghost Hunters Society (AGHS) held an investigative weekend at the mansion and confirmed that the place is indeed still haunted. The Monte Cristo Homestead is located off the Hume Highway in Junee. For more information, telephone 02-6924-1637 or E-mail montecristohomestead@bigpond.com.au.

Picton

MUSHROOM TUNNEL This tunnel was in use from 1867 to 1919, when the railway line it served was abandoned. It was used to store munitions during World War II and to grow mushrooms after the war. Today it is known simply as the Mushroom Tunnel. Almost every night for the last few years, "ghost lights" have been seen flitting about at the east end of the tunnel, and sometimes the lights coalesce into the apparition of a

Mushroom Tunnel, Picton, Australia (Liz Vincent, Picton Ghost Tours)

Lady in White. The ghost of the Mushroom Tunnel is Emily Bollard, a fifty-year-old woman who was killed in the tunnel in 1916. She was on her way to visit her brother, when she decided to take a shortcut through the tunnel. She was hit by a train halfway into the tunnel and killed instantly. In 1999, a witness passed out from fear when the ghost approached her with outstretched arms. That same year, a twenty-year-old woman was momentarily possessed by the lights, and the apparition seemed to be able to more fully materialize because of it.

Picton is located southwest of Sydney, near Campbelltown. The Picton Ghost Hunt is conducted by paranormal investigator Liz Vincent on most Friday and Saturday nights. Information can be obtained by calling 02-4677-2044, faxing 02-4677-3289, or E-mailing Liz Vincent at lizv@fastlink.com.au.

ST. MARK'S CHURCH This Anglican church and graveyard is haunted by the apparitions of two children and a woman dressed in old-fashioned clothing. The little boy appears to be about six years old, while the girl is around twelve, and the woman seems to be their mother. Recently, a woman parked near the graveyard with her husband at dusk one night noticed two children walking around the graves, holding hands. The witness saw them walking around the graveyard for about ten minutes and saw them disappear behind some gravestones. Then she realized the children were dressed in early-twentieth-century clothes, and the children were nowhere to be found.

UPPER PICTON SCHOOL This school was struck by lightning in 1914 and several pupils were injured, but in the mid-1950s, a little girl burnt to death in a fire in the building. It is thought to be her presence that haunts the place. The current custodian reports being followed by footsteps, and sometimes doors open and close by themselves. She has also encountered an eerie white light and often hears ghostly voices drifting through the corridors. Recently, an invisible presence slapped her hard on her arm one night.

WOLLONDILLY SHIRE HALL The Wollondilly Shire Hall does not sound like a scary place, but nearly everyone in Picton would tell you that it has long been haunted. The present building was constructed around the original Picton School, which was built in 1869. Today, the place is used by the Picton Theatre Group for their performances. At least three ghosts are believed to inhabit the old building.

"Ted" is the name given the apparition of a man, who appears as a black silhouette in the farthest corner backstage. Another apparition is a young girl, whose crying can be heard coming from underneath the stage. The ghost of a small boy also haunts the building. His fleeting presence is usually sighted out of the corner of the eye.

Willondilly Shire Hall, Picton, Australia (Liz Vincent, Picton Ghost Tours)

Sydney

PRINCE HENRY HOSPITAL Prince Henry Hospital is an isolated complex sitting on five hundred acres of sand dunes in the Little Bay area outside Sidney. It was established in 1881 as the Coast Hospital and was built so far from the city of Sydney because it was intended as a treatment center for patients with contagious diseases. After extensive renovations in the 1960s, the ghosts of former employees and patients began showing up.

In the Delaney Ward (B Block), walks the apparition of a former matron called Gracie. She was a neurotic woman who immediately washed herself after being touched or bumping into someone. She died in B Block under mysterious circumstances from a fall into an abandoned elevator shaft. But she still makes her rounds. Her apparition is regularly seen in B Block, and patients there report being taken care of by a nurse with an old-fashioned white veil. She tops off glasses of water, adjusts blankets, and has even placed bedpans under patients and removed them afterwards. Most patients do not realize she is a ghost, but the nurses are terrified of encountering her. Nurses report feeling her presence scrutinizing their work and monitoring their coffee breaks. When Gracie's ghost appears, the clocks in the area stop functioning, with their hands pointing at two o'clock for some reason. Once, two nurses working the night shift left milk boiling on a stove, while they stepped into the hall for a few seconds to check on things. When they returned to the tearoom, they found the stove turned off, the boiling pot emptied in the sink, and all the cups and saucers and condiments put back on the shelves. No other staff members were on the floor, and no one could have entered the room without being seen. The clock had been reset to two o'clock.

The ghost of an aboriginal boy haunts the stairway of B Block and has been known to trip employees using the stairs. Sometimes the boy's giggling apparition is spotted sitting at the foot of the stairs. Other ghosts in the hospital include an unidentified man who walks the deserted halls at night. His sinister presence manifests as a moving shadow accompanied by heavy footsteps. When intravenous drips and medical equipment turn off mysteriously, nurses blame his presence. Ghostly patients buzz nurses late at night from locked, unoccupied wards. Other ghosts are seen in the abandoned cemetery on the premises where over one thousand former patients and nurses who died at the hospital are buried.

QUARANTINE STATION The Australian Quarantine Station is located across the harbor from Sydney. It is considered by investigators to be the most haunted place in Australia. Established in 1832 to isolate immigrants and prevent the spread of contagious disease among the population of Australia, it became impractical with the rise of air travel in the 1960s. The compound was finally closed down in 1984. The only residents of the Quarantine Station today are its ghosts—plenty of them. Sightings are so frequent that in 1996, a service was held to try to bring peace to the souls of the estimated six hundred people buried on the grounds.

The station was not a happy welcome for people coming to Australia. They were fumigated with poisonous fumes, forced into showers and scrubbed with phenol solution, and then herded into a fenced compound, where soldiers were ordered to shoot anyone trying to escape. The sick, including children, were whisked away to isolated cells where friends and parents could not visit. Priests also were not allowed to visit the sick or perform services for the dead, who were buried late at night under cover of darkness. Tombstones were taken off the graves to avoid offending patients, but the bodies were never disinterred and moved elsewhere for fear of spreading disease.

Disembodied screams still issue from the Bathhouse and a feeling of despair overcomes visitors to the area. White-gowned apparitions float over the graveyards at night, and the apparition of a former gravedigger and his dog keep them company. Old-time music waifs through the Third-Class Social Hall, where dancing footsteps can sometimes be heard coming from the abandoned room. The Medical Superintendent Building is haunted by the apparitions of a woman in a red velvet gown from the 1890s and a man in a long white coat. An invisible presence traipses up and down the stairs and on the second floor, where the medical staff's living quarters were once located. The station's two sick wards are haunted by the ghosts of children and adults sitting up in their beds. Sometimes large smallpox ulcers and scars can be seen on the apparitions' faces. The specter of a young nurse in an old-fashioned white uniform is often reported still attending to the sick and dying in the wards. The apparitions of doctors are also encountered in the wards, tour groups

participating in sleepovers report invisible hands trying to sit them up in their beds in the middle of the night or being awakened by the sounds of the tea or medicine cart being pulled up the aisle.

One strong presence attached to a bed in the corner of one ward is a dark-skinned child with long black hair. The girl is extremely distraught, and some visitors have even sat on her bed tying to comfort her tortured spirit. During an investigation by psychic Michael Williams in 1996, a recording of the sounds of someone playing a xylophone and infrared photos of a spiraling blue mist were detected near the haunted bed. The ghosts of sailors have also been reported in front of this building on the porch and in the yard. Entire ships suspected of carrying diseases were sometimes quarantined along with their crew and passengers in the station's sandy harbor.

In 1900, during an outbreak of bubonic plague in Sydney, all the Chinese people were forced to move to the Quarantine Station, where they lived under the most squalid conditions. They were assigned to an old dormitory and allotted a small outdoor kitchen and dining area. The ghosts of those poor souls still haunt the Chinese Dormitory and are known for their sadness and violence toward white people. The apparition of a middle-aged Chinese man sneaks up behind tourists and pushes them violently from behind, and as they turn around, glares into their faces and disappears. Recently, a museum staff member was nearly pushed over a nearby cliff by an unseen presence that came up behind her and pushed her hard between the shoulder blades. The woman quit her job the next day.

The Station Morgue is haunted by the apparition of an Aboriginal man whose body was brought there after a violent storm hit the area in the late 1920s. His body was placed on the autopsy table and left overnight, but the next morning, he was found lying dead on the floor in another part of the room. He had apparently not been dead and recovered enough to seek a way out of the dark room. His spirit still believes he is alive trying to find a way out of the room. The grief-stricken apparition is seen staring out the morgue's windows and photographs in the area have shown an unexplainable blue vapor that takes the form of a man's face. Daily tours are available from the National Parks and Wildlife Service. The Sydney Quarantine Station Historical Site is on North Head Scenic Drive in Manly. For more information, phone 02-9977-6522 or visit the Australian Ghost Hunters Society Web site at hompages.tig.com.au.

VICTORIA

Melbourne

BLOCK ARCADE The Block Arcade is a popular shopper center in downtown Melbourne that is haunted by ghosts from another structure that once stood on the property. In the early 1900s, three firemen lost their lives trying to put out a fire that erupted by spontaneous combustion in a grain storage warehouse that used to be where the Block Arcade now sits. Their apparitions and a variety of paranormal effects haunt merchants of the shopping arcade.

CHINATOWN A narrow passageway between buildings here called "Death Alley" is haunted by people whose bodies were dumped here after they were killed by gangsters in the early 1930s. Asian residents refuse to walk down this and other alleys because they believe ghosts can use them to pass through to our side. There is an old garage in Chinatown open for free parking but nobody takes advantage of the offer because it is haunted. Even security guards in the garage have reported hearing strange voices and seeing strange luminous beings inside the garage at night. Today no security guard wants to work there, so there is no longer any kind of security on the place. Upstairs in the garage is an apartment where the apparition of a woman has been seen and heard. Now no one will rent the apartment either. For more information, visit the Ghosts and Other Haunts Web site at homepages.ihug.co.nz/~dp.jod.

COBB & CO BUILDING The multilevel parking garage where the old Cobb & Co building used to sit still carries trauma of that place. Apparently, a bloody murder occurred in the building and was kept secret. Only psychics have detected evidence of the dreadful deed. Today, parking attendants and security guards have seen a menacing white vaporous being lingering in certain areas of the parking garage. Several employees have quit after encountering the evil entity.

FLINDERS STREET RAILROAD STATION Built in the early 1900s, this picturesque old railway station sits on the banks of the Yarra River. The station was a popular fishing site in the early years and many anglers could be seen attempting to catch dinner. Today, train passengers often report seeing a short, elderly man carrying a fishing pole and a wooden bucket filled with perch. He stands on the busy platform but never boards a train. If approached, he vanishes from sight and many travelers have been so upset by the encounter that they missed their trains.

HAUNTED BOOKSHOP The Haunted Bookshop at 15 McKillop Street in Melbourne is a small bookshop lined with old wooden bookshelves and occult books from around the world. Owner Drew Sinton offers many courses on demonology and ghosthunting. Angelica Danton is the resident clairvoyant, and the pair's séances are open to the public. Melbourne's two-and-a-half-hour Ghost Tour also leaves from here. For more information, phone 03-9670-2585 or fax 03-9670-2595.

MELBOURNE GAOL The old Melbourne Gaol (jail) is considered one of the most haunted places in Melbourne, and tours are so popular they have to be booked through Ticketmaster. It was here where the famous "bushranger" Ned Kelly was hanged in 1888, and his ghost, along with many of his fellow inmates, still haunt the place. Ned's body was originally buried there underneath the flagstones near the old gallows. In 1929, a steam shovel doing work in the area accidentally struck Ned's coffin and tore the lid off. When word got out, there was a mad rush as souvenir seekers came to grab one of his bones. What remained of his corpse was relocated to Pentridge Prison. No wonder Ned's ghost seems a little upset when people encounter him. For more information, visit the Gaol's homepage at home.vicnet.net.au/~omgaol. For bookings, phone Ticketmaster at 11-613-9694-0567.

MITRE TAVERN The historical Mitre Tavern is haunted by the apparition of a lady dressed in white clothes who is thought to be a former manager. She is most often seen presiding over the restaurant area as if she were still in charge. In 1998, three managers saw her ghost and all three resigned afterwards.

NATIONAL GALLERY A strong presence that has possessed performing artists and their instruments is encountered at Melbourne's National Gallery. Recently, the distinguished pianist Stephen McIntyre was giving a concert when an invisible being took over the piano. Stephen fought through the concert to regain control but could not overcome the entity. The audience clearly heard the strange sounds being made by the possessed piano and whispered amongst themselves. During intermission, a technician checked the piano and could find nothing amiss. The ABC was recording the concert, but when it was played back, no extraneous noises from the piano could be heard.

PRINCESS THÉATRE The famous ghost of the Princess Theatre is Frederici (Frederick Baker), an actor who died of a heart attack on March 3, 1888, while playing Mephistopheles in the opera "Faust." The Italian-born Englishman was only thirty-eight years old at the time, and his spirit never surrendered his best role. The haunting started on the night that the opera resumed after the death of Frederici. Cast members felt his presence throughout the performance, and the actor who took Frederici's place said that every time he stepped forward to take a bow, invisible hands would push him backwards. After that, Frederici's ghost never left, and his apparition was often seen sitting in the Dress Circle during rehearsals. Others claimed the ghost brushed by them in the hallways. Finally, the owners of the theater offered a hundred pounds to anyone who would spend a night alone in the theatre, although no one ever took up the challenge.

In the early 1900s, a fire department employee on fire watch at the theater opened a sliding section of the roof to ventilate the building when he saw Frederici's apparition standing on center stage in the bright moonlight. He described this figure as "a tall, well-built man with distinguished features, dressed in evening clothes with a long cloak and a top hat." In 1917, the wardrobe mistress who was working late and a fireman on duty in the theater witnessed the Frederici's ghost sitting in the middle of the second row of the Dress Circle. In 1919, another fireman saw the ghost standing in the same spot on two separate occasions. In the years since, scores of employees, actors, security personnel, and patrons have seen Frederici's apparition. Today, it is considered good luck if the ghost is seen on opening night, and the theater even leaves a particular seat vacant in the Dress Circle for him on an opening night.

STATE LIBRARY There are many ghosts in Melbourne's State Library building. The Arts Library is haunted by the apparition of a woman. A black shadow moves about in the Music Books section. A sinister presence is felt in Room S200. Poltergeist phenomena occurs in the Newspaper Room. Mysterious figures and glowing balls of light are witnessed on the stairways. And in the rest of the library, dark shadowy forms hide between bookshelves, and white misty figures are seen in the halls. Security personnel report seeing, hearing, and even smelling a wide variety of paranormal phenomena when no one else is around. Tour groups taken on ghost tours through the library have also reported unusual happenings, especially in the upper dome area. For information on the ghost tours, visit www.haunted-com.au/resources/ghosttour/ghosttour.html or phone 03-9670-2585.

VICTORIA MARKETS The Victoria Market in Melbourne is built on top of the city's first cemetery. The unceremonious usurping of this holy ground has resulted in a fairly active haunting from the ten thousand souls buried here. Reports of ghostly encounters at the market go back to the 1840s and continue to this day. The most active ghosts seem to be those "undesirables" who were buried outside the fence of the general graveyard. Three bushwhackers who were caught and hanged beside their graves outside the fence are often encountered in the present flower pavilion or near the fruit and vegetable stands.

TASMANIA

Cleveland

ST. ANDREWS INN This former inn on the Hobart-Launceston Highway is now a popular restaurant and coffee house haunted by the ghost of a young prostitute stabbed to death in an upstairs room in the 1860s. The wayside inn used to be the hangout of escaped convicts and bushrangers robbing people traveling through the Epping Forest. For many years, the forest was haunted by the ghost of a headless man. The haunting is thought to have originated with an incident in 1883, when two young men murdered and scalped a lemonade vendor driving his horse cart through the forest.

The room at the St. Andrews where the prostitute died is plagued by strange noises that include chairs and tables being shoved about when no one is in the room and disembodied voices. Sometimes the girl can be heard begging for her life. Her apparition likes to follow people up and down the stairs, and witnesses report bumping into an invisible person on the stairs. Some men have said the ghost goes so far as to strip them naked when she catches up with them.

Derby

DORSET HOTEL The large lake behind the town of Derby marks the location of the Briseis Tin Mine. The open-pit mine was one of the largest in Tasmania, and workers built a high dam on the Cascade River to provide the great amounts of water necessary for its operation. During torrential downpours in the month of April 1929, the dam burst and sent a twenty-meter (sixty-five-foot) high wall of water down towards the mine. Supervisor William Beamish was one of the first to see the wave of water and lost his life trying to warn others.

Despite his efforts, many workers died that day, and a temporary morgue had to be set up at the Dorset Hotel. To this day, the apparitions of stunned and confused miners wander through the corridors of the hotel. Not long ago, a guest at the hotel reported being transported back in time to that day when relatives and friends gathered at the hotel to identify the bodies. The ghosts of the Briseis miners are even seen walking somberly down the streets of the town, and recently, a woman saw a few of them riding the buses.

Fingal

THE GARTH A stone building called "The Garth" is haunted by the frustrated apparition of a lonely settler. The building is located on the banks of the South Esk River, just outside Fingal in Tasmania. The settler hanged himself in the building when the bride he sent for from England wrote him to say she no longer loved him and would not be joining him in Australia.

Hobart

BISHOPSCOURT The large Victorian mansion at 26 Fitzroy Place in Hobart is the official residence of the Anglican bishop of Tasmania. The original house built in 1840, now just one wing of the mansion, is the part that is haunted. The home was occupied by Judge Thomas Horne and his family, but it is haunted by the Gray Lady, the mother of a young man whom the judge sentenced to the gallows, supposedly for a crime he did not commit. The sad apparition floats through the oldest wing, still mourning for her son. The father of the famed World War II British officer Field Marshal Montgomery admitted his family had seen the ghost several times when they lived there at the turn of the nineteenth century.

GOVERNMENT HOUSE The elegant manor home of Tasmania's governors was known to be haunted long before it opened its doors to the public in 1989. Servants and former residents told of unexplainable footsteps and eerie moaning sounds that sometimes erupted from nowhere into very loud and distinct sentences. In the 1920s, several visitors reported hearing a disembodied voice in the vestibule asking, "What is the time?" In 1951, the wife of Governor Sir Hugh Binney admitted that the place was haunted and that she often heard an ethereal voice asking about the time or pronouncing in a panicked voice, "It's quarter past eleven!" Investigators determined that the time-obsessed spirit was Lady Strickland, wife of an early governor by the name of Sir Gerald Strickland. The woman was said to be very upset over a public hanging, and she constantly inquired about the time on the day it occurred.

PARLIAMENT HOUSE The Speaker's Room in Tasmania's parliament building is haunted by an unidentified politician who emerges from the shadows and disappears just as quickly. The apparition is also seen in the undercroft museum area. Sometimes, an invisible presence blocks the door to the Speaker's Room and prevents people from entering. The ghost is usually encountered by custodians working late at night in the deserted building.

ST. JOHN'S CHURCH St. John's Church in the New Town section of Hobart is haunted by a pathetic presence called "Gwennie." The child's ghost dates back to a time when the church was the chapel for the King's Orphan School. Built with convict labor in 1834, the chapel was connected to the school by two walkways—one for girls and the other for boys. A similar segregation was practiced in the church. The main floor held the town's upstanding citizens, the locked and guarded south gallery was for convicts, and the north gallery was reserved for the equally disrespected orphaned children of convicts, Aborigines, and the poor.

The children might have had it a little worse than the convicts. Since they could not be forced to work, they were malnourished and lived in wretched conditions. Nonetheless, they were forced to attend church and sing the praises of God. One particularly beautiful, high treble voice

is still heard coming from the north gallery. It has been described as a union of singing and crying—the eerie sounds of a young girl's voice that issues from the farthest corner of the orphan's gallery.

ST. MICHAEL'S COLLEGIATE SCHOOL Built in 1825, this impressive townhouse was built by a former chief justice and later became the residence of the Roman Catholic bishops of Hobart. Since 1880, the building has been used as an Anglican boarding and day school. At the turn of the century, one of the Anglican nuns was making her nightly rounds when she slipped at the top of the stairs and fell to her death. The ghostly glow from her oil lamp and the light patter of her footsteps are still encountered on the stairway and in the dormitories. The devoted nun is still making her rounds, checking on her girls late at night.

THEATRE ROYAL Built in 1834, the Theatre Royal is the oldest theater in Australia. As a matter of pure convenience, a pub was built in the basement of the building. It was originally called the "Shades" but was later changed to the "Shakespeare," although today it sits unused and deserted. Back in the mid-1800s, it was a rip-roaring tavern that attracted loose women and gruff men. The ghost of the theater dates back to those days and is said to be a whaler stabbed to death by a prostitute. However, another incident might also be responsible for the ghost here. About that same time, an actor died in a pistol duel with another actor over one of the ladies.

In any case, the presence manifests as the bright white specter of a young man, whom employees have nicknamed "Fred." Fred is most often seen sitting in the third row from the back or walking down the main aisle in the auditorium, although he has also shown up in the Dress Circle and back stage. The ghost can also manifest as an invisible chill that moves chandeliers or raises and lowers seats. Theatre Royal's ghost is credited with putting out what could have been a devastating fire that erupted backstage in June 1984. For some unexplainable reason, the theater's fire curtain descended in front of the stage and prevented the flames from spreading into the auditorium.

Launceston

PENQUITE ROAD The ghost of a mistreated Aborigine haunts the area between Penquite Road and the Esk River near Launceston, Tasmania. The tall, hunched apparition is a mutilated black man, who was hunted down and burned alive by British settlers. The ghoulish figure's skin is burnt to a crisp and his ear lobes are melted away. Sometimes, it is just his invisible presence that people see moving through the tall grass and leaving footprints in the dirt. Another area known for its Aborigine ghosts is Suicide Bay, at Woolnorth in northwest Tasmania. Cattlemen herded together an entire tribe of Aborigines and drove them off the cliffs of the bay.

PRINCESS THEATRE The ghost at the Princess Theatre did not start manifesting here until 1972, when the place was remodeled from a live playhouse into a movie theater. Employees and guests started reporting strange scratching sounds, sudden unexplainable drops in room temperature, and the sounds of piano playing when no one is in the theater. Many believe the ghost is Max Oldaker, an accomplished actor who worked at the theater and died in Launceston in 1970.

New Norfolk

ROYAL DERWENT HOSPITAL Ward 5 of Willow Court at this forty-year-old hospital is haunted by a violent male apparition. Mysterious lights float through the ward, sudden chill spots form, and the form of a man moves about the corridors. In July 1991, four employees saw the apparition and watched in terror as it picked up a male nurse and threw him against the wall three times. After that, the management was forced to install security cameras in the ward to placate employees. That section of the hospital is for mentally disabled patients, but was formerly a ward for the terminally ill. The hospital is located off Lyell Highway in the town of New Norfolk. For more information, visit the Ghosts and Other Haunts Web site at homepages.ihug.co.nz/~dp.jod.

TYNWALD MANSION This old Gothic Victorian house looks so haunted, it was the centerpiece for an ABC-TV series called *The Willow Bend Mystery*. Today, it is an opulent restaurant full of playful ghosts. The building is located on the Willow Bend Estate and is the former manor house for the Lachlan River Mills property. It was the private residence of the Plunkett family for fifty years, and it is the Plunkett children who haunt the place. The children's presence has been sensed in the first floor lounge, tower room, former bedrooms, and in the upstairs halls. The apparition of a lovely twenty-year-old girl appears at the top of the stairway, peeking around the banister pole and waving at people to come up to join her.

Port Arthur

ISLE OF THE DEAD There is nothing on the Isle of the Dead except old graves and ghosts. Located off Port Arthur, the uninhabited islet is home to nearly two thousand dead convicts, public officials, and military personnel. There used to be a small caretaker's hut on the island but by the late 1870s, no caretaker would spend the night alone on the island, and it has long since disappeared. The island sat abandoned for over a hundred years, until recently it was opened as a tourist. Still, no one ever stays overnight.

PORT ARTHUR PRISON HISTORICAL SITE A small, heavily guarded road and the great blue ocean are the only way to escape from this former prison. Iron-barred gates impossible to budge suddenly open and close by themselves, a ghostly old lady rocks back and forth in a guard's cottage, and tourists sometimes find a few extra faces in photographs taken at the site. Bells ring from nowhere near the old church ruins. The screams of a fourteen-year-old boy hanged here still echo through the corridors, and the presence of a man who hanged himself still haunts his former cell. Some unseen presence terrifies people in Cell 4, and so many visitors have become "frozen in terror" in the center of the cell, that authorities had to board it up. The prison was completed in 1852 and was considered a model prison in terms of its treatment of convicts. Apparently, the ghosts would disagree.

Richmond

PROSPECT HOUSE RESTAURANT This 150-year-old inn and restaurant was built by James Kestall Buscombe, a wealthy local businessman. It is his wife, however, who haunts the place, and she seems to be spending eternity looking for her jewelry, which is said to be still hidden somewhere on the property. Her apparition, dressed in a distinctive crinoline dress, has been seen throughout her former residence. She sits on the edge of beds upstairs, reclines in chairs in the former parlor, and is seen climbing the stairs. The old key to Mrs. Buscombe's jewelry box was found many years ago, but the whereabouts of the box itself remains a mystery.

Another ghost of Prospect House dwells in the old basement servant's quarters. The violent presence is blamed for flinging a child out of bed in the middle of the night and sitting on top of people's chest so they cannot breathe. In 1989, an Anglican priest performed an exorcism in the basement, and encounters with the spiteful specter declined noticeably.

RICHMOND BRIDGE The stone bridge spanning the Coal River in Richmond is the oldest bridge in Australia and also the most haunted. The bridge was built in 1824 using convict labor, and its construction was supervised by an ex-convict overseer by the name of George "the Flagellator" Grover. Grover was a sadistic man who loved using leather whips on people. He worked as the official flagellator at the Richmond Gaol, where he punished prisoners with a cat-o'-nine-tails whip starting at 9:00 A.M. each morning.

One day, a dense fog enveloped the bridge, and the convicts took the opportunity to seize Grover, beat him mercilessly, and throw him to his death on the rocks below the bridge. Those responsible for his death could never be identified and no one was punished, but Grover's ghost has not forgotten. When a fog covers the old Richmond Bridge, the apparition of the Flagellator crawls up the rocks along the riverbank and onto the bridge. Only one thing is on his mind: revenge.

RICHMOND GAOL Cell 3 in solitary confinement in this 1820s prison is haunted by the unsettling presence of an unknown man who was confined there in the nineteenth century. Visitors and employees are locked in the cell by some unseen force or are overcome by dizziness and other eerie effects. Sometimes a man's groaning can be heard coming from the empty cell. The building became the city jail in 1928 and was opened as a historical site in 1950.

ST. LUKE'S ANGLICAN CHURCH The wispy white apparition of a man haunts the tower at St. Luke's Church. He has also been seen at the entrance to the old city graveyard and strolling on the grass of the Congregational Cemetery. Some locals believe the ghost of St. Luke's is an unidentified man known only as "Old Daddy," who used to roam the streets of town. Others believe the spirit is one of the convicts, settlers, or military personnel who lie in the many unmarked graves in the old city graveyard near the church.

SOUTH AUSTRALIA

Adelaide

OLD SPOT HOTEL This old hotel near Adelaide in the town of Gawler is haunted by the presences of a little girl named Elizabeth, who died of pneumonia, and an old man named George, who is dressed like a coachman. The building was constructed in 1836 as the town morgue but became a hotel when additions were made in the late nineteenth century. When renovations were made at the turn of the century, the apparitions started being reported by guests and employees.

Recently, a professional photographer named Scott Pearson, who is also a gifted psychic, was

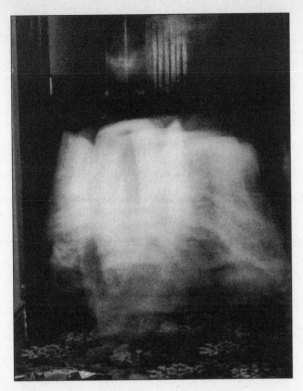

Old Spot Hotel, Adelaide, Australia (Scott Pearson)

able to capture the spirits on film. The case made headlines across South Australia and in 1998 was featured on an Australia news program called "A Current Affair." "I definitely felt something," said Scott, "force or a presence, like a chill through your whole body."

QUEENSLAND

Alice Springs

CORROBOREE SPRINGS One of Australia's best documented ghosts is known simply as the "Ghost of the Outback." It has been seen scores of times in a clearing near Corroboree Springs, which is 161 kilometers (100 miles) from Alice Springs. The short, dark-featured spirit is thought to be a member of the Arunta Aboriginal Tribe, which used the site for secret and occasionally fatal initiations.

Brisbane

BOGGO ROAD GAOL The Boggo Road Gaol is located on Annerly Road in Dutton Park near the center of Brisbane. Originally used as a holding tank for prisoners being shipped to St. Helena Island, it soon became a place of permanent incarceration for notorious prisoners. The jailhouse was closed down several years ago and only the ghosts remained behind. Punishment at the prison was severe, and suicides were commonplace. Hangings took place here until 1922, when capital punishment was abolished in Australia.

Boggo Road Gaol, Brisbane, Australia (Jim Sim, Brisbane Ghost Tours)

One of the most active presences here is Ernest Austin, a convicted murderer hanged at the prison in 1913. There was only one official report of a guard's encounter with his ghost on rounds one night, but a recent investigation turned up scores of other sightings by guards in the eighty years the prison was open after his execution. Most of the encounters took place in the old gallows area. A recent investigation turned up photographic evidence of continuing paranormal activity. The old gaol is now under the care of the National Trust and several tours are available. More information can be found at the Brisbane Ghost Tours Web site at members.tripod.com/~Ghost_Tours, the Brisbane Ghost Walk at www.ghost-tours.com.au, or the Castle of Spirits site at members.tripod.com/~cluricaun/main.htm.

BRISBANE ARCADE Brisbane Arcade is a two-story shopping arcade that runs from the Queen Street Mall through to Adelaide Street. The apparition of a former shopkeeper has been seen walking on the second level of the arcade, looking through the iron latticework to the floor below. She is most often spotted on the part of the second floor balcony that has the center cut out so people can look down on the first floor. Her shop was closed when she died, but she still keeps an eye on the place.

The Brisbane Ghost Walk assembles under the Queen Victoria statue at Brisbane Park at 7:30 P.M. Tours take place on Sunday and Wednesday at 7:30 and 9:30 P.M. at the main gate. Bus tours of Redlands and Ipswitch sites are also available. For more information, go to www.ghost-tours.com.au or contact Jack Sim at enquiries@ghost-tours.com.au or call 6234-617-3272.

Bulimba Cemetery, Brisbane, Australia (Dorothy O'Donnell, Gryphon)

BRIDGEMAN DOWNS CEMETERY Many different apparitions have been reported darting across the paved and dirt roads in Bridgeman Downs Cemetery. The ghosts are most often sighted at dawn and dusk.

BROOKFIELD CEMETERY Brookfield Cemetery is on Brookfield Road in the Brisbane suburb of Brookfield. It dates back to the early 1880s and is now being remodeled with a more modern layout. The construction work has stirred up a lot of other sightings of misty shapes since it began. The ghosts move rapidly from the older part of the cemetery to the newer part, as if they are looking forward to some new faces about the place.

BULIMBA CEMETERY This foreboding nineteenth-century cemetery sits on Wynnum Road on top of a hill in Morningside. There are no reported sightings of apparitions here, but visitors often report feeling uncomfortable as if something were watching them. Even drivers in cars on the road that circles the cemetery get the same feeling. For information on other cemeteries in Brisbane, visit the Ghosts and Other Haunts Web site at homepages.ihug.co.nz/~dp.jod.

CITY HALL Brisbane City Hall has at least three ghosts. One is of a female apparition dressed in old-fashioned clothes. She is most often seen on the main staircase or at the top of the stairs overlooking the foyer. The second ghost is a workman who occasionally appears in the elevator. He was killed during installation of the elevator in the 1930s. The third apparition here hangs around in the Red Cross Tea Room. It is the ghost of an American sailor killed by another sailor in a fight over an Australian girl. Sometimes, the angry voices of their argument and the gruesome sounds of a knife being thrust into a person's chest can be heard in rooms next to the Tea Room. City Hall does have its own tours that sometimes mention the ghostly activity here. For more information, call 07-3225-4890. The Brisbane Ghost Tours also have tours here.

LUTWYCHE CEMETERY The graves at the Lutwyche Cemetery on Gympie Road in Lutwyche date back to the 1870s, and ghostly experiences here are presaged by a musty odor of death and decay. Many have reported vague feelings of dread and oppression here. The cemetery has fallen into disrepair and has become a hangout for derelicts.

MOGGILL CEMETERY Moggill Cemetery is a small graveyard on Moggill Road across from a large shopping center. It has a reputation for putting out some very bad vibrations. The cemetery started around 1850 and holds many early pioneers of Brisbane, but it is overgrown now and many of the tombstones have been stolen or damaged by vandals. Perhaps that is why the spirits are so upset here.

MOUNT GRAVATT CEMETERY Mount Gravatt Cemetery is next to Griffith University in the Mount Gravatt area. The 1880s cemetery has different sections for different ethnic groups and the majority of graves are from the 1960s. The cemetery is further segregated into lawn, monument, and crypt sections. There are numerous impressive stone crypts and tombstones. Encounters with apparitions are rare, and most of the spirits seem content to stay in their own sections.

NEWSTEAD HOUSE Historic Newstead House was built in 1846 on the banks of the Brisbane River. Today, it is a fully restored homestead site on Breakfast Creek Road in the town of Newstead. The place is haunted by the spirits of former residents. Disembodied footsteps are heard, lights go off and on of their own accord, and objects get moved about by some unseen presence. The most active ghost seems to be a former maid, who still tries to keep the house in order. While she is harmless, she is an annoyance to the staff because she keeps moving things around.

OLD GOVERNMENT HOUSE The present headquarters of the National Trust of Queensland used to be the Governors Office up until 1910. Now known as the Old Government House, it is located at the end of George Street in Brisbane, next to the Queensland University of Technology, Gardens Point campus. The mansion was built in 1860 and has beautifully manicured gardens to this day. It is haunted by a frequent visitor to the estate, George Ferguson Bowen, who died in 1899 in England. He must have loved it here, because his spirit keeps returning.

PARLIAMENT HOUSE Parliament House, located on the corner of George and Alice Streets in Brisbane, has been the seat of power in Queensland since it was first built in 1868. The plush sandstone building is haunted by three ghosts. One of the ghosts is an unidentified male apparition who just moves about the building as if he were still going about his business. Another ghost haunts the Speakers Room. He is thought to be a man who committed suicide by shooting himself there. The third ghost is believed to be the spirit of a man who died in his office at Parliament House in 1879. Tours of the building are available when Parliament is not in session.

PLOUGH INN The Plough Inn at Southbank in East Brisbane is a popular pub with a lot of ghost stories to tell. Built in the late 1800s, the Plough Inn has become a favorite nightspot for Brisbane citizens. The ghost here is a young woman who was strangled here by her boyfriend back in the 1920s. Her apparition has never been spotted but her distinctive voice has been heard throughout the building. She is most often encountered near Room 7 of the inn.

TOOWONG CEMETERY This large cemetery in the Birdwood district of Toowong was opened in 1871. It is a peaceful cemetery that is haunted by eerie, singing white lights that investigators believe represent the souls of those interred here. Like many Australian cemeteries, it is divided into separate ethnic sections and exhibits a wide variety of languages and tombstone design.

Cooktown

BLACK MOUNTAIN This notoriously haunted mountain in the Black Trevethan Range is located

Toowang Cemetery, Brisbane, Australia (Dorothy O'Donnell, Gryphon)

in Queensland, twenty-six kilometers (sixteen miles) south of the town of Cooktown. The road between Cooktown and Cairns crosses a low ridge in the mountain at five hundred feet (152 meters) above sea level. The foreboding mountain is inhabited by all kinds of nasty creatures, including gigantic pythons and a strange beast that has been dubbed the "Queensland Tiger." Sometimes the sounds of millions of frogs that live on the mountain can be deafening. The mountain is sacred to the Aborigines, who call it "Kalkajaka" or "mountain of death." A ravine here was the site of a massacre of Aborigines by European settlers, and the ghosts of the murdered Aborigines still haunt it. Both white men and their cattle who have wandered on Black Mountain have disappeared without a trace. The first record of such a disappearance was in 1877, when a carrier and his horse vanished without a trace. In 1890, a constable stationed at Cooktown tracked a criminal into the mountains and both men disappeared. Over the years numerous prospectors, cowboys, policemen, campers, hikers, and travelers have been sucked up by the mysterious mountain.

Fremantle

OLD FREMANTLE PRISON Australia was used as a prison colony by England and some of the first prisoners were sent to Fremantle. The ghosts of some of the world's most notorious and violent men are still seen in the old gaol (jailhouse),

kitchen, roundhouse, and in the many tunnels in the compound. The apparitions of executed inmates are reported most frequently, although other powerful presences include a few men who went insane behind bars. There are even a few Aboriginal spirits tied to the property before it was a prison. The Fremantle Ghost Walk commences from outside the Town Hall at 7:00 P.M. from November 11 through December 14.

Parramatta

OLD GOVERNMENT HOUSE This manor house, the first public building in Australia, was built in 1799 and was the Governor's country residence in Parramatta until 1855. The house is located at the beginning of George Street between Pitt and Macquarie Streets. The center of all the ghostly activity in the house seems to be the upstairs "Blue Room." The blue painted bedroom is home to an apparition in a blue dress called—you guessed it—the Blue Lady. She is thought to be Mary Bligh because a witness identified her from a sketch made of her when she was alive. She is also seen walking down the small hallway outside the Blue Room with a small dog in her arms, in the doorway to the Blue Room, and standing at the top of the stairs. Psychics visiting the room insist a violent rape took place in the left-hand corner of the Blue Room, and visitors often feel sick or upset when they stand in the affected area. Visitors also complain of bad smells that float through the room and feeling suddenly ice cold. Security guards have reported that the door to the Blue Room opens and closes by itself or sometimes the doorknob vibrates violently.

Other ghosts have also been encountered here. A workman installing a chandelier saw a disembodied face staring at him through one of the windows, and when he glanced at the window to the left, he saw the same face glaring at him. During an investigation by the Australian Ghost Research Society (AGRS), two psychics walking through the house detected a very negative presence that left marks on the arm of one of the women. One of the managers of Government House often heard voices coming from the old Dining Room, and a guard on duty there saw the ghost of a servant girl standing next to the dining table. On a ghost tour one night a group and guide observed a ghostly apparition circle the outside of the group and then exit through a doorway into a dark hall. Another guide was letting a couple out one of the back doors, and encountered the apparition of a man in the hallway next to him. During another ghost tour, an apparition was spotted in a corner of the cellar. Ghost tours through the building fill up fast. For reservations, call 02-9635-8149.

NORTHERN TERRITORY

AYERS ROCK Ayers Rock, also known by its aboriginal name Uluru, is the biggest monolith in the world. Located about 444 kilometers (275 miles) southeast of Alice Springs, it is not hard to find. The one-and-a-half-mile-long, five-mile-wide rock rises abruptly 1,100 feet from the surrounding plains. Discovered by explorer Ernest Giles in 1872, it was named in honor of Sir Henry Ayers, premier of South Australia, in 1883. The Aborigines visited it since time immemorial and hidden away in shadowy crevasses are sacred relics and offerings dating from the dawn of time. Occult activity has been reported in the area for decades, and over a dozen people camping or visiting the rock have vanished without a trace.

In August 1980, a baby named Azaria Chamberlain disappeared from her parents' tent at Ayers Rock. A massive search failed to find the child. In

Ayers Rock, Northern Territory, Australia (Andrew Hayden)

1986, a British tourist who had written to relatives that he had discovered evidence of "occult activity" at the site was found dead under mysterious circumstances at the foot of the rock. Amazingly, the blood-covered jacket of Azaria was found not far from his body. The dead man's family believes he stumbled across a satanic cult in the area that engaged in human sacrifice and was murdered, although police concluded he accidentally fell to his death from the rock. Even stranger is the fact that the name Azaria means "sacrifice in the desert." For more information, visit the Ghosts and Other Haunts Web site at homepages.ihug.co.nz/~dp.jod.

WEST AUSTRALIA

York

OLD YORK HOSPITAL York is an old settlement town located about one hundred kilometers (sixty-two miles) east of Perth in West Australia. The town is full of old stone buildings, but it is the former hospital that is known to be haunted. Even when the hospital was in operation, it was considered haunted. A former matron who worked there in the 1920s recalled: "There was always something terrifying about the upstairs rooms. The hospital staff refused to go up there alone, and even when the ward was full of patients, the nurses always made their rounds in pairs." The large gray building is surrounded by trees, but birds and other animals rarely venture near the place. In recent years, the building has been turned into a hostel and many tour groups rent out the whole place. Many members of these groups have reported ghostly encounters.

In 1980, members of a children's athletic club and their adult supervisors made the mistake of staying for a week in the building. Late on the first night of their stay, the sounds of moaning started emanating from inside the walls, then a horrendous scream was heard. The source of the frightening sounds was never determined, but it repeated several nights in a row. The next morning at breakfast, a large china jug levitated from the countertop and smashed to pieces on the floor in front of two women cooking breakfast. Right after breakfast, two of the youngest children were attacked by an unseen presence in the hallway. One of the girls started screaming, "Hold me! Hold me! I can't sit down. Stop them! Stop them!" Then, she was thrown against a glass-paneled door at the end of the hall. The impact shattered the thick glass, gashing her arm to the bone when she tried to protect her head with her hand. She was rushed to the hospital and stitched to stop the bleeding. The next day, a boy went into shock when he saw the apparition of a partial human figure materialize with its hand on the doorknob of the broken door.

The intensity of haunting seemed to increase that afternoon. One of the adults was kicked in the back by an invisible force, doors slammed shut injuring people as they walked through doorways, painful invisible needles seemed to inject themselves into an adult woman's flesh, and the horrible stench of rotting flesh filled the building. By the third day, both adults and children were sleeping in one room to protect themselves from the invisible presence. After that the phenomena seemed to be concentrated in the downstairs lounge area, near the stairway, and in an upstairs room known as the Dying Room. The Dying Room had been bolted shut when the group arrived, but had somehow unlocked itself on the third day.

The caretaker kept downplaying the group's complaints of a haunting, although he did admit that other groups had reported similar events. He could offer no explanations and seemed genuinely mystified when the Dying Room was found open. Finally, he agreed to provide them with a guard dog at night, but the fierce dog refused to enter the building, even when the owner tried to drag it in. The case was investigated by Miriam Howard-Wright, a local ghost researcher, who found the testimony of the witnesses highly credible.

NEW ZEALAND

New Zealand was settled by Polynesians around A.D. 1000. Native Maori tribe leaders ceded their islands to Britain in 1840, and New Zealand was a British colony until 1907, when it became the Dominion of New Zealand. The country consists of a North Island, a South Island, and numerous smaller islands. More information can be found at Gryphon's New Zealand Ghosts Web site at homepages.ihug.co.nz/~dp.jod.

NORTH ISLAND

CAMP WAIOURU This New Zealand Army training camp, located in the middle of North Island, is haunted by the presence of a young man who hanged himself in the barracks in the 1960s. The ghost began manifesting within a week of the suicide. The men in the barracks started complaining of being awakened in the middle of the night by an invisible force pressing down on their bodies. One man nearly suffocated when his face was pushed into his pillow for several minutes. Then the men began reporting a white floating cloud "shaped like a ten-pin bowling pin" that wandered through the barracks. All the encounters were accompanied by a sudden drop in air temperature, and after the event was over, the temperature of the air returned to normal. The encounters with the ghost of Camp Waiouru are so common that later soldiers nicknamed the ghost "Harvey."

Wellington

WELLINGTON OPERA HOUSE Wellington Opera House was built in the early 1900s. The architect was a perfectionist by the name of Albert Liddy, who spent many lonely hours fretting over his drawings and plans in his design office at the back of the theater. One day he simply could not take the pressure any more and committed suicide there. However, he never could give up his attachment to the beautiful opera house, and his spirit still haunts the place, especially in the backstage area near his former office. He is still sensitive to criticism, however, and anyone who says anything bad about the theater is apt to suffer the worse for it. On several occasions, people have been hurt in mysterious accidents immediately after voicing complaints about the theater, and both employees and managers have learned to keep their mouths shut.

SOUTH ISLAND

Arahura River

TE-WAI-POUNAMU (GREENSTONE WATERS) This area is named for a sacred landmark on the Arahura River, which runs through the Westlands area on South Island. Known simply as the Greenstone, the legendary green boulder was said to protect the Maori tribe, but was lost for many years. In 1970, Hori Ngawai, a *tahunga* (shaman) and *kamatua* (tribal elder) had a vision of the stone's location. Standing on the bank near the mouth of the Arahura River, he predicted that the stone would appear after the eighth wave. "When the eighth ripple comes," he predicted, "you will see the Greenstone." As the eighth wave receded, the water cleared, and there for all to see was the long-lost Greenstone, which was retrieved at low tide by tribe members. It is said the spirit of Hori Ngawai is still connected to the ancient stone.

Christchurch

BARBADOS STREET CEMETERY The gravestone of Margaret Burke would never let the upper-class citizens of Christchurch forget her murder. The poor Irish immigrant had worked as a maid in several of their homes. Then on January 9, 1871, she was brutally raped and murdered by a Panamanian servant by the name of Simon Cadeno. Cadeno worked as a manservant for a rich New Zealander named William Robinson and was charged with the murder in March 1871. The following month, he was found guilty and hanged at the Lyttleton Jail.

Margaret was buried in a potter's grave on January 11, but after their servant was found guilty of her murder, the respectable Robinson family felt it only fitting that they should pay for a granite headstone for her grave. The tombstone was completed and erected over Margaret's grave in September 1871. A month later, a reddish-brown mark that resembled a large bloodstain appeared on the stone. No amount of scrubbing would remove the stain, and the stone had to be replaced. Before long, the new tombstone was also "bleeding." Rumors started that Margaret's spirit was returning to haunt those who had taken her for granted. For many years, the haunted headstone was a macabre tourist attraction in Christchurch, but in recent years, the stone was frequently vandalized. Finally, the Department of Parks and Reserves removed the granite marker for safekeeping. After requests from citizens that it be returned to Margaret Burke's grave, the department said that it had mysteriously disappeared.

CRACROFT HOUSE Cracroft House, also known as the Old Stone House, sits at the foot of the Cashmere Hills in Christchurch. It was built by Sir John Cracroft Wilson, whose apparition is sometimes seen standing on the stairway. The sightings peaked when his former mansion was remodeled into private apartments, and later when it was turned into artist's studios. In 1969, several artists working in the building saw his elderly, bearded apparition. Today, the distinctive dwelling is the headquarters of the New Zealand Girl Guide Movement, but no one there has yet reported any run-ins with his tall, bearded ghost.

In May 1969, an article appeared in the Christchurch Press that the Old Stone House had a ghost. Several artists working in the building had reported seeing an elderly bearded man standing on the stairs. Yet when they investigated he could not be found and the rooms at the top of the stairway were dusty and spider webbed and had obviously not been used for years. According to some students, the story behind the ghost was that in the days of the original owner, Sir John Cracroft Wilson had an Indian baker in his employ who became very jealous when one of the other Indians began to pay attention to his wife. The baker killed his compatriot and burned his remains in the oven. The students claim that the haunting began after it was decided to remove the old baker's oven in the course of reconstruction. During the excavation some old bones were dug out, but before they could be examined properly, they disappeared. So we shall never know whether they were animal or human.

Recently, a Malaysian student went out to the back of Old Stone House to the restroom. As he washed his hands he glanced up into the mirror and saw someone looking over his shoulder. He whipped around, but there was no one there. Another time, a group of visitors approaching the house saw the apparition of a man standing in the window on the second floor. The room in which the ghost appeared was locked because it had no floorboards and was under renovation. Frequently, visitors to Old Stone House report hearing the sounds of an organ being played echoing through the halls, when in fact there is no organ in the house.

DUNEDIN HOSPITAL The infamous Gray Lady of the old Dunedin Hospital is thought to be a young mother, who gave up her baby to adoption here. After giving birth, she fell into a deep depression and died shortly afterwards. Her despondent apparition is seen wandering the hallways between Ward One and the Victoria Ward and on the stairway to the Jubilee wing. Many nurses have reported seeing her shadowy form late at night looking for her baby.

HANNAH PLAYHOUSE Hannah Playhouse was built in 1973, and during construction, one of the workers fell and was killed on the site. It is his displaced spirit that now haunts the theater. Downstage director Ellie Smith admitted that many actors feel the presence of the construction worker in that corner of the stage. Recently, actor Steven Ray was on a metal catwalk looking for a stage prop when he backed into someone with a sudden bump. He turned around to apologize and there was no one there.

ASIA

CAMBODIA

The Khmer state gradually rose to supremacy here in the seventh century and ruled the entire Mekong Valley by the twelfth century. It became a French protectorate in 1863 and an independent country in 1954.

Angkor

ANGKOR RUINS The temple complex at Angkor in Cambodia is one of the most haunted places in Asia. Hardly anyone who visits the spot does not experience some encounter with spirits. Most people visiting Angkor feel the energy here is more earthy and grounded than other sacred sites, and many report somewhat unsettling encounters with animal or warrior ghosts. The moat that surrounds the two-square-mile city has been called a portal to another world outside of time.

The site was built by Khmer rulers between A.D. 879 and 1191. Thai soldiers conquered Angkor in 1432 and for the next few centuries the site lay abandoned in the jungle. Legends of a ghostly city in the Cambodian jungle spread throughout the world, until the site was rediscovered by a French explorer in 1860. Massive renovations

Angkor Wat, Angkor, Cambodia (Martin Gray)

were begun by the French and continue to this day. Angkor Wat is the largest and most impressive temple in the ancient city. The intricately carved Bantay Seray Temple is another spot where visitors have unusual experiences.

Phnom Penh

KHMER ROUGE Cambodia is still haunted by ghosts from the Khmer Rouge killing fields in the northern part of the country. In the 1970s, over a million people were killed during the genocidal rule of rebel Pol Pot. Photographs of victims are permanently displayed in the city of Phnom Penh, and Buddhist shrines have been erected all around the country to help survivors cope with the lingering trauma.

Gruesome apparitions are seen emerging from the mists along the banks of the Mekong River, and there have also been reports of apparitions of victims walking befuddled through the streets of Koulen and Stung Treng. Much of northern Cambodia was turned into a giant forced labor camp by the Khmer Rouge guerillas, and those who did not cooperate were immediately eliminated. On the "bodies" of some of the apparitions, ancient Buddhist tattoos can be discerned. Young men had themselves tattooed in the belief that the sacred symbols would act as armor against the bullets of the Khmer Rouge, as well as protect their spirits in the afterlife.

CHINA

Chinese civilization began in the Huang River valley around 3000 B.C. It was ruled by a series of dynasties beginning with the Hsia dynasty in 2000 B.C. Revolutionaries overthrew the Ching dynasty and established the Chinese Republic in 1912. A civil war after World War II resulted in the establishment of the communist People's Republic of China.

Chengde

YUN SHAN FAN DIAN HOTEL This formidable old building is haunted by the Empress, the apparition of a woman wearing the ancient gown of a Chinese empress. She is always seen at the end of the hall on the eighth floor of the building. Sometimes she is seen on the balcony on that same floor looking down over the edge, and several ghosts of her servants have been observed in her company. She is thought to be Chinese royalty who visited the building long ago, but exactly who she is has never been determined. Recently, the ghost of a man in modern Western clothing has started showing up in the lobby and at other places in the grand old hotel.

Kweilin

WHA CHEE The mountains near this village in western China are haunted by a strange apparition called the Devil Tiger. Located about 40 kilometers (twenty-five miles) southwest of the city of Kweilin, the village has lost several of its members to the phantom, which was described by American writer Ernest Bentley as a "dull cloudlike, amoeba thing." Bentley witnessed the phantom when he was stationed in China with the U.S. Army in 1945. Today, the phantom the villagers euphemistically call the Devil Tiger still roams the few remaining forested hills in the area that have not been harvested of trees. Whatever the "amoeba thing" is, its territory is shrinking every year.

PUSALU A luminous apparition, about the size of a man, has been seen floating above the buildings of this tiny farm town located about forty-eight kilometers (thirty miles) from Beijing. The ghostly figure shimmers with a golden light and ascends slowly from the barren hills behind the town into the dark skies above. In December 1999, the apparition was witnessed by dozens of villagers. "It was so beautiful," remarked witness Wang Cunqiao, "sort of yellow. It looked like someone flying up to heaven."

Xian

MOUNT LI TOMB COMPLEX The emperor of the province of Qin, Shi Huangdi (also known as Zheng), unified China in the middle of the second century B.C. and became one of its most powerful rulers. He was a firm believer in spiritual powers and often received prophetic messages in his dreams. His court contained many mystics and alchemists who sought to increase his spiritual as well as material powers, and he firmly believed that the world after death was just as real as the physical world. In order to prepare himself for his journeys in the afterlife, the emperor hired the best artisans in Asia to create an army of more than 7,500 full-sized figures of soldiers and horses in full battle gear to be buried with him. He died in 210 B.C. and his army was waiting for him.

The ghostly army was not discovered until 1974, when flabbergasted archeologists discovered a maze of underground vaults surrounding the emperor's magnificent mausoleum. Pit One of the ongoing excavation contains six thousand figures—the mass of the emperor's army positioned in military phalanxes ready for battle. Each soldier is unique, with his own face, hairstyle, and clothing, and the detail is absolutely superb. The eyes seem able to move in their sockets, and some workers felt as if the eyes of the figures followed them around. Pit Two contains a mobile reserve army of nearly 1,500 soldiers and horses. Pit Three contains sixty-eight giant, bearded figures thought to be the emperor's military commanders. Pit Four is empty. Some think the emperor died before the chamber could be filled. However, some occult researchers believe that Pit Four does contain soldiers, for it is here where workers report the eerie feeling of not being alone or of being watched. According to some, Pit Four contains the invisible spirits of the emperor's most elite bodyguards—his invisible Ghost Brigade.

Zhejiang Province

PUJI SI TEMPLE Spirits are sensed and seen at the Puji Si Temple on the 284-meter (932-foot) high Pu Tuo Shan mountain in eastern China. The temple was built in A.D. 1080 and has been the scene of many profound spiritual experiences by

Puji Si Temple, Zhejiang Province, China (Martin Gray)

visitors. The Buddhist sacred mountain of Pu Tuo Shan is located on a small island and is dedicated to the Bodhisatva Kuan-Yin, whose spirit is thought to dwell here. Kuan-Yin was a male holy person who wandered through India and Tibet. When he reached this mountain in China, he attained total enlightenment and also changed into a woman, which demonstrated that he had successfully balanced the masculine and feminine energies within.

FIJI

Fiji was inhabited since prehistoric times and was discovered by Dutch explorers in 1643. It was annexed to Great Britain in 1874 and became an independent republic after a coup in 1987.

Suva

PARLIAMENT HOUSE The seat of government on the island nation of Fiji is haunted by the apparition of an unidentified man. Custodians had long reported strange noises and feelings of not being alone late at night in the building, but in recent years the presence has begun to manifest in other ways. In the 1990s, poltergeist activity such as unaccountable footsteps, lost objects that reappear in odd places, and unexplainable electrical problems started occurring with increasing frequency.

In 1993, the apparition was caught on security cameras monitoring one of the meeting rooms. Three astonished guards watched for five minutes as the ghostly figure walked about and then disappeared into thin air. One of the guards told reporters the image caught on film was a "kalou vu" (ancestral spirit) that had manifested to protect its descendents from government control. The videotape was examined by Prime Minister Sitiveni Rabuka and Opposition Leader Jai Ram Reddy, but neither man could offer any explanation. The tape was shown on national television, and most residents agreed that a "kalou vu" was doing some spectral lobbying.

INDIA

An urban culture flourished in northern India around 3000 B.C., though India remained ruled by feudal lords for centuries. Mogul invaders conquered the country but lost their power by 1707, when a loose confederacy of states was formed. The country was virtually ruled by early Western traders, especially the British East India Trading Company. Gradually rule passed to the British government. A sovereign state of India was finally created in 1947.

Calcutta

DAKSHINESWAR TEMPLE The immense spiritual presence of a former priest at the Kali Temple of Dakshineswar in Calcutta is sensed by nearly everyone who visits this unique site. Some have even experienced his spirit taking form in front of them during meditation. Ramakrishna became the head priest of the temple in 1856, after the former head served only a year in the newly opened temple. He was soon relieved of his duties, however, when it became obvious his soul was destined for greater service. Ramakrishna practiced a kind of divine union in which he felt himself becoming one with the object of his concentration and devotion—the ultimate divine force in the universe. All the various forms of gods and goddess appeared to him, including Christ, Mohammed, Shiva, and dozens of other Hindu deities. He entered profound ecstatic trances that were said to have made him a conduit of higher consciousness and energy, and his fame as an avatar spread throughout Asia. He died at the age of fifty in 1886, but his pure spirit remains at Dakshineswar.

Gompti River

CREMATION GROUNDS The entire community surrounding the ancient Hindu Cremation Grounds on the bank of the Gompti River is haunted. Today, the Indian government has restricted the traditional crematoria grounds to a quarter square kilometer area; however, they have not been able to control the many wandering spirits that show up in the neighboring homes. Re-

Dakshineswar Temple, Calcutta, India (Martin Gray)

ports of ghosts taking up residence in the houses surrounding the grounds are numerous. Most of the homes are over a hundred years old, although a few are really nothing more than flimsy huts that are destroyed by the storms of each monsoon season. The quality of the homes seems to make little difference to the otherworldly interlopers, who seem attracted by large and noisy families. Dozens of residents report seeing the apparitions of unknown Hindu men and women, mysterious sulfurous odors, and unaccountable footsteps walking through their homes late at night.

Jaipur

AMBER PALACE The ruins of this ancient palace are haunted by the ghost of a clown. The Maharajah of Amber ruled the entire province of Jaipur, but the dynasty was on its last legs by the 1750s, when Prince Marwar ruled. The prince was so obese that he could not get off his couch and had to be waited on like an invalid. In 1754, a French circus touring India stopped at the Amber Palace to entertain the prince.

One performer, Pepe Dindoneau, performed the wondrous feat of walking on air (actually a camouflaged tightrope), and the prince was so enamored of the man that he paid him to stay with him in the palace after the circus had moved on. Pepe married the gardener's daughter and they had three sons together. Then, one year during the festival of Kali at the palace, Pepe's wife and a son were murdered by Thuggees, a violent Indian cult who sacrificed humans to Kali. Pepe was never the same. Today, amongst the ruins of the old palace, his apparition is still seen. Sometimes he is a young man performing in the open courtyard. At other times, usually during a full moon or just before dawn in the morning, he is seen as an older man peering over the broken walls or walking through the ravine at the foot of the palace.

Mirzapur

TEMPLE OF KALI The ghosts of sadistic cult members known as Thuggees haunt this temple, which was their chief sanctuary in the nineteenth century. Their violent energy can still overcome visitor to the temple. Thuggees were a band of thieves and assassins (our word "thug" comes from their name) who believed Kali, the goddess of blood and violence, had founded their organization. Thuggees slowly strangled their victims to death with a cord, releasing and tightening it to keep the victim suffering as long as possible and give the goddess time to witness their deed. They rarely attacked women because their goddess was female. Today, a similar cult known as the Dacoits practice their devotion to Kali in the Chambal Valley area south of the city of Agra.

JAPAN

The Japanese island was inhabited by humans as long ago as thirty thousand years. Early Chinese rule was replaced by a military government of feudal lords and shoguns (military dictators). The first modern emperor took control of the country in 1868. A new constitution was adopted after World War II.

Hachioji

HACHIOJI CASTLE Hachioji is a suburb of Tokyo that has a long history. If you follow the Shiroyama Rindo dirt road into the woods near town, you will come upon the ruins of Hachioji Castle, built in 1570 by the feudal lord Hojo Ujiteru. The trauma that never left this site occurred on June 23, 1590, when the castle was attacked by an army under the command of shogun Toyotomi Hideyoshi. Rather than be taken prisoner and subjected to rape and torture, the women of Hachioji Castle leapt to their deaths from the ramparts. There was so much blood in the ravine below that it ran like a stream and created rock-staining waterfalls.

The castle was immediately haunted by screams and the sickening thud of bodies hitting the rocks, and no one would live there. It remained deserted for four hundred years. In 1951, the place was made a historical site, and archeological studies have been taking place since 1977. However, the haunting sounds of death and terror have never left this traumatized site.

OTSUKAYAMA PARK Otsukayama is a 213-meter (699-foot) high hill located about two kilometers (one and a quarter mile) from the Hachioji train station. In a clearing near the top of the hill once stood the Doryodo Temple, a nineteenth-century site erected with funding provided by area silk merchants. Ever since 1965, the temple ruins have been haunted by the apparition and crying sounds of a female caretaker who was murdered here in September 1963. Asai Toshi was an eighty-two-year-old widow who was known to hoard large sums of money. After someone robbed her of her life savings, they cut her throat and plunged a knife into her heart. She was buried in a small graveyard behind the temple. In 1983, the abandoned temple was demolished, but that did not stop the haunting of its ruins. In 1990, the city made the hillside area a public park.

Hokkaido Island

MANNENJI TEMPLE The Mannenji Temple at Saporro on Hokkaido Island is haunted by a doll. A miraculous doll here is thought to be possessed by the soul of a young girl named Okiku Eikichi, who died in 1918. Shortly after the death of their child, the parents noticed that the doll's hair started to grow as if it were infused with a life force. In 1938, the haunted doll was given to Shinto priests at the Mannenji Temple. By that time the formerly close-cropped doll's head had grown hair down to its knees. Every March 21 at the Spring Equinox, the priests give the doll a trim, but the hair continues to grow several inches a year. The Japanese believe that dolls have "souls." They give old family dolls to priests to have them exorcised or burnt. For more information on Japanese Ghosts, visit the Web site www.revanche-hoya.de/html/g4.html.

Honshu Island

MOUNT HAGURO The spirit of a former prince named Kokai is sensed at his grave and near a six hundred-year-old, five-story pagoda on top of Mount Haguro in the Yamagata Prefecture of northern Honshu. The seventh-century prince renounced his titles and possessions and became a wandering mystic who founded Shugendo Buddhism. A vision guided him to Mount Haguro, where he spent the rest of his life. The mountain is also the home of the Yudono Hot Springs where a deity lives. Pilgrims bathe in the springs to replenish their spiritual energies.

TONO RIVER The Tono River, which flows through Tono City in Iwate Prefecture, is haunted by mysterious water spirits called Kappa. Usually

Mount Haguro, Honshu Island, Japan (Martin Gray)

considered evil phantoms, the Kappa are depicted with webbed fingers, scaly skin, and a desire to rape and kill humans. They pull people into the river and kill them by evisceration. Local residents believe the entities truly exist and there are records of women becoming pregnant by them.

CROS HONE Near this village in Gunma Prefecture on Honshu Island, a highway tunnel is haunted by many different spirits. The Cros Hone Tunnel is built through a hill that served as an execution area during the Edo regime in the nineteenth century. Many people were beheaded there, and their spirits are said to have gone into the hill. Many paranormal encounters, such as disembodied laughter and feelings of a sinister presence, have been reported by drivers going through the tunnel, and there is an usually high rate of traffic accidents there.

The most frequently sighted apparition, however, is of a modern woman who died in an accident in the tunnel. Drivers have reported her apparition stepping in front of their cars, and many strike her, but when they stop, there is no victim to be found. Back in their cars, they see the mutilated face of a woman in their rearview mirrors.

Kanzaki

YOSHINOGARI Yoshinogari is an archeological site near the town of Kanzaki in Saga Prefecture. This area was the site of a settlement of ancient Japanese called the Yayoi. The ghosts of these ancient warriors and their athletic children playing have been reported ever since the excavating began. In the first and second centuries A.D., the Yayoi built all manner of battlements and weapons. One unusual implement found at the dig is a form for casting an unusual saucer-shaped emblem or weapon with three winglike blades angling off from it.

Kawasaki City

NAKAHARA FIRE STATION The Gyokusen branch of the Nakahara Fire Station in Kawasaki City is haunted by the ghosts of a man and woman, who sometimes climb into bed with sleeping firemen. The male apparition is naked, about thirty-five years old, with a long, serious face. The female apparition wears a kimono and has a round face with a passive look. Sometimes the apparitions appear only from the waist up. There is a tall watchtower next to the fire station, and the sounds of an invisible person ascending the stairs are often heard.

The haunting started in 1959, immediately after the current structure was completed. The fire station is located next to an old graveyard that is part of the Hottaji Temple, and many bones and hidden underground burial vaults were discovered during its construction. The watchtower was destroyed in 1980 but was soon replaced, and the construction seemed to increase the ghostly activity. In 1982, a memorial to the bodies disturbed during construction on the property was made, and on the first and fifteenth of every month, special prayers are said to placate the restless spirits.

Kitakyushu

INANAKI PASS AND MEJI TUNNEL The highway at Inanaki Pass near Kitayushu and the narrow, old Meji tunnel are haunted by an unidentified woman. She is described only as "a woman in white," and she is usually observed just standing alongside the pavement late at night.

MOJI COAST Off the coast here in the twelfth century, a fierce sea battle was fought between the Genji and Heike feudal families. The Heike were wiped out, including an eight-year-old prince, who is said to have drowned in his mother's arms. Today, visitors to the sea here and drivers on the coast highway, including hardened taxi drivers, see the apparitions of the devastated Heike warriors.

Kokotoke

KOKOTOKE TOGE The tunnel entrance to Highway 20 (the Koshu Kaido Highway), which runs out of Tokyo towards Mount Takao, used to be a checkpoint gate that was set up to restrict travel within Japan. From 1623 to 1869, people only passed through this point during daylight hours by showing proper authorization. Violators were crucified on the spot. But the apparition seen here is of a woman dressed in modern clothing holding a baby. The mother and child phantom appears out nowhere in the middle of the road and has been known to cause serious accidents. At other times, she is seen walking alongside the road with her baby. Often, she smiles at passing drivers. When a male driver stopped to offer assistance, she looked at him through the side window of the car and intoned the words "wrong man." Then she disappeared.

Kyushu Island

FUKUOKA JO GAKUIN COLLEGE Fukuoka Jo Gakuin College, a woman's College at Ogori on Kyushu Island, is haunted by the ghosts of soldiers who died in a battle on the school grounds centuries ago. In a single afternoon in July 1359, over five hundred men met their deaths in a battle between feuding warlords that took place on this field in Fukuoka Prefecture. The ground was never the same after that; nothing grew and no one would live there. Finally, a cemetery was built on part of the field and a monument erected to those who died in the fierce fighting.

A military training school was then built on the property, and that is when the real problems began. Almost immediately, apparitions of dead warriors started showing up ready for battle. The soldiers heard voices coming from nowhere or saw ghostly figures of restless warriors. The neighboring farmers began to see ancient warriors floating through the empty fields. In the early 1970s, an officer sleeping on the grounds awoke to see three dark figures standing outside the screen door of his quarters. One kept begging "Omizu, Omizu, kudasai!" ("Water! Water, please!"). The puzzled officer got up from his bed and opened the door so that the three could get some water, but they had vanished. In response to the increased hauntings, the town of Ogori has paid for Shinto exorcisms to be performed yearly at the battle site.

According to Jesse Glass, a teacher at the Fukuoka Jo Gakuin Collage, which sits across from the military school, the exorcisms have not helped. "Town officials say that this has solved the problem, but still the sightings of these restless warriors continue. The security guards at the school are a stoic bunch," he said. "They have their own small guard house by the front gate of the school, and they man this from early morning to late at night. But even they have seen these ghosts floating, single file down the road on an early Sunday morning. They reported their sighting to the school chaplain."

Miyajima Island

TORI GATE For the Japanese, mountains are the home for all kinds of spirits and ghosts. When someone dies, their spirits ascend to mountaintops in a process of purification for assimilation back into the divine. Corpses were often simply laid or covered with dirt at the base of mountains to make the journey as short as possible. Spirits of dead people were believed to gather on mountaintops and even hold meetings there. Many mountains in Japan have shrines built on them by a number of different sects, and pilgrimages to mountains were part of every person's duty to become more spiritually aware. Tori Gates are placed in lakes to merge the energies of water and mountain.

Furthermore, Japanese traditional belief views every object in the manifested world as having its

Tori Gate, Miyajima Island, Japan (Martin Gray)

own inherent spirit called a "kami." These invisible presences influence human events and humans in turn can influence their world by meditation and prayer. Kami spirits were especially concentrated on mountains, and many mountains in Japan are considered sacred because of the presence of powerful kami energies.

Nagasaki

NAGASAKI RIVER To this day, on the anniversary of the dropping of the bomb on Nagasaki (August 9), the phantom of a black crane flies through the air above the city and lands on the river that runs through the city. After the bombing, many victims of the atomic blast sought relief for their burns in the cool river water. Those who see the phantom say that it disappears and reappears as if it were made of black mist.

Nagasaki Prefecture

ISAHAYA SHRINE This ancient shrine is haunted by a terrifying presence that has been experienced by scores of witnesses, and while tourists visit the shrine, locals know better and stay away. The disagreeable ghost of Isahaya is thought to be a lion spirit that possesses people. At a smaller shrine nearby, located in a cave on the hillside near the famous "Eyeglasses Bridge" (Meganebashi), the feral spirit of fox can also follow people home. People returning from the shrines report feeling as if they were "no longer alone" or are being followed by something. Often the spirit appears during sleep and attacks the person's dreambody.

In 1993, tourist Jesse Glass returned from visiting the shrines and found his life suddenly in turmoil. He had recurring, exceptionally vivid dreams about something dragging him from his

Isahaya Shrine, Nagasaki Prefecture, Japan (Jesse Glass)

bed and throwing him off the eighth-floor balcony of his hotel. When he awoke, he found long claw marks on his back. It got so bad, he forced himself to stay awake rather than succumb to the horrifying dreams. "I could distinctly see the grotesque faces of the stone lions at Isahaya Shrine," he said of his visions. "They seemed to have a fierce intelligence about them and were observing me, even as I had observed them. Some 'thing' I could not see exerted incredible force and dragged me by my bedclothes toward the balcony, where it hiked me up over the railing and let me go. I could clearly see the details of the surrounding buildings and the white lines of the parking lot below."

Oita Prefecture

BEPPU The large stone Buddha on the roadside near the resort city of Beppu in Oita Prefecture is an animated spirit that knows when fatal accidents are about to happen. The statue predicts automobile accidents by the position of its arms. Normally, the right arm of the statue points up, but just before a fatal car accident happens, its right arm assumes a downward-pointing position. Within a few days a traffic fatality always occurs. The paranormal phenomena has been documented on film with the arm in its "before" and "after" positions. The statue is solid stone, carved from one granite slab, and there is no way to explain the arm's movement.

Okinawa Island

AWASE A boxy white house locals call "Three Day House" stands near a string of cheap motels along Highway 22 near Awase in central Okinawa. It is haunted by the apparitions of a man and small boy. The boy is seen playing with a ball in the living room, while the man is observed committing suicide by hanging himself there. Poltergeist effects have also been reported. One male tenant awoke in the middle of the night when he felt his mattress bounce. When he turned on the light, he found five knives stuck in the mattress all around his body. The house is now rented out only to Americans, because no Okinawan will stay there.

Nonetheless, even the Americans are said to sense something is not quite right and move out in a few days. That is how the house earned the nickname "Three Day House."

MAEHARA Kakazu Takadai Park is a public park off Highway 330 at the Shuri/Maehara exit that was the scene of bloody fighting during World War II. Scores of Americans and Japanese soldiers died in the Battle of Kakazu Ridge and it is their spirits that are encountered here. Even people in their cars driving through the park report paranormal effects such as the air becoming electrically charged and sudden icy cold spots that enter the car and will not leave. For more information on Okinawa haunted sites, visit Jane Hitchcock's Okinawa Web site at www.geocities.com/Silicon-Valley/6006/okinawa.htm

NAHA Camp Schwab Road is a mountain road leading to the old U.S. Marines base from the village of Nago, near the capitol city of Naha. It is haunted by the apparition of a twenty-year-old woman in black slacks. The phantom is seen in the middle of the road but disappears before being hit by oncoming traffic. The girl ghost has even flagged down taxi cabs and asked to be taken to Nago, but by the time they arrive, she has vanished into thin air. No one has been able to identify the spirit, but sightings of her are so frequent that the stretch of road where she appears is now called Ghost Corner and she has been nicknamed the "Nightwalker of Nago."

NAKAGUSKU CASTLE The ruins of this seven hundred-year-old castle are located off Highway 146, about ten miles north of Naha between the two United States military bases known as MCAS Futenma and MCB Camp Foster. The castle walls are still mostly intact, although not much else remains of the old fortress. There have been some reports of ghostly happenings here, but for the most part, the spirits in this area seem to have checked into an abandoned hotel adjacent to the castle.

The hotel was built in the early 1980s in the form of a small village and theme park. When the construction moved too close to a sacred cave in the area, problems began and building was halted because no one wanted to work on the haunted property. There were numerous unexplainable injuries and many workers experienced eerie feelings of intense hostility inside the hotel. Even though Buddhist monks had warned him about the spiritual presence in the cave, the owner insisted on pursuing his dream hotel. The man lost all his money in the venture and also lost his mind. He was committed to a mental hospital. Today, a Buddhist monk has taken up residence in the abandoned building to protect the disturbed spirits. Still, passersby have reported floating balls of light in the darkened windows and the sounds of people talking and having fun, as if the place were open for business. Marines from Futenma who have trespassed on the property have reported hearing whispering voices and seeing the apparition of a man walking through the deserted rooms.

PIPELINE ROAD The part of Pipeline Road that parallels Highway 58 near the MCAS Futenma intersection is haunted by the apparition of an elderly Okinawan man, who materializes in old-fashioned clothes without any legs. The man seems mischievous or downright evil. Many drivers have reported catching glimpse of the ghost as they pass through this section of road, which is alongside an old graveyard.

URASOE The Nakanishi High School in the city of Urasoe in south Okinawa is haunted by numerous unidentified apparitions and paranormal events. Located between Highway 58 and Highway 330 off Yafuso Dori Road, the high school was blessed by local shamans and even rebuilt from the ground up in 1990, but the haunting still continues. During the construction of the foundation for the original building, dozens of human skeletons were unearthed in what was assumed to be an unmarked burial ground.

Sasebo

HUIS TEN BOSCH Huis Ten Bosch is a European Village theme park in the town of Sasebo in Nagasaki Prefecture. The entertainment complex has museums, windmills, canals, and several European-style hotels, including the haunted Hotel Europa. Many visitors to the park who stay in Room 470 of the hotel experience a terrific flash of intense lightning, followed by the sounds of a child's footsteps running across the room above them. The hotel was on marshland where many victims of the atomic bomb are said to have been buried.

Shikoku

MOUNT KOYA The apparition of one of Japan's great spiritual leaders is seen near his tomb on Mount Koya. His presence is also felt at his birthplace in Zentsuji. Kobo Daishi, also known as Kukai, was a ninth-century homosexual mystic who blended the beliefs of Buddhism and Shintoism to create a powerful faith that portrayed everything as possessing an intelligent spiritual essence. He took a vow of poverty and traveled throughout Japan trying to awaken others to the spiritual forces in every particle of creation. Kukai was adept at controlling these unseen forces and became renowned for his ability to enter deep states of meditation and for his skill at performing almost instant exorcisms.

Somo

SAKURA SOGORO The ghost of Sakura Sogoro is said to still roam the hills of Somo prefecture in Japan. Long ago, an oppressive lord named Hotta Kozuke raised taxes to the point where his subjects could not survive, and the peasants signed a petition for relief. The petition was presented to Kozuke by Sogoro, who was the leader of one of the larger villages. In response, Kozuke had Sogoro and his wife seized and forced to watch as their three young sons were beheaded. Then he crucified Sogoro's wife and finally Sogoro himself. Before Sogoro died, he vowed that he would haunt Kozuke through all eternity. That, apparently, is what has happened. For in the years before Kozuke died, he was plagued by Sogoro's apparition, and long afterwards, the villager's ghost is still seen scouring the countryside for Kozuke.

Tazawako

TOMB OF PRINCESS TAKIYASHA For some reason the spirit of a young princess is starting to manifest after being silent for a thousand years. Sightings of her apparition at her gravesite in the village of Tazawako in Akita Prefecture started in the early 1990s, and in 1992, a visitor captured her image on videotape. She appears as a young woman in a white kimono and most often holds the palms of her hands pointed upward in the old Japanese style of prayer. Her ghost was also seen by a nun from the Ryugenji Temple who described the apparition as that of a seventeen-year-old girl with red lips and long hair and wearing a white kimono. The Japanese are taking the reappearance of Princess Takiyasha very seriously. She is the daughter of one the strongest supernatural entities in Japan, the great samurai Tairo no Masakado (see Tokyo, Otemachi District, below).

Tokyo

DIET The eighth floor of the Japanese Diet (parliament) is haunted by the presence of a woman who committed suicide there. During the American occupation, the eighth floor was used as a social club and dance floor. During one of the dances, a woman got into an argument with her boyfriend and started crying uncontrollably. Suddenly, the hysterical woman leapt to her death through an open window. Within a few days, the sounds of her weeping could be heard coming from the empty dance floor. The situation got so bad that authorities closed off the floor, and it remains sealed to this day.

FUKOKU SEIMEI BUILDING This modern office building is haunted by the apparition of a former female employee, who in a moment of despair, jumped out of a window to her death. But even in death, she failed. No one saw her do it or missed her presence, and her body lay for several weeks hidden in a clump of bushes. Finally, passersby noticed the odor of rotting flesh and complained to police, who found the badly decomposed body. Now the woman's ghost haunts the lobby and elevators in the building. People report feeling an invisible female presence beside them in the elevators, where the buttons to the upper floors light up by themselves. Perhaps the confused woman's spirit is trying to get back in the building to attempt another suicide—only this time to do it right.

HIGASHI IKEBUKURO CENTRAL PARK During construction of this six thousand-square-meter park, workers reported an unusual number of freak accidents and sensed negative presences around them. Workers heard ghostly moaning sounds, and a man working in an old tomb on the property went insane and ran screaming from the park. He was later found and committed to a mental institution. Another worker took a photo of a wall about to be torn down that showed the incongruous image of Buddha wearing a Japanese military cap. Today, people in the park report hearing strange voices coming from nowhere, and occasionally, a spirit fireball is seen drifting through the area. It is thought the disturbances resulted from the opening of a tomb on the grounds of a former prison that was torn down in 1966. Others surmise the paranormal activity has something in common with the mysterious lights seen nearby at the Sunshine 60 Building. After many unexplainable delays, the park was finally completed in 1980.

NAKANO BEACH The area of beach at the southeast corner of Tokyo Bay, near the village of Nakano, is haunted by the apparitions of Japanese swordsmen. A group of four Samurai warriors, mounted on horseback, has been known to attack people and even leave witnesses with bleeding wounds from the ethereal blades. Neither the fierce warriors nor their steeds ever leave any tracks in the soft sand. In September 1990, a Sensei and his student were practicing sword stances late on the night of the full moon. The four spirit-warriors attacked and cornered the student on a large boulder, where he fought them off for several hours. "I know there were four mounted horsemen on that beach," the student told investigators, "and they attacked me."

OIWA Tokyo's most famous ghost is Oiwa, a sad woman in white, whose face is usually hidden by her long, flowing hair. She has been encountered on sidewalks all over the city. When people approach her, she turns to reveal a hideously twisted and scarred face. As witnesses run away in terror, her mocking laughter is sometimes heard.

The gruesome haunting is based on a true story. In the nineteenth century, Oiwa and her husband, Iyemon, made their living as humble paper umbrella makers. Iyemon, however, was a frustrated man, a "defrocked" or masterless samurai, who eventually began an affair with a young girl neighbor. Together with a male accomplice, Iyemon plotted the murder of his wife so he could be with his new love. They prepared a virulent poison and put it in Oiwa's food, and she died a slow and painful death with the right side of her face and body paralyzed first and then the rest of her body gradually losing its life force. But Oiwa had time to realize what had happened, time to feel rage and long for revenge. The merciless Iyemon then nailed Oiwa's body to one side of a wooden door, and killed his accomplice and nailed his body to the other side of the door. Then, he tossed the door into a nearby river. Almost immediately, the horrific ghost of Oiwa started appearing to Iyemon and following him everywhere he went. Finally, late one night, he confronted the ghost with his samurai sword and cut her head off, only to find that he had really murdered his lovely bride to be.

The story of Oiwa has caught the imagination of the Japanese and is retold in several kabuki-style plays. One of them called the "Tokaido Yotsuya Ghost Story" was made into a film that is shown on television at midnight during the Obon celebration every August. This production and nearly every other staged retelling of Oiwa's story has been considered haunted by her spirit and plagued with a myriad of unexplainable problems. The poltergeist problems quickly subside, however, if the cast and crew take the time to say prayers in her memory or visit the Oiwa Shrine in Yotsuya to offer their respect.

OTEMACHI DISTRICT There is a haunted gravesite in the middle of this busy financial district. Just behind the headquarters of the Mitsui Trading Company is a small monument marking the burial site of the head of a famous samurai warrior. Tairo no Masakado was killed in A.D. 940 in a battle between two factions trying to set up new capitol cities for Japan. His body was beheaded and his head displayed in Kyoto, but according to reports of the time, his head started glowing one night and flew off in the heavens and landed in Shibazaki, where villagers buried it beneath a mound of dirt in the Kanda Myolin Shrine. One evening, ten years later, the mound of dirt began shaking and the glowing ghost of the samurai walked from his grave every night afterwards until special prayers of remembrance were said over the site.

Eventually, the shrine was moved and the city of Tokyo grew up around the old gravesite. In 1923, the Finance Ministry building was erected on the site and the tomb was destroyed, although a temporary marker was put in place. Construction was plagued by weird accidents and odd poltergeist activity. After all fourteen of the finance ministers involved in the decision to erect the building died under mysterious circumstances, a decision was made to stop construction so a purification ritual could be held. Construction was resumed, but the ritual was held annually thereafter. Then, on June 20, 1940, exactly one thousand years after the murder of Tairo, the Finance Ministry building caught fire. A special remembrance ceremony was ordered and the site was treated with unusual respect by authorities, until 1945, when occupation forces from the United States built a parking lot on top of it. Almost immediately, strange things began to be reported and there were several deaths and injuries among the construction crew.

In 1961, Japanese authorities removed the parking lot, purified it with rituals, and once again dedicated the spot to the memory of Tairo no Masakado. However, employees working in newly constructed offices that faced the tomb reported eerie feelings and nausea. Finally, some of the largest banks and corporations in Japan banded together to finance improvements to the memorial and offer regular dedications and prayer ceremonies. Today, prayers are said at the tomb on the first and fifteenth of every month, and no one dares show any disrespect to Tairo's spirit. Even when the site is shown or mentioned in news stories, reporters visit the site to pray. Nobody in Tokyo wants an angry supernatural presence in the middle of the nation's crucial finance district. While Tairo may have found peace, the ghost of his daughter has only recently begun to be seen (see Tazawako, Japan, the Tomb of Princess Takiyasha).

SUNSHINE 60 BUILDING This 240-meter (788-foot) tall building in the Ikebukuro district in Tokyo was built in 1978 on the site of the prison where seven high-ranking Japanese war criminals, including the notorious Hideki Tojo, were executed on December 23, 1948. In 1979, on the anniversary of the end of World War II, mysterious balls of light representing departed spirits (called "hinotama" by the Japanese) started appearing in the area over and around the Sunshine 60 Building (see Higashi Ikebukuro Central Park, above).

Yamanahsi Prefecture

OIRAN BUCHI GORGE Oiran Buchi Gorge literally means "prostitute gorge," and it is the ghosts of murdered prostitutes that haunt it. During the nineteenth century a private gold mine was operated by the Takeda family in the hills near the gorge. The mining operation attracted prostitutes, whose clients moved on to spread rumors about all the gold being found in the hills here. The family wanted to stop the word of the gold from spreading, so they invited all fifty-five prostitutes in the area to an elegant feast that was to take place on a wooden viewing platform constructed high above the gorge. When all the prostitutes had shown up and were busy talking and eating, the support cables to the platform were cut, dumping the screaming women over the edge to their deaths. Today their spirits haunt Oiran Buchi Gorge and have been known to try to push visitors, especially men, over the edge.

KOREA

The Korean peninsula was conquered by the Chinese in 108 B.C., but in the following centuries a series of dynasties ruled. It became a Japanese protectorate in 1905 and after World War II was divided into two separate countries.

No Gun Ri

RAILWAY UNDERPASS A concrete railroad underpass in the countryside outside the village of No Gun Ri, a hundred miles south of Seoul in South Korea, is haunted by the victims of a massacre that took place in the first few weeks of the Korean War. In July 1950, hundreds of local villagers were machine-gunned by American soldiers, who were under orders to shoot civilians as a precaution against North Korean infiltrators. Soldiers from the U.S. Army First Calvary Regiment were herding the peasants off a road onto parallel railroad tracks, when U.S. Air Force F-80 fighters began strafing the area. People ran for cover in the tunnel, where infantrymen opened fire on them. As many as three hundred men, women, and children died. The victims tried to shield the children by huddling around them, and several children survived by burrowing into the mass of dead bodies.

Today, desperate screams mixed with gunfire still echo from the concrete walls of the tunnel, and the apparitions of white-clad peasants are sometimes reported. Many blessings have been performed at the tunnel to try to heal the site of

No Gun Ri Tunnel, No Gun Ri, South Korea (Wide World Photos)

its trauma. In 1999, the bullet holes inside the tunnel were finally plastered over. Over sixty witnesses, including survivors and U.S. soldiers, have come forward describing the deadly encounter, and negotiations are under way for reparations to the families of those killed.

MALAYSIA

Malaysia is an independent country consisting of eleven states in the South China Sea. It was formed in 1963 to include Singapore, which broke away in 1965 to become an independent country.

Ipoh

SYDNEY APARTMENTS The Sydney apartment building in the Old Town section of the city of Ipoh is haunted by the ghosts of people whose bodies were once stored there. At one time, the upper floor of the building was used to keep corpses and prepare them for Chinese funerals. Residents of the building have reported numerous paranormal happenings, including icy cold spots that move around like people, portraits that appear to drip blood only late at night, and quarrelsome spirits who argue when asked to leave. The "hantu" (ghost) of an elderly man is the most active in recent years.

Melaka Pindah Hill

OLD RUBBER PLANTATION The abandoned rubber plantation at Melaka Pindah is haunted by presences associated with the site's heyday and the deplorable conditions under which its workers labored. Many deaths from accidents and disease plagued the plantation, whose overseers were known to be unsympathetic and harsh. The apparitions seen in the forests and crossing the roads in the area are of the traditional spook variety, that is, they are described as "white-sheeted" humanoid figures without any distinctive features. In 1977, a group returning from a wedding party had their entire automobile blanketed by the white ectoplasm as they approached the top of Melaka Pindah Hill. They had to stop, at which time, the "white 'something' flew towards the treetops of the old rubber plantation."

Pahang Province

GENTING HIGHLANDS Genting Highlands is a popular recreation theme park located at six thousand feet above sea level on a hill in the state of Pahang. The park perimeter is haunted by a dead military guard who is still on duty. Dressed in a World War II uniform, the apparition patrols the grounds late at night and has been spotted by several witnesses. Not long ago, two tourists out for a stroll after midnight encountered the lifelike ghost. The ghost approached them and told them to turn back because there was "a war zone ahead." They obeyed his orders and turned around when they suddenly realized how odd was his comment about the war zone. They assumed he meant "war games" or something. By the time they turned around, he had disappeared.

TEMPLER PARK The ghosts of four men dressed in all white clothing haunt the campground area of this park. Sometimes the apparitions can be heard speaking in a very old Japanese dialect. Recently, a group of scouts camping in the park encountered the quartet of spirits, who have also been witnessed by other visitors to the park. They are thought to be the ghosts of Japanese monks from an ancient monastery that once stood in the area.

Penang Island

PENANG BRIDGE Penang Bridge, at 13.5 kilometers (8.3 miles) the longest bridge in Asia, connects the island of Penang with the Malaysian mainland. By the time the bridge was completed in 1979, seven workers had died in accidents during its construction. Their ghosts still haunt the engineering marvel, and they have apparently brought along a few friends that met in the spirit world. The sightings occur most frequently at the mainland exit side of the bridge and at the pillars midway.

Automobile drivers and people who fish off the bridge often report encounters with the ghosts of mutilated workmen and headless phantoms. In the 1980s, the mysterious apparition of a White Lady started appearing in the middle of the bridge thoroughfare. No one has been able to explain who she is or what she wants, although several psychics have proposed that the ghosts of Penang Bridge have opened a portal to the Other Side and all sorts of paranormal phenomena can be expected.

In 1996, the apparition of a pale-faced woman appeared in the back seat of a car as it approached the center of the bridge. The two occupants of the car, a daughter and her mother, were sitting in the front seat. The daughter, who was driving, saw the ghost in her rearview mirror and at first thought it was her mother because it looked so much like her. She immediately pulled into the emergency lane and stopped the car to try to figure out what was going on. Before she could get her seat belt undone, her mother calmly opened the door on the passenger side, walked to the bridge railing, and leapt over the side to her death in the icy water below. The bizarre details of the case were released by police investigators, who bruled the death a suicide. For more information, visit the Asian Horror Web site at members.tripod.com/~DragonKid.

Miri

MIRI HOSPITAL The original hospital in Miri is on the opposite side of the river from town, and patients had to catch a ferry to go to see a doctor. The newer hospital is easier to get to, but there are still people who use the old hospital. Apparently, there are a few ghosts who still go to the old hospital too. The apparitions of patients, doctors, and even their vehicles have been seen waiting for the ferry in front of the main building.

Sarawak Province

TAMAN NEGARA LAMBIR The Lambir Forest Preserve has been called the most haunted spot in the state of Sarawak. The region is said to be haunted by the mysterious ghost of the Green Man. Sometimes witnesses report seeing the apparition of a man in a green shirt, while other times they only see a green or orange form moving about in the woods. At other times, the invisible presence of a man is sensed walking beside hikers or following them closely.

In June 1997, a Form 4 Prefects Camp from the town of Miri was set up at a chalet in the forest. The group consisted of eight teachers and forty-two students. One of the assignments given the students was to hike to the Pantu Waterfall, but the trip proved to be an encounter with the paranormal. Many students and teachers reported baffling encounters with green or orange lights, the apparition of a man in a green plaid shirt, an invisible presence walking beside them on the paths, and a frightening "dark shape" that followed them by leaping from tree to tree.

Sibu

SUNGEI MERAH The Sungei Merah district of the village of Sibu in Sarawak province is haunted by the phantom of a woman in a sarong on a motorbike. Most of the sightings are late at night on the roads near the cemetery. She is believed to be a local woman who died giving birth to a son in 1992. She does not realize she is dead but realizes her son is missing and drives frantically around the graveyard neighborhood looking for him.

Not long ago, a policeman patrolling the area saw the scantily clad woman on her motorbike late at night and stopped her to see if she needed assistance. She told him that she was looking for her seven-year-old son. He offered to help in the search but followed her from some distance behind and soon lost sight of her. After cruising around looking for her, he came upon her motorbike parked outside a house. Assuming she had found her child, he knocked on the front door to check with her. A groggy man answered and the officer inquired about the woman and her child. The man told him that his wife had died giving birth to his then seven-year-old son, who was sleeping soundly in his bed.

NEPAL

This ancient country developed dynastic rule in the fourth century A.D. It became an independent country in 1923 and a constitutional monarchy in 1962. A new constitution in 1990 restricted royal powers and granted more rights to citizens.

Kathmandu

SWAYAMBHUNATH STUPA This ancient stupa predates the arrival of Buddhism to the valley. From time immemorial, there has been an intelligent spiritual force or entity attached to this place. Even the name Swayambhu suggests this. It means "self-existent" or "self-created." It is said to have been founded by a previous Buddha or previous incarnation of Buddha. This sacred site is known for its paranormal light that manifested from a lotus plant planted by the previous Buddha in the marshes here. The light could be seen for miles around, and people came from throughout Asia to see it. The entire valley was drained to allow easier access to the light, and the stupa was built to commemorate it. The face on the stupa has a third eye but no ears, because the entity here does not need to hear either praise or prayers.

Near the stupa is a smaller temple called Shan-

Shantipur and emerged with the mandala. As soon as it was brought into the light of day, it began to rain. For more information, visit Martin Gray's Sacred Sites Web site at www.sacredsites.com.

PALMYRA ISLAND

Palmyra Island is a large atoll in the center of the Pacific Ocean that is considered by many to be one of the most malevolent pieces of real estate on the planet. The island's West Lagoon has been the site of more than its share of violence. Nobody has ever managed to conquer this thirteen-square-mile ghost island, located one thousand miles south of Hawaii and 350 miles north of the equator, and roads and a landing strip built during World War II are now broken and overgrown by lush jungle vegetation. The island is surrounded by a large shark population, and its lagoons contain a poisonous algae that makes most of the fish inedible to humans. But even more threatening, visitors to this uninhabited island are often overcome by feelings of dread and doom and forced to leave.

Palmyra Island was discovered in 1798 by the American Edmond Fanning, but he was so moved by a feeling of impending danger that he weighed anchor and set sail in the middle of the night just to get away from the place. In the following years, several sailing vessels wrecked on the island's reefs and disappeared with all hands on board. Before long the island gained a reputation for swallowing up ships with no sign of survivors or wreckage. It became known as the Cursed Island and a place where only pirates ventured to hide their treasure. When the United States took possession from 1941 to 1947, the weird reputation was reconfirmed, as pilots reported disconcerting effects approaching the landing strip and several planes that crashed in the water disappeared without a trace like they had dropped off the face of the earth.

In 1951, after Palmyra became private property under the protection of the United States, several attempts were made to develop the island. No one succeeded. In the early 1970s, an ex-convict tried to take up residence on the island, but he was

Swayambhunath Stupa, Kathmandu, Nepal (Martin Gray)

tipur or "place of peace," but it is known to visitors for its ominous and slightly threatening atmosphere. This is the home of Tantric alchemist and magician Shantikar Acharya, who is said to be still alive, although he was born in the eighth century. Shantikar lives in a chamber beneath the temple that is always kept locked. It is said that he is engaged in a deep meditation that has lasted centuries. Sometimes, Shantikar may be interrupted in his meditation if the Kathmandu Valley is threatened. In that case, the King of Nepal must enter the underground chamber and disturb the avatar, who will then make a magical mandala. This last occurred in 1658, when the valley was threatened by a terrible drought. The king visited driven mad by the place. When a San Diego married couple docked their sailboat in the lagoon, he seized their ship and brutally tortured and murdered them. Dozens of others who have tried to establish a home on the island in the years since have ended up leaving feeling lucky to have survived. However, if you would like to try your luck against the Cursed Island, it was put up for sale in 1998. The price is $47 million.

PHILIPPINES

The Philippines were discovered in 1521 by the Portuguese explorer Ferdinand Magellan and were under Spanish control until the twentieth century. The Commonwealth of the Philippines was established in 1935, and the islands became a country in 1946.

Corregidor Island

SOUTH BEACH This section of the island of Corregidor is haunted by the insane ghost of a woman in a nurse's uniform who chases people with a big glass syringe in her hand. The woman's uniform dates from World War II, and she is thought to be a Filipino nurse who fell in love with an American serviceman who died in action during the war. The woman went into a deep depression from which she never recovered, and spent the remainder of her days in an insane asylum. To this day, her ghost is seen along the beach looking for her lover or waiting for him by a giant narra tree in front of the ruins of a concrete bomb shelter.

Manila

GIRLS CATHOLIC SCHOOL This Catholic girls' boarding school was founded in 1632 and is haunted by the apparition of one of its founding fathers. The ghost of a man in a black, colonial suit has been encountered by both students and nuns. His distinctive apparition is most often is sighted in the balcony in the auditorium, though sometimes he appears as a swirling mist in other areas of the school. The library and veranda area is haunted by the apparition of a young girl, and the ghost of a nun has been seen floating around on the main floor of the dormitory.

MARCOS STADIUM The large, modern sports stadium built by President Ferdinand Marcos in the 1970s for the Asian Games has many ghosts. Stadium construction was rushed to make the deadline for the Asian Games, and the entire floor was just paved in fast-setting cement when the stadium was opened. The structure collapsed and several hundred people suffocated in the wet cement. The body parts of people half-encased in the cement were cut off with chainsaws and construction continued as if nothing happened. Today, many gruesome apparitions are reported in the stadium and the basement refreshment areas.

SINGAPORE

Singapore is a former British colony that is now a city-state that gained its independence from Malaysia in 1965.

CHANGI BEACH This area in east Singapore is believed to be haunted by the ghosts of executed Chinese killed during the Japanese occupation. Bypassers often report hearing strange crying and screaming, and some witnesses have seen the grisly executions replayed in front of them. The beach houses on Changi Beach are also haunted. The ghosts are thought to be former residents who do not take kindly to new renters. Residents have reported feeling being stared at or even slapped by unseen hands. Weeping and other frightening sounds have also been heard in the middle of the night. In a few cases, residents have been attacked while taking baths or even possessed by the angry spirits.

EAST COAST BEACH This area is haunted by the apparition of an unidentified Lady in White, who is seen floating about the beach at night. Screaming and other strange noises seem to accompany the haunting. There are also several of Singapore's infamous "White Houses" here. White Houses are abandoned buildings that are considered haunted or where some traumatic event has made people stop wanting to live in them.

LOR HALUS This sand and stone storage area of Singapore is known for its pollution and grime. However, people fishing overnight from piers here often report paranormal phenomena such as strange voices, balls of blue light, and apparitions. For some reason, there have been several instances of ghosts asking for food from fishermen. For more information on Singapore hauntings, visit the Singapore Ghosts Web site at www.cyberway.com.sg/~leo81/main.htm.

MRT STATIONS Several of Singapore's MRT stations are haunted by workers who died during their construction. People in late night trains report seeing the headless apparitions of men in work clothes wandering through the stations. Unexplainable screams and voices are also heard in the middle of the night in the deserted stations.

POLICE ACADEMY The men's dormitory at the Singapore Police Academy is haunted by the apparition of a woman carrying a baby. At one point in the mid-1990s, ninety percent of the men staying in the building admitted they thought it was haunted. Today, the ghost is such a frequent visitor that the men have nicknamed her "Pontianak." Lake at night, the woman can be heard singing lullabies. No one has yet done a thorough investigation to find out who the woman might be.

RAFFLES HOTEL This prestigious international hotel is haunted by the sounds of a young girl's voice singing a nursery rhyme. The voice sings in English and is most often heard in rooms and halls in the back wing of the hotel. Many guests and employees have reported hearing the disembodied voice in recent years, and some reports go back nearly fifty years. The source of the eerie singing is thought to be in an English boarding school that stood at this location in 1897. The unidentified girl's spirit is tied to those days when she lived here.

ST. JOHN ISLAND The abandoned buildings on St. John Island are haunted by former residents. Visitors to the island hear voices calling them from the deserted buildings and loud thumping sounds and the running of tap water when no plumbing is connected.

TAI PAK KONG SAN CEMETERY The Tai Pak Kong San Cemetery near Canning Garden in Singapore is a cemetery haunted by itself. Witnesses report seeing the phantom of an old wooden house sitting in an open field where the cemetery now stands. Sometimes, disembodied voices are heard and the sounds of children laughing echo from nowhere. Apparently, the cemetery is haunted by how it used to be many years ago.

SOCIETY ISLANDS

The Society Islands are near the Tropic of Capricorn in the South Pacific. They are part of French Polynesia and became a French protectorate in 1843.

Moorea Island

BELVEDERE LOOKOUT POINT The heart-shaped island of Moorea is haunted by the presence of its former ruler, Princess Eimeo. At one time, the island was named Eimeo, and residents still honor her spirit. Before she died, she promised she would always look over the island and its inhabitants and would be there for them if they would only ask. She described the island as being her own heart, with the two north bays (Cook's Bay and Opunohu Bay) representing the pathways to her heart. All residents have to do is ask twice to receive her help, although she reserved the right to refuse those whom she judged selfish. Through the centuries, there have been many tales of Eimeo coming to the assistance of villagers and granting their wishes. She is thought to be buried at the Belvedere Lookout Point, where her apparition has been sighted on several occasions. Her presence has also been sensed comforting souls in the old hospital graveyard near Vaire in the Afareaitu District on the southeast coast, as well as at other towns along the coastal highway.

TAIWAN

Taiwan (Formosa) is a former Chinese island ceded to Japan from 1895 to 1945. It became the seat of the Chinese Nationalist Government in 1949.

Tianan

TIANAN TAOIST TEMPLE The apparition of a man seems to be haunting a huge stuffed crocodile that is the centerpiece of a Taoist temple here. The giant animal was brought from a temple in Thailand over fifteen years ago, and for the last twelve years, the ghost of a tall man has been spotted standing next to the huge stuffed beast. The crocodile is a good luck symbol for the Taoists, and it is supposed to drive away spirits. Unless, of course, the man is someone it may have eaten while alive.

THAILAND

Thailand (formerly Siam) was settled by Thai people from China. It came under Khmer control in the ninth century and finally became a constitutional monarchy in 1932.

Bangkok

MERCK PHARMACEUTICALS In the back yard of the manufacturing plant of pharmaceutical giant Merck in Bangkok stands a gaily painted miniature house on top of a long pole. It is known in Thailand as a "Spirit House," a tiny substitute home designed to lure evil spirits away from the main building or dwelling. They can be seen throughout the city, and even businesses use the miniature houses to protect themselves from wandering ghosts and negative spiritual influences. Merck managers hired a shaman to insure the proper placement of the Spirit House, and in 1964 it was moved from the front of the building to the back. That adjustment, according to business manager Ted Sienicki, resulted in a noticeable lift in morale, smoother production, and increased business.

QUEEN SIRIKIT CONVENTION CENTER Ratchadaphisek Road in front street of the Queen Sirikit Convention Center in Bangkok is a favorite hangout for body snatchers. Motorcyclists often drag race down the road at night, and there have been many fatalities. When someone is seriously injured, there is a mad rush by the body snatchers to see who can get to him first. Body snatchers are everywhere in the city. They patrol the streets in cars, rickshaws, and motorbikes looking for newly deceased people. The reason? There is a competition between the Ruam Katanyu, Por Teck Tung, and other Buddhist groups in the city to perform religious rites for the dead, so the groups welcome the opportunity to donate funeral services for unclaimed bodies.

The body snatchers deliver bodies to morgues, where an official report is issued. If no one claims the body, one of the Buddhist organizations handles the funeral for free. The higher the number of free burials, the higher the prestige of the organization and the more donations it receives. Thai businessmen are eager to finance body snatchers, because the wealthy men believe they are doing a service that will reap spiritual benefits for them. The cycle of body recovery also helps the police and emergency personnel, for body snatchers often clean up the scene of an accident or crime and collect evidence.

The only flaw in the system is that many body snatchers take advantage of the situation to rob victims of their money and jewelry. Many tourists believe that is the real motive behind the enthusiastic attention to the dying or seriously injured. Accident victims have survived tell of being picked up by body snatchers, who rifle through the victim's pockets and belongings while the person is writhing in pain or semi-conscious. In 1991, there was a frenzy of looting by body snatchers when a Lauda Airlines jet crashed that killed 223 people, and in 1993, when a hotel collapsed, so many wallets were stolen that many bodies could not be immediately identified. There are even reports of victims coming back to haunt overzealous body snatchers. Some say they are constantly followed by dark shadows or apparitions of their former "clients."

WAT MAHABUT TEMPLE Wat Mahabut is a Buddhist temple in the town of Ayutthaya, which is just north of Bangkok. The ancient temple is known for its beautiful shrine of Maae Nak Phrakahnong and a unique stone head of Buddha that is embedded in the roots of a tree. It is also famous for its ghost. A female apparition called the "Manak" has appeared at the temple in front of hundreds of witnesses over the centuries. She is thought to be the spirit of a woman buried on the temple grounds over two hundred years ago.

Lahus

TAWS The mountainous Lahus region of Thailand borders Burma to the north and is inhabited by the Lahus tribe. The area is haunted by shapeshifting phantoms known as "Taws," who have the ability to resemble human beings or large wolves. Taws are known to raid the outskirts of villages and carry away tribesmen to feed on their flesh and souls. The ghostly beings appear to exist at the edge between body and spirit, and are distinguished from humans and animals by their eerily glowing red eyes. During certain times of the month, the Lahus never leave their villages, even to hunt.

VIETNAM

Vietnam was under Chinese control until the fifteenth century and has been a pawn of the larger powers ever since. It became a French protectorate in the 1880s, but after much resistance, the French finally evacuated the country in 1954. It was partitioned in two separate countries. After the Vietnam War, the southern part fell to the communist north in 1975 and the Socialist Republic of Vietnam was created in 1976.

Quang Tri Province

KHESAN VALLEY The Khesan Valley in Quang Tri Province in Vietnam is haunted by a glowing ghost that appears on moonless nights. The unidentified apparition has a definite illumination, but no distinct features can be seen. It is shaped like a human figure and makes no sounds as it moves about. The figure was first reported by U.S. Marines on Hill 689 in the valley in 1968, during the Vietnam War, and for that reason is thought to be an American soldier killed during the heavy combat there.

LA VANG CATHOLIC SHRINE Over two hundred years ago, a group of Catholic worshipers saw the apparition of the Virgin Mary appear in a small brick chapel here. The church, located a half hour outside the town of La Vang in Quang Tri Province, was destroyed in 1972 when the area was in the middle of a fierce combat zone. The ruins of the church can still be seen, however, and a large statue of the Virgin Mary with Christ child marks the site. As many as two hundred thousand people a year make the pilgrimage to the sacred site. Early Catholics in Vietnam were persecuted and often forced to worship in remote locations, but today, they make up over ten percent of the country's population.

Thuc Duc

SUICIDE TURN This section of road in the town of Thuc Duc is haunted by the apparition of a small boy kicking a ball back and forth from one side of the road to the other. In the late 1980s, children in the town used to take advantage of rain showers to go out to "take a bath" or just play in the rain. One day a boy kicked his ball into a puddle of water at the exact instant the wind blew a sheet of roofing off a home that severed a power line. One end of the line fell into the puddle and killed the boy instantly, charring his body black. As a memorial, the community buried the boy under a granite marker on the side of the road where he died, although the spot soon became known as Suicide Turn because of its connection with death.

Sightings of the boy's ghost started not long afterwards. The sightings take place most often at night around 10:00 P.M. Villagers know of the ghost and few people venture in the area after dark, even though a modern hospital was built over part of the original site. Not long ago, a man took a shortcut through the small road late at night and ended up possessed by the spirit of the boy. He suddenly started talking like a child and complaining he was bored with no one to play with. A priest was hired to perform an exorcism, but the ritual did not work, and reportedly, the man is still possessed and unable to work.

EURASIA

IRAQ

Iraq is the home of the ancient Babylonian Empire. In modern times, it became part of Turkey and then a British protectorate in 1921. It became an independent country in 1932.

Baghdad

BABYLON The ruins of the ancient city of Babylon are located eighty-nine kilometers (fifty-five miles) south of Baghdad near Al Hillah on the Euphrates River. Babylon was first settled around 3000 B.C. and became the capital of Mesopotamia from 612 B.C. The ruins are said to be haunted by the two vampire spirits called Utukku and Ekimmu. It is also the dwelling place of the defunct Babylonian gods, including the god of death, Uggae, and the horrific god of the sea, Tiamat. A demon called Lilitu is also supposed to roam these grounds.

ISRAEL

Israel was founded in 1948 as a home for displaced Jews from around the world. It was created out of a division of Palestine between Arabs and Jews.

Jerusalem

CHURCH OF THE HOLY SEPULCHER Jerusalem was first settled around 3000 B.C. and today is a sacred city to three religions (Christianity, Islam, and Judaism). Religious fervor is so high here that the Jerusalem police have a special unit for dealing with people suffering from religious overexcitement. In many ways, the city has become a symbol of the cosmos. The city's temples above ground represent heaven, but Dante's Inferno is supposed to exist below the city, extending all the way to Mount Purgatory in the Southern Hemisphere.

The living presence of Christ is said to be felt

Church of the Holy Sepulcher, Jerusalem, Israel (Martin Gray)

in the small Church of the Holy Sepulcher in Jerusalem, and devoted visitors report having a variety of supersensory experiences near the altar. In 335, during excavations for the church, workers supposedly unearthed the cross on which Jesus was crucified, and below that they found hidden the skull of Adam. There are other entities encountered here, including some pagan energies dating from the time when a temple to Aphrodite stood on this spot.

Ramle

KIBBUTZ SCHOOL The Kibbutz School located between the towns of Ramle and Rechovot in Israel is haunted by the apparition of an ugly old woman. Her phantom head was seen floating around in the male dormitory in September 1980. She was squinting and her lower lip hung down, and she seemed confused. The apparition is thought to be a woman who died at the kibbutz on the same night of the haunting.

SAUDI ARABIA

Saudi Arabia was formed as a dual kingdom out of Arabian lands in 1927 and became a unified kingdom in 1932.

ALJUBAIL AIRPORT Ghosts were transported to this Middle East airport from South America in 1990. After the Jim Jones suicides in Jonestown, Guiana, the bodies were flown back to the United States in a huge C-5 cargo plane. After unloading the bodies, crewmembers noticed many paranormal indicators such as sudden loud banging sounds, whispering voices, and even a sadistic laughter from nowhere. The plane's next trip was to Saudi Arabia, and by the time it landed, Air Force crewmembers refused to linger or rest in the cargo hold and wanted nothing to do with the plane.

Marines stationed at the airport took up the challenge and cleared everything and everyone out of the plane and then shut themselves inside. Soon a deafening banging sound like a sledgehammer hitting an empty oil drum was heard, and the Marines evacuated the plane. No explanation was discovered, and the plane was nearly dismantled to find a cause for the strange noises. After that, apparitions began to manifest in the cargo hold, and were sensed at a hangar and other spots in the airport. The plane was then sealed and sentries posted from two hundred yards around it. After the plane returned to the United States, there were no further reports of haunting, though authorities at the airport would not comment as to whether the ghostly passengers were now their problem.

SYRIA

Syria was settled around 3000 B.C. and became part of the Persian Empire in the sixth century B.C. It became part of Turkey in the nineteenth century and became an independent nation in 1918.

Damascus

DAMASCUS APARTMENTS An eighth-floor apartment in this building on the western border of the city of Damascus is haunted by a violent entity that takes the shape of a large black hound that witnesses describe as "misty" or "borderless." In 1990, fifteen people witnessed poltergeist effects in the apartment that included lights flashing or going on and off by themselves, an invisible hand that slapped people in the face, heavy disembodied footsteps that stomped through the apartment, as well as objects flying across rooms and smashing against walls. Psychics from Yeman were brought into the place to try to exorcize the demon but their efforts were not much help. The source of the poltergeist activity might have been a seventeen-year-old girl living in the apartment at the time, but an investigation of the case was never made.

TURKEY

Turkey was home to the Hittite civilization, which flourished between from 1700 B.C. to 1200 B.C., and then home to the Ottoman Empire. A revolution against the Ottomans took place in 1920 and the Turkish Republic was proclaimed in 1923.

Gallipoli Peninsula

GALLIPOLI NATIONAL PARK This public park is haunted by soldiers who died in battle during the British Palestine campaigns of 1915–1917. Both British and Turkish apparitions are seen. Other more ancient visions are seen here too. Australian author Ion Idriess recalled one paranormal incident that occurred at Gallipoli in December 1916 when he was stationed in Palestiene. "After the battles of Maghdaba and El Arish," he wrote in his book *The Desert Column*, "troops riding back the thirty miles from Maghdaba were enveloped in blinding clouds of dust. Nearly the whole column was riding in snatches of sleep; no one had slept for four nights and they had ridden ninety miles. Hundreds of men saw the queerest visions—weird-looking soldiers were riding beside them, and many were mounted on strange animals. Hordes walked right amongst the horses, making not the slightest sound. The column rode through towns with lights gleaming from the shuttered windows of quaint buildings. The country was all waving green fields, and trees and flower gardens. Numbers of the men are speaking of what they saw in a most interesting, queer way. "There were tall stone temples with marble pillars and swinging oil lamps—our fellows could smell the incense—and white mosques with stately minarets."

BIBLIOGRAPHY

Adams, Norman. *Haunted Scotland*. Edinburgh: Mainstream Publishing, 1998.

Athony, Wayne. *Derbyshire Ghosts*. London: J.H. Hall & Sons, 1992.

Belyk, Robert. *Ghosts II: More True Stories from British Columbia*. Winnipeg: Kromar Printing Ltd., 1997.

Belyk, Robert. *Ghosts: True Stories from British Columbia*. Victoria, British Columbia: Horsdal & Schubart Publishers Ltd., 1994.

Brookesmith, Peter. *Ghosts*. London: Orbis Publishing, 1980.

Brookesmith, Peter. *Great Hauntings*. London: Macdonald & Co., 1988.

Brooks, J.A. *Britain's Haunted Heritage*. Norwich, England: Jarrold Publishing, 1990.

Brooks, John. *The Good Ghost Guide*. London: Jarrold Publishing, 1994.

Cavendish, Richard. *The World of Ghosts and the Supernatural*. New York: Facts On File, 1994.

Christensen, Jo-Anne. *Ghost Stories of British Columbia*. Toronto: Hounslow Press, 1996.

Cohen, Daniel. *The Encyclopedia of Ghosts*. New York: Dorset Press, 1984.

Columbo, John Robert. *Ghost Stories of Ontario*. Toronto: Hounslow Press, 1995.

Columbo, John Robert. *Haunted Toronto*. Toronto: Hounslow Press, 1996.

Columbo, John Robert. *Mysterious Canada*. Toronto: Doubleday Canada Ltd., 1989.

Day, A. Grove, and Kirtley, Bacil. *Horror In Paradise: Grim and Uncanny Tales from Hawaii and the South Seas*. Honolulu: Mutual Publishing, 1986.

Dunne, John. *Haunted Ireland*. Belfast, Ireland: Appletree Press, 1989.

Emberg, Buck and Joan. *Ghostly Tales of Tasmania*. Launceston, Tasmania: Regal Publications, 1998.

Findler, Gerald. *Ghosts of the Lake Counties*. Lancaster, England: Dalesman Publishing, 1975.

Gillese, John Patrick. "The Virgin's Visit to Garabandal." *Fate Magazine* (December 1965 and January 1966). St. Paul, Minnesota: Llewellyn Publishing.

Giordano, Margaret. *Tasmanian Tales of the Supernatural*. Launceston, Tasmania: Regal Publications, 1994.

Gray, Martin. *Places of Peace and Power*. Sedona, Arizona: Gray, P.O. Box 4111, Sedona, AZ, 86340, 1998.

Green, Andrew. *Ghosts of Today*. London: Kaye & Ward, 1980.

Green, Andrew. *Haunted Houses*. London: Shire Publications, 1991.

Green, Andrew. *Haunted Inns & Taverns*. London: Shire Publications, 1996.

Guiley, Rosemary Ellen. *The Encyclopedia of Ghosts and Spirits*. New York: Facts On File, 1992.

Harpur, James. *The Atlas of Sacred Places: Meeting Points of Heaven and Earth*. New York: Henry Holt & Co., 1994.

Haslam, David. *Ghosts and Legends of Nottinghamshire*. Berks, England: Countryside Books, 1998.

Hauck, Dennis William. *Haunted Places: The National Directory*. New York: Penguin, 1996.

Hervey, Sheila. *Canada: Ghost to Ghost*. Toronto: Stoddart Publishing Co., 1996.

Hitchcock, Jane. *The Ghosts of Okinawa*. Crofton, Maryland: Shiba Hill, 1996.

Holzer, Hans. *Ghosts: True Encounters with the World Beyond*. New York: Black Dog & Leventhal Publishers, 1997.

Holzer, Hans. *Haunted House Album*. New York: Dorset Press, 1992.

Hough, Peter. *Supernatural Britain: A Guide to Britain's Most Haunted Places*. London: Macnab Camera Press, 1995.

Hough, Peter. *Supernatural Britain: A Guide to Britain's Most Haunted Places*. London: July Piatkus Publishers Ltd., 1995.

Innes, Brian. *The Catalogue of Ghost Sightings*. London: Wellington Press, 1996.

Iwasaka, Michiko, and Barre, Toelken. *Ghosts and the Japanese*. Logan, Utah: Utah State University Press, 1994.

Jackson, Robert. *Great Mysteries: Ghosts*. New York: Smithmark Publishing, 1992.

Lightburn, Martin. *A Gazetter of British Ghosts*. London: Pan Books, 1973.

Lyal, Adam. *Witchery Tales: The Darker Side of Edinburgh*. Edinburgh, 1988.

Lyal, Adam. *Witchery Tales: The Darker Side of Edinburgh*. Edinburgh: Moubray House Press, 1988.

Marsden, Simon. *The Journal of a Ghosthunter*. New York: Cross River Press, 1994.

Mason, John. *Haunted Heritage*. London: Collins & Brown Ltd., 1999.

Mead, Robin. *Weekend Haunts: A Guide to Haunted Hotels in the UK*. London: Impact Books, 1994.

Michael, Prince. *Living with Ghosts*. New York: W.W. Norton & Co., 1995.

Price, Harry. *The Most Haunted House in England*. London: Longmans, Green, & Co., 1940.

Pugh, Jane. *Welsh Ghostly Encounters*. Gwynedd, Wales: Gwasg Carreg Gwalch, 1990.

Reynolds, James. *Gallery of Ghosts*. New York: Grosset & Dunlap Inc., 1965.

Ross, Catrien, *Supernatural and Mysterious Japan*. Tokyo: Yenbooks, 1996.

Smith, Barbara. *Ghost Stories from Alberta*. Willowdale, Ontario: Hounslow Press, 1993.

Smith, Barbara. *Ghost Stories of Manitoba*. Edmonton, Alberta: Lone Pine Publishing, 1998.

Underwood, Peter. *Ghosts and How to See Them*. London: Anaya Publishers Ltd., 1993.

Underwood, Peter. *The A–Z of British Ghosts*. London: Chancellor Press, 1992.

Underwood, Peter. *The Ghost Hunters Almanac*. Orpington, Kent, England: Eric Dobby Publishing, 1993.

Vincent, Liz. *Ghosts of Picton Past*. Picton, New South Wales: Alted Printing, 1997.

Walker, John Anthony and Clarke, Andy. *Ghostly Guide to the Lake District*. Lancaster U.K.: White Rabbit Press, 1999.

Yeates, Geoff. *Cambridge College Ghosts*. Cambridge, England: W. Heffer & Sons, 1994.

INTERNET SOURCES FOR MORE INFORMATION

Asian Horror (members.tripod.com/~DragonKid/main.html).

Australian Ghost Hunters Society (www.aghs.org.au).

Austrian Society for Parapsychology (www.t0.or.at/~psi/index.htm).

Belgium Ghost Hunters Society (welcome.to/bghs).

Borley Rectory (www.borleyrectory.com).

Brisbane Ghost Tours (www.ghost-tours.com.au).

Brisbane Ghost Hunters (members.tripod.com/~cluricaun/main.htm).

Castle of Spirits (www.castleofspirits.com).

Cornish Ghost Stories (www.connexions.co.uk/culture/html/ghosts.htm).

David Haslam's British Ghosts (www.geocities.com/Area51/Station/9814/ghostmain.html).

Derby Ghosts (www.derbycity.com/ghosts/ghosts.html).

Edinburgh Witchery (www.witcherytours.com).

Finnish Poltergeists (personal.inet.fi/tiede/poltergeist/english.htm).

Ghost Club of Britain (dspace.dial.pipex.com/town/lane/xmo85/gc_fr.htm).

Ghost Research Society (www.ghostresearch.org).

Ghost and Other Haunts in New Zealand and Australia (homepages.ihug.co.n2/~sp.jod).

Haunted Melbourne (www.haunted.com.au/resources/ghosttour/ghosttour.html).

Haunted Places—Dennis W. Hauck (www.haunted-places.com).

Haunted Scotland (www.highlanderweb.co.uk/haunted/haunt3.htm).

Haunted Valley Webcam (www.hauntedvalley.com/webcam.htm).

International Ghost Hunters Society (www.ghostweb.com).

International Society for Paranormal Research (www.ispr.net).

Judy Farncombe's Ghost Index (homepage.virgin.net/martin.farncombe/ghost_index.htm).

Mystical WWW (www.mystical-www.co.uk).

New Zealand Ghosts (homepages.ihug.co.nz/~dp.jod).

Paranormal Society of the North Atlantic (webhost.avint.net/hardticket/psna.htm).

Places of Peace and Power (www.sacredsites.com).

Singapore Ghosts (www.cyberway.com.sg/~leo81/main.htm).

Tom Slemen's Strange But True (www.ghostcity19.freeserve.co.uk).

Toronto Ghosts (www.torontoghosts.org).

White Rabbit British Ghosts (www.afallon.com/pages/whiterabbit1.html).

INDEX

FOR THE BEST IN PAPERBACKS, LOOK FOR THE

In every corner of the world, on every subject under the sun, Penguin represents quality and variety—the very best in publishing today.

For complete information about books available from Penguin—including Puffins, Penguin Classics, and Arkana—and how to order them, write to us at the appropriate address below. Please note that for copyright reasons the selection of books varies from country to country.

In the United Kingdom: Please write to *Dept. EP, Penguin Books Ltd, Bath Road, Harmondsworth, West Drayton, Middlesex UB7 0DA.*

In the United States: Please write to *Penguin Putnam Inc., P.O. Box 12289 Dept. B, Newark, New Jersey 07101-5289* or call 1-800-788-6262.

In Canada: Please write to *Penguin Books Canada Ltd, 10 Alcorn Avenue, Suite 300, Toronto, Ontario M4V 3B2.*

In Australia: Please write to *Penguin Books Australia Ltd, P.O. Box 257, Ringwood, Victoria 3134.*

In New Zealand: Please write to *Penguin Books (NZ) Ltd, Private Bag 102902, North Shore Mail Centre, Auckland 10.*

In India: Please write to *Penguin Books India Pvt Ltd, 11 Panchsheel Shopping Centre, Panchsheel Park, New Delhi 110 017.*

In the Netherlands: Please write to *Penguin Books Netherlands bv, Postbus 3507, NL-1001 AH Amsterdam.*

In Germany: Please write to *Penguin Books Deutschland GmbH, Metzlerstrasse 26, 60594 Frankfurt am Main.*

In Spain: Please write to *Penguin Books S. A., Bravo Murillo 19, 1° B, 28015 Madrid.*

In Italy: Please write to *Penguin Italia s.r.l., Via Benedetto Croce 2, 20094 Corsico, Milano.*

In France: Please write to *Penguin France, Le Carré Wilson, 62 rue Benjamin Baillaud, 31500 Toulouse.*

In Japan: Please write to *Penguin Books Japan Ltd, Kaneko Building, 2-3-25 Koraku, Bunkyo-Ku, Tokyo 112.*

In South Africa: Please write to *Penguin Books South Africa (Pty) Ltd, Private Bag X14, Parkview, 2122 Johannesburg.*